APPLIED CONSUMPTION ANALYSIS

REVISED AND ENLARGED EDITION

ADVANCED TEXTBOOKS IN ECONOMICS

VOLUME 5

Editors:

C.J. BLISS

M.D. INTRILIGATOR

Advisory Editors:

D.W. JORGENSON

M.C. KEMP

J.-J. LAFFONT

J.-F. RICHARD

NORTH-HOLLAND
AMSTERDAM · NEW YORK · OXFORD · TOKYO

APPLIED CONSUMPTION ANALYSIS

REVISED AND ENLARGED EDITION

LOUIS PHLIPS

C.O.R.E.

NORTH-HOLLAND
AMSTERDAM · NEW YORK · OXFORD · TOKYO

ELSEVIER SCIENCE PUBLISHERS B.V.
Sara Burgerhartstraat 25
P.O. Box 211, 1000 AE Amsterdam, The Netherlands

Distributors for the United States and Canada:
ELSEVIER SCIENCE PUBLISHING COMPANY, INC.
655 Avenue of the Americas
New York, N.Y. 10010, U.S.A.

First edition: 1974
Revised edition: 1983
Second impression: 1990

Library of Congress Cataloging in Publication Data

Phlips, Louis.
    Applied consumption in analysis.

    (Advanced textbooks in economics; v. 5)
    Bibliography: p.
    Includes index.
    1. Demand (Economic theory)   2. Consumption
(Economics)   3. Statics and dynamics (Social
sciences).   I. Title.   II. Series.
HB801.P47   1982   338.5'21   82-18834
ISBN 0-444-86531-4 (U.S.)

ISBN: 0 444 86531 4

Printed in The Netherlands

Introduction to the series

The aim of the series is to cover topics in economics, mathematical economics and econometrics, at a level suitable for graduate students or final year undergraduates specializing in economics. There is at any time much material that has become well established in journal papers and discussion series which still awaits a clear, self-contained treatment that can easily be mastered by students without considerable preparation or extra reading. Leading specialists will be invited to contribute volumes to fill such gaps. Primary emphasis will be placed on clarity, comprehensive coverage of sensibly defined areas, and insight into fundamentals, but original ideas will not be excluded. Certain volumes will therefore add to existing knowledge, while others will serve as a means of communicating both known and new ideas in a way that will inspire and attract students not already familiar with the subject matter concerned.

The Editors

To Lucie

Preface

This is not a book on demand theory. Nor is it a book on the econometrics of demand systems. Rather, what I have tried to write is a text on the subject matter between theory and estimation, that is on the art of reformulating pure theory to make it suitable for econometric applications. In my experience, it is not sufficient to offer a price theory course and an econometrics course: most students find it very difficult to bridge the gap between the two without appropriate training.

As in the art of piano playing, the art of consumption analysis requires a lot of practising. That is why many exercises are offered to the reader while only a few answers are given (for the more important ones). The reader is strongly requested to work out all answers for himself. His background is assumed to include some knowledge of calculus and of elementary textbook economics. Purely econometric considerations have been avoided. The starred sections are more advanced and sometimes require some matrix algebra: they can be used for a 'special topics' course.

My intellectual debt to Hendrik S. Houthakker, one of the pioneers in the field, should be obvious. His work on additive functions fascinated me and is at the core of the static part of this book. His more recent contributions, with Lester D. Taylor, to the dynamization of demand systems provided the framework for my own work, which would never have come from the ground without their help and encouragement.

I am most heavily indebted for research assistance and intellectual support to E. de Souza, J. Garcia dos Santos, Ph. Rouzier, R. Sanz Ferrer and D. Weiserbs, whose personal contributions have been indicated – I hope – at the appropriate places in the next. The editors of this Series, C. Bliss and M.D. Intriligator, offered many suggestions and constructive criticism during the various stages of elaboration.

Thanks are also due to A.P. Barten and A. Deaton for comments on the final manuscript.

Competent programming assistance was given by M. Vuylsteke-Wauters over a number of years, and more recently by J.P. Lemaître. Ph. Rouzier and P. Rousseaux. Last but not least, I wish to thank B. de Schaetzen, B. de Rochelée and F. De Beir for cheerful secretarial assistance.

De Haan, July 1973   LOUIS PHILIPS

Preface to the second edition

This second edition is also an enlarged one. Part I now offers a brief discussion of duality and flexible forms, in particular of Deaton and Muellbauer's 'almost ideal demand system'. There is also an introduction to Muellbauer's treatment of the 'aggregation problem'. Part II includes my work on the demand for leisure and money and on true wage indexes (a new Chapter X). The second half of the final chapter, on intertemporal utility maximization, is completely rewritten and largely draws from my work with Frans Spinnewyn. Throughout, I have done my best to update the references. The list of references now extends till 1981.

I wish to thank Simone Clemhout, Wouter Keller, Wilhelm Krelle, A. H. Q. M. Merkies and Ricardo Sanz-Ferrer for pointing out errors in the first edition.

After correcting a distressingly large number of printing errors, I'll bet none appear in this edition. Or am I too optimistic?

De Haan, April 1982   LOUIS PHILIPS

Contents

Part I

Statics

I

Utility functions

In order to analyse statistical data on consumption we need to start from some hypothesis. The one that is both natural and fruitful is to assume the existence, for each (or for the average) consumer, of a continuous utility function

$$u = f(x_1, x_2, \ldots, x_n)$$

and to give it certain properties that make it easy to maximize with the usual mathematical tools.

It will be assumed that there are only a finite number of commodities, say n; and that each commodity can be characterized numerically. It will further be assumed that there exists a unit of measure for each commodity, for example in kilogrammes or in litres or simply in quantity. This being so, any assortment or bundle or packet of the n commodities can be numerically expressed as a vector with n components: $(x_1, x_2, \ldots, x_n)$. Each component always refers to the same commodity.

It is useful to consider each commodity as being linked with an axis in the space of dimension, n, of real numbers, R^n. In this way all the properties of this space will be at our service. However, the commodity set will not be considered as covering the entire space, R^n. We shall limit it by imposing 3 properties which define the *commodity set*:

(1) A commodity may not be characterized by strictly negative numbers. Hence the commodity vector, $x = (x_1, \ldots, x_n)$ can have no negative components.

(2) Let $x^0 = (x_1^0, x_2^0, \ldots, x_n^0)$ be a bundle (or n-tuple) available to the consumer. Then any bundle of the form $\alpha x^0 = (\alpha x_1^0, \ldots, \alpha x_n^0)$, $0 \leqslant \alpha \leqslant 1$, can be extracted from this bundle. This is known as the property of *divisibility*.

(3) The commodity set contains the bundle, $(0, 0, \ldots, 0)$: moreover, if a bundle x^1 belongs to the set then any bundle, x^2, where $x_i^2 \geqslant x_i^1$, $i = 1, \ldots, n$, belongs to the set. The commodity set is, therefore, unbounded from above.

The symbol 'u' can be interpreted as measuring the 'satisfaction' derived from the consumption of alternative consumption bundles. More precisely, 'u' is a number that facilitates the ordering of the commodity bundles according to the preferences of the consumer. The utility function is indeed a numerical representation of a preference ordering, in the sense that 'u' is a number associated with each possible consumption bundle, such that if one bundle, say $x^0 = (x_1^0, x_2^0, \ldots, x_n^0)$, is preferred to another bundle, say $x' = (x_1', x_2', \ldots, x_n')$, the number associated with x^0 is greater than the number associated with x'.

1.1. Basic axioms on the preference relation

The first question to ask is: what are the conditions that make such a representation possible? In other words, we want to know what properties the consumer's preferences should have to make it possible to associate a number with each commodity bundle in the way described above.

It is intuitively clear that restrictive assumptions will have to be made: some possible irregular properties will have to be excluded from the analysis. The reader is requested to ask himself whether he is ready to consider the assumptions introduced below as acceptable, i.e. whether the inevitable loss in realism is not exaggerated.

Economic theory formulates these assumptions as *axioms*, i.e. as statements that are accepted as being true without proof. This means that theorists consider these as intuitively plausible foundations on which a scientific theory can be built. All sciences start from a set of axioms, as one has to start somewhere. There is no reason why economic science should be an exception to this rule.

Some *definitions* and a minimum of *notation* are required. The basic concepts are those of preference and indifference, which are supposed to have an immediate intuitive meaning. Let x^0 and x' be two vectors representing two commodity bundles. We say that

$$\langle\!\langle\, x^0 \precsim x' \,\rangle\!\rangle \text{ means } \langle\!\langle\, x^0 \text{ is \textit{not preferred} to } x' \,\rangle\!\rangle$$

The relation 'is not preferred to' is taken as the elementary or primitive concept. The following relations are derived from it:

$\langle\!\langle\, x^0 \precsim x'$ and $x' \precsim x^0 \,\rangle\!\rangle$ means $\langle\!\langle\, x^0 \sim x' \,\rangle\!\rangle$, i.e. $\langle\!\langle\, x^0$ *is indifferent to* $x' \,\rangle\!\rangle$,

$\langle\!\langle\, x^0 \precsim x'$ and not $x' \precsim x^0 \,\rangle\!\rangle$ is written $\langle\!\langle\, x' \succ x^0 \,\rangle\!\rangle$ and means $\langle\!\langle\, x'$ *is preferred to* $x^0 \,\rangle\!\rangle$.

With this notation, we are able to state the three basic axioms that are needed to establish the 'existence' of a continuous utility function. (The word existence is put between quotation marks to indicate that it is used in a strict sense, without any metaphysical connotation. This point is taken up below at the end of Section 1.4.)

A.1. AXIOM OF COMPARABILITY: *For any pair of commodity bundles* x^0 *and* x' *in the commodity set* X, *the consumer is able to say* $x^0 \precsim x'$ *or* $x' \precsim x^0$.

Notice that the term 'or' means that at least one of the statements must hold. Both statements may therefore hold simultaneously, in which case we have $x^0 \sim x'$.

A.1 aims at excluding the case where the consumer would be unable to make comparisons about some bundless. In other words, A.1. makes the preference relation *complete*.

A.2. AXIOM OF TRANSITIVITY: $x^0 \precsim x'$ *and* $x' \precsim x''$ *imply* $x^0 \precsim x''$.

If the bundle x^0 is not preferred to the bundle x', and the latter is not preferred to x'', then x^0 is not preferred to x''. In other words, the consumer's preferences are *consistent*: he never contradicts himself.

Technically speaking, these two axioms give us a *preordering* (or 'weak' ordering). A preordering is indeed a binary relation which is reflexive and transitive. The binary relation $\precsim$ – just defined as transitive – is also reflexive, as clearly $x \precsim x$ for any x in X according to A.1. In order to follow standard terminology, we will use the word 'ordering' instead of 'preordering' in later sections, although this is technically incorrect.[1]

A.2. excludes from the analysis a number of preference relations that may (perhaps frequently) exist and are not necessarily irrational.

---

[1] A (strong) 'ordering' is such that $\langle\!\langle\, x^0\, R\, x'$ and $x'\, R\, x^0 \,\rangle\!\rangle$ implies $x^0 = x'$, where R is a binary relation on a set. In that case indifference is ruled out and replaced by equality.

EXERCISES

1.1. Discuss the example given by Pearce (1964, p. 20) of behaviour that seems to be inconsistent with A.2. A colleague is invited to dinner. At the end of the meal, he has to choose between a small and a large apple: he takes the small one (although he is still hungry). Then, choosing between a large pear and a small apple, he takes the pear (because he is so hungry). But when offered a large pear and a large apple, he takes the apple (because he prefers apples).

Answer: The preordering appears as intransitive: large apple $\succ$ large pear $\succ$ small apple $\succ$ large apple. Nevertheless, the choices are all perfectly rational: his first choice (the small apple rather than the large one) is based on the desire to be polite (i.e. not to be considered greedy); the two other choices are explained above. The example is perhaps not inconsistent with A.2 given the additional information that the colleague is hungry, and the fact that, in the first alternative, a sociological constraint (politeness) comes in. To take account of this constraint and make A.2 operational, one should recognize that the large apple in the first choice is not really on the same footing (the same commodity) as the large apple in the third choice.

1.2. Give a few examples of strong orderings.

A.1 and A.2 give a complete preordering. One is tempted to conclude that A.1 and A.2 are sufficient conditions for the existence of a utility function, i.e. that one can now associate a real number with each commodity bundle, in such a way that the natural order of the real numbers corresponds to the preordering. There is a complication, however: one can imagine preorderings that are complete but cannot be represented by a real-valued function.

Consider the following situation. I am a dipsomaniac. Consequently I systematically prefer any bundle that contains alcohol. Needless to say, if two bundles contain alcohol, I prefer the one which contains more of it. I am interested in the other commodities if and only if the two bundles contain the same quantity of alcohol.

Let there be two bundles x^0 and x', each with two goods: beer (x_1) and bread (x_2).

If there is more beer in x^0 than in x', i.e. if $x_1^0 > x_1'$, then I prefer x^0 to x'. Let there be a third bundle x'' such that $x_1'' = x_1^0$. I prefer x'' to x^0 only if $x_2'' > x_2^0$, i.e. if there is more bread in x'' than in x^0.

Figure 1.1. represents the situation.

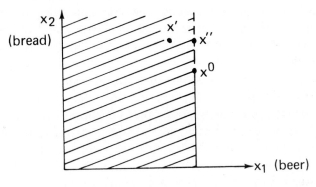

Fig. 1.1.

x^0 Is preferred to x' (which contains less beer) and x'' is preferred to x^0 (same quantity of beer but more bread). Notice that x^0 is preferred to any bundle located in the shaded area *and* on the segment from x^0 to the horizontal axis. Notice also that the dotted line represents bundles that are preferred to x^0. As there are no points indifferent to x^0, it is impossible to trace a continuous curve separating x^0 from the bundles that are preferred to x^0 and the bundles to which x^0 is preferred. x' and x'' may come as close to x^0 as one wishes without becoming indifferent to it.

EXERCISE

1.3. Does the example given above belong to the family of preorderings? *Hint:* check for reflexivity and transitivity. You will find that the answer is: yes.

We have here an example of what has been called a *lexicographic ordering* (see Debreu, 1954). The adjective is well chosen, as commodity bundles are ordered in the same way as words are in a dictionary. To exclude it – and possible similar preorderings – it suffices to accept the following axiom:

A.3. AXIOM OF CONTINUITY: *The set of bundles not preferred to x^0 and the set of bundles to which x^0 is not preferred are both closed in X, for any x^0.*

Take any point x' not preferred to x^0. A.3 says that it is possible to let x' come close enough to x^0 for x^0 not to be preferred to x', i.e. to be indifferent to x'. This is exactly what was impossible in Figure 1.1. Indeed, the set of points not preferred to x^0 was not closed, i.e. it did not contain its boundaries. The same was true for the set to which x^0 was not preferred.

Debreu (1959, p. 60–63) shows that A.1, A.2 and A.3 are sufficient conditions for the existence of a real-valued utility function, which is a continuous function of the quantities consumed, such that $u(x^0) \leqslant u(x')$ when $x^0 \precsim x'$. Note that the Debreu theorem does not imply uniqueness of the utility function: any monotonic transformation of a utility function is also a utility function (i.e. we obtain ordinal rather than cardinal utility). This will be discussed further in Section 1.3.

1.2. Additional axioms

The result obtained in the preceding section is quite nice. However, the utility function whose existence is now beyond doubt still does not have all the desired properties. As was said in the first sentence of this chapter, we want to have a utility function because we want to maximize it, in the belief that the properties of this maximum are a good description of the observed behaviour of the consumer in the market. The commodity bundles purchased in the market will indeed be considered as 'optimal' i.e. as bundles corresponding to a maximum of the utility function (given a budget constraint to be introduced later on).

To make this maximization feasible, we will introduce three additional axioms.

A.4. AXIOM OF DOMINANCE (OR MONOTONICITY): *When two bundles x^0 and x' in X are such that x^0 dominates x', then x^0 is preferred to x'.*

Let $x^0 = (x_1^0, x_2^0)$ and $x' = (x_1', x_2')$. We say that x^0 dominates x' if
$$x_1^0 \geqslant x_1' \quad \text{and} \quad x_2^0 > x_2'$$
or if
$$x_1^0 > x_1' \quad \text{and} \quad x_2^0 \geqslant x_2'.$$

In one word, the consumer is supposed to prefer the bundle that contains more of one of the two goods and not less of the other good. He always prefers more to less, hence the term 'monotonicity': this axiom makes u a *strictly increasing* function of the quantities consumed. You will have noticed that the way lexicographic preferences were defined was consistent with the dominance axiom. As you did not protest at the time we discussed Figure 1.1, A.4 probably seems reasonable to you.

EXERCISES

1.4. Can you explain why A.4 implies the absence of saturation?

1.5. Draw the commodity set X, consisting of all bundles composed of x_1 and x_2. Locate a point $x^0 = (x_1^0, x_2^0)$ and shade the area of points to which x^0 is preferred and the area of points preferred to x^0 according to A.4. If an indifference curve (the locus of all points indifferent to x^0) were to be drawn, what would be its shape, given that it has to pass through x^0?

Your knowledge of elementary textbook economics may have led you, while working out exercise 1.5, to draw an indifference curve through x^0 that is not only downward sloping but also convex to the origin. To be allowed to do this, however, we need a further axiom.

A.5. AXIOM OF STRICT CONVEXITY: *If two bundles x' and x^0 are indifferent, then a linear combination of these bundles is preferred to x' and x^0.*

Remember that a set S is said to be 'convex' if a line segment between any two points P_1 and P_2 in that set belongs entirely to it. If all the points

$$P = aP_1 + (1 - a)P_2 \quad \text{where} \quad 0 \leqslant a \leqslant 1$$

belong to S, then S is convex. The linear combination (or weighted mean) P indeed defines all the points on a straight line drawn between P_1 and P_2. Applied to a (convex) consumption set X, this means that preferences are convex if

$$ax' + (1 - a)x^0 \gtrsim x^0 \quad \text{when} \quad x' \gtrsim x^0 \qquad (0 \leqslant a \leqslant 1) \qquad (1.1)$$

or

$$ax' + (1 - a)x^0 \succ x^0 \quad \text{when} \quad x' \succ x^0 \qquad (0 < a \leqslant 1). \qquad (1.2)$$

Then the set of all points (in X) at least as desired as x^0 is a convex set. The same is true for the set of points preferred to x^0. Figures 1.2a and 1.2b illustrate this.

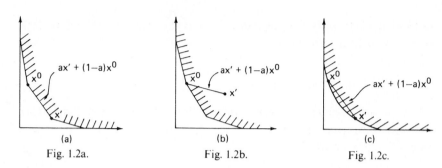

(a)	(b)	(c)
Fig. 1.2a.	Fig. 1.2b.	Fig. 1.2c.

A.5 is however an axiom of *strict* convexity, and implies that

$$ax' + (1 - a)x^0 \succ x^0 \quad \text{when} \quad x' \sim x^0 \quad (0 < a < 1).$$

The indifference curves have to be smooth (see Figure 1.2c), which is of course a stronger condition and corresponds to the sort of curve we had in mind when we started this discussion.

What does A.5 imply in terms of the utility function? We know that

$$u(x') > u(x^0) \quad \text{when} \quad x' \succ x^0.$$

A.5 therefore implies

$$u(ax' + (1 - a)x^0) > u(x^0) \quad \text{when} \quad x' \sim x^0,$$

i.e. when $u(x^0) = u(x')$ and $0 < a < 1$. $\qquad\qquad$ (1.3)

A utility function with property (1.3) is said to be *strictly quasi-concave*.

A.6. AXIOM OF DIFFERENTIABILITY.

We will finally assume that the strictly increasing (A.4) and quasi-concave (A.5) utility function is also *twice differentiable*. Together with A.4 and A.5, this assumption has important consequences for applied work, some of which may already be indicated.

Take the first order partial derivative $\partial u / \partial x_i$, which is called the 'marginal utility' of good i. Because of A.4, marginal utilities have always to be positive! When drawing a curve representing marginal utility of good i as a function of its quantity, we should therefore be careful not to cross the horizontal axis!

On the other hand, Young's theorem implies that the second-order derivatives are such that

$$\frac{\partial^2 u}{\partial x_i \, \partial x_j} = \frac{\partial^2 u}{\partial x_j \, \partial x_i}, \qquad\qquad (1.4)$$

so that the matrix of second-order derivatives, called 'Hessian matrix' is symmetric (see (1.9) below).

1.3. Ordinalism versus cardinalism

Now that we have a (well-behaved) utility function at our disposal, to represent a given preference ordering, a natural question is: is this representation unique?

The answer is: no. A whole family of transformations can do equally well, i.e. represent equally well the same preference ordering. To see this, it may be useful to start from the interpretation of u as a measure of the satisfaction derived from the consumption of a commodity bundle, and to ask what sort of measure it could be. A digression on the notion of 'measure' and its properties is then in order. This digression opens with the following exercise.

EXERCISE

1.6. A 'measure' is a number associated with an entity. Let there be the entities A, B, C, D, E, F, G and the measures associated with each of these as indicated in column (1) of the following table.

Entity	(1)	(2)	(3)	(4)	(5)
A	1				
B	2				
C	3				
D	4				
E	5				
F	7				
G	10				

(a) Multiply the numbers in column (1) by 2, and write down the result in column (2). What sort of measures allow transformations of this type?

(b) Add the number 5 to the numbers of column (1) and write down the result in column (3). Example of measure where this sort of addition is currently made?

(c) Multiply column (1) by 2, add the number 3 to each result, and fill in column (4). If you have travelled from Anglo-Saxon to European countries, you have had to make this sort of transformation (to get an idea of the temperature).

(d) Column (1) is related to columns (2), (3) and (4) respectively by linear increasing transformations of the type $y = ax + b$, $(a > 0)$, where the x's are the measures in column (1). Fill in column (5), using a transformation of x that is non-linear.

A measure is said to be '*cardinal*' when it is subject to linear (increasing) transformations only. It is '*ordinal*' when all monotonic (increasing) transformations (which of course include linear transformations) are allowed. Clearly, to know whether a measure is cardinal or ordinal, one has to be informed about the type of permissible transformations, it being understood that all usual measures are subject to transformations.

What then about u, our 'measure' of satisfaction? The authors who introduced this concept in economics (Menger, Gossen, Walras) implicitly or explicitly considered it as a cardinal measure. The immediate implication is that u is determined *up to a linear (increasing) transformation*. In terms of exercise 1.6, this means the following. Interpret the entities A, B, ..., G as different commodity bundles, and the numbers in column (1) as values of u associated with these bundles. The cardinal nature of u then implies that the numbers in colums (2), (3) and (4) express the satisfaction derived from the consumption of A, or B, etc. as well as do the numbers in column (1). In fact, any linear increasing transformation of column (1) does equally well. But column (5) could not replace column (1).

Cardinalism was soon very strongly objected to (in particular by Irving Fisher and Vilfredo Pareto). The decisive attack came in the thirties with the work of Hicks (1936), who showed that a rigorous analysis can be built on the assumption of a utility function defined *up to a monotonic increasing transformation*, which is of course much less restrictive. Defining u as an ordinal measure has at least two advantages. First, as a matter of scientific strategy, a less restrictive hypothesis is always to be preferred, because of the greater generality of the results derived from it. Second, it is not realistic to suppose that satisfaction is measurable in a cardinal way.

The more recent development of the axiomatic approach, defining the axioms necessary for establishing the existence of a well-behaved utility function, has laid the foundations for the ordinal approach. Indeed, any monotonic increasing transformation of u can serve as a representation of the underlying preference ordering. It is the preference ordering that counts. In what follows, the utility function will therefore *always* be defined as ordinal, i.e. as determined up to an increasing monotonic transformation. The implications of this will become clear as we proceed.

EXERCISES

1.7. Suppose a utility function in terms of x_1 and x_2 is specified as

(1) $u = x_1 x_2$

Let there also be the following utility functions:

(2) $u = x_1^2 x_2^2$
(3) $u = x_1^2 x_2^3$
(4) $u = 4x_1 x_2$
(5) $u = 4x_1 x_2 + 17$
(6) $u = \log(x_1 x_2)$

(a) Which functions are transformations of (1)?
(b) Which transformations can replace (1) from a cardinal point of view? From an ordinal point of view?
(c) Fill in the following table, in which each column corresponds to one of the six utility functions specified above.

x_1	x_2	(1)	(2)	(3)	(4)	(5)	(6)
1	1	1	1				
1	2	2	4				
2	1	2	4				
2	2	4	16				
3	2	6	36				

1.8. Let u be a utility function satisfying the axioms enumerated in Sections 1.1 and 1.2
   (a) Show that, if v is a monotonic increasing transformation of u, v satisfies the axiom of dominance.
   (b) What about the other axioms?
Answer: (a) By assumption, $v = F(u)$ such that $F' = dF/du > 0$. (F designates the transformation). The axiom of dominance implies $\partial u/\partial x_i > 0$. To show that v satisfies the axiom, one has to prove that $\partial v/\partial x_i > 0$. Now $\partial v/\partial x_i = F' \cdot \partial u/\partial x_i$, i.e. the product of two

positive terms, which is positive. Q.E.D. Notice that $F' > 0$ implies that the transformation has to be *strictly* increasing. In other words, $F' \geqslant 0$ would not do.

The reader should be convinced by now that our axioms establish the existence of a *class* of utility functions, in the sense that, given a member of that class, any (strictly) increasing monotonic transformation of it also represents the underlying preference ordering. It is important then to verify to what extent the properties of a given utility function are invariant under monotonic increasing transformations, i.e. to what extent the properties of one utility function are shared by the other members of its class.

Let us consider the first and second order partial derivatives of u and of $v = F(u)$, with $F' > 0$, where $v = F(u)$ designates the whole class of utility functions representing the same preference ordering, and set up the following table:

u	v
$\dfrac{\partial u}{\partial x_i}$	$\dfrac{\partial v}{\partial x_i} = F' \dfrac{\partial u}{\partial x_i}$
$\dfrac{\partial^2 u}{\partial x_i^2}$	$\dfrac{\partial^2 v}{\partial x_i^2} = F' \dfrac{\partial^2 u}{\partial x_i^2} + F'' \left(\dfrac{\partial u}{\partial x_i}\right)^2$
$\dfrac{\partial^2 u}{\partial x_i \partial x_j}$	$\dfrac{\partial^2 v}{\partial x_i \partial x_j} = F' \dfrac{\partial^2 u}{\partial x_i \partial x_j} + F'' \dfrac{\partial u}{\partial x_j} \dfrac{\partial u}{\partial x_i}$

where $F'' = \mathrm{d}^2 F/\mathrm{d}u^2$. When F is linear, F' is a positive constant and $F'' = 0$.

Looking at the first order partial derivatives, we see that their absolute value is never invariant within the class of utility functions considered. The absolute value of the marginal utility of a good is not determined. But the sign of these derivatives is always invariant (and positive), whether F is linear or not.

As for the second order direct derivatives, it is clear that their absolute value is not invariant, whether $F'' = 0$ or not. Their sign, however, is invariant if $F'' = 0$, i.e. if u is cardinal. Indeed, F' being positive, $\partial^2 v/\partial x_i^2$

will be negative if $\partial^2 u/\partial x_i^2$ is negative, when $F'' = 0$. This is not necessarily so when $F'' \neq 0$. That is the reason why the famous 'law of decreasing marginal utilities' is cardinal.

EXERCISES

1.9. The preceding statements can be illustrated with the help of the following table, in which the utilities listed in column (1) are transformed linearly into those listed in column (2) and non-linearly into those of column (3). Compute the first and second differences corresponding to (2) and (3) respectively. Compare their absolute values and signs with those of the first and second differences of (1).

(1)	First diff.	Second diff.	(2)	First diff.	Second diff.	(3)	First diff.	Second diff.
1			5			1		
6	5		15			36		
10	4	−1	23			100		
13	3	−1	29			169		
15	2	−1	33			225		
16	1	−1	35			256		
16.5	0.5	−0.5	36			272.25		

1.10. Use the transformations listed in exercise 1.7 to illustrate the preceding conclusions with respect to the invariance of the absolute value and the sign of the first and second order (direct and cross) partial derivatives. Which utility function obeys the law of decreasing marginal utilities?

Given that the absolute value of $\partial u/\partial x_i$ is not determined, ordinal demand theorists are anxious to avoid the concept of 'marginal utility' and replace it by the concept of 'marginal rate of substitution' between goods i and j, which is simply the ratio $(\partial u/\partial x_i)/(\partial u/\partial x_j)$. The latter's absolute value (just as its sign) is indeed invariant under monotonic transformations of u (why?).

For analogous reasons, orthodox ordinal theorists avoid concepts defined in terms of the absolute value or the sign of the second order derivatives of u. One example is the concept of independence or 'additivity', defined by the property that $\partial^2 u/\partial x_i \partial x_j = 0$. (Section 3.1 will be devoted to it.) A good deal of recent applied econometric analysis in the field is however based on utility functions specified as being additive. for reasons to be explored. This indicates that econometricians find it worthwhile to investigate and to tests empirically certain cardinal properties of a given utility function, although these properties are known not to be invariant under monotonic transformations. This is probably a transitory state of affairs: a day will come when these properties will have been redefined in ordinal terms. Some progress in that direction is reported in Section 3.4. Another example is the law of decreasing marginal utilities. Again, applied econometricians are happy to discover that their estimates of the second order partial direct derivatives of the utility function (on which their estimates are based) show up with a negative sign. They know that some transformation(s) may change this sign and are careful not to utilize these members of the class of utility functions considered.

1.4. Maximization of the utility function

The quantities purchased by a consumer are supposed to be optimal quantities, i.e. quantities determined by maximizing his utility function under a budget constraint. Formally, he is thus supposed to maximize $u = f(x_1, \ldots, x_n)$ subject to the linear constraint

$$\sum_i p_i x_i = y \tag{1.5}$$

where p_i represents the price of the ith commodity and y designates his total expenditures, called 'income'. All prices are supposed to be given: the consumer cannot influence them. y is fixed: the problem of how much to spend (and therefore how much to save) out of disposable income is not taken up here, to concentrate attention on the *allocation* of a given budget among n goods. In the final chapter of Part II, we will try to solve the difficult problem of simultaneously determining total expenditures (y) and their allocation among n goods.

Here, we reduce the analysis to the simple classical calculus problem of finding a constrained maximum of u, the constraint being linear. The successive steps are: (a) find the first order or necessary conditions for a local interior maximum; (b) verify the second order conditions for a local maximum; (c) make sure that the conditions for a global maximum are satisfied. Our interest is indeed in the global maximum which, after all, is *the* maximum.[2]

To find the *first order conditions* for a local maximum, we form the Lagrangian function

$$L = u - \lambda(\sum_i p_i x_i - y) \tag{1.6}$$

where λ is a Lagrange multiplier and we differentiate L with respect to x_i and λ, to obtain

$$\frac{\partial L}{\partial x_i} = \frac{\partial u}{\partial x_i} - \lambda p_i$$

$$-\frac{\partial L}{\partial \lambda} = \sum_i p_i x_i - y.$$

Putting all derivatives equal to zero, we obtain the $(n + 1)$ first order conditions:

$$\frac{\partial u}{\partial x_i} = \lambda p_i \qquad (i = 1, 2, \ldots, n)$$

$$\sum_i p_i x_i = y. \tag{1.7}$$

On the assumption that the conditions for a global maximum are satisfied – which is a valid assumption as we shall see in a moment – the solution of system (1.7) provides us with the n optimal values of x_i and the equilibrium value of λ. The n equilibrium values of x_i appear as functions of all prices and of y.[3] These functions are the *demand functions*, which describe the behaviour of the consumer in the market. These are therefore the functions we are interested in, whose properties we will analyse in Chapter II and whose parameters we will want to estimate in subsequent chapters.

Notice that the first n equations can be written as

$$\frac{\partial u/\partial x_1}{p_1} = \frac{\partial u/\partial x_2}{p_2} = \ldots = \frac{\partial u/\partial x_n}{p_n} = \lambda \tag{1.8a}$$

---

[2] For a general exposition of these conditions, see Intriligator (1971) or Lancaster (1968).
[3] This can be proved, using the implicit function theorem. See e.g. Intriligator (1971, Chapters 3 and 7).

which expresses the well-known cardinal principle that, at equilibrium, all marginal utilities divided by the corresponding prices are equal. In an ordinal approach, these conditions are rewritten as

$$\frac{\partial u/\partial x_i}{\partial u/\partial x_j} = \frac{p_i}{p_j} \tag{1.8b}$$

where the ratio at the left hand side is interpreted as a marginal rate of substitution (invariant under monotonic transformations of u).

EXERCISES

1.11. Maximize the utility functions (1), (2), (4), (5) and (6) of exercise 1.7, subject to the constraint $p_1 x_1 + p_2 x_2 = y$, and derive in each case the 2 demand equations and the equilibrium value of λ.

Answer: For $u = x_1 x_2$, the first order conditions are

$x_2 = \lambda p_1$
$x_1 = \lambda p_2$
$p_1 x_1 + p_2 x_2 = y.$

To solve this system, insert the first two conditions in the budget constraint, to obtain $p_1(\lambda p_2) + p_2(\lambda p_1) = y$. The equilibrium value of λ is therefore

$$\lambda^0 = \frac{y}{2p_1 p_2}.$$

Inserting this value in the first two conditions, we obtain the system of demand equations:

$$x_1^0 = \frac{y}{2p_1}$$

$$x_2^0 = \frac{y}{2p_2}.$$

The maximization of the other utility functions leads to exactly the same solutions. This is not at all surprising, as these utility functions all belong to the same class (i.e. are monotonic transformations of each other) and therefore represent the same preference ordering. One and the same preference ordering should lead to the same behaviour in the market, whatever its numerical representation. The general proof of this central result is given in exercise 1.15 below.

The demand functions just obtained have a very special and uncommon feature: the quantity demanded of each good depends only upon its own price. Normally *all* prices appear in each demand equation. We shall have to wait until Chapter III (Section 3.5) to find out why these demand equations have this special property.

1.12. Maximize $u = x_1 x_2$ given the constraint $2x_1 + 5x_2 = 100$ and draw (on graph paper) the map of indifference curves representing u, the budget constraint and the equilibrium point.

Hint: Remember that $x_1^0 = 100/2 \times (2)$ and $x_2^0 = 100/2 \times (5)$, and that the indifference curve passing through the equilibrium point has the utility index $25 \times 10 = 250$ associated with it.

1.13. (a) Show that the marginal rate of substitution is equal to minus the slope of the indifference curve to which it relates and, at equilibrium, to minus the slope of the budget line.

(b) What is the equation of the slope of the indifference curves defined by the utility functions (1), (2), (4) and (6) of exercise 1.7? Do you notice anything special?

Answer: (a) An indifference curve is defined by the property that $du = 0$. From

$$du = \frac{\partial u}{\partial x_1} dx_1 + \frac{\partial u}{\partial x_2} dx_2 = 0,$$

we derive

$$-\frac{\partial u}{\partial x_2} dx_2 = \frac{\partial u}{\partial x_1} dx_1$$

$$-\frac{dx_2}{dx_1} = \frac{\partial u/\partial x_1}{\partial u/\partial x_2}.$$

dx_2/dx_1 is the slope of the indifference curve. At equilibrium (see the first order conditions above),

$$\frac{\partial u/\partial x_1}{\partial u/\partial x_2} = \frac{p_1}{p_2}$$

while the budget constraint can be written $x_2 = (y - p_1 x_1)/p_2$. The slope of the budget line is therefore $-p_1/p_2$.

(b) The slopes are all equal to x_2/x_1. Along a line passing through the origin, i.e. for a given ratio x_2/x_1, all indifference curves have the same slope. These utility functions are thus 'homothetic'. On this, see Section 3.5.

1.14. Take the utility function $u = x_1 x_2$ and modify it in the following way. Replace x_i by $(x_i - \gamma_i)$ where γ_i is a constant, and allow each variable to have an exponent $\beta_i \neq 1$. You get $u = (x_1 - \gamma_1)^{\beta_1}$ $(x_2 - \gamma_2)^{\beta_2}$. Apply a logarithmic transformation to get another member of its class and generalize to n goods. You end up with $u = \sum_i \beta_i \log (x_i - \gamma_i)$. This is the well-known *Stone-Geary utility function* (about which more will be said in Chapter IV). Derive the system of demand equations, on the normalizing assumption that $\sum_i \beta_i = 1$.

Answer: From the first order conditions we derive

$$\beta_i = \lambda p_i(x_i - \gamma_i)$$
$$\sum_i \beta_i = 1 = \lambda \sum_i p_i(x_i - \gamma_i)$$

$$\lambda = \frac{1}{y - \sum_i p_i \gamma_i}.$$

(No confusion should arise from the fact that, from now on, we write the equilibrium λ^0 as λ and x_i^0 as x_i, to save on notation.) Substituting, we find

$$\beta_i = \frac{p_i(x_i - \gamma_i)}{y - \sum_j p_j \gamma_j}$$

or

$$x_i = \gamma_i + \frac{\beta_i}{p_i}(y - \sum_j p_j \gamma_j)$$

which is the famous '*linear expenditure system*' to be analysed extensively in Chapter IV. Now, each quantity demanded is a function of y and of *all* prices (the price p_i *and* the prices of all other goods).

Before taking up the second order conditions for a (local) maximum, we want to pause a moment and ask what may be the meaning, from the point of view of the economist, of the (somewhat mysterious) La-grange multiplier λ. It is possible and useful to give it an economic interpretation.

You will have noticed that λ appears as a factor of proportionality equal – at equilibrium – at the marginal utility of any good divided by its price. At equilibrium, λ is therefore the utility provided by the 'last dollar' spent, or 'the marginal utility of money' (in the terminology introduced by Alfred Marshall). To see this, consider that

$$\frac{\partial u}{\partial x_i} = \lambda p_i$$

may be written as

$$\frac{\partial u}{\partial (p_i x_i)} = \lambda$$

as p_i is a constant. The product $(p_i x_i)$ is the expenditure on good i. At equilibrium, an additional dollar spent on any good (i may be any commodity) therefore provides the same increase in utility λ. We can therefore say[4] that λ is the change in the maximized value of utility as income changes, or

$$\lambda = \frac{\partial u}{\partial y}$$

at equilibrium.

It is also illuminating to interpret λ as a number that converts money into utility, as

$$\lambda = \frac{1}{p_i} \frac{\partial u}{\partial x_i}$$

and $1/p_i$ is the number of units of good i that can be bought with one dollar (one monetary unit).

Finally, we notice that the equilibrium λ is a function of income and all prices (see exercises 1.11 and 1.14) and that this function is homo-geneous of degree minus one in prices and income. (Check in exercises 1.11 and 1.14 by multiplying all prices and income by a constant). This property of λ is related to the fact (to be established in the next chapter)

---

[4] The proof will be given in exercise 1.22 using the 'indirect' utility function.

that the quantities demanded remain unchanged when all prices and income increase or decrease proportionally, i.e. that the demand functions are homogeneous of degree zero. The solution of the first order conditions being unchanged, $\partial u/\partial x_i$ remains unaffected by a proportional change in prices and income, so that λ has to be *divided* by the constant by which p_i is multiplied for $\partial u/\partial x_i = \lambda p_i$ to remain true.

EXERCISES

1.15. u may be replaced by a monotonic transformation of it. It should be true, therefore, that the demand equations obtained by maximizing a transformation of u are the same as those obtained by maximizing u. In working out exercise 1.11, we saw that this was indeed the case. You are well equipped, by now, to give a general proof.

Answer: Constrained maximization of $v = F(u)$, with $F' > 0$, leads to the first order conditions

$$\frac{\partial v}{\partial x_i} - \lambda^* p_i = 0 \quad \text{and} \quad \sum p_i x_i = y,$$

where λ^* is the Lagrange multiplier associated with the maximization of v. The first n conditions can be rewritten as

$$F' \frac{\partial u}{\partial x_i} - \lambda^* p_i = 0$$

or

$$\frac{\partial u}{\partial x_i} - \frac{\lambda^*}{F'} p_i = 0.$$

As both λ (utilized in the maximization of u) and λ^* have to be positive (why?), we can replace λ^*/F' by λ, since $\lambda^* = F'(\partial u/\partial y) = F'\lambda$. We therefore end up with the same first order conditions as those obtained by maximizing u. The solution of these conditions, i.e. the system of demand equations, must therefore be the same. Q.E.D.

1.16. (a) Derive the equilibrium values of λ^* associated with each of the utility functions (2), (4), (5) and (6) of exercise 1.7, given that you know the λ associated with $u = x_1 x_2$ (exercise 1.11).

(b) Does the evolution of λ or λ^* as a function of y, in exercise 1.11, appear realistic to you? Compare with exercise 1.14.

(c) Are the absolute value and the sign of the marginal utility of money invariant under monotonic increasing transformations of the utility function?

(d) What about the absolute value and the sign of the derivative of the marginal utility of income with respect to income?

(e) What about the elasticity of the marginal utility of income with respect to income $\partial\lambda/\partial y . \; y/\lambda$?

The entire preceding discussion has been based on the assumption that the second order conditions for a local maximum and the conditions for a global maximum are satisfied. The time has come to look at these conditions, which will be given without proof.

Sufficient conditions for the second order conditions are as follows: for a constrained maximum, with one constraint, the determinant of the bordered Hessian should have the sign of $(-1)^n$, where n is the number of variables, the largest principal minor should have a sign opposite to this, and successively smaller principal minors should alternate in sign, down to the principal minor of order 2.

We already know that the 'Hessian' is the symmetric matrix of second order partial derivatives of the utility function. The bordered Hessian is defined here as

$$\begin{bmatrix} 0 & p_1 & \cdot & \cdot & \cdot & p_n \\ p_1 & u_{11} & \cdot & \cdot & \cdot & u_{1n} \\ \cdot & \cdot & \cdot & \cdot & \cdot & \cdot \\ p_n & u_{n1} & \cdot & \cdot & \cdot & u_{nn} \end{bmatrix}$$

where

$$u_{ii} = \frac{\partial^2 u}{\partial x_i^2}, \qquad u_{ij} = \frac{\partial^2 u}{\partial x_i \partial x_j}.$$

We see that the Hessian U

$$U = \begin{bmatrix} u_{11} & \cdot & \cdot & \cdot & u_{1n} \\ \cdot & \cdot & \cdot & \cdot & \cdot \\ u_{n1} & \cdot & \cdot & \cdot & u_{nn} \end{bmatrix} \qquad (1.9)$$

is bordered by a row and a column containing a zero and the partial derivatives (with respect to x_i) of the budget constraint $\sum\limits_i p_i x_i - y = 0$.

The principal minors referred to are obtained by deleting the *last* 1, 2, ..., *r* ... rows and columns of the bordered Hessian.

In the particular case where $n = 2$, the sufficient condition is thus that

$$\begin{vmatrix} 0 & p_1 & p_2 \\ p_1 & u_{11} & u_{12} \\ p_2 & u_{21} & u_{22} \end{vmatrix} = 2u_{12}p_1p_2 - p_1^2 u_{22} - p_2^2 u_{11} > 0 \qquad (1.10)$$

and

$$\begin{vmatrix} 0 & p_1 \\ p_1 & u_{11} \end{vmatrix} = -p_1^2 < 0.$$

Looking more closely at the determinant of the bordered Hessian for $n = 2$, we see that the sign condition can be rewritten as

$$p_1^2 u_{22} + p_2^2 u_{11} - 2u_{12}p_1p_2 < 0. \qquad (1.11)$$

Now, a well known mathematical result is that, if the utility function is (strictly) *concave*, then the Hessian U is negative semi-definite[5] so that (1.11) is satisfied. None of our axioms, however, implies the concavity of the utility function. The axiom of convexity guarantees that the utility function is *quasi-concave* (or '*concave-contoured*'). Remember that quasi-concavity is defined according to (1.3) as

$$u(ax' + (1 - a)x^0) > u(x^0) = u(x')$$

which means that an indifference curve (i.e. a contour) is a lower boundary of a convex set[6]. (Strict) concavity, on the other hand, is defined as

$$u(ax' + (1 - a)x^0) > au(x') + (1 - a)u(x^0) \quad \text{for} \quad x' \neq x^0. \qquad (1.12)$$

In (1.12), it is *not* supposed that x' and x^0 are equally preferred bundles. Concavity therefore depends both on the contours *and* on the way utility changes from contour to contour: it should change in such a way

---

[5] I.e. $z'Uz \leq 0$ for any vector $z \neq 0$. See e.g. H.G. Eggleston, *Convexity*, Cambridge University Press, 1958, p. 51.

[6] Quasi-concavity implies $z'Uz \leq 0$, where z is not an arbitrary vector but the difference between x' and x^0, *these being equally preferred bundles*.

that marginal utilities are decreasing. In applied work we shall often introduce the assumption of concavity.

However, concavity is too restrictive for theoretical purposes. It is more general to assume that the indifference curves are convex from below (i.e. that the utility function is quasi-concave). The sufficient conditions are then also satisfied. To show this, remember that the slope of an indifference curve is equal to[7]

$$\frac{dx_2}{dx_1} = -\frac{u_1}{u_2} \tag{1.13}$$

where $u_i = \partial u / \partial x_i$. Convexity implies $d^2 x_2 / dx_1^2 > 0$. Now (please check)

$$\frac{d^2 x_2}{dx_1^2} = -\frac{1}{u_2^3}(u_{11}u_2^2 - 2u_{12}u_1 u_2 + u_{22}u_1^2)$$

$$= -\frac{1}{u_2 p_2^2}(u_{11}p_2^2 - 2u_{12}p_1 p_2 + u_{22}p_1^2) \tag{1.14}$$

on substituting $u_1 = p_1 u_2 / p_2$. $d^2 x_2 / dx_1^2$ is positive if and only if (1.11) is satisfied, since $u_2 p_2^2$ is positive.

EXERCISE
1.17. Verify that condition (1.11) is satisfied in exercises 1.11 and 1.14, even when the second order direct derivatives of u are not negative.

It remains for us to consider the *conditions for a global maximum*. For a problem concerned with maximizing a continuous function $f(x)$ over a closed feasible set K, every local maximum is also a global maximum if: (a) f is a concave function and (b) K is a convex set. And if f is strictly concave over a convex feasible set the global maximum is unique. Furthermore, it is sufficient for satisfaction of the global optimum conditions for a maximum that $f(x)$ be a monotonic increasing transformation of a concave function, and K a convex set (Lancaster, 1968, p. 17–19).

As any quasi-concave function $f(x)$ which is an increasing function of every component of the vector x can be expressed as a monotonic increasing transformation of some concave function, all utility functions obeying our axioms are monotonic increasing transformations of some concave utility function. Any local maximum is therefore also a global maximum.

---

[7] See exercise 1.13.

1.18. Verify that the utility functions (1), (2), (4) and (5) of exercise 1.7 are (a) quasi-concave and (b) monotonic increasing transformations of the strictly concave utility function (6) $u = \log(x_1 x_2)$. *Hint:* apply (1.12) and (1.3).

To conclude this section, it may be useful to say a word about the *epistemology* of utility maximization. Some readers may have the impression that the preceding exposition is purely 'formal', without any relation to 'reality'. They may wonder whether the utility function exists 'really' – (not just formally); if it does, whether the consumer wants to maximize it; and even if he does, whether he would be able to do so.

The answer to each of these questions is probably: no. Negative answers to these sorts of questions are not considered relevant by the economist. The utility function is a formal concept useful to the economist, not to the consumer. By postulating (and possibly specifying) a utility function, the economist wants to create a tool useful for a correct description of observed consumer behaviour in the market and a reasonably good forecast of future behaviour. In the present state of the art, the best descriptions and therefore the best forecasts are obtained when using the assumption (or the implications) of utility maximization (as we shall see in later chapters); this fact is sufficient to reject criticisms based on the alleged 'formal' or 'unrealistic' character of our approach. This fact also confirms a more general observation, according to which 'reality', as it appears in the available statistical data, becomes intelligible only to the extent that it is interpreted with the help of a formal hypothesis that is *imposed* on the observed data. 'Reality' has to be remodeled to become interesting. Needless to say, further progress of economic science may (and probably will) one day put up an assumption – and corresponding axioms – that leads to even better descriptions and forecasts. At the moment, many refinements are already available, as will become clear in Part II of this book where we shall dynamize the utility function and put the problem in an intertemporal framework.

In the limit, one may say that the utility function exists because we postulate it. Its maximization is the logical consequence of our axioms. It is the *economist* who maximizes utility to find the 'optimal' quantities corresponding to the quantities that the consumer effectively purchases in the market. The optimization technique is thus simply a procedure that is utilized because it works, i.e. because it leads to operational hypotheses which turn out to be valid. Its justification lies in the conclusions that can be derived from it. (For an analogous argument, see Kuenne (1963, p. 16).)

These conclusions obviously refer to the demand equations, and take the form of *restrictions* to be imposed on these equations. Chapter II derives the 'general' restrictions that result from utility maximization as such. Chapter III discusses the additional 'particular' restrictions (as we shall call them) that result from the use of utility functions specified as having particular properties, and shows how to incorporate these restrictions in the empirical estimation of price and income elasticities. In this philosophy, applied consumption analysis appears then as the art of constructing and effectively utilizing interesting theoretical restrictions in the (econometric) estimation of demand equations. That this art is worth practising and developing is indicated by the observation that stronger (more particular that is) restrictions produce more precise estimations and better forecasts.

1.5. Indirect utility functions

All utility functions introduced above are 'direct': they have x_i ($i = 1, \ldots, n$) as arguments. We know that constrained maximization leads to a system of demand equations of the type

$$x_i^0 = \phi_i(p_1, \ldots, p_n, y).$$

When we replace x_i by the optimal x_i^0 in the direct utility function, we obtain an alternative description of a given preference ordering, called the indirect utility function, which we write as

$$
\begin{aligned}
u^* &= f[\phi_1(p_1, \ldots, p_n, y), \phi_2(p_1, \ldots, p_n, y), \ldots, \phi_n(p_1, \ldots, p_n, y)] \\
&= f^*(p_1, \ldots, p_n, y)
\end{aligned}
\tag{1.15}
$$

for $i = 1, \ldots, n$. The indirect utility function has prices and income as arguments.

EXERCISES

1.19. Write down the indirect utility functions corresponding to the direct utility functions (1), (2), (4), (5) and (6) of exercise 1.7.

1.20. What is the indirect utility function corresponding to the Stone-Geary function?

  Hint: See exercise 1.14.

We now investigate the properties of $f^*(p_1, \ldots, p_n, y)$. First of all, we want to emphasize that f^* is obtained by substituting x_i^0 for x_i in $f(x_1, \ldots, x_n)$. x_i^0 being optimal quantities that maximize u, u^* represents the *highest* utility that may be obtained with alternative (given) prices and incomes.

Another interesting property is the following. We will show that the demand functions ϕ_i are homogeneous of degree zero (in income and prices). Consequently, the indirect utility function is also *homogeneous of degree zero:* as a proportional change in all prices and income does not affect x_i^0, it cannot affect u^* either. The price-income indifference surfaces

$$f^*(p_1, \ldots, p_n, y) = \text{constant}$$

can therefore be represented by cones whose summit lies on the origin, in a three-dimensional diagram with y on the vertical axis and prices on the horizontal axes (see Figure 1.3).

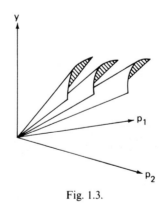

Fig. 1.3.

Figure 1.3 represents three indifference surfaces corresponding to three different constant values of u^*.

EXERCISE

1.21. Verify that the indirect utility functions derived in exercises 1.19 and 1.20 are indeed homogeneous of degree zero in income and prices.

Furthermore, there is a duality relation[8] between $f(x_1, \ldots, x_n)$ and $f^*(p_1, \ldots, p_n, y)$. (This is not surprising, given that both represent the same preference ordering.) Maximization of f with respect to the x's, with given prices and income, leads to the same demand equations as minimization of f^* with respect to prices and income, with given quantities. This property is the more useful as we can, to derive the demand equations from $f^*(p_1, \ldots, p_n, y)$, apply a formula known as *Roy's identity*[9]. Roy derives his identity in the following way. At equilibrium, we must have

$$\mathrm{d}u^* = 0 \quad \text{and} \quad \sum_i x_i \mathrm{d}p_i = \mathrm{d}y,$$

or

$$\frac{\partial f^*}{\partial p_1}\mathrm{d}p_1 + \frac{\partial f^*}{\partial p_2}\mathrm{d}p_2 + \ldots + \frac{\partial f^*}{\partial p_n}\mathrm{d}p_n = -\frac{\partial f^*}{\partial y}\mathrm{d}y$$

and

$$x_1^0\,\mathrm{d}p_1 + x_2^0\,\mathrm{d}p_2 + \ldots + x_n^0\,\mathrm{d}p_n = \mathrm{d}y$$

which implies

$$\frac{\partial f^*/\partial p_1}{x_i^0} = \ldots = \frac{\partial f^*/\partial p_n}{x_n^0} = -\frac{\partial f^*}{\partial y}$$

or

$$x_i^0 = -\frac{\partial f^*/\partial p_i}{\partial f^*/\partial y}. \tag{1.16}$$

Once f^* has been specified, it suffices to apply this identity to obtain the demand functions.

EXERCISES

1.22. In Section 1.4 we have interpreted λ as being the marginal utility of money or $\partial u/\partial y$ *at equilibrium*. The time has come to show that indeed $\lambda^0 = \partial u^*/\partial y$.

---

[8] A treatment of this and related duality relations is to be found in Bronsard (1971) and Lau (1972).

[9] See Roy (1942, p. 21) or Roy (1961, p. 22–23).

Answer: Differentiating u^* with respect to y, we have

$$\frac{\partial u^*}{\partial y} = \sum_i \frac{\partial f^*}{\partial x_i} \frac{\partial x_i}{\partial y}.$$

Differentiating the budget constraint with respect to y, we obtain

$$\sum_i p_i \frac{\partial x_i}{\partial y} = 1 \quad \text{or} \quad \lambda^0 \sum_i p_i \frac{\partial x_i}{\partial y} = \lambda^0.$$

Subtracting the second result from the first, we find

$$\frac{\partial u^*}{\partial y} = \sum_i \frac{\partial f^*}{\partial x_i} \frac{\partial x_i}{\partial y} - \lambda^0 \sum_i p_i \frac{\partial x_i}{\partial y} + \lambda^0 = \lambda^0 + \sum_i \left(\frac{\partial f^*}{\partial x_i} - \lambda^0 p_i \right) \frac{\partial x_i}{\partial y}.$$

As $\partial f^*/\partial x_i - \lambda^0 p_i = 0$ for all i, $\partial u^*/\partial y = \lambda^0$. Q.E.D.

1.23. Apply Roy's identity to the indirect utility functions obtained in exercises 1.19 and 1.20 to verify that you obtain the same demand equations as in exercises 1.11 and 1.14.

1.24. Let $u^* = \sum_i a_i(y/p_i)^{b_i}$ be the indirect 'addilog' utility function as specified by Houthakker in (1960b).
Derive the demand equations. Are these linear? If not, could you transform the demand equations into linear expressions (suitable for econometric estimation)?
Answer: From Roy's identity, the demand equations are

$$x_i = \frac{a_i b_i y^{b_i} p_i^{-b_i - 1}}{\sum_j a_j b_j y^{b_j - 1} p_j^{-b_j}}.$$

These are non-linear expressions. It would be very hard – and probably impossible – to imagine a workable method of estimating the coefficients a_i and b_i. The non-linearity is due to the presence of the sum in the denominator. How can we get rid of it?
Notice that the *same* sum appears in each demand equation. Why not divide one equation by another? One gets

$$\frac{x_i}{x_j} = \frac{a_i b_i y^{b_i} p_i^{-b_i - 1}}{a_j b_j y^{b_j} p_j^{-b_j - 1}}.$$

This is still non-linear, but a few additional manipulations suffice to give us a linear expression. Multiplying the numerator and the denominator by y we obtain

$$\frac{x^i}{x_j} = \frac{a_i b_i (y/p_i)^{b_i + 1}}{a_j b_j (y/p_j)^{b_j + 1}}$$

and, taking logarithms,

$$(\log x_i - \log x_j) = (\log a_i b_i - \log a_j b_j) + (1 + b_i) \log(y/p_i)$$

$$- (1 + b_j) \log\left(\frac{y}{p_j}\right).$$

Now $(1 + b_i)$ and $(1 + b_j)$ are slope coefficients in the multiple regression of the dependent variable $(\log x_i - \log x_j)$ on the independent variables $\log (y/p_i)$ and $\log (y/p_j)$. From the estimate of each slope coefficient estimates of b_i and b_j can be computed. Is it possible to estimate a_i and a_j?

A final word has to be said about the interest of the indirect as compared with the direct utility function. We saw that they are equivalent representations of the underlying preference ordering and that maximization of the latter and minimization of the former leads to the same observable behaviour in the market, i.e. to the same demand equations. In Houthakker's words (1960b, p. 245): 'While the direct utility function probably has greater intuitive appeal, the indirect utility function is not without its claims to interest also, for it is the foundation of 'constant-utility' index numbers of the cost of living. If we try to determine what change in income is necessary to compensate for a given change in prices (to mention one of the problems to which such index numbers can be applied) we are in effect trying to keep the *indirect* utility function constant'. Chapter V will make this clear.

II

Demand functions: general restrictions

In Chapter I, we assumed the existence, for a given price and income situation, of a solution $(x_1^0, \ldots, x_n^0, \lambda^0)$ for the first order conditions (1.7). For variable prices and income, this solution appears therefore as a system of n demand functions

$$x_1^0 = \phi_1 (p_1, \ldots, p_n, y)$$
$$x_2^0 = \phi_2 (p_1, \ldots, p_n, y)$$
$$\cdot$$
$$\cdot \qquad\qquad\qquad\qquad\qquad\qquad\qquad (2.1)$$
$$\cdot$$
$$x_n^0 = \phi_n (p_1, \ldots, p_n, y)$$

together with

$$\lambda^0 = \lambda^0 (p_1, \ldots, p_n, y). \qquad\qquad\qquad (2.2)$$

The existence of these functions, i.e. the fact that quantities are completely determined by prices and total expenditure, is guaranteed by the implicit function theorem,[1] System (2.1) is the system of demand equations or, shortly, the *demand system*. Applied consumption analysis is mainly concerned with the estimation of the parameters of one equation, or, when possible, of all equations in (2.1).

The present chapter is devoted to the analysis of the properties (of these demand equations) which result from the fact that a demand system is obtained by utility maximization. These properties will take the form of mathematical restrictions on the derivatives of the demand functions. These are always effective, whatever the form of the utility

---

[1] This theorem requires (a) the existence of the solution $(x_1^0, \ldots, x_n^0, \lambda^0)$ and (b) quasi-concavity of the utility function (which implies the non-singularity of the bordered Hessian). See Intriligator (1971, Chapters 3 and 6) or Lancaster (1968, p. 327–328).

function, and are therefore put together under the heading 'general restrictions'.

We shall discover that the general restrictions are deceptive because too general from the point of view of the applied economist. When it comes to estimation, one wants to have stronger restrictions to work with, such as conditions on the signs of the income and price derivatives (and elasticities) of the demand functions, or even conditions on the absolute value of certain parameters. The more restrictive are the conditions, the greater the chances are that our model will be rejected by the data; and the greater is the confidence we may attach to our estimates if they nevertheless turn out to be valid. Hence our interest in the 'particular restrictions' (Chapter III) which result from particular specifications of the utility function, and our interest in algebraic specifications, as should be clear to the reader who has gone through the exercises of Chapter I.

It is only after a full discussion of these matters that we shall be able to understand the intricacies of the analysis of the structure of preferences, i.e. of separability, independence, substitutability and complementarity. In Chapter III we introduce the reader to important recent developments on that front, while deferring a discussion of empirical implementations to Chapter IV.

Before proceeding, a word of caution may be in order. One should always recall that a demand system is defined for a given preference ordering. When preferences change the demand system also changes, as the form of the given utility function (or rather the properties of the given class of utility functions, to take account of the fact that a particular utility function is defined up to a monotonic transformation) determines the form of the demand functions. If then, in an empirical study, one tries to estimate the parameters of a demand equation or system, one should be conscious of the implicit assumption that the utility function remained unchanged over the observation period (or the sample space). Now, the preference ordering may in fact change a lot over time or from one household to another, so that it is very important to incorporate these changes in the analysis. The second part of this book is entirely devoted to this question.

The issue just discussed is not to be confused with the phenomenon of so-called shifts in elementary textbook 'demand curves' defined as

$$x_i = \phi_i(p_i) \tag{2.3}$$

where quantity demanded of good *i* appears as a function of its price. It should be evident that (2.3) is based on the assumption that the prices of all other goods and total expenditures are held constant. If y or one of the other prices came to vary, the curve representing (2.3) would of course shift. If is often said that (2.3) is defined *ceteris paribus* (all other things constant). The methodological and economical implications of the *ceteris paribus* assumption have been brilliantly discussed by Friedman (1949) to which the interested reader is referred.

2.1. Homogeneity of degree zero

Every demand equation must be homogeneous of degree zero in income and prices. In other words, if all prices and income are multiplied by a positive constant *k*, the quantity demanded must remain unchanged. In applied work, only those mathematical functions which have this property can be candidates for qualification as demand functions.

It is easily seen that this restriction is the direct result of utility maximization. It suffices us to take a closer look at the first order conditions. Multiplying all prices by *k* in the $n - 1$ equations

$$\frac{\partial u/\partial x_i}{\partial u/\partial x_j} = \frac{p_i}{p_j}$$

we see that the *k* drops out from the numerator and the denominator of the price ratio. As for the budget constraint, multiplying income and all prices by *k* we find (putting *k* before the summation sign)

$$ky = \sum_i kp_i x_i = k\sum_i p_i x_i$$

Again *k* can be eliminated. All first order conditions remain unaffected.

EXERCISE

2.1. Give an example from recent monetary history that illustrates the preceding exposition. Is the homogeneity restriction realistic?
   Answer: General De Gaulle's monetary reform, putting one hundred old French Francs equal to one new Franc. This is a change in the monetary unit and implies a multiplication of all prices and incomes by $k = 1/100$. (As such, it has nothing to do with inflation, except if inflation were to raise all prices and incomes proportionally.)
   The restriction says that the French should continue to consume

exactly the same quantities after the reform as though nothing happened. Consumers are supposed to have no 'money illusion': they should realize that a commodity priced '1 (new) F.' is *not* cheaper than a commodity priced '100 F.F.'. Whether the condition is realistic is hard to say. On average it probably is.[2]

The knowledge that all demand functions are homogeneous of degree zero is not very useful as such. To make it operational, we want to express it as a restriction on the derivatives of the demand functions. Euler's theorem, stating that if a function $z = \psi(x, y)$ is homogeneous of degree r then

$$x\frac{\partial z}{\partial x} + y\frac{\partial z}{\partial y} = rz,$$

is helpful. Take the demand function $x_1 = \phi_1(p_1, p_2, p_3, y)$. Straightforward application of the theorem gives

$$p_1\frac{\partial x_1}{\partial p_1} + p_2\frac{\partial x_1}{\partial p_2} + p_3\frac{\partial x_1}{\partial p_3} + y\frac{\partial x_1}{\partial y} = 0$$

or, in general,

$$\sum_j p_j\frac{\partial x_i}{\partial p_j} + y\frac{\partial x_i}{\partial y} = 0 \qquad (i, j = 1, \ldots, n) \tag{2.4}$$

Dividing all elements in (2.4) by x_i, we obtain price and income elasticities and the restriction becomes

$$\sum_j \frac{p_j}{x_i}\frac{\partial x_i}{\partial p_j} = -\frac{y}{x_i}\frac{\partial x_i}{\partial y} \tag{2.5}$$

The sum of all direct and cross elasticities with respect to prices of any commodity i has to be equal to minus its income elasticity. This condition has to be exactly fulfilled if we want to maintain that our computations produce estimates of derivatives or elasticities of demand functions.

EXERCISES

2.2. Compute, for the demand functions obtained in exercise 1.11
    (a) the direct (or own) price elasticities;

---

[2] See Section 2.5 below. However Branson and Klevorick (1969) found a significant degree of money illusion in the *aggregate* consumption function for the United States.

(b) the cross price elasticities:
(c) the income elasticities.
(d) Verify the homogeneity restriction.

Answer: No computation whatsoever is required. The elasticity of a variable x with respect to a variable y is equal by definition to $d \log x / d \log y$, while the demand functions $x_i = y/np_i$ can be written as $x_i = (1/n)y^1 p_i^{-1}$. The exponents are elasticities. Therefore

(a) all own price elasticities are equal to minus one:
(b) all cross price elasticities are zero, as the demand for commodity i is a function of its own price (and income) only:
(c) all income elasticities are unitary:
(d) $-1 + 1 = 0$. Q.E.D.

2.3. Same exercise with respect to the linear expenditure system $x_i = \gamma_i + \beta_i/p_i(y - \sum_j p_j\gamma_j)$ derived in exercise 1.14. Now some algebra is required.

Answer:

$$\frac{\partial x_i}{\partial p_i} = -\frac{\beta_i y}{p_i^2} + \frac{\beta_i}{p_i^2} \sum_{j \neq i} p_j\gamma_j$$

$$\frac{\partial x_i}{\partial p_j} = -\frac{\beta_i}{p_i}\gamma_j$$

$$\frac{\partial x_i}{\partial y} = \frac{\beta_i}{p_i}$$

$$-\frac{\beta_i}{p_i}y + \frac{\beta_i}{p_i}\sum_{j \neq i}p_j\gamma_j - \frac{\beta_i}{p_i}\sum_{j \neq i}\gamma_j p_j = -\frac{\beta_i}{p_i}y. \text{ Q.E.D.}$$

It is worth emphasizing that the demand equations *automatically* satisfy the homogeneity restriction (as well as the other general restrictions) when the demand system is obtained by constrained maximization of an algebraically specified utility function. As exercises 2.2 and 2.3 suggest, computations automatically produce derivatives (and therefore elasticities) such that conditions (2.4) or (2.5) are satisfied. In the case of the linear expenditure system for example, the values of β_i and γ_i, estimated from a time series of expenditures and prices for n goods, will be such that the estimated elasticities will sum up to zero for any good. This is a great comfort to the applied economist and explains his interest in demand systems derived from a particular utility function.

The possible loss of generality resulting from the choice of a particular utility function is (at least partly) compensated by the fact that one does not have to care about the general restrictions.

Where is the snake in this Eden? Unfortunately, complete demand systems can only be estimated (in the present state of the art) for a limited number of commodities (ten to twenty, say), if only because the available statistical data cover at most thirty to forty years. These commodities must therefore be large aggregates. One very often has to set up a demand equation for a much more disaggregated commodity ('beer' rather than 'food', 'automobiles' rather than 'durables', etc.), which it would be impossible to estimate in the framework of a complete system. What then?

One way out is to suppose separability and multi-stage maximization, and to construct a sub-system (for 'food', say) derived by maximization of a branch utility function (see Chapter III). But even this may be asking too much, given that one may wish to enter into the subtleties of the demand for a particular good. Some particular features may not be shared by other demand equations in the subsystem: the demand for good i may be a function of a number of variables that do not appear in the other demand equations. It is preferable then not to try to estimate a complete system (or sub-system), as all equations in a system have the same characteristics (same functional form, same independent variables).

In the analysis of the demand for a particular commodity taken in isolation, an *ad hoc* specification of the demand function has to be found. Furthermore, this specification has to be such that conditions (2.4) or (2.5) are again satisfied. (Otherwise, it would be impossible to pretend that the estimated elasticities refer to a *demand* function.) A few standard tricks are presented in the following exercises.

EXERCISES

2.4. The double-logarithmic specification

$$x_1 = A p_1^{\beta_{11}} p_2^{\beta_{12}} p_3^{\beta_{13}} y^\gamma,$$

in which good 1 is the particular commodity to be analysed, and goods 2 and 3 are close substitutes or complements, is very popular. How would you impose the homogeneity restriction?

Answer: The restriction is

$$\beta_{11} + \beta_{12} + \beta_{13} + \gamma = 0.$$

It is sufficient to make sure that $\gamma = -\beta_{11} - \beta_{12} - \beta_{13}$. This is obtained by writing the demand equation as

$$x_1 = A p_1^{\beta_{11}} p_2^{\beta_{12}} p_3^{\beta_{13}} y^{-\beta_{11} - \beta_{12} - \beta_{13}} \; = \; A \left(\frac{p_1}{y}\right)^{\beta_{11}} \left(\frac{p_2}{y}\right)^{\beta_{12}} \left(\frac{p_3}{y}\right)^{\beta_{13}}$$

and to run the multiple regression

$$\log x_1 = \log A + \beta_{11} \log\left(\frac{p_1}{y}\right) + \beta_{12} \log\left(\frac{p_2}{y}\right) + \beta_{13} \log\left(\frac{p_3}{y}\right).$$

Minus the sum of the estimates of β_{11}, β_{12} and β_{13} is the estimate of γ. Why is the double-logarithmic specification so popular? (See the answer to exercise 2.2).

2.5. You are asked to produce estimates of the price and income elasticities of good 1, for which good 2 is the only close substitute. You assemble statistical time series on x_{1t}, p_{1t}, p_{2t} and total expenditures per capita y_t and bring these data to the computer centre. A programmer – who is not an economist – suggests that you compute the multiple regression $x_{1t} = a + b_{11}p_{1t} + b_{12}p_{2t} + cy_t$. Would you agree? See Klein (1962, Chapter 2).

Answer: No, as the suggested linear equation is not homogeneous of degree zero. If you had good reason to use an equation linear in the variables (I cannot think of any good reason, though), you would have to make it homogeneous of degree zero, for example by dividing all independent variables by p_{1t}, or p_{2t}, or by the index of consumer prices.

2.2. Adding-up

The budget constraint has to be satisfied over the observed (or predicted) range of variation of prices and income. The demand equations have therefore to be such that the sum of the estimated (or predicted) expenditures on the different commodities equals total expenditures in any period. Such a system is sometimes said to be 'additive': it should be clear that a statement of that sort is not to be confused with statements about the additivity of the utility function (as defined in Chapter III).

The adding-up restriction can be expressed in terms of income derivatives in the following way. Differentiating the budget constraint with respect to y we get

$$\sum_i p_i \frac{\partial x_i}{\partial y} = \sum_i \frac{\partial(p_i x_i)}{\partial y} = 1 \tag{2.6}$$

where $p_i x_i$ is the expenditure on good i. $\partial(p_i x_i)/\partial y$ is called[3] the marginal propensity to consume good i (or its 'marginal budget share'). According to (2.6) the marginal propensities to consume must sum to one. In other words, an increase in total expenditure must be entirely allocated to the different commodities.

In applied work this is by no means a trivial matter. To see this, consider a forecast to be made for the expenditures on each of n goods. The restriction implies that the sum of the forecasts for the individual expenditures has to exactly equal the predicted total expenditures over the entire forecasting period. Again (and fortunately) this will be automatically the case if the demand system is derived by constrained maximization of a duly specified utility function. Otherwise one has to resort to appropriate mathematical devices (such as the use of linear functions) which ensure additivity.

EXERCISES

2.6. Verify that the adding-up condition is satisfied in the demand systems obtained in exercises 1.11 and 1.14.

2.7. In working out exercise 2.6, you will have noticed that β_i is the marginal propensity to consume in the linear expenditure system. However, the β's were normalized from the beginning by the assumption that $\sum_i \beta_i = 1$. Would the adding-up condition still be satisfied if the β's were not normalized?

Answer: Yes, of course. Insert the n first order conditions

$$x_i = \gamma_i + \frac{\beta_i}{\lambda p_i}$$

in the budget constraint and solve for λ:

$$\lambda = \frac{\sum_i \beta_i}{y - \sum_i p_i \gamma_i}.$$

---

[3] $p_i x_i / y$ is the average propensity to consume good i or its average budget share.

Substitute back to obtain

$$x_i = \gamma_i + \frac{\beta_i}{p_i(\sum_j \beta_j)}(y - \sum_j p_j\gamma_j).$$

Then

$$\sum_i \frac{\beta_i}{\sum_j \beta_j} = 1$$

or equivalently

$$\sum_i p_i x_i = \sum_i p_i\gamma_i + \frac{\sum_i \beta_i}{\sum_i \beta_i}(y - \sum_i p_i\gamma_i) = y.$$

It is evident that the normalization of the β's was based on the knowledge that $\partial(p_i x_i)/\partial y$ is equal to $\beta_i/\sum_j \beta_j$ (where the β's are not normalized).

2.3. The Slutsky equation: an intuitive approach

The remaining general restrictions are implications of the so-called 'Slutsky equation', which also bears the well-deserved name of 'fundamental equation of the theory of value'. The matter is so important that we will first approach it in an intuitive way, to make the economic implications clear. In the next section, we will proceed to a technical treatment with the help of the matrix algebra notation introduced by Anton Barten. By the same token a compact and unified presentation of all general restrictions will be given.

The basic idea is that the price derivatives of a demand equation can be decomposed. Slutsky (1915), in a now famous article that was rediscovered after some twenty years of neglect, was the first to show that the reaction of the quantity demanded of a good to a change in its price (*or* to a change in the price of *any* other good) can be decomposed into an *income effect* and a *substitution effect*. The first effect designates the variation (in the quantity demanded) due to the fact that a price change implies a change in the real income of the consumer: if a price increases, for example, the consumer has his purchasing power reduced. He will therefore adjust his demand. Generally (but not

necessarily) the reduction in purchasing power will lead to a reduction
of demand.

The substitution effect is that part of the variation in quantity demanded that is due to the fact that if the price of one good changes, its
relative price also changes, with the result that less will be consumed of
the good whose relative price increases (and more of the goods which
are substitutes to it), *if* one ignores the income effect.

Both effects are the result of one and the same price change. Their
sum is equal to the observed variation of quantity demanded. It may be
worth emphasizing that the income effect is a *quantity* change, which
results from a change in *price* (not in income).

The decomposition can be obtained in the following heuristic way.
Take any demand equation

$$x_i = \phi_i(p_1, \ldots, p_n, y)$$

and suppose p_i increases by dp_i, the other prices and y remaining constant. As a result, our consumer's purchasing power is reduced. Let us
imagine that we give him compensation, dy, which exactly makes up
for his loss in purchasing power. Two approaches are possible: we can
give compensation that keeps utility constant or one that allows him
to buy the same commodity bundle as the one he bought before the
price change. In the limit, both definitions give the same results. We
start with the second, so that the compensation is equal to

$$dy = x_i \, dp_i$$

where x_i is the quantity demanded before the price change. The price
change is now said to be 'compensated'.

Given a compensated price change, there are two variations dp_i and
dy, so that

$$dx_i = \frac{\partial x_i}{\partial p_i} dp_i + \frac{\partial x_i}{\partial y} dy$$

or

$$\left(\frac{dx_i}{dp_i}\right)_{y'} = \frac{\partial x_i}{\partial p_i} + \frac{\partial x_i}{\partial y}\frac{dy}{dp_i}$$

where $(dx_i/dp_i)_{y'}$ is the response of x_i to a compensated price change,
evaluated at $y' = y + dy$. By definition, the compensation given to the

consumer has eliminated the income effect. Thus $(dx_i/dp_i)_{y'}$ must be the substitution effect.

However, the compensation is such that $dy/dp_i = x_i$. On the other hand, $\partial x_i/\partial p_i$ is the derivative that we want to decompose. We can therefore write

$$\frac{\partial x_i}{\partial p_i} = \left(\frac{dx_i}{dp_i}\right)_{y'} - x_i \frac{\partial x_i}{\partial y} = k_{ii} - x_i \frac{\partial x_i}{\partial y}. \tag{2.7}$$

$\partial x_i/\partial p_i$ being uncompensated and $(dx_i/dp_i)_{y'}$ being the substitution effect (which we will henceforth call k_{ii} or k_{ij}) we end up with an income effect equal to $(-x_i \, \partial x_i/\partial y)$. Equation (2.7) is the Slutsky equation for the case where it is the commodity's own price that changes.

EXERCISE

2.8. Write the Slutsky equation for the case where it is the price of another good (p_j) that varies.

Answer: As $dy/dp_j = x_j$ we find

$$\frac{\partial x_i}{\partial p_j} = k_{ij} - x_j \frac{\partial x_i}{\partial y}.$$

Can we derive restrictions on the income effect? No. All we can say is that the greater $\partial x_i/\partial y$ or x_i, the greater it is in absolute value. The presence of the former element is not surprising. The presence of x_i can be understood intuitively: when the price of a matchbox rises I do not lose much purchasing power (x_i is small) but when my rent (large x_i) is increased things are very different as my rent represents a large part of my budget.

Economic theory has nothing to say about the sign of the income effect, in the absence of a particular specification of the utility function. If $\partial x_i/\partial y$ is positive, the income effect is negative; if $\partial x_i/\partial y$ is negative, the income effect is positive. But there is no general restriction on the sign of the income derivative. By definition, $\partial x_i/\partial y > 0$ when i is not an inferior good, and $\partial x_i/\partial y < 0$ when i *is* an inferior good. It is an empirical question to know to which category i belongs, i.e. to know what the sign of the income derivative (and therefore of the income effect) is.

Let us now imagine that the consumer is given such compensation in revenue as keeps his utility level unchanged. Important general restrictions on the substitution effects can then be easily worked out. We take the simple case where the utility function has only two arguments x_1 and x_2. Total differentiation of the first order conditions (1.7) leads, after rearrangement, to the system (x, x_2)

$$
\begin{aligned}
u_{11}\,dx_1 + u_{12}\,dx_2 - p_1\,d\lambda &= \lambda\,dp_1 \\
u_{21}\,dx_1 + u_{22}\,dx_2 - p_2\,d\lambda &= \lambda\,dp_2 \\
-p_1\,dx_1 - p_2\,dx_2 &= -dy + x_1\,dp_1 + x_2\,dp_2
\end{aligned}
\tag{2.8}
$$

Let D be the determinant

$$
\begin{vmatrix}
u_{11} & u_{12} & -p_1 \\
u_{21} & u_{22} & -p_2 \\
-p_1 & -p_2 & 0
\end{vmatrix}
= 2u_{12}p_1p_2 - p_1^2 u_{22} - p_2^2 u_{11}
$$

which we know to be positive from (1.10). Let D_{11}, D_{12}, etc. designate the cofactors of the element in the first row and the first column, of the element in the first row and the second column, etc. Then by Cramer's rule (see e.g. Henderson and Quandt, 1958, Appendix A–1),

$$
dx_1 = \frac{\lambda D_{11}\,dp_1 + \lambda D_{21}\,dp_2 + D_{31}(-dy + x_1\,dp_1 + x_2\,dp_2)}{D}.
$$

If now p_1 is the only price that changes ($dy = dp_2 = 0$), and dividing by dp_1, we obtain

$$
\begin{aligned}
\frac{\partial x_1}{\partial p_1} &= \frac{\lambda D_{11}}{D} + x_1 \frac{D_{31}}{D} \\
&= \frac{\lambda D_{11}}{D} - x_1 \frac{\partial x_1}{\partial y}
\end{aligned}
\tag{2.9}
$$

as $\partial x_1/\partial y = -D_{31}/D$. When the price change is compensated, $du = 0$ which implies $p_1\,dx_1 + p_2\,dx_2 = 0$ (why?) and therefore $-dy + x_1\,dp_1 + x_2\,dp_2 = 0$. Therefore

$$
\left(\frac{\partial x_1}{\partial p_1}\right)_{u=\text{constant}} = k_{11} = \frac{\lambda D_{11}}{D} = -\frac{\lambda p_2^2}{D} < 0,
\tag{2.10}
$$

which identifies $\lambda D_{11}/D$ as the substitution effect. (Instead of giving compensation that allows the purchase of the 'old' quantities, i.e. the quantities consumed before the price change, we are now giving compensation that holds u constant. For infinitesimal changes, this amounts to the same.)

We can now establish the general restriction that *the own (or direct) substitution effect is negative*. Indeed, λ and D are positive while D_{11} is negative, since $D_{11} = -p_2^2$.

The second general restriction says that *the matrix of substitution effects K,*

$$K = \begin{bmatrix} k_{11} & k_{12} & \ldots & k_{1n} \\ k_{21} & k_{22} & \ldots & k_{2n} \\ \cdot & & & \\ \cdot & & & \\ \cdot & & & \\ k_{n1} & k_{n2} & \ldots & k_{nn} \end{bmatrix}$$

is symmetric, or

$$k_{ij} = k_{ji} \tag{2.11a}$$

or

$$\frac{\partial x_i}{\partial p_j} + x_j \frac{\partial x_i}{\partial y} = \frac{\partial x_j}{\partial p_i} + x_i \frac{\partial x_j}{\partial y}. \tag{2.11b}$$

Indeed, in the simple two-commodity case above, we have from (2.8) and its counterpart

$$dx_2 = \frac{\lambda D_{12}\, dp_1 + \lambda D_{22}\, dp_2 + D_{32}(-dy + x_1\, dp_1 + x_2\, dp_2)}{D}$$

that

$$\frac{\partial x_1}{\partial p_2} = \frac{\lambda D_{21}}{D} + x_2 \frac{D_{31}}{D} = \frac{\lambda D_{21}}{D} - x_2 \frac{\partial x_1}{\partial y}$$

$$\frac{\partial x_2}{\partial p_1} = \frac{\lambda D_{12}}{D} + x_1 \frac{D_{32}}{D} = \frac{\lambda D_{12}}{D} - x_1 \frac{\partial x_2}{\partial y}.$$

As $D_{12} = D_{21}$, since the bordered Hessian matrix is symmetric, $k_{12} = k_{21}$.

A few caveats are in order. First, it should be noted that the sign of the cross substitution effect k_{ij} is not determined. As this sign is sometimes utilized to define substitution or complementarity relationships (see Section 3.4 on the structure of preferences), these relationships are to be determined empirically as long as no specific utility function is brought into the analysis. Secondly, the signs of $\partial x_i/\partial p_i$ and $\partial x_i/\partial p_j$ are also not determined. $\partial x_i/\partial p_i$ being the slope of the demand curve (2.3), this means that demand curves are *not* necessarily downward sloping. While the element k_{ii} is always negative, the element $(-x_i\,\partial x_i/\partial y)$ may be positive, in which case $\partial x_i/\partial p_i$ may be positive if the absolute value of the income effect is large enough. Finally, it will be remembered that the first order conditions are invariant under monotonic transformations of the utility function (exercise 1.15). The Slutsky equation is therefore also invariant.

EXERCISES

2.9. (a) Derive the Slutsky equation for the demand equations obtained by constrained maximization of $u = x_1 x_2$.
   (b) Verify that $k_{ii} < 0$ and $k_{12} = k_{21}$.
   (c) Explain why p_i is the only price that appears in the demand equation for good i.

Answer: (a) Total differentiation of the first order conditions

$$x_2 - \lambda p_1 = 0$$
$$x_1 - \lambda p_2 = 0$$
$$y - p_1 x_1 - p_2 x_2 = 0$$

gives

$$dx_2 - p_1\,d\lambda = \lambda\,dp_1$$
$$dx_1 \qquad\quad - p_2\,d\lambda = \lambda\,dp_2$$
$$-p_1\,dx_1 - p_2\,dx_2 \qquad\quad = -dy + x_1\,dp_1 + x_2\,dp_2$$

so that

$$D = \begin{vmatrix} 0 & 1 & -p_1 \\ 1 & 0 & -p_2 \\ -p_1 & -p_2 & 0 \end{vmatrix} = 2p_1 p_2$$

$$D_{11} = -p_2^2 \qquad D_{21} = p_1 p_2 \quad \text{and} \quad D_{31} = -p_2.$$

$$dx_1 = \frac{-p_2^2\lambda\,dp_1 + p_1 p_2\lambda\,dp_2 - p_2(-dy + x_1\,dp_1 + x_2\,dp_2)}{2p_1 p_2}$$

and for $dp_2 = dy = 0$

$$\frac{\partial x_1}{\partial p_1} = -\frac{p_2\lambda}{2p_1} - \frac{x_1}{2p_1}.$$

(b) λ, p_1 and p_2 being positive, $k_{11} = -p_2\lambda/2p_1 < 0$.
What about k_{22}?
As for symmetry, we find

$$\frac{\partial x_1}{\partial p_2} = \frac{1}{2}\lambda - \frac{x_2}{2p_1}$$

and

$$\frac{\partial x_2}{\partial p_1} = \frac{1}{2}\lambda - \frac{x_1}{2p_2}$$

so that

$$k_{12} = k_{21} = \tfrac{1}{2}\lambda.$$

Notice that you could have used (2.11b) to find directly $k_{12} = k_{21} = 0 + y/4p_1p_2 = \lambda/2$.
Similarly k_{ii} can be computed directly from (2.7) as

$$k_{ii} = \frac{\partial x_i}{\partial p_i} + x_i \frac{\partial x_i}{\partial y} = \frac{-2y}{4p_i^2} + \frac{x_i}{2p_i} = -\frac{y}{4p_i^2} < 0.$$

(c) Using the knowledge that $\lambda = y/2p_1p_2$ and $x_i = y/2p_i$, we find

$$\frac{\partial x_1}{\partial p_2} = \frac{y}{4p_1p_2} - \frac{y}{4p_1p_2} = 0$$

$$\frac{\partial x_2}{\partial p_1} = \frac{y}{4p_1p_2} - \frac{y}{4p_1p_2} = 0.$$

The cross substitution effect and the income effect happen to have the same absolute value and opposite sign. That is why each quantity demanded is a function of its own price only.

2.10. Suppose then you want to estimate the demand function $x_i = a + b_{11}p_{1t} + b_{12}p_{2t} + cy_t$ (in which the independent variables are constructed in such a way that the function is homogeneous of degree zero). Does your knowledge of the general restrictions allow you to determine in advance (a) the order of magnitude of the coefficients b_{11}, b_{12} and c?; (b) the sign of each of these coefficients?; (c) the sign of some of these, given the sign of one of them?

Answer: The answer to each of these questions is: no. The order of magnitude never entered our discussion. The signs of $\partial x_i/\partial p_i$, $\partial x_i/\partial p_j$ and $\partial x_i/\partial y$ being undetermined, the same is true for the corresponding coefficients (here b_{11}, b_{12} and c). Even if we knew that $c < 0$, i.e. that the commodity analysed is an inferior good, we could not infer from this that b_{11} is positive (why?). All this is the more deceptive as these are precisely the sort of questions which the applied economist would like to be answered *before* embarking upon econometric work. For he would then have strong hypotheses to test on a given sample. As long as signs and magnitudes of regression coefficients are undetermined, any empirical result looks as good as any other. Hence the quest for particular restrictions.

2.4.* The fundamental matrix equation[4]

Let x and p be $(n \times 1)$ vectors and y a scalar. Maximization of $u = f(x)$ under the constraint $p'x = y$ leads to the system of first order conditions

$$\begin{aligned} u_x &= \lambda p \\ p'x &= y \end{aligned} \tag{2.12}$$

where $u_x = \partial u/\partial x = [u_1, \ldots, u_n]'$. The solution of (2.12) is

$$\begin{aligned} x &= x(y, p) \\ \lambda &= \lambda(y, p). \end{aligned} \tag{2.13}$$

The total differential of the vector of marginal utilities can be written $\mathrm{d}u_x = U\,\mathrm{d}x$, where U is the $(n \times n)$ Hessian matrix

$$U = \left[\frac{\partial^2 u}{\partial x_i\,\partial x_j}\right] = [u_{ij}]$$

introduced in equation (1.9) of Chapter I. With this notation, total differentiation of the first order conditions gives

$$\begin{aligned} U\,\mathrm{d}x &= p\,\mathrm{d}\lambda + \lambda\,\mathrm{d}p \\ \mathrm{d}y &= p'\,\mathrm{d}x + x'\,\mathrm{d}p \end{aligned}$$

or

$$\begin{bmatrix} U & p \\ p' & 0 \end{bmatrix} \begin{bmatrix} \mathrm{d}x \\ -\mathrm{d}\lambda \end{bmatrix} = \begin{bmatrix} 0 & \lambda I \\ 1 & -x' \end{bmatrix} \begin{bmatrix} \mathrm{d}y \\ \mathrm{d}p \end{bmatrix} \tag{2.14}$$

---

[4] See Barten (1964a, 1966) or Goldberger (1967).

which Barten (1966, p. 14) calls the fundamental matrix equation of the theory of consumer demand in terms of infinitesimal changes.

EXERCISE

2.11. Write out (2.14) in algebraic notation for $n = 2$ to find system (2.8).

On the other hand, total differentiation of (2.13) shows that

$$dx = x_y\,dy + X_p\,dp$$
$$d\lambda = \lambda_y\,dy + \lambda'_p\,dp$$

where dx and dp are vectors, or

$$\begin{bmatrix} dx \\ -d\lambda \end{bmatrix} = \begin{bmatrix} x_y & X_p \\ -\lambda_y & -\lambda'_p \end{bmatrix}\begin{bmatrix} dy \\ dp \end{bmatrix} \tag{2.15}$$

where

$$x_y = \begin{bmatrix} \dfrac{\partial x_i}{\partial y} \end{bmatrix}, \qquad \lambda_y = \dfrac{\partial \lambda}{\partial y}, \qquad \lambda_p = \begin{bmatrix} \dfrac{\partial \lambda}{\partial p_i} \end{bmatrix} \quad \text{and} \quad X_p = \begin{bmatrix} \dfrac{\partial x_i}{\partial p_j} \end{bmatrix}.$$

Since (2.14), after having substituted (2.15) into it, holds for arbitrary dy, dp, we can write the fundamental equation in terms of partial derivatives as

$$\begin{bmatrix} U & p \\ p' & 0 \end{bmatrix}\begin{bmatrix} x_y & X_p \\ -\lambda_y & -\lambda'_p \end{bmatrix} = \begin{bmatrix} 0 & \lambda I \\ 1 & -x' \end{bmatrix}. \tag{2.16}$$

The solution of (2.16) for x_y, X_p, λ_y and λ_p permits the deduction of the general restrictions which a complete system of demand equations will satisfy regardless of the underlying utility function. To solve (2.16) one has to compute the inverse of the first matrix to the left. This inverse is:[5]

$$\begin{bmatrix} U & p \\ p' & 0 \end{bmatrix}^{-1} = (p'U^{-1}p)^{-1}\begin{bmatrix} (p'U^{-1}p)U^{-1} - U^{-1}pp'U^{-1} & U^{-1}p' \\ p'U^{-1} & -1 \end{bmatrix}$$

$$= R \tag{2.17}$$

---

[5] One has to apply the following rule for the inversion of a matrix in partitioned form. Let

$$A = \begin{bmatrix} E & F \\ G & H \end{bmatrix}$$

and $D = H - GE^{-1}F$, and suppose that A, E and D are nonsingular. Then

$$A^{-1} = \begin{bmatrix} E^{-1}(I + FD^{-1}GE^{-1}) & -E^{-1}FD^{-1} \\ -D^{-1}GE^{-1} & D^{-1} \end{bmatrix}.$$

The proof can be found in Goldberger (1964, p. 27).

so that

$$\begin{bmatrix} x_y & X_p \\ -\lambda_y & -\lambda_p' \end{bmatrix} = R \begin{bmatrix} 0 & \lambda I \\ 1 & -x' \end{bmatrix}$$

or

$$\lambda_y = (p'U^{-1}p)^{-1} \tag{2.18}$$

$$\lambda_p = -\lambda_y(\lambda U^{-1}p + x) \tag{2.19}$$

$$x_y = \lambda_y U^{-1}p \tag{2.20}$$

$$X_p = \lambda U^{-1} - \lambda\lambda_y U^{-1}pp'U^{-1} - \lambda_y U^{-1}px'. \tag{2.21}$$

Substitution of (2.20) in (2.19) and (2.21) finally gives

$$\lambda_y = (p'U^{-1}p)^{-1} \tag{2.22}$$

$$\lambda_p = -(\lambda x_y + \lambda_y x) \tag{2.23}$$

$$x_y = \lambda_y U^{-1}p \tag{2.24}$$

$$X_p = \lambda U^{-1} - \lambda\lambda_y^{-1}x_y x_y' - x_y x'. \tag{2.25}$$

Equation (2.25) is the Slutsky equation and can be written

$$X_p = K - x_y x' \tag{2.26}$$

where

$$K = \lambda U^{-1} - \lambda\lambda_y^{-1}x_y x_y' \tag{2.27}$$

is the substitution matrix (i.e. the matrix of substitution effects) and $-x_y x'$ the matrix of income effects.

This exposition has the important advantage of showing that the substitution effect can be decomposed into two components. The first component

$$\lambda u^{ij}$$

(where u^{ij} denotes the i, j element of U^{-1}) is called the *specific substitution effect*. The second component

$$-\left(\lambda/\frac{\partial\lambda}{\partial y}\right)\frac{\partial x_i}{\partial y}\frac{\partial x_j}{\partial y}$$

is the *general substitution effect*, in the terminology introduced by Houthakker (1960, p. 248, footnote 8). When $i = j$, the decomposition refers to the direct substitution effect. When $i \neq j$, it refers to the cross-substitution effect.

EXERCISE

2.12. Are the signs of the specific and the general substitution effects determined? Discuss separately the cases where $i = j$ and $i \neq j$.
   Hint: Remember our discussion of the invariance of u_{ij} under monotonic transformations of u (in Section 1.3) and of λ_y in exercise 1.16.

2.13. We know that the (total) substitution effect k_{ij} is not affected by monotonic increasing transformations of the utility function. Explain why its components in (2.27) are not invariant.
   Hint: We know that k_{ij} is invariant because it can be written as $\partial x_i / \partial p_j + x_j(\partial x_i / \partial y)$. All the elements in this expression are indeed invariant. To answer the question, it suffices therefore to look more closely at the different elements in (2.27).

The adjectives 'specific' and 'general' are well chosen. The first indicates that the corresponding component depends upon the specific relation (in terms of u_{ij}) between good i and good j. The second emphasizes that the component

$$-\left(\lambda \bigg/ \frac{\partial \lambda}{\partial y}\right) \frac{\partial x_i}{\partial y} \frac{\partial x_j}{\partial y}$$

represents an overall effect, for which it is possible to give an appropriate compensation. This can be seen as follows.

Substituting (2.26) into (2.15) we have

$$\begin{aligned}
\mathrm{d}x &= x_y \, \mathrm{d}y + (K - x_y x') \mathrm{d}p \\
&= x_y \, \mathrm{d}y + (\lambda U^{-1} - \lambda\lambda_y^{-1} x_y x_y' - x_y x') \mathrm{d}p \\
&= x_y[\mathrm{d}y - x' \, \mathrm{d}p - (\lambda\lambda_y^{-1}) x_y' \, \mathrm{d}p] + \lambda U^{-1} \, \mathrm{d}p.
\end{aligned}$$

(2.28)

To define the (total) substitution effect as the response to a compensated price change, we introduced a compensation equal to $x' \, \mathrm{d}p$. If now we give a compensation equal to

$$\mathrm{d}y = x' \, \mathrm{d}p + (\lambda\lambda_y^{-1}) x_y' \, \mathrm{d}p$$

(2.29)

we find $dx = \lambda U^{-1} dp$, which is the specific substitution effect. On the other hand, substitution of (2.23) in (2.15) gives

$$\begin{aligned} d\lambda &= \lambda_y \, dy - \lambda x_y' \, dp - \lambda_y x' \, dp \\ &= \lambda_y (dy - x' \, dp - \lambda \lambda_y^{-1} x_y' \, dp) \end{aligned} \tag{2.30}$$

so that $d\lambda = 0$ when the compensation is as in (2.29). That is why the specific substitution effect λU^{-1} is also defined as the response to a marginal-utility-of-income compensated price change.

We now derive the general restrictions from (2.22)–(2.25). The *adding-up* restriction (often called 'Engel aggregation' condition in the terminology of Frisch (1959)) is obtained by premultiplying (2.24) by p':

$$p' x_y = \lambda_y p' U^{-1} p = 1 \tag{2.31}$$

in view of (2.22). Equation (2.31) corresponds to equation (2.6).

Postmultiplication of the transpose of (2.25) by p gives what Frisch calls the 'Cournot aggregation' condition:[6]

$$\begin{aligned} X_p' p &= \lambda U^{-1} p - \lambda \lambda_y^{-1} x_y x_y' p - x x_y' p \\ &= \lambda \lambda_y^{-1} x_y - \lambda \lambda_y^{-1} x_y x_y' p - x x_y' p \\ &= \lambda \lambda_y^{-1} x_y - \lambda \lambda_y^{-1} x_y - x \\ &= -x \end{aligned} \tag{2.32}$$

in view of (2.24) and (2.31). This result will be used in a moment.

The *symmetry* of K ($K = K'$) follows directly from the fact that

$$\lambda U^{-1} - \lambda \lambda_y^{-1} x_y x_y'$$

is a symmetric matrix. From (2.26) we may therefore write

$$X_p + x_y x' = X_p' + x x_y'. \tag{2.33}$$

which corresponds to (2.11b).

It is now easy to establish the *homogeneity* condition. Postmultiplication of K by p gives

$$\begin{aligned} Kp &= X_p p + x_y x' p \\ &= X_p' p + x x_y' p \\ &= -x + x \\ &= 0 \end{aligned} \tag{2.34}$$

in view of (2.33), (2.32) and (2.31). $Kp = 0$ corresponds to equation (2.4).

---

[6] This condition was not discussed above, because it can be derived from the other general restrictions.

Finally, we have to establish the *negativity* of the own substitution effect k_{ii}. This is perhaps the most important restriction as it establishes the negativity of the slope of the demand curves whenever the income derivative is not negative, i.e. for all goods that are not inferior. The proof is based on the fact that the substitution matrix K is negative semidefinite, or

$$y'Ky \leqq 0, \qquad y \neq 0. \tag{2.35}$$

To prove negative semidefiniteness, we have to go back to the quasi-concavity of the utility function, which implies that $z'Uz < 0$, where z is the difference between two equally preferred bundles x' and x^0, or[7]

$$z'Uz < 0, \qquad u_x'z = 0, \qquad z \neq 0$$

or

$$z'Uz < 0, \qquad p'z = 0, \qquad z \neq 0. \tag{2.36}$$

given that $u_x = \lambda p$. To take advantage of this knowledge, we transform $y'Ky$ in an expression of the form $z'Uz$.

Using (2.27), (2.18) and (2.20), we can write (2.17) as

$$\begin{bmatrix} U & p \\ p' & 0 \end{bmatrix}^{-1} = \begin{bmatrix} \dfrac{1}{\lambda}K & \lambda_y U^{-1}p \\ \lambda_y p'U^{-1} & -\lambda_y \end{bmatrix} \tag{2.37}$$

so that, by the definition of the inverse of a partitioned matrix

$$\frac{1}{\lambda}UK + p\lambda_y p'U^{-1} = \frac{1}{\lambda}UK + px_y = I.$$

Premultiplying this result by $(1/\lambda)K$, we find

$$\left(\frac{1}{\lambda}K\right)U\left(\frac{1}{\lambda}K\right) = \left(\frac{1}{\lambda}K\right), \tag{2.38}$$

in view of (2.34). We have thus found a way to transform K into an expression involving U.

Consider then the quadratic form

$$y'\left(\frac{1}{\lambda}K\right)y = \left(\frac{1}{\lambda}y'K\right)U\left(\frac{1}{\lambda}Ky\right) = z'Uz \tag{2.39}$$

---

[7] Consider the Taylor expansion $u(x') = u(x^0) + u_x'z$, where the vector u_x is evaluated at a point x'' of the linear interval between x^0 and x'. Indifference implies $u(x') = u(x^0)$ or $u_x'z = 0$. The Property $z'Uz < 0$ is valid for almost every commodity bundle.

with $z = (1/\lambda)Ky$. From (2.36) we know that $p'z = 0$. The z's are then restricted as required by the definitions of quasi-concavity, so that the quadratic form (2.39) is negative if $z \neq 0$. If $z = 0$, $(1/\lambda)Ky = 0$. However, we know that $(1/\lambda)Kp = 0$ from (2.34). Therefore, since the null space of K is of dimension 1, $z = 0$ only if $y = \alpha p$ where α is some real scalar. But then $y \neq 0$. This establishes that

$$y'\left(\frac{1}{\lambda}K\right)y \leqq 0, \qquad y \neq 0 \tag{2.40}$$

which itself implies (2.35), as λ is positive[8].

It immediately follows that

$$e_i'Ke_i = k_{ii} < 0 \tag{2.41}$$

where e_i is a vector of n elements with all elements equal to zero except the ith one which is unity. Indeed, since *all* prices are positive, $e_i \neq \alpha p$, so that the quadratic form (2.41) must be negative.

2.5. Concluding remarks: evidence and significance

Equations (2.31), (2.33), (2.34) and (2.41) or their counterparts (2.6), (2.11b), (2.4) and (2.10) are the general restrictions or 'Slutsky conditions'[9] that each demand system must satisfy. The time has come to pause and enquire about the precise meaning of the preceding statement. Do we mean to say that observed demand behaviour does in fact always satisfy these conditions? If not, in what sense do we say that the general conditions 'must' be satisfied?

Each of the general restrictions defines a relationship that is exact. The sum of marginal propensities to consume exactly equals 1. The cross substitution effect k_{ij} exactly equals k_{ji}. The sum of all price and income elasticities exactly equals zero. All k_{ii} are negative. As these are derived from theoretical arguments, there is no reason why measured behaviour[10] should obey them, as theory is always a simplification of reality. A thousand particular circumstances may ensure that the sum of measured marginal propensities to consume does not exactly equal one, if only because statistical data always contain some errors of

---

[8] See Barten, Kloek and Lempers (1969).

[9] In the terminology suggested by Barten (1967) in honour of Eugen Slutsky who was the first to state them explicitly.

[10] The observed behaviour of rats, though, does satisfy the general restrictions of demand theory: see Kagel et al. (1975 and 1977). Since human beings are much more complex animals, they are less likely to behave according to our axioms.

measurement. And similarly for the other restrictions. All we can hope is that rough estimates, computed without imposing these constraints, will not be inconsistent with them.

Theil (1967, Chapter 7) has specified a system of demand equations[11] that permits a direct empirical testing. Start from the differential (2.28), written as

$$dx_i = \frac{\partial x_i}{\partial y}(dy - \sum_h x_h\, dp_h) + \sum_j k_{ij}\, dp_j \qquad (2.42)$$

in algebraic notation, where $h, i, j = 1, \ldots, n$. Using the equality $dx = x\, d\log x$, where log denotes natural logarithms, it can be shown that (2.42) is equivalent to

$$w_i\, d\log x_i = B_i(d\log y - \sum_k w_k\, d\log p_k) + \sum_j S_{ij}\, d\log p_j \qquad (2.43)$$

where $w_i = p_i x_i/y$, the share of expenditure on commodity i in total expenditure, $B_i = p_i(\partial x_i/\partial y)$ and $S_{ij} = (1/y)p_i p_j k_{ij}$.

The adding-up condition can now be written as

$$\sum_i B_i = 1 \qquad (2.44)$$

while the new version of the homogeneity condition is given by

$$\sum_j S_{ij} = 0. \qquad (2.45)$$

The transformation from k_{ij} to S_{ij} leaves the symmetry untouched, hence

$$S_{ij} = S_{ji}. \qquad (2.46)$$

Finally, because prices and income are strictly positive

$$S_{ii} < 0. \qquad (2.47)$$

If one is ready to treat B_i and S_{ij} as constants, these constants can be estimated by ordinary least squares, equation by equation.

Using time series on expenditure and prices for four aggregate commodity groups (food, pleasure goods, durables and remainder) in the Netherlands, covering the years 1922–1939 and 1949–1961, Barten (1967) finds that:

(a) all estimated S_{ii} coefficients are negative;

---

[11] Known as the 'Rotterdam model'. It can also be found in Barten (1967). See Barnett (1979a) on the theoretical foundations of this model.

(b) although the homogeneity condition is not exactly satisfied, the empirical data used are not inconsistent with it;

(c) the B_i almost sum to one;

(d) the empirical validity of the symmetry condition, which is not exactly satisfied, cannot be rejected.

Further tests, based on the same model, were carried out by Byron (1970a, b) and Barten (1969) using maximum likelihood methods and seemed to suggest rejection of the theoretical restrictions. However, Deaton (1972) has shown that these rejections are largely due to the inappropriate use of asymptotically valid test criteria. After correction, the general restrictions appear consistent with the empirical evidence, except for the homogeneity restriction.[12]

We find it difficult to take the results of these tests very seriously. The logic of the tests seems to be to compare the likelihood of the restricted data with the likelihood of the unrestricted data. However, it should be realized, as we shall emphasize in a moment, that the estimation of demand equations such as those defined in (2.43) implies particular restrictions in terms of the preference ordering so that the data are not really unrestricted. Given that the demand equations have to be specified in some way, a valid testing against unrestricted data is probably impossible.[13] We therefore think that, if we want measurement to be meaningful, we must *impose* the general restrictions whatever the results of the sort of tests just referred to.

To impose a restriction means that the computations are arranged in such a way that it is *exactly* satisfied. The easiest way to impose all general restrictions simultaneously, as several exercises have already made clear, is to derive the demand equations from a specified utility function, for then the form of the demand equations will be such that all general restrictions are *automatically* satisfied. The disadvantage of this procedure is a possible loss of generality implied in the choice of a particular utility function.

The alternative is to start from an appropriate specification of the demand equations such as (2.43) and to impose the restrictions as

[12] The same conclusions emerge in more recent tests by Deaton (1974a) and Deaton and Muellbauer (1980b). However, Christensen, Jorgenson and Lau (1975) conclude that the theory of demand is rejected *in globo*, without noticing that their tests might as well reject the 'translog' model used (See Section 4.3.4 below).

[13] A further critique of the logic of these tests can be found in Phlips (1975). On the statistical level, Laitinen (1978) and Bera, Byron and Jarque (1981) notice that the asymptotic tests used are biased towards rejection.

constraints in the regressions, as was done by Barten (1967, 1969) and Byron (1970a, b). The disadvantage is that the computational burden is very high, very sophisticated econometric methods becoming indispensable. Furthermore, there is the danger that the generality of the method may be only apparent: while the procedure apparently avoids the necessity of using a particular utility function, assumptions made in specifying the demand equations may involve the adoption of particular restrictions typical for a certain class of utility functions. For example when the demand equations are linear in prices and income, the implicit assumption is that the utility function belongs to the same class as the 'Stone-Geary' function $\sum_i \beta_i \log (x_i - \gamma_i)$ (see Section 4.3.3). In the Barten case, the constancy of B_i and S_{ij} has even more restrictive consequences, as will become clear in the next chapter, Section 3.5. Given this danger, it is probably better to specify the utility function right from the start. This is at any rate the approach we have chosen.

Whatever the method adopted to impose the general restrictions, it should be clear that they lead to important economies of parametrization. The strength of the theory exposed in this chapter is to reduce the number of 'free' coefficients in a demand system. As soon as we know $(n - 1)$ marginal propensities to consume, we can compute the nth propensity as one minus the sum of the others. Once the off-diagonal elements of the substitution matrix K have been computed on one side of the main diagonal, there is no need to estimate those on the other side, as we know that $k_{ij} = k_{ji}$. Exercise 2.4 has given an example of how the homogeneity condition can help to reduce the number of elasticities to be estimated. These economies are the more welcome as statistical observations are always limited in number: the smaller the number of parameters to be estimated, the greater our chances are of being able to derive statistically significant estimates.

Furthermore, the theoretical restrictions provide very useful checks of the accuracy of the computations made. If, when the restrictions are imposed, some estimated k_{ii}, say, turn out to be positive, some computational error must have been made.

Finally, an important theorem in the theory of econometrics (see Theil, 1965 or Goldberger, 1964) shows that gains in 'efficiency', i.e. increases in the precision and hence in the significance of the estimates, are present whenever restrictions are imposed on regressions by ordinary least squares. Any effort on the theoretical scene, leading to operational restrictions, is therefore rewarding from the point of view of the econometrician: a restriction, however general, is better than no restriction.

III

Demand functions: particular restrictions

In this chapter, our efforts concentrate on the specification of the utility function. Our objective is to derive specifications leading to interesting and operational restrictions, capable of moulding the available statistical data in a form that can easily be tested by current econometric methods and therefore rejected by the same methods. A first specification that comes to mind, because it is the first step to the analysis of the structure of human wants and has been widely used in the empirical work of the sixties, is that of an additive utility function.

3.1. Additive utility functions[1]

Up to now, we have left the utility function entirely unspecified in the theoretical exposition. (Particular specifications appeared only in the exercises.) The utility function was therefore written as $u = f(x_1, x_2, \ldots, x_n)$.

To introduce the (strong) assumption that the utility provided by the consumption of one good is not influenced by (independent of) the consumption of any other good, we write the direct utility function as

$$u = f_1(x_1) + f_2(x_2) + \ldots + f_n(x_n) \tag{3.1}$$

where f_i designates a function peculiar to commodity i (not to be confused with a partial derivative of f!). A function obeying (3.1) is called 'additive'. However, any monotonically increasing transformation $F(u)$ also represents the underlying preference ordering. We therefore say that a preference ordering, represented by a utility function $u = f(x_1, \ldots, x_n)$,

---

[1] The basic reference is Houthakker (1960b).

is additive if there exists a differentiable function F, $F' > 0$, and n functions $f_i(x_i)$, such that

$$F[f(x_1, \ldots, x_n)] = \sum_i f_i(x_i) \qquad (i = 1, \ldots, n), \qquad (3.1a)$$

i.e. if one member of the class of utility functions representing the preference ordering is additive.

It can easily be seen that (3.1) implies independence of the marginal utility of good i from the consumption of any other good. As $\partial u/\partial x_i = df_i/dx_i$,

$$\frac{\partial^2 u}{\partial x_i \, \partial x_j} = 0 \qquad (i \neq j). \qquad (3.2)$$

EXERCISES

3.1. (a) For what sort of commodities can the additivity assumption be considered as a good approximation of reality?
(b) Is any of the utility functions listed in exercise 1.7 additive?
(c) What about the Stone-Geary utility function introduced in exercise 1.14?
Answer: (a) The additivity assumption is defensible if the arguments of the utility function are taken to be broad aggregates of goods such as 'food', 'clothing', 'housing' rather than individual commodities. It is precisely for these aggregates that statistical data can be found in the national accounts.

3.2. In applied work, one often encounters the quadratic utility function. For two goods, it is written as

$$u = a_1 x_1 + a_2 x_2 + \tfrac{1}{2}(a_{11} x_1^2 + 2a_{12} x_1 x_2 + a_{22} x_2^2).$$

(a) What does the equation look like in algebraic and in matrix notation for n goods?
(b) How can it be made additive?
(c) What is the typical feature of marginal utilities?
(d) How can one ensure that marginal utilities are decreasing?
(e) Take the additive form of the quadratic utility function. Assume that prices are constant and equal to 1 and $n = 2$ (to simplify the arithmetic). Maximize subject to the budget constraint and solve for the demand equations. You should discover that these

equations (called 'Engel curves' because the quantities demanded are functions of income only) are linear.

Answer: (a) $u = \sum_i a_i x_i + \frac{1}{2} \sum_i \sum_j a_{ij} x_i x_j$

and

$$u = a'x + \tfrac{1}{2}x'Ax$$

where x is the column vector $[x_1, x_2, \ldots, x_n]'$, a is the column vector of constants and A is a symmetric matrix of constants with the elements a_{ii} on its main diagonal and the a_{ij}'s as off-diagonal elements ($a_{ij} = a_{ji}$).
(b) Put all $a_{ij} = 0$ ($i \neq j$). Then the matrix A is diagonal.
(c) Marginal utilities are linear and can become negative.
(d) Impose $\partial^2 u / \partial x_i^2 = a_{ii} < 0$.
(e) I find the system

$$x_1 = \frac{a_2 - a_1}{a_{11} + a_{22}} + \frac{a_{22}}{a_{11} + a_{22}} y$$

$$x_2 = \frac{a_1 - a_2}{a_{11} + a_{22}} + \frac{a_{11}}{a_{11} + a_{22}} y.$$

Adding up these two linear Engel curves, I find that the two intercepts sum to zero (the first is the negative of the second) and that the slopes sum to one. Why should this be?

It is worth noting that the early marginalist writers worked with additive utility functions. Because of the impact of ordinalism, these functions disappeared from the scene for many years (to reappear in the sixties, only, with the development of applied econometric work in the field). Additivity, defined as above, is indeed a cardinal property. The reader who has gone carefully through the material of Section 1.3 should have no difficulty to prove this.

EXERCISE

3.3. (a) Show that the condition (3.2) is invariant under linear transformations (of the utility function) only.
   (b) Illustrate (a) by comparing the second order partial cross derivatives computed in exercise 1.10.

Answer: (a) For $v = F(u)$ with $F' > 0$, we have

$$\frac{\partial^2 v}{\partial x_i\, \partial x_j} = F' \frac{\partial^2 u}{\partial x_i\, \partial x_j} + F'' \frac{\partial u}{\partial x_j} \frac{\partial u}{\partial x_i}$$

which is zero only if $F'' = 0$ ($\partial u/\partial x_i$ and $\partial u/\partial x_j$ being positive).

The additivity assumption is a first step towards a better understanding of the structure of preferences. It is a progress, in the sense that it allows as to take the independence of certain aggregates (groups of commodities) into account. But it is unfortunate in having additive utility functions defined in a cardinal way. Suppose, indeed, that a preference ordering is additive. It is a pity to have its representation cast in a form that is not invariant under non-linear transformations.

One possible attitude is to say that this fact should not prevent us from analysing and testing its empirical implications, as it is important to get a better understanding of the structure of preferences (which a purist ordinal approach would prevent us from analysing). This is the current attitude and we will adopt it in the chapters devoted to empirical studies.

A further possibility is to reject the definition of additivity in terms of the second order cross-partial derivatives of the utility function (equation (3.2)), and to define additivity in terms of the particular restriction which it implies. This restriction is derived below in equation (3.13) and is cast in terms of price and income derivatives of the demand equations, which are invariant.

Another more courageous attitude is to try to redefine independence (together with the other possible relationships among goods, which are substitutability and complementarity) in ordinal terms, exploiting the groupwise structure of preferences. Barten (1971) has done original work in this direction and we will try to get the flavour of it in Section 3.4.

For the time being, we are interested in the empirical implications of additivity, i.e. in the restrictions on the derivatives of the demand equations that result from direct additivity. To simplify the notation, we will analyse a two-commodity case, and generalize while proceeding.

Maximization of $u = f_1(x_1) + f_2(x_2)$ subject to the budget constraint gives the first-order conditions

$$\begin{aligned}
f_1' &= \lambda p_1 \\
f_2' &= \lambda p_2 \\
p_1 x_1 &+ p_2 x_2 = y.
\end{aligned} \tag{3.3}$$

where $f'_i = \partial f_i/\partial x_i$. Differentiation of (3.3) with respect to y leads to

$$f''_1 \frac{\partial x_1}{\partial y} = p_1 \frac{\partial \lambda}{\partial y}$$

$$f''_2 \frac{\partial x_2}{\partial y} = p_2 \frac{\partial \lambda}{\partial y} \tag{3.4}$$

$$p_1 \frac{\partial x_1}{\partial y} + p_2 \frac{\partial x_2}{\partial y} = 1$$

as the cross-derivatives vanish. System (3.4) implies

$$p_1 \left(\frac{p_1}{f''_1}\right) + p_2 \left(\frac{p_2}{f''_2}\right) = \frac{1}{\partial \lambda/\partial y}. \tag{3.5}$$

Differentiation of (3.3) with respect to p_1 gives

$$f''_1 \frac{\partial x_1}{\partial p_1} = \lambda + p_1 \frac{\partial \lambda}{\partial p_1}$$

$$f''_2 \frac{\partial x_2}{\partial p_1} = p_2 \frac{\partial \lambda}{\partial p_1} \tag{3.6}$$

$$x_1 + p_1 \frac{\partial x_1}{\partial p_1} + p_2 \frac{\partial x_2}{\partial p_1} = 0$$

or, after some manipulation,

$$p_1 \left(\frac{p_1}{f''_1}\right) + p_2 \left(\frac{p_2}{f''_2}\right) = \frac{-x_1 - p_1(\lambda/f''_1)}{\partial \lambda/\partial p_1} \tag{3.7}$$

Similarly, differentiation of (3.3) with respect to p_2 gives

$$p_2 \left(\frac{p_2}{f''_2}\right) + p_1 \left(\frac{p_1}{f''_1}\right) = \frac{-x_2 - p_2(\lambda/f''_2)}{\partial \lambda/\partial p_2}. \tag{3.8}$$

Comparing (3.5), (3.7) and (3.8), we see that

$$\frac{1}{\partial \lambda/\partial y} = \frac{-x_1 - p_1(\lambda/f''_1)}{\partial \lambda/\partial p_1} = \frac{-x_2 - p_2(\lambda/f''_2)}{\partial \lambda/\partial p_2} \tag{3.9}$$

$$= \frac{-x_k - p_k(\lambda/f''_k)}{\partial \lambda/\partial p_k} \quad (k = 1, \ldots, n)$$

or

$$\frac{\partial \lambda}{\partial p_k} = \frac{\partial \lambda}{\partial y}\left(-x_k - p_k \frac{\lambda}{f_k''}\right)$$

$$= \frac{\partial \lambda}{\partial y}\left(-x_k - \frac{\lambda}{\partial \lambda/\partial y}\frac{\partial x_k}{\partial y}\right) \tag{3.10}$$

using (3.4). From (3.6) we know that $\partial x_i/\partial p_k = (p_i/f_i'')(\partial \lambda/\partial p_k)$. Therefore

$$\frac{\partial x_i}{\partial p_k} = -\frac{p_i}{f_i''}\frac{\partial \lambda}{\partial y}\left(x_k + \frac{\lambda}{\partial \lambda/\partial y}\frac{\partial x_k}{\partial y}\right)$$

$$= -\frac{\partial x_i}{\partial y}\left(x_k + \frac{\lambda}{\partial \lambda/\partial y}\frac{\partial x_k}{\partial y}\right) \quad (i \neq k). \tag{3.11}$$

Clearly, we also have

$$\frac{\partial x_j}{\partial p_k} = -\frac{\partial x_j}{\partial y}\left(x_k + \frac{\lambda}{\partial \lambda/\partial y}\frac{\partial x_k}{\partial y}\right) \quad (j \neq k).$$

so that

$$\frac{\partial x_i/\partial p_k}{\partial x_j/\partial p_k} = \frac{\partial x_i/\partial y}{\partial x_j/\partial y} \quad (i \neq k;\ j \neq k). \tag{3.12}$$

This is the particular restriction we were looking for: *the direct utility function can be written in the additive form if and only if*[2] *the cross-price derivatives are proportional to the income derivatives.* To understand what this means, write (3.12) as

$$\frac{\partial x_i}{\partial p_k} = \mu \frac{\partial x_i}{\partial y} \quad \text{with} \quad \mu = \frac{\partial x_j/\partial p_k}{\partial x_j/\partial y}, \quad i \neq k, \tag{3.13}$$

and suppose i designates food and k designates housing. The restriction says that the change in the demand for food induced by a change in the price of housing is proportional to the change in the demand for food induced by a change in income. *The factor of proportionality μ does not depend on the good (food) whose quantity reponse we are considering* (but it does depend on the good (housing) whose price has changed). If i were to designate another good, say clothing, the factor of proportionality would be the same, as long as it is the price of housing that is changing.

---

[2] For a proof of sufficiency, see Houthakker (1960b).

Notice also that we can express the same restriction in terms of the cross-substitution effect. In general, the cross substitution effect is equal (see exercise 2.8) to

$$k_{ij} = \frac{\partial x_i}{\partial p_j} + x_j \frac{\partial x_i}{\partial y}.$$

Using (3.11), we find that in the case of direct additivity it reduces to

$$
\begin{aligned}
k_{ij} &= -\frac{\partial x_i}{\partial y}\left(x_j + \frac{\lambda}{\partial \lambda/\partial y}\frac{\partial x_j}{\partial y}\right) + x_j \frac{\partial x_i}{\partial y} \\
&= -\frac{\lambda}{\partial \lambda/\partial y}\frac{\partial x_i}{\partial y}\frac{\partial x_j}{\partial y} \qquad (i \neq j)
\end{aligned}
\tag{3.14}
$$

which we identified in Section 2.4 as the '*general*' cross substitution effect. The specific cross-substitution effect is zero.

This is an important result. First of all, it shows that the independence of the marginal utility of good i from the consumption of any other good j does *not* imply that a change of the price of good j leaves the demand of good i unaffected: *the cross-substitution effect does not vanish*! Even under additivity, a change in the price of any other good will affect the demand of good i. Why is this? Because all goods 'compete for the consumer's dollar', to put it in simple terms. In other words, there always remains an overall effect, which we call the general substitution effect, and which is proportional to the income derivatives $\partial x_i/\partial y$ and $\partial x_j/\partial y$. The factor of proportionality is a function of the marginal utility of money and its response to a change in income.

On the other hand, we established in Chapter II that the Slutsky equation is invariant under monotonic increasing transformations of the utility function. This means, in particular, that the substitution effects are invariant. All the utility functions belonging to the same class as a given additive utility function (i.e. including the non-linear transformations of it which are *non*-additive) have therefore the same cross-substitution effects (for given i, j). In the case of the additive function, the 'total' effect reduces to one of its components, which is not invariant (as the ratio $\lambda/(\partial\lambda/\partial y)$ is invariant under linear transformations only). When we transform the additive member of the class non-linearly, the general substitution effect changes, but simultaneously the specific effect becomes non-zero in such a way that the sum of the general and the specific effect, i.e. the ('total') substitution effect, remains unaltered.

EXERCISES

3.4. (a) Verify that the cross-substitution effects (for given i, j) are the same for the utility functions (1), (2), (4), (5) and (6) of exercise 1.7. (b) Check that the last of these utility functions, namely $u = \log (x_1 x_2)$, is the only one to have cross-substitution effects obeying equation (3.14).

3.5. (a) Prove the following proposition: when the marginal utility of each good is a function of its own quantity only and decreases when the consumption of the good increases, then consumption of each good increases with income.
(b) What is the sign of the cross-substitution effect in the case described under (a)?
Hint: (a) Prove that $\partial x_i / \partial y$ is positive, starting from the system (2.8) and using Cramer's rule, for $n = 2$.

Up to now, we discussed direct additivity. When it is the *indirect* utility function that is additive, the resulting particular restriction has been shown by Houthakker (1960b) to be

$$\frac{\partial x_i / \partial p_k}{x_i} = \frac{\partial x_j / \partial p_k}{x_j}, \qquad (i \neq k, j \neq k) \tag{3.15}$$

which is quite different from restriction (3.12). Here, the cross-price derivatives are proportional to the quantities affected. Indirect additivity has other implications than direct additivity! (3.15) can in turn be written as

$$\frac{\partial x_i}{\partial p_k} \frac{p_k}{x_i} = \frac{\partial x_j}{\partial p_k} \frac{p_k}{x_j} \tag{3.16}$$

so that all cross-price elasticities with respect to p_k are the same.

What if *the direct and the corresponding indirect* utility functions are both additive? Combining (3.12) and (3.15), one finds

$$\frac{\partial x_i / \partial p_k}{\partial x_j / \partial p_k} = \frac{\partial x_i / \partial y}{\partial x_j / \partial y} = \frac{x_i}{x_j}$$

or

$$\frac{\partial x_i}{\partial y} \frac{y}{x_i} = \frac{\partial x_j}{\partial y} \frac{y}{x_j}, \tag{3.17}$$

that is to say, *all elasticities with respect to total expenditure are equal and hence unitary*[3]. As will become clear in the next chapter, this implies that all Engel curves are straight lines through the origin: at all income levels, a constant proportion of total expenditures is allocated to each commodity, which is in contradiction with all empirical findings. Fortunately, the indirect utility function corresponding to an additive direct utility function is not, in general, additive. This is fortunate, because otherwise additive utility functions would be entirely unrealistic and not suitable for empirical work.

EXERCISES

3.6. (a) How would you write the additive indirect utility function, taking account of the fact that it is homogeneous of degree zero in income and prices?

(b) In earlier exercises we came across an additive direct utility function whose corresponding indirect utility function is also additive. Which one is it? Convince yourself that all income elasticities are unitary.

Answer: (a) $\quad u^* = f_1^*\left(\dfrac{y}{p_1}\right) + f_2^*\left(\dfrac{y}{p_2}\right) + \ldots + f_n^*\left(\dfrac{y}{p_n}\right).$

(b) see exercise 1.19, utility function (6).

3.7. The preceding exercise made it clear that, while direct additivity is defined in terms of the x's, indirect additivity is defined in terms of income and prices. The Stone-Geary utility function and the corresponding indirect utility function are not additive in these variables. You will have noticed, however, that the preference orderings described by these utility functions are additive in other variables. Which are these? Show that restriction (3.17) applies to them.

Hint: see exercises 1.14 and 1.20.

The reader who has gone through exercises 3.6, 1.19 and 2.9, will have discovered that the class of utility function to which $u = \sum_i \log x_i$

belongs leads to demand functions with not only unitary income

---

[3] For a further discussion of this restriction, see Samuelson (1965), Houthakker (1960b) and Section 3.5.

elasticities, but also *unitary own price elasticities*[4] *and zero cross-price elasticities*. This is an implication of 'simultaneous' direct and indirect additivity, as has been shown by Samuelson (1965).[5]

In fact, each of these properties implies any of the other, as the demand functions must be of the form $x_i = k_i(y/p_i)$, where k_i is a constant, in order to have $p_i x_i = k_i y$. Once this is realized, the reader should conclude that something is wrong with the derivation of (3.17), which is based on a combination of (3.12) and (3.15). Indeed, knowing that simultaneous direct and indirect additivity implies zero cross-price elasticities, the ratios

$$\frac{\partial x_i/\partial p_k}{\partial x_j/\partial p_k} = \frac{0}{0}$$

become indeterminate forms and one cannot legitimately manipulate their equality as if they were regular numbers, as was pointed out by Samuelson (1969). A correct proof of (3.17) should proceed otherwise, by using the duality properties of direct and indirect utility functions. It is beyond the scope of this book to develop these duality relations.

The utility functions which are directly and indirectly additive are also 'homothetic' and will be further discussed in the final section of this chapter.

3.2. Separable utility functions

The aggregates that appear as arguments in additive utility functions are groups of commodities. A natural question is to ask under what conditions the arguments of the utility functions may be aggregated. In particular, is not additivity too strong a condition, in the sense that a grouping is possible without supposing that the groups are independent? The answer is: yes.

It is intuitively clear that what we would like to do is to partition the consumption set into subsets which would include commodities that

---

[4] To be entirely correct, one should draw attention to the existence of an exceptional case, discovered by Hicks (1969) and further analysed by Samuelson (1969), where at most one commodity may have a non-unitary price elasticity.

[5] The adjective 'simultaneous' is used here to indicate the case where the indirect utility function corresponding to an additive direct utility function is additive. We have 'non-simultaneous' direct and indirect additivity when the corresponding indirect utility function is non-additive but can be transformed into an additive one.

are closer substitutes or complements to each other than to members of other subsets. (Independence from one subset to another would not be required.) Instead of writing, say

$$u = f(x_1, x_2, x_3, x_4, x_5)$$

we would like to group the variables in the function to make it expressible as, say

$$u = F(A, B)$$

where

$$A = f_a(x_1, x_2)$$
$$B = f_b(x_3, x_4, x_5).$$

Commodities 1 and 2 would, in this example, belong to group A and commodities 3, 4 and 5 to group B. The utility function would then be 'separable' (in two groups, in the example) without necessarily being additive. The term 'expressible' indicates an important condition: we want the value of u to be the same with or without grouping, i.e. whether u is expressed as a function of all elementary variables or as a function of the groups.

Under what conditions can this be done? Following Green (1964, p. 11), we start from a simple numerical example, in which the consumer is supposed to consume the following three commodities: commodity A (food), commodity D_1 (housing) and D_2 (automobiles). We seek the conditions under which $u = f(A, D_1, D_2)$ can be written as $u = F(A, D)$ where D is a function of D_1 and D_2 and aggregates D_1 and D_2 into the group 'durable goods'.

Let us agree to represent two combination of D_1 and D_2, combined with a constant amount of A, by the same value of D if and only if they provide the same satisfaction (when combined with the given amount of A). This is in keeping with the requirement that a grouping of the variables should not modify u. Thus, we shall say that $D(20, 5) = D(18, 6)$ from the point of view of utility, if the following figures are given:

A	D_1	D_2	u
100	20	5	1.000
100	18	6	1.000

Suppose the quantity of A consumed doubles. If we find

A	D_1	D_2	u
200	20	5	1.800
200	18	6	1.700

our convention obliges us to say that D (20, 5) $\neq D$ (18, 6). It is then impossible to say anything more about D: there is no basis for grouping D_1 and D_2 into 'durables'. But if the two combinations of D_1 and D_2, when consumed with the new (or any other) quantity of A, still provide the same utility, then we are sure (and only then) that the durables are separable from food. This is the case if the following figures hold:

A	D_1	D_2	u
200	20	5	1.800
200	18	6	1.800

Now, to say that the two combinations of D_1 and D_2 provide the same utility, whatever the consumption of A, is to say that the marginal rate of substitution of one durable for another $(20 - 18 = 2D_1$ for $6 - 5 = 1D_2)$ is independent of A. Generalizing, this leads to the criterion that *it is a necessary and sufficient condition for a function to be separable, that the marginal rate of substitution between any two variables belonging to the same group be independent of the value of any variable in any other group.*

This theorem is due to Leontief (1947). To prove necessity, let the n commodities be partitioned in m groups, and let there be n_r ($r = 1$, ..., m) commodities in each group $(n = \sum_{r=1}^{m} n_r)$. The utility function

$$u = f(x_{11}, \ldots, x_{1n_1}, \ldots, x_{r1}, \ldots, x_{rn_r}, \ldots, x_{m1}, \ldots, x_{mn_m}) \qquad (3.18)$$

is to be expressed in the form

$$u = F[f_1(x_1), f_2(x_2), \ldots, f_r(x_r), \ldots, f_m(x_m)] \qquad (3.19)$$

where each f_r is a 'branch' utility function. Each x_r is in turn a function of $x_{r1}, x_{r2}, \ldots x_{rn_r}$.

We want to show that (3.18) can be expressed as (3.19) if and only if

$$\frac{\partial}{\partial x_{qk}}\left(\frac{\partial f}{\partial x_{ri}}\bigg/\frac{\partial f}{\partial x_{rj}}\right) = 0 \tag{3.20}$$

for all q, r, i, j, k $(q, r = 1, \ldots, m; q \neq r; k = 1, \ldots n_q; i, j = 1, \ldots, n_r)$.

We start from the condition that the grouping should not affect u, and that therefore

$$df = \sum_r \sum_j \frac{\partial f}{\partial x_{rj}} dx_{rj} \equiv dF = \sum_r \frac{\partial F}{\partial x_r} dx_r = \sum_r \sum_j \frac{\partial F}{\partial f_r} \frac{\partial f_r}{\partial x_{rj}} dx_{rj}.$$

For any group r, and any members i and j, it follows that

$$\frac{\partial f}{\partial x_{ri}} = \frac{\partial F}{\partial f_r} \frac{\partial f_r}{\partial x_{ri}} \quad \text{and} \quad \frac{\partial f}{\partial x_{rj}} = \frac{\partial F}{\partial f_r} \frac{\partial f_r}{\partial x_{rj}}$$

so that

$$\frac{\partial f}{\partial x_{ri}}\bigg/\frac{\partial f}{\partial x_{rj}} = \frac{\partial f_r}{\partial x_{ri}}\bigg/\frac{\partial f_r}{\partial x_{rj}}$$

But since f_r is a function only of the members of group r, the same is true for the ratio of its derivatives and for the marginal rate of substitution to which this ratio is equal. Q.E.D.

The proof of sufficiency is rather cumbersome and, in order to save space, will not be given here (see Green, 1964, p. 13–15).

In the exposition above, goods i and j belong to the same group r, while good k belongs to a different group q. It is clear that one could define another type of separability, in which i, j and k belong each to a different group. This is called 'strong separability'. Then, the partition is such that the marginal rate of substitution between any two goods belonging to two different groups is independent of the consumption of any good in any third group. As a result, the marginal utility of a commodity in one group is independent of the consumption of any good in any other group, which is a very strong condition indeed. Strong separability thus implies independence between groups or 'groupwise independence'. (By contrast, functional separability as defined by condition (3.20) has been called 'weak separability'.) A strongly separable utility function is written

$$u = f_1(x_1) + f_2(x_2) + \ldots + f_r(x_r) + \ldots + f_m(x_m) \tag{3.21}$$

where each f_r is a branch utility function.

EXERCISES

3.8. Utilize one of the algebraically specified utility functions, intro-
      duced in earlier exercises, to construct:
      (a) a weakly separable utility function;
      (b) a strongly separable utility function.
      Answer: Why not take the quadratic utility function? (You might
      as well try the Stone-Geary function.) To get a clear distinction
      between the two cases, we have to introduce at least three commo-
      dities, one of which is an aggregate. Let $x_1 = b_1 x_{11} + b_2 x_{12}$, i.e.
      commodity 1 is a linear combination of two more disaggregated
      commodities.
      (a) Then $u = a_1 x_1 + a_2 x_2 + a_3 x_3 + \frac{1}{2}(a_{11} x_1^2 + 2a_{12} x_1 x_2 + 2a_{13} x_1 x_3 + 2a_{23} x_2 x_3 + a_{22} x_2^2 + a_{33} x_3^2)$ is weakly separable.
      Indeed

      $$\frac{\partial u}{\partial x_{11}} \bigg/ \frac{\partial u}{\partial x_{12}} = \frac{\partial u}{\partial x_1} \frac{\partial x_1}{\partial x_{11}} \bigg/ \frac{\partial u}{\partial x_1} \frac{\partial x_1}{\partial x_{12}} = \frac{b_1}{b_2}$$

      is independent of x_2 and x_3. Notice that

      $$\frac{\partial u}{\partial x_{11}} = (a_1 + a_{11} x_1 + a_{12} x_2 + a_{13} x_3) b_1$$

      is *not* independent of x_2 or x_3. The same is true for $\partial u / \partial x_{12}$.
      (b) By putting $a_{ij} = 0$ $(i \neq j)$, we obtain a strongly separable
      utility function. Then

      $$\frac{\partial u}{\partial x_{11}} \bigg/ \frac{\partial u}{\partial x_2} = \frac{(a_1 + a_{11} x_1) b_1}{(a_2 + a_{22} x_2)}$$

      is independent of x_3. Now $\partial u / \partial x_{11}$ is independent of x_2 and x_3.

3.9. Is strong separability synonymous with additivity?
      Answer: Formally, strong separability implies additivity between
      groups. It is only when each group comprises only one commodity
      that strong separability reduces to additivity. From an economic
      point of view, however, additivity is defensible only if the arguments
      of the utility function are broad aggregates (see exercise 1.19). In
      applied work, strong separability, groupwise independence and
      additivity therefore designate one and the same situation.

3.10. Specify algebraically a utility function that is strongly separable ($m = 3$), but with a first branch that is weakly separable ($n_1 = 2$). *Hint:* This can be obtained by adding an additive quadratic utility function to a non-additive one.

Weak separability is of great interest to the economist as a prerequisite for the consistency of the *two-stage maximization procedure* discussed by Strotz[6]. The basic idea is appealing and seems highly plausible. Households are supposed to proceed in two steps, the first being an optimal allocation of income among broad commodity groups (the m groups in equation (3.19), say) corresponding to 'branches' of the utility function. There is thus a budget allotment $y_r(\sum_r y_r = y)$ to each branch.

The second step implies the optimal spending of each budget allotment in its branch, with no further reference to purchases in other branches. This amounts to maximizing each branch utility function subject to the budget constraint

$$\sum_j x_{rj} p_{rj} = y_r \qquad (j = 1, \ldots, n_r). \tag{3.22}$$

The (weakly) separable utility function appears, in the terminology introduced by Strotz, as a *utility tree*, with branches corresponding to $f_1, f_2, \ldots, f_m$.

The time has come to ask ourselves what are the implications for observed consumer behaviour of the separability hypothesis. These implications can be derived in a simple way with the help of so-called 'conditional demand functions', which we introduce in the next section, following Pollak (1969) and especially (1971a). These functions have the additional advantage of placing emphasis on the implications of separability for the demand functions themselves, by facilitating the derivation of restrictions not only on the derivatives of the demand equations, but also on the number of variables that appear as arguments in the demand equations.

---

[6] In his 1957 article, Strotz defined the utility function as being weakly separable. Gorman (1959a, b) tried to show – and Strotz (1959) subsequently agreed with this – that the two-stage procedure has to be based, for three or more groups, on a strongly separable function. Recently, however, Blackorby et al. (1970) made it clear that the Strotz-Gorman conditions refer only to the existence of group price indices and showed that the budgeting procedure described by Strotz is consistent if, and only if, the utility function is weakly separable. Anderson (1979) shows how to use theoretically correct price indices in a complete demand system. See also the price index $\pi(c_t)$ used in Section 11.12.

3.3. Conditional demand functions and the implications of separable utility

Let us partition the set of all commodities into two subsets, θ and $\bar{\theta}$. The individual's consumption of the goods in $\bar{\theta}$ has been determined before he enters the market: these goods have been 'preallocated'. We assume that the consumer is not allowed to sell any of his allotment of the preallocated goods, and that he cannot buy more of them. The goods in θ are available on the market. Total expenditure on the goods available on the market is denoted by y_θ. The consumer is supposed to maximize $u = f(x_1, \ldots, x_n)$ subject to the constraint

$$\sum_{i \in \theta} p_i x_i = y_\theta \tag{3.23}$$

and the additional constraints

$$x_k = \bar{x}_k \qquad (k \in \bar{\theta}). \tag{3.24}$$

Hence, his demand for the goods available on the market depends on the prices of these goods (P_θ), total expenditure on them (y_θ), and his allotment of the preallocated goods ($\bar{x}$ say). Then the conditional demand function for the ith good is

$$x_i = \psi_i(P_\theta, y_\theta, \bar{x}) \qquad (i \in \theta). \tag{3.25}$$

Suppose now that the allotment of the preallocated goods is precisely equal to the amounts he would have purchased in the absence of a pre-allocation, i.e. to the amounts determined by the ordinary demand equations $x_k = \phi_k(p_1, \ldots, p_n, y)$, and that $y_\theta = y - \sum_k p_k \theta_k$ $(k \in \bar{\theta})$. Then the consumer will purchase the same quantities of each of the goods available (in θ) as in the absence of a pre-allocation. That is

$$\phi_i(p_1, \ldots, p_n, y) = \psi_i(P_\theta, y_\theta, \Phi_\theta) \tag{3.26}$$

where Φ_θ designates the vector of ordinary demand equations for the preallocated goods.

Coming back to the case where the utility function is a *tree*, i.e. is weakly separable according to (3.19), we assume that the goods in one branch (the branch 'food') are available on the market, while all other goods are preallocated. The conditional demand functions are determined by maximizing (3.19) subject to

$$\sum_{j=1}^{n_r} x_{rj} p_{rj} = y_r$$

which is the constraint (3.22), r being the branch ('food') in which the goods are available on the market, and the additional constraints

$$x_{qk} = \bar{x}_{qk}. \qquad (qk \in \bar{\theta}) \tag{3.27}$$

If we absorb the constraints (3.27) into (3.19), we obtain

$$u = F[f_1(\bar{x}_1), f_2(\bar{x}_2), \ldots, f_r(x_r), \ldots, f_m(\bar{x}_m)]. \tag{3.28}$$

Our problem now reduces to the constrained maximization of (3.28), which itself reduces to the constrained maximization of the branch utility function $f_r(x_r)$ so that the utility maximizing values of $(x_{r1}, x_{r2}, \ldots, x_{rn_r})$ are independent of the levels of the preallocated goods. Hence, the conditional demand functions for the goods in θ, i.e. in branch r, are of the form

$$\psi_{ri}(P_r, y_r, \bar{x}) = \psi_{ri}(P_r, y_r),$$

while, using (3.26), the ordinary demand functions for the goods in branch r are such that

$$x_{ri} = \phi_{ri}(P, y) = \psi_{ri}(P_r, y_r) \tag{3.29}$$

where P is the vector of all prices $(p_{11}, \ldots, p_{1n_1}, \ldots, p_{r1}, \ldots, p_{rn_r}, \ldots, p_{m1}, \ldots, p_{mn_m})$.

Equation (3.29) is important. It is a restriction on the nature of the arguments that appear in the demand equations: (3.29) says that *the demand for a commodity in a branch can be expressed as a function of the prices in and the budget allotment to that branch.*

We do *not* say that the quantities demanded in one branch are independent of the prices of commodities in other branches or of total expenditures. What we say is that total income and the prices of goods outside the branch enter the demand functions for goods in the branch only through their effect on y_r, the budget allotment to that branch. And that, when the budget allotment to the branch is known, we can ignore the prices of goods outside the branch.

This restriction is very useful in applied work. To the extent that the hypothesis of a utility tree, and the corresponding assumption of multi-stage maximization, can be maintained, *and* if the branch structure of a specified utility function is known, then a subset of demand equations inside a branch can be estimated using only the prices of the goods in the branch and total expenditures on goods in the branch.

EXERCISES

3.11. Pollak (1971a) illustrates the preceding discussion by supposing that r = food and ri = Swiss cheese.

(a) To what extent will a change in the price of shoes ($= qk, q \neq r$) cause a change in Swiss cheese consumption?

(b) Suppose that a change in the price of another non-food item, say, tennis balls, has the same effect on y_r as the change in the price of shoes. Will both price changes have the same effect on the consumption of Swiss cheese?

(c) What if a change in total income y has the same effect on y_r as the two price changes just considered? Will it also have the same effect on Swiss cheese consumption?

3.12. Suppose you have estimated a system of demand equations for the branch food. What additional information do you need to compute

(a) the cross-price elasticity between Swiss cheese and shoes?

(b) the elasticity of Swiss cheese with respect to total income y?

The implications of the utility tree hypothesis for the partial derivatives of the demand functions can now be derived without difficulty. Differentiating (3.29) with respect to p_{qk} and y we obtain

$$
\frac{\partial x_{ri}}{\partial p_{qk}} = \frac{\partial \psi_{ri}}{\partial y_r} \frac{\partial y_r}{\partial p_{qk}} \qquad (q \neq r)
$$

$$
\frac{\partial x_{ri}}{\partial y} = \frac{\partial \psi_{ri}}{\partial y_r} \frac{\partial y_r}{\partial y}
$$

(3.30)

taking account of the fact that y_r is a function of all prices and of total income y. That is, *the change in the consumption of a good in branch r caused by a change in the price of a good in another branch is proportional to the change in the budget allotment of the branch caused by that price change. And similarly for a change in total income.* (Notice that this restriction is implicitly contained in the answer to exercise 3.12.)

On eliminating $\partial \psi_{ri}/\partial y_r$ from (3.30) and supposing that $\partial y_r/\partial y \neq 0$ we can write

$$\frac{\partial x_{ri}}{\partial p_{qk}} = \frac{\partial y_r/\partial p_{qk}}{\partial y_r/\partial y} \frac{\partial x_{ri}}{\partial y}$$

$$= \mu_r \frac{\partial x_{ri}}{\partial y} \tag{3.31}$$

That is, the change in the demand for Swiss cheese induced by a change in the price of shoes is proportional to the change in the demand for Swiss cheese induced by a change in income. *The factor of proportionality is the same for all food items* (but it does depend on the good (shoes) whose price has changed).

Introducing a second food item j, we can express (3.31) as

$$\frac{\partial x_{ri}/\partial p_{qk}}{\partial x_{rj}/\partial p_{qk}} = \frac{\partial x_{ri}/\partial y}{\partial x_{rj}/\partial y} \qquad (q \neq r) \tag{3.32}$$

EXERCISE
3.13. Compare equations (3.31) and (3.13) on the one hand, and (3.32) and (3.12) on the other hand. Notice the similarities *and* the differences.

We now turn to the case of strong separability or 'groupwise independence' (also called 'block additivity') defined in equation (3.21). It implies weak separability: as the marginal rate of substitution between any two goods belonging to two different groups is independent of the consumption of any good in any third group, the marginal rate of substitution between two goods belonging to *the same* group depends only on the goods in that group. The restriction derived above therefore applies directly to groupwise independence: the demand for a particular commodity can be written as a function of the prices in the branch and of the budget allotment to the branch to which it belongs. As groupwise independence is a stronger condition than weak separability, it must have *additional* implications.

Pollak (1971, p. 248) derives these from the following consideration: 'If a utility function is a tree with m branches, in general, we cannot combine two branches into a single branch. For example, if 'food' and 'recreation' are two branches of a tree, it is not in general true that the demand for Swiss cheese can be written as a function of food prices, recreation prices, and total expenditure on food and recreation. But if the utility function is block additive, it is always permissible to treat the goods in two (or more) blocks as a single block. [...] More generally, if a block additive utility function has m blocks, and if some of these blocks are combined to form m^* superblocks, $m^* < m$, then the utility function is block additive in the superblocks. Hence, a block additive utility function with m blocks is a utility tree with m^* branches'.

Suppose, then, than r is a group combining all blocks except one, which is group q. The latter contains the preallocated goods, say all 'clothing'. Then the demand for Swiss cheese may be written as a function of the prices of all non-clothing goods and total expenditure on all goods other than clothing. Restriction (3.30) applies, together with (3.31) and (3.32). But the interpretation is different: as r now indicates any 'superblock', the group to which good i belongs is irrelevant. Equation (3.31) should therefore be rewritten as

$$\frac{\partial x_{ri}}{\partial p_{qk}} = \mu \frac{\partial x_{ri}}{\partial y}, \tag{3.33}$$

where *the factor of proportionality has no subscript, to indicate that it is independent of the good whose quantity response we are considering.*

It now suffices for us to imagine that each group contains only one commodity ('food', 'clothing', 'recreation', 'housing', ...), to be back in the case considered in Section 3.1. The results obtained for the case of block additivity carry over directly. In particular, we may use any partition of the goods which is convenient. For example, we can write the demand for food as a function of the price of food, the price of clothing, and total expenditure on food and clothing. Or, if we prefer, we can write the demand for food as a function of all goods except clothing and total expenditure on all goods other than clothing. As for the restriction on the price and income derivatives, it can now be derived without effort using conditional demand functions. The reader is invited to work this out for himself in the following exercise.

EXERCISE

3.14. Derive equations (3.13) and (3.12) by differentiating a conditional demand equation defined in the appropriate way. Give an economic interpretation of each of your results.

   Hint: Suppose all goods are in θ, except good k, which is pre-allocated.

It remains for us to express the restrictions on the derivatives, in the weak and strong separability cases, in terms of the cross-substitution effects k_{ij}, as we were able to do in equation (3.14) for the additivity case. Goldman and Uzawa (1964) have done pioneering work in this respect. As the matter is a difficult one, and the derivation is highly technical, the reader will have first to assimilate the material of the next section, at the end of which the said restrictions are derived.[7]

3.4.* The structure of preferences: substitution, complementarity and independence

The hypothesis of independence between goods (whether particular commodities or groups of commodities) gives no more than a first approximation to the structure of preferences, even for very large aggregates. Inside these groups, complementarity and substitutability certainly exist. And it is highly likely that such relationships also exist between groups, at all levels of aggregation. This is at least the impression one gets after carrying out a test of the additivity hypothesis, as explained in Section 8.5 of Part II.

The hypothesis of weak separability seems therefore to give a more realistic description of the structure of preferences and to provide the appropriate framework to discuss complementarity and substitutability. It has the additional advantage of eliminating a number of paradoxes and contradictions that characterize the more traditional approaches. The old cardinal definition of, say, complementarity, is indeed different from the (by now traditional) ordinal definition. Furthermore, two commodities which appear as complements under one definition may appear as substitutes under another definition. Before presenting the new approach based on the separability hypothesis, we examine more closely the traditional definitions.

The cardinal definitions proceed in terms of second order cross-partial derivatives of the utility function. As we have seen in Section 3.1, independence between commodities i and j is defined by the fact that

$$\frac{\partial^2 u}{\partial x_i \, \partial x_j} = 0.$$

---

[7] See equations (3.45) and (3.46).

We may now add that, in the same spirit, complementarity implies

$$\frac{\partial^2 u}{\partial x_i \, \partial x_j} > 0.$$

Two commodities are complements if the increased consumption of j increases the marginal utility of i (and vice-versa). This definition probably corresponds to the reader's intuitive concept of complementarity. In a similar way, a negative second order cross-partial derivative defines substitutability.

However, the sign of these cross-partial derivatives is not invariant under monotonic increasing transformations of the utility functions, as we have demonstrated in Section 1.3 and re-emphasized in exercise 3.3. It is invariant under linear transformations only. That is why the above definitions are cardinal.

From an ordinal point of view, the demand equations have the advantage of being invariant under any monotonic increasing transformation (see exercises 1.11 and 1.15). As a consequence, the derivatives – and in particular the substitution effects – of the demand equations are invariant. Furthermore, the sign of the cross-substitution effect is not only invariant but also undetermined: it may be positive, negative or zero (see Section 2.3). This immediately suggests that one might use the sign of the cross-substitution effect k_{ij} and say that i and j are substitutes whenever k_{ij} is positive. Indeed, a compensated increase in the price of j (margarine) leads to an increase in the demand for i (butter). We end up with the following invariant conditions:

$k_{ij} > 0$ indicates substitutability
$k_{ij} < 0$ indicates complementarity
$k_{ij} = 0$ indicates independence.

These are definitions suggested[8] by Hicks (1936). They are to be found in most textbooks.

Notice that independence is *not* defined by the fact that the demand for commodity i is independent of the price of commodity j, i.e.

$$\frac{\partial x_i}{\partial p_j} = 0 \qquad (i \neq j)$$

---

[8] In fact, Hicks uses three different definitions of complementarity.

For p_i to be the only price that appears in the demand equation of commodity i, it is indeed necessary that the cross-substitution effect be positive and equal in absolute value to the income effect (which is negative in the absence of inferior goods), so that their sum be equal to zero. We came across such a case in exercise 2.9. We then discovered that the utility function $u = \prod_i (x_i)$ belongs to the class of functions leading to demand equations with unitary own price and income elasticities, all cross-price elasticities being zero. According to the Hicksian definitions, all commodities would then appear as substitutes, as the cross-substitution effects are positive.

For some time, economists thought that this settled the matter. On second thoughts, they came to realize that the Hicksian definitions were not satisfactory.

First of all, they are biased in favour of substitutability. The use of the cross-substitution effect implies that all goods can be substitutes but not complements. To see this, recall that the homogeneity restriction implies

$$\frac{\partial x_i}{\partial y} y + \sum_j p_j \frac{\partial x_i}{\partial p_j} = 0 \qquad (i, j = 1, \ldots, n)$$

while the Slutsky equation gives

$$\frac{\partial x_i}{\partial p_j} = k_{ij} - \frac{\partial x_i}{\partial y} x_j.$$

Hence

$$\frac{\partial x_i}{\partial y} y + \sum_j p_j \left(k_{ij} - \frac{\partial x_i}{\partial y} x_j \right) = 0$$

$$\frac{\partial x_i}{\partial y} y + \sum_j p_j k_{ij} - \frac{\partial x_i}{\partial y} \sum_j p_j x_j = 0$$

or

$$\sum_j p_j k_{ij} = 0. \tag{3.34}$$

This result is also implied in (2.34).

As $k_{ii} < 0$, all k_{ij} (for $i \neq j$) cannot be negative (complementarity). But all k_{ij} could be positive.

Furthermore, in the particular case of a directly additive utility function, the substitution effect reduces to the 'general' substitution effect

$$k_{ij} = -\frac{\lambda}{\partial\lambda/\partial y}\frac{\partial x_i}{\partial y}\frac{\partial x_j}{\partial y}.$$

On the assumption that marginal utilities are decreasing, all income derivatives are positive (see exercise 3.5), while λ is positive and $\partial\lambda/\partial y$ is negative, so that k_{ij} is positive. In this case of independent marginal utilities, all goods are substitutes according to the Hicksian definitions. Clearly, this so-called substitutability has nothing in common with the preference relationships that are typical for the pairs of goods under consideration. It simply reflects the fact that all goods 'compete for the consumer's dollar'.

This result suggests another drawback of the Hicksian approach: it leads us away from the intuitive (cardinal) concepts to the point of giving contradictory and often confusing results. In the preceding paragraph, goods that are 'independent' (in a cardinal sense) appear as substitutes. In exercise 2.9, goods that are complements according to common sense (positive second order cross-partial derivatives of the utility function $u = x_1 x_2$) are again gratified with positive cross-substitution effects (Hicksian substitutability).

In a recent paper, Barten (1971) has derived concepts that combine the intuitive appeal of the cardinal criteria with the ordinal character of the Hicksian definitions. To do this, Barten starts from the groupwise structure of preferences.

Consider a partition of the n commodities in m groups and let the utility function be a *utility tree* (or weakly separable) according to

$$u = F[f_1(x_1), f_2(x_2), \ldots, f_r(x_r), \ldots, f_m(x_m)].$$

Then

$$\frac{\partial u}{\partial x_i} = \frac{\partial u}{\partial f_r}\frac{\partial f_r}{\partial x_i} \tag{3.35}$$

for $i \in r$, where r is any group. For $i \in r$, $j \in q$ and $r \neq q$, one has

$$\frac{\partial^2 u}{\partial x_i\,\partial x_j} = \frac{\partial^2 u}{\partial f_r\,\partial f_q}\frac{\partial f_r}{\partial x_i}\frac{\partial f_q}{\partial x_j}$$

$$= \left(\frac{\partial^2 u}{\partial f_r\,\partial f_q}\bigg/\frac{\partial u}{\partial f_r}\frac{\partial u}{\partial f_q}\right)\frac{\partial u}{\partial x_i}\frac{\partial u}{\partial x_j}. \tag{3.36}$$

At equilibrium, $\partial u/\partial x_i = \lambda p_i$ ($i = 1, \ldots, n$). Therefore

$$\frac{\partial^2 u}{\partial x_i \, \partial x_j} = \tau_{rq} p_i p_j \tag{3.37}$$

where

$$\tau_{rq} = \lambda^2 \frac{\partial^2 u}{\partial f_r \, \partial f_q} \bigg/ \frac{\partial u}{\partial f_r} \frac{\partial u}{\partial f_q}.$$

Let us call τ_{rq} the interaction coefficient between groups r and q. The sign of τ_{rq} is not invariant under non-linear (monotonic increasing) transformations of the utility function. However, the sign of the *difference* between two interaction coefficients is invariant! The proof will be given in a moment. We notice immediately that it is possible to say (in an ordinal way) that wine and cheese, for example, complement each other better than wine and toothpaste, or, beer and wine are closer substitutes than pencils and butter. These statements can be translated in the ordinal statements that the wine–cheese interaction coefficient is larger than the wine-toothpaste interaction coefficient, or that the wine–beer coefficient is smaller than the pencils–butter one.

In each of these two examples, the second pair has been deliberately chosen such as to include goods taken from groups that appear intuitively as independent (wine – toothpaste, pencils – butter). The idea is that the interaction coefficient of one pair of groups may be taken as a standard to calibrate all other coefficients. And that this pair is to be chosen among those which are independent, i.e. where there are no specific relations between the commodities from the user's point of view. By definition, the independent pairs have equal interaction coefficients.

Given a standard interaction coefficient, two groups are independent if the difference between their interaction coefficient and the standard coefficient is zero. For substitution, this difference is to be negative. For complementarity, it is positive. And since we can push the partition to the point where each group consists of only one commodity, these definitions apply also to individual commodities. The analogy with the signs of the cross-partial derivatives in the cardinal approach is perfect.

We now turn to the proof of the invariance of the difference between two coefficients of interaction.

Before proceeding, we obtain from (3.35) for $i, j \in r$

$$
\frac{\partial^2 u}{\partial x_i\,\partial x_j} = \frac{\partial u}{\partial f_r}\frac{\partial^2 f_r}{\partial x_i\,\partial x_j} + \frac{\partial^2 u}{\partial f_r^2}\frac{\partial f_r}{\partial x_j}\frac{\partial f_r}{\partial x_i}
$$

$$
= \frac{\partial u}{\partial f_r}\frac{\partial^2 f_r}{\partial x_i\,\partial x_j} + \left(\frac{\partial^2 u}{\partial f_r^2}\Big/\left(\frac{\partial u}{\partial f_r}\right)^2\right)\frac{\partial u}{\partial x_i}\frac{\partial u}{\partial x_j}
$$

(3.38)

or, at equilibrium,

$$
\frac{\partial^2 u}{\partial x_i\,\partial x_j} = \frac{\partial u}{\partial f_r}\frac{\partial^2 f_r}{\partial x_i\,\partial x_j} + \tau_{rr}p_i p_j
$$

(3.39)

where

$$
\tau_{rr} = \lambda^2 \frac{\partial^2 u}{\partial f_r^2}\Big/\left(\frac{\partial u}{\partial f_r}\right)^2.
$$

The results (3.37) and (3.39) can be presented in matrix notation in the following way. Arrange the row vector of quantities x' and the row vector of prices p' such that $x' = [x'_1, x'_2, \ldots, x'_r, \ldots, x'_m]$ and $p' = [p'_1, p'_2, \ldots, p'_r, \ldots, p'_m]$ with x_r and p_r being the subvectors of quantities and prices. One then defines the matrices

$$
P = \begin{bmatrix}
p_1 & 0 & \ldots & 0 & \ldots & 0 \\
0 & p_2 & \ldots & 0 & \ldots & 0 \\
\cdot & & & \cdot & & \\
\cdot & & & \cdot & & \\
\cdot & & & \cdot & & \\
0 & 0 & \ldots & p_r & \ldots & 0 \\
\cdot & \cdot & & & & \cdot \\
\cdot & \cdot & & & & \cdot \\
\cdot & \cdot & & & & \cdot \\
0 & 0 & \ldots & 0 & \ldots & p_m
\end{bmatrix}
\qquad
T = \begin{bmatrix}
\tau_{11} & \tau_{12} & \cdots & \tau_{1m} \\
\tau_{21} & \tau_{22} & \cdots & \tau_{2m} \\
\cdot & \cdot & & \cdot \\
\cdot & \cdot & & \cdot \\
\cdot & \cdot & & \cdot \\
\tau_{m1} & \tau_{m2} & & \tau_{mm}
\end{bmatrix}
$$

where P is $(n \times m)$ and T is $(m \times m)$ and symmetric. The Hessian matrix of second order (direct and cross) partial derivatives can now be expressed as follows, using (3.37) and (3.39):

$$
U = U_D + PTP'
$$

(3.40)

where U_D is a symmetric block diagonal matrix. The typical element of the rth diagonal block is the first term on the right-hand side of (3.39).

Let $v = F(u)$, $F' > 0$, to designate the whole class of differentiable utility functions associated with the same preference ordering as u. As in Section 1.3, the monotonic increasing transformation F is assumed to be at least twice differentiable. We know that

$$\frac{\partial^2 v}{\partial x_i \, \partial x_j} = F' \frac{\partial^2 u}{\partial x_i \, \partial x_j} + F'' \frac{\partial u}{\partial x_i} \frac{\partial u}{\partial x_j}$$

or, in matrix notation,

$$V = F'U + F''u_x u'_x$$

where V is the matrix of second order partial derivatives of v and u_x the vector of first order partial derivatives of u. At equilibrium

$$V = F'U + F''\lambda^2 pp'$$

or, using (3.40)

$$\begin{aligned} V &= F'U_D + F'PTP' + F''\lambda^2 pp' \\ &= F'U_D + P[F'T + F''\lambda^2 ii']P' \\ &= F'U_D + PT^*P' \end{aligned} \tag{3.41}$$

where i is a vector with all (m) elements equal to unity.

In T^* we have the element

$$\tau^*_{rq} = F'\tau_{rq} + F''\lambda^2 \tag{3.42}$$

so that, for $(s, t) \neq (r, q)$

$$\tau^*_{rq} - \tau^*_{st} = F'(\tau_{rq} - \tau_{st}). \tag{3.43}$$

We are glad to discover that, F' being positive, the sign of the difference between two reaction coefficients remains unaltered after an increasing monotonic transformation of the utility function. Q.E.D.

It remains for us to derive the implications of separability in terms of the substitution effects, and to replace the Hicksian definitions by other (ordinal) definitions that are not contradictory with those in terms of interaction coefficients.

Remembering that the matrix of substitution effects can be written as

$$K = \lambda U^{-1} - \left(\lambda \Big/ \frac{\partial \lambda}{\partial y}\right) x_y x'_y$$

where x_y is the vector of income derivatives and using (3.40), Barten (1971, Appendix A) obtains

$$K = \lambda U_D^{-1} + X_y \Phi X_y' \qquad (3.44)$$

where

$$\Phi = -\lambda \left[\hat{\gamma}^{-1} (T - TP'U^{-1}PT) \hat{\gamma}^{-1} + \left(1 / \frac{\partial \lambda}{\partial y} \right) u' \right],$$

$$X_y = \begin{bmatrix} \dfrac{\partial x_1}{\partial y} & \cdot & 0 & 0 \\ & \cdot & & \\ 0 & \cdot & \dfrac{\partial x_r}{\partial y} & \cdots & 0 \\ \cdot & & \cdot & & \cdot \\ \cdot & & & \cdot & \cdot \\ \cdot & & & & \cdot \\ 0 & & 0 & & \dfrac{\partial x_m}{\partial y} \end{bmatrix}$$

and $\hat{\gamma}$ is the representation of the vector $\gamma = \lambda_y \iota - TP'x_y$ as a diagonal matrix. For $i \in r$, $j \in q$ and $r \neq q$, (3.44) implies

$$k_{ij} = \phi_{rq} \frac{\partial x_i}{\partial y} \frac{\partial x_j}{\partial y}. \qquad (3.45)$$

The factor of proportionality ϕ_{rq} is the same for all cross-substitution effects between pairs of commodities with one member belonging to group r and one member belonging to group q.

We know that k_{ij} is invariant under monotonic increasing transformations of the utility function. It is important to realize that here ϕ_{rq} is also invariant. Indeed, replacing U by V one finds

$$K = \left(\frac{\lambda^*}{F'} \right) U_D^{-1} + X_y \Phi^* X_y'$$
$$= \lambda U_D^{-1} + X_y \Phi^* X_y'$$

since

$$\lambda^* = F'\lambda, \quad \text{so that} \quad \Phi = \Phi^*.$$

When all elements of the matrix T are equal, all elements of Φ are also equal. Indeed, let $T = \alpha \iota \iota'$. Then, since $\iota' P x_y = p' x_y = 1$:

$$\gamma = \lambda_y \iota - TP'x_y = \lambda_y \iota - \alpha \iota \iota' P' x_y$$
$$= (\lambda_y - \alpha)\iota = \beta \iota$$

with $\beta = \lambda \gamma - \alpha$. Therefore, $\hat{\gamma} = \beta I$ and

$$\Phi = -\lambda[(1/\beta)^2(\alpha \iota \iota' - \alpha^2 \iota' P' U^{-1} P \iota') + (1/\lambda_y)\iota \iota']$$
$$= [-\lambda(\alpha - \alpha^2 p' U^{-1} p)/\beta^2 - \lambda/\lambda_y]\iota \iota'$$
$$= [\lambda/(\alpha - \lambda_y)]\iota \iota'$$

since, as follows from (2.22), $p'U^{-1}p = 1/\lambda_y$. In other words, when all groups are independent,

$$k_{ij} = \phi \frac{\partial x_i}{\partial y} \frac{\partial x_j}{\partial y} \tag{3.46}$$

for all $i \in r, j \in q$ and all r and q, $r \neq q$. Under groupwise independence, *there is one single factor of proportionality, common to all groups.*

Again, we may reduce each group to one single commodity and apply (3.46) to the case of additivity, i.e. independence between individual commodities.

EXERCISE

3.15. (a) Check the invariance of $\phi = \lambda/(\alpha - \lambda_y)$ under monotonic increasing transformations of the utility function, using (3.42) and the answer to exercise 1.16d.

(b) Explain why the invariance of ϕ is not in contradiction to equation (3.14), where the expression $(-\lambda/(\partial \lambda/\partial y))$ is not invariant.

Finally, Barten (1971) shows that $(\phi_{rq} - \phi_{st})$ has the opposite sign of $(\tau_{rq} - \tau_{st})$, when the interaction between groups s and t is the standard case. If then we apply the Hicksian definitions to the difference $(\phi_{rq} - \phi_{st})$ instead of the sign of k_{ij}, a pair of commodities or commodity groups that are substitutes according to the cardinal definitions (and their ordinal counterpart in terms of differences between reaction coefficients) are also substitutes according to the modified Hicksian definition. Consistency in thus achieved. The reader is referred to Barten's paper for the proof and further details and qualifications.

3.5. Homothetic utility functions

To make this exposition reasonably complete, we should say a few words about homothetic utility functions, the more as we have used functions with this property in several exercises. The basic reference[9] is Lau (1970) to which the reader is referred for more details and proofs.

We first define homotheticity: a function is homothetic if it can be written in the form $u = F[f(x_1, \ldots, x_n)]$, where F is a positive, finite, continuous and strictly monotonically increasing function of one variable with $F(0) = 0$, and f is a homogeneous function of n variables. F is said to be positively homothetic or negatively homothetic depending on whether f is positively homogeneous or negatively homogeneous, respectively.

We immediately infer that all homogeneous utility functions are homothetic, as the function F that appears in the definition belongs to the class of admissible transformations.

EXERCISE

3.16. Do you know any utility function that is homothetic?

Answer: All utility functions in exercise 1.7 are homothetic (see exercise 1.13b). Functions (1), (2), (4), (5) and (6) in that exercise all belong to the same class. The homothetic function (3), however belongs to another class and describes therefore another preference ordering.

3.17. Do you know any utility function that is both homothetic and additive?

Answer: The functions (1), (2), (4), (5) and (6) in exercise 1.7, as they are transformations of each other. The transformation (6) shows that they represent an additive preference ordering.

From the exercises based on the utility function $u = \prod_i (x_i)$ and transformations of it, the reader is already familiar with the properties of homothetic utility functions. The time has come to take a closer look at these properties.

To begin with, $\lambda' = ru$ if, and only if, the direct utility function is homogeneous of degree r, where $\lambda' = \lambda y$ and λ is the Lagrangian

---

[9] See also Samuelson (1942).

multiplier associated with *u*. The proof is very simple. Write the first order conditions as:

$$\frac{\partial u}{\partial x_i} - \lambda' \frac{p_i}{y} = 0$$

$$\sum_i \frac{p_i}{y} x_i - 1 = 0$$

Therefore

$$\frac{p_i}{y} = \frac{\partial u / \partial x_i}{\lambda'}$$

and

$$\lambda' = \sum_i \frac{\partial u}{\partial x_i} x_i \tag{3.47}$$

$$= ru$$

by Euler's theorem. The converse is proved similarly. Lau (1970) also shows that a utility function is homothetic if, and only if, $\lambda' = g(u)$ where *g* is a function of one variable.

EXERCISE
3.18. Check that (3.47) is satisfied by the utility functions of exercise 1.7.
    Hint: To save time, use your answers to exercise 1.16a.

Homotheticity also has an important implication for the form of the demand equations: the demand equations $x_i = \phi_i(p_1/y, \ldots, p_n/y)$ are *homogeneous of degree* −1 *in the p_i's* if, and only if, the utility function is homothetic. This implies that the demand equations can be written as:

$$x_i = \phi_i(p_1, \ldots, p_n)y \tag{3.48}$$

where ϕ_i is homogeneous of degree −1 in the prices, while all commodities have constant income elasticity of one. The reader has already checked this for the class to which $u = \prod_i (x_i)$ belongs in exercise 2.2.

In view of restriction (3.17), we may infer that simultaneous direct and indirect additivity implies that the utility function is homothetic. However, the converse is not true: homotheticity does not imply simultaneous direct and indirect additivity, as was emphasized by Samuelson (1965).

As noted earlier, the assumption of unitary income elasticities is entirely unrealistic: when all income elasticities are equal to one, a constant proportion of total expenditures is allocated to each commodity, which is in contradiction with facts. That is why economists are anxious to avoid homothetic utility functions in the construction of allocation models.[10] The early introduction of a class of homothetic functions in this book is entirely for pedagogical reasons: these functions are easy to handle *and* help the student to understand the advantages of the generalization of $u = \sum_i \log x_i$ into the Stone-Geary function $u = \sum_i \beta_i \log (x_i - \gamma_i)$.

We end this discussion by drawing the reader's attention to a well-known group of utility functions, which Samuelson (1965) called the 'Bergson family' in honor of Bergson (1936) who seems to have been the first to explore their properties. These are the functions which are additive and homothetic. Here they are:

$$u = \sum_i \beta_i \log x_i \qquad \beta_i > 0, \quad \sum \beta_i = 1, \qquad (3.49)$$

$$u = -\sum_i \beta_i x_i^\alpha, \qquad \beta_i > 0, \qquad \alpha < 0, \qquad (3.50)$$

$$u = \sum_i \beta_i x_i^\alpha, \qquad \beta_i > 0, \quad 0 < \alpha < 1. \qquad (3.51)$$

Equation (3.49) obviously corresponds to $\sum \log x_i$, except for the normalization rule $\sum \beta = 1$, and is of the 'Cobb-Douglas' type.[11]

EXERCISE

3.19. Let the utility function be $u = x_1^{1/2} + x_2^{1/2}$. Show that it implies expenditure proportionality.

Equation (3.49) is also implied in the 'Rotterdam model' presented in Section 2.5 (see Theil, 1967, Chapter 7 and Barten, 1967, 1969). The demonstration is due to Goldberger (1969). Goldberger first proves that if the consumer's utility function is directly additive, and if the expend-

---

[10] These functions may be useful, though, in the derivation of a consumption function in an intertemporal context. See, e.g. Friedman (1957).

[11] For further details, see Pollak (1971b). The indifference maps of (3.49), (3.50) and (3.51) are identical with the isoquant maps of the constant-elasticity-of-substitution production functions and can be found in Chipman (1965).

iture functions $q_i = p_i x_i = q_i(p_1, \ldots, p_n, y)$ display constant marginal budget shares (or marginal propensities to consume), so that the

$$\mu_i = \frac{\partial q_i}{\partial y} = \frac{\partial p_i x_i}{\partial y} = p_i \frac{\partial x_i}{\partial y}$$

are constant with respect to variation in $y, p_1, \ldots, p_n$, the utility function must be of the Stone-Geary form, that is $u = \sum_i \beta_i \log (x_i - \gamma_i)$.

From exercise 1.14, we know that the associated marginal utility of income is

$$\lambda = \frac{\sum_i \beta_i}{y - \sum_j p_j \gamma_j}$$

so that the 'income flexibility' (reciprocal of the elasticity of λ with respect to y) is

$$1 \Big/ \frac{\partial \lambda}{\partial y} \frac{y}{\lambda} = - \frac{(y - \sum_j p_j \gamma_j)}{y}.$$

Suppose now that, as in the Rotterdam model, utility is directly additive, marginal budget shares are constant and income flexibility is constant, (with the result that k_{ij} and therefore S_{ij} is constant). We see that this requires

$$\gamma_1 = \ldots = \gamma_i = \ldots = \gamma_n = 0,$$

in which case the Stone-Geary function specializes to $\sum_i \beta_i \log x_i$. The income flexibility is then equal to -1.

EXERCISE

3.20. It should be clear to you that, for $u = \sum_i \beta_i \log x_i$, the expenditure functions are of the form $q_i = (\beta_i/\sum_i \beta_i)y$, or $q_i = \beta_i y$ if the β's are normalized.
Hint: Look at the answers to exercises 1.14 and 1.11.

In view of the lack of realism in the Bergson functions, one may question the acceptability of the Rotterdam model.[12] Some authors,

---

[12] The reader should notice that, in empirical applications, the Rotterdam model is is not written in the continuous version given in equation (2.43). In fact, a finite approximation is used. That is the reason why the estimated elasticities are not unitary.

such as Yoshihara (1969) simply reject it. Barten (1969, p. 13, 14) argues that it remains a useful tool for testing the general restrictions. He thinks that the model can be justified as the first terms in a Taylor expansion of arbitrary demand functions and that the approximation will be good enough provided real income and relative prices do not change too much over the period of estimation. Barten also emphasizes that, in applied work, one is always using data of an aggregated type and that it is therefore of limited interest to look for the underlying utility function. If this were true, the efforts made in this chapter (and throughout this book) to derive particular restrictions from specified utility functions would lose most of their empirical relevance. This raises the problem of aggregation over individuals, about which more will be said in the next chapter.

IV

Empirical implementations

This chapter is devoted to the analysis of a limited number of empirical studies, chosen among the classics in the field. The choice has been made on the basis of pedagogical considerations. Our purpose is not to 'illustrate' the theory of consumer's behaviour or to survey the field[1], but rather to show how to bridge the gap between a theoretical reasoning and an empirical study. To attain this goal, it is useful to provide a feeling of the (slow) historical learning process that has been going on since the first pioneering attempts were made in the thirties.

The basic philosophy of this chapter is that 'facts do not speak for themselves'. Statistical data convey a message only to the extent that they have been re-arranged and transformed in a way adapted to a theoretical hypothesis. As a result, theoretical refinements are a necessary condition for progress in the interpretation of facts. That is, theoretical restrictions have to be *imposed* on the empirical estimates. Conversely, as should be clear from Chapters II and III, the choice of a particular demand model for estimation purposes automatically involves theoretical restrictions. To quote from the survey of applied consumption analysis by Brown and Deaton (1972):

Strong *a priori* notions are built into the analysis by the choice of model and these will interact with the data to yield results which to some extent will be affected by the model chosen. At the same time such strong preconceptions are inevitable; *some* functional form must serve as a basis for estimation, and even then when it has been chosen it will in most circumstances be possible to estimate only a few parameters for each commodity. This constraint, which is due to the lack of independent variation in the prices and income in most time series, rules out the possibility of overcoming some of the specification problems by estimating an equation involving all the prices simultaneously. Faced with all these considerations, and with the necessity of justifying the demand function chosen, it is perhaps natural that the investigators have turned to the theory of demand as a tool

---

[1] An excellent survey is to be found in Brown and Deaton (1972).

for deriving the necessary constraints and for organising their *a priori* assumptions. Because the theory is well worked out and well understood, demand equations which embody it will be guarded from some of the absurdities and inconsistencies which may arise from pragmatic models if the latter are used without considerable care and expertise.

4.1. Economic theory and empirical analysis

Before taking a closer look at particular empirical studies, we must pause and ask ourselves what are the theoretical questions – leaving aside all purely statistical or mathematical considerations – that the economist has to raise (and possibly solve) before embarking upon an empirical analysis of consumer's behaviour.

Take the following example. You have a time series of annual consumption of a commodity, say for the period 1950–1970, at your disposal. You also have an annual price index for that commodity over the same period. That makes 21 pairs of observations which you represent on a 'scatter diagram'. The scatter has a descending general shape. By some least squares method, you fit a regression line, say

$$x_{it} = \alpha_i + \beta_i p_{it}$$

where x_{it} is annual consumption and p_{it} is the annual price index. To what extent can you be confident that $\beta_i(p_{it}/x_{it})$ is an estimate of the price elasticity in year t?

Some fifty years ago, economists would probably have said that you indeed get an estimate of price elasticity, provided the statistical fit is sufficiently good. The reader who has gone through the preceding chapters, would probably raise a number of questions *before* discussing the statistical significance of the computed regression coefficients.

First of all, the *theoretical plausibility* of the demand equation used in the computations has to be established. Does it satisfy the general restrictions of the theory of consumer's demand, so that it could be derived by maximizing a utility function? If so, how is the use of a linear function to be justified? Are the particular restrictions resulting from linearity acceptable?

Having established the theoretical plausibility, the economist still has his doubts: how can he make sure that the estimated equation is a demand equation, and not something else? This is the *identification problem.* What allows us to identify the fitted line as a demand function? When β_i turns out to be negative, this is a first indication that it is the slope of a demand function. But as the consumption data are simultaneously sales data, and prices are realized prices, resulting from the intersection of a demand and a supply curve, a negative β_i may also indicate that both curves have been shifting in such a way that the intersection points are located around a downward sloping line. If that were the case, the computed value of β_i would be different from the 'true' slope to be estimated.

Economic theory also warns us that to write the demand of good i as a function of its own price p_i only, one has to accept a number of assumptions, put together under the label '*ceteris paribus*'. Income should certainly appear in it. To leave it out is implicitly to assume that it has been constant over the period considered. Was this in fact the case? What about the other prices? What about the implicit assumption of unchanged preferences?

Finally, statistical data in most cases refer to markets in which several individuals operate. However, demand theory describes the behaviour of 'a' consumer. There might thus be a problem of *aggregation over individuals*.

Each of these questions is sufficiently important for us to indicate briefly what sort of answers can be given, in order to avoid an understandable but sterile attitude of scepticism.

4.1.1. Theoretical plausibility

To ensure the theoretical plausibility of empirical demand equations, the natural procedure seems to be to specify a particular utility function and to derive the 'estimating' equations (i.e. the equations to be estimated) from it by constrained maximization. All general restrictions are then automatically satisfied. Furthermore, the particular class of utility functions chosen gives additional particular restrictions. By an appropriate choice, one obtains the particular restrictions deemed useful or necessary for economic or statistical reasons. One may of course have doubts about the suitability of adopting a particular specification and try out alternative specifications, (as was done by Parks (1969) and Deaton (1973), for example).

This procedure is not without its problems, though. The number of known and well behaved utility functions is very limited, in the present state of the art. The derivation of demand equations is not always possible. The demand equation one ends up with may be too complicated to permit estimation, because of non-linearities or because of the number of parameters to be estimated.

One therefore often proceeds otherwise, specifying directly the demand equations that seem appropriate for the problem at hand, and taking care to impose general restrictions which ensure their theoretical plausibility. This is typically the approach followed in the analysis of a particular commodity, where the particularities of an individual market (such as the automobile or the housing market) are to be taken into account. It is also typical for the analysis of complete systems of demand equations by the 'Rotterdam School', as was shown in Section 2.5. Here, the difficulty is to be aware of the particular restrictions that are implicitly imposed (such as the assumption of a homothetic utility function implied in the Rotterdam model) and to keep the computational burden down to reasonable proportions.

4.1.2. Identification[2]

The identification problem was raised by Working (1927) in his classic paper What do statistical demand curves show?'. In principle, the answer is simple: to identify a given relationship one has to take other possible relationships into account. To be able to identify a demand function with the help of statistical data, one has to realize that supply has simultaneously influenced the same data, for the simple reason that the observed prices are the result of the equalization of demand and supply, while the observed quantities have been bought and therefore sold. A simultaneous model should be constructed.

EXERCISE

4.1. Consider a market that can be described by the following simple model:

$$x^D = 20 - p + t$$
$$x^S = p + 4t$$

where x^D represents the quantity demanded, x^S is the quantity supplied, p is the price and t is an exogenous variable measuring time. Determine the time path of prices and the quantities at equilibrium ($x^D = x^S$) on the assumption that $t = 1, 2, 3, \ldots$. Show that a regression line connecting the interaction points would be different from both the demand and the supply curve.

---

[2] The discussion in this section is entirely non-technical. See any econometrics textbook for a more rigorous treatment.

Clearly, certain conditions have to be satisfied for the demand curve to be identified. Suppose, for example, that the demand curve is stable over time, while the supply curve is systematically shifted in one direction, as in the following exercise.

EXERCISE

4.2. (a) The variable t appears in the supply equation only, so that the model becomes

$$x^D = 20 - p$$
$$x^S = p + 4t.$$

Convince yourself that the demand equation coincides with a regression line connecting the intersection points (and is therefore identified), as a result of the elimination of t in the demand equation.
(b) Give examples of commodities for which the supply function is subject to displacements over time, while the demand function is stable.
Hint: See Section 4.3.1.

If one curve is stable, while the other is subject to shifts, the former can be identified. Shifts are due to the presence, in the equations, of exogenous or 'predetermined' variables such as 'time', or 'weather conditions' (rainfall per square inch, for example), or more generally any variable not explained by the model. From a technical point of view, the problem therefore boils down to determining whether predetermined variables, that appear elsewhere in the model, are eliminated from the equation to be identified. We will not pursue the matter any further. Firstly, because we want to avoid econometric considerations. Secondly, because identification problems are ignored in practice, whenever complete systems of demand equations (or several demand equations) are to be estimated. Indeed, it is entirely unpractical to specify supply equations for a number of commodities, the more as a solid theoretical underpinning as well as appropriate data are often lacking on the supply side.[3]

---

[3] A number of econometric considerations also indicate that the gain to be expected from work on the identification front is often negligible. See Stone (1953, p. 248-249). For a contrary view, see Summers (1959) and Williams (1978).

4.1.3. Ceteris paribus

Economic theory, as any theory, simplifies reality. In particular, it is concerned with a limited number of variables, those which we hope are the most important ones. All the variables excluded from the analysis are implicitly or explicitly supposed to be constant by the condition 'ceteris paribus'. The economist who is working with observed data should therefore be aware of the following two requirements.

First of all, he should recognize the incomplete character of the theoretical hypotheses, given the complexities of the 'real world'. Formally, this means that he should always add an error term to the equations to be estimated, and write for example

$$x_{it} = \alpha_i + \beta_i p_{it} + \varepsilon_{it}.$$

The error ε_{it} is a variable summarizing the impact of those variables that are not explicitly introduced in the theoretical model and whose effects tend to compensate each other, so that ε_{it} may be considered as stochastic. He should analyse the properties of ε_{it}, in order to specify the properties of its probability distribution (zero mathematical expectation, independence of p_{it}, constant variance and absence of correlation, for example). Although the knowledge of these properties is a prerequisite for the correct application and interpretation of regression techniques, it is essentially the economist's job – not the statistician's! – to specify these in detail for the problem at hand.

Secondly, the economist should have a precise knowledge of the systematic sources of variation in the sample to be analysed. Very often, economic theory includes in the 'ceteris paribus' condition a variable or several variables that did in fact vary a lot over the observation period and had a systematic impact on consumption. Their influence being observable, these variables have to be 'extracted' from the error term and introduced explicitly in the estimating equation, over and above the 'theoretical' variables.

Suppose, by way of example, that economic theory suggests that the demand for commodity i is a function (homogeneous of degree zero) of the price of this commodity, the prices of all other commodities and of the consumer's income. Suppose also that, for lack of imagination, theory has nothing to say about the form of the demand equation (no particular restrictions available). Some ad hoc reasoning and experience with regression techniques may then suggest the adoption of the following specification:

$$x_{it} = p_{it}^{\beta_{ii}} p_{jt}^{\beta_{ij}} p_{kt}^{\beta_{ik}} y_i^{\gamma} e^{\varepsilon_{it}}. \tag{4.1a}$$

Commodities j and k are a close substitute and a close complement respectively. The estimating equation is

$$\log x_{it} = \log \alpha + \beta_{ii} \log p_{it} + \beta_{ij} \log p_{jt} + \beta_{ik} \log p_{kt}$$
$$+ \gamma \log y_t + \varepsilon_{it}, \tag{4.1b}$$

so that the regression coefficients directly provide estimates of the price and income elasticities on the assumption that (4.1) is identified.

In writing the demand equation as (4.1), we implicitly considered that the impact of all other variables one may think of may be subsumed under the error term ε_{it}. It should also be clear that prices are relative prices and income is real income, to satisfy the homogeneity condition.

The point we want to make is that specification (4.1) is based on the implicit assumption of unchanged preferences. The most casual empiricism suggests, however, that changes in tastes are frequent and sometimes considerable. Taste changes lead to shifts of the demand curves, and these shifts may have an impact on x_i that is as important, if not more important, than that of prices and income. Examples are easy to find. World War II had the effect of importing American consumption patterns to the continent of Europe (chewing gum, Coca-Cola, whisky, ...). There are the familiar phenomena of habit formation (pipe smoking, travel by car, ...), fashion, advertising, ...

Whenever the observation period is not very short, taste changes almost certainly occurred. Their impact has to be introduced in the empirical analysis. How can this be done? In principle, one would prefer to reformulate the theory by allowing for changes in the utility function. Most of Part II of this book is devoted to a discussion of how to proceed. In practice, this is not always possible and, as in our example, one may wish to directly reformulate the demand equations.

To take account of sudden upheavals such as those resulting from a war, a common trick is to use 'dummy variables' (which take the value 0 before the critical year and the value 1 afterwards). The procedure amounts to a single displacement of the intercept for the period beginning in the year in which the change occurred. That is, the coefficient of the dummy variable d is added to the intercept. The procedure has of course no theoretical standing. The same can be said about the introduction of a time trend to represent the effects of continuous changes in tastes. A very common representation is

$$x_{it} = \alpha p_{it}^{\beta_{ii}} p_{jt}^{\beta_{ij}} p_{kt}^{\beta_{ik}} y_t^{\gamma} e^{\rho t + \varepsilon_{it}} \tag{4.2}$$

where ρ is the annual rate of growth of x_i due to unidirectional taste changes. Needless to say, variables other than time may be used, if they can be defined and observed.

4.1.4. Aggregation over individuals

Demand theory and the restrictions derived from it relate to a particular individual. But statistical data almost inevitably relate to groups of consumers (the buyers on a particular market, for example) or to all consumers in an economic community. The problem is to know whether demand theory is relevant for the interpretation of such aggregates and if so, to what extent and in what sense.

A first possibility would be to reinterpret the theory as relating to the group of consumers as such. The group as a whole would be supposed to maximize a 'community' utility function representing a community preference field. All restrictions would then be valid for group behaviour without qualification. Unfortunately, the implications for individual behaviour would conflict with observed behaviour, so that this simple solution has to be disregarded. (See Gorman, 1953 and Green, 1964.)

At the other extreme, one may want to start from demand equations defined as relating to particular individuals, and investigate under what conditions the properties for the individual equations carry over to the aggregate equation obtained by summation over the individuals.

Suppose, for example, that we want to find a sufficient condition for the aggregate income elasticity to be equal to the individual income elasticities. We find that the equality of all individual income elasticities is not sufficient: in addition, individual incomes have to grow in the same proportion so that the income distribution remains unchanged. Indeed, let there be three consumers in the market for commodity i, and let $y^{(1)}$, $y^{(2)}$ and $y^{(3)}$ be the incomes of these individuals, so that aggregate income y is

$$y = y^{(1)} + y^{(2)} + y^{(3)},$$

while aggregate consumption x_i is

$$x_i = x_i^{(1)} + x_i^{(2)} + x_i^{(3)}.$$

Clearly, if

$$\frac{dy^{(1)}}{y^{(1)}} = \frac{dy^{(2)}}{y^{(2)}} = \frac{dy^{(3)}}{y^{(3)}} = \frac{dy}{y}$$

and

$$\frac{dx_i^{(1)}/x_i^{(1)}}{d_y^{(1)}/y^{(1)}} = \frac{dx_i^{(2)}/x_i^{(2)}}{dy^{(2)}/y^{(2)}} = \frac{dx_i^{(3)}/x_i^{(3)}}{dy^{(3)}/y^{(3)}}$$

so that

$$\frac{dx_i^{(1)}}{x_i^{(1)}} = \frac{dx_i^{(2)}}{x_i^{(2)}} = \frac{dx_i^{(3)}}{x_i^{(3)}} = \frac{dx_i}{x_i},$$

then aggregate income elasticity is equal to each individual income elasticity, These conditions are of course unrealistic.

Suppose, on the other hand, we want to know under what conditions aggregate demand functions exist, so that it is possible to write aggregate demand as a function of prices (the same for all consumers) and of aggregate outlay. Once these conditions are found, we could ask whether they could be rationalized as resulting from the maximization of some utility function and hence have the same properties as individual demand functions. New insights on these questions were obtained by Muellbauer[4] (1975b and 1976).

Aggregate demand functions exist (are the exact sum of individual demand equations) if we can write

$$\bar{x}_i = \phi_i(\bar{y}, p),$$

where $\bar{x}_i$ is average demand (a function of all individual incomes and of prices)

$$\bar{x}_i = f_i(y^1, y^2, \ldots, y^H, p) = \frac{1}{H} \sum_h \phi_i^h(y^h, p),$$

the superscript h denotes the hth household, H is the total number of households, and $\bar{y}$ is average income. The function f_i indicates that $\bar{x}_i$ depends on the distribution of incomes. The function ϕ_i, to the contrary, does not refer to the income distribution: for it to hold, a change in the income distribution should not affect average demands! It should be clear, then, that all consumers should have the same marginal propensities to consume for any

---

[4] See Deaton and Muellbauer (1980a, Chapter 6 or 1980b, Appendix) for a summary.

good, i.e. that all individual demand equations must be linear in y^h and have the same slope with respect to y^h, or

$$x_i^h = \alpha_i^h(p) + \beta_i(p)y^h, \tag{4.3}$$

a very stringent condition indeed (as we shall see in Section 4.2.4).

To show that (4.3) is consistent with utility maximization, Muellbauer notes that it can be derived (by differentiation) from the cost function

$$C^h(p, u^h) = a^h(p) + u^h b(p), \tag{4.3a}$$

using duality theory. The reader is referred to Section 4.3.4 for an introduction to the use of cost functions (see especially equation (4.42)) to generate demand functions that are compatible with utility maximization[5]. The cost function (4.3a) happens to have what is called the *Gorman polar form*, a form introduced by Gorman (1961, 1976).

To get away from the unrealistic linearity condition (4.3), Muellbauer asks a still different question: under what conditions can we say that aggregate demand functions reflect the behavior of a 'representative consumer', in the sense that they would be a function, not of average income $\bar{y}$, but of a representative level of income y_0, *which itself can be a function of the income distribution* and of prices. (Once these conditions are known, characteristics (parameters, for example) of the income distribution could be introduced into the analysis in a way that is compatible with demand theory). It turns out that each household should have a cost function of the form

$$C^h(p, u^h) = \theta^h[u^h, a(p), b(p)] + \phi^h(p), \tag{4.4}$$

where $a(p)$, $b(p)$ and $\phi^h(p)$ are linearly homogeneous functions of prices and θ^h is linearly homogeneous in a and b. This is a generalization of the linear cost function (4.3a). In the special case where y_0 depends only on the distribution of incomes (not on the prices) – a case of price independent generalized linearity or 'PIGL' – a special form of the representative cost function is the PIGLOG form

$$\log c(u_0, p) = (1 - u_0)\log a(p) + u_0 \log b(p), \tag{4.4a}$$

where $u_0 = f^*(p, y_0)$. Since the 'almost ideal demand system' described in Section 4.3.5 has a cost function, equation (4.48), that belongs to the PIGLOG family, this system can be made to add up exactly over households (and thus to generate aggregate demand functions that are directly com-

---

[5] Please check at this point that differentiation of the cost function (4.3a) with respect to p_i gives equation (4.3), with $\beta_i(p) = \partial \log b(p)/\partial p_i$ and $\alpha_i^h(p) = \partial a^h(p)/\partial p_i - a^h(p)\beta_i(p)$.

patible with individual utility maximization) or to reflect the distribution of household budgets. It will also be seen to be compatible with the observed behavior of household expenditures.

The difficulties encountered when proceeding from individual demand equations to aggregate demand equations are generally referred to as 'the aggregation problem'. The attitude of most applied econometricians (including myself) is simply to ignore this aggregation problem and adopt a third approach by formulating aggregate relationships directly from the theory of the individual consumer.

When we use aggregate expenditure data divided by population to implement models derived from the theory of the individual consumer, we think of them as relating to a 'representative' consumer whose behaviour is supposed to reflect the average behaviour of the population.[6] It is supposed that this average consumer as such has a specific behaviour, different from the behaviour of actual persons. The question whether properties of the individual utility functions carry over to the 'representative' utility function is ignored.

To quote from Hicks, *A Revision of Demand theory* (1956, p. 55):

The statistical information on consumers' behaviour, which is available to us, always relates to the behaviour of groups of individuals – such, for instance, as the consumers of a particular commodity in a particular region. It is always material of this character which we have to test; and indeed it is material of this kind which we want to test, for the preference hypothesis only acquires a prima facie plausibility when it is applied to a statistical average. To assume that the representative consumer acts like an ideal consumer is a hypothesis worth testing; to assume that an actual person, the Mr. Brown or Mr. Jones who lives round the corner, does in fact act in such a way does not deserve a moment's consideration.

To this methodological point of view, we might add the comment that the 'aggregation error' involved in our procedure is probably of little importance. The following quotation from Houthakker and Taylor's recent book on dynamic demand analysis (1970, p. 200) is revealing, and we close this discussion with it:

The theory of the dynamic preference ordering given here is strictly in terms of a single individual, yet we apply it to entire countries. In so doing we ignore the aggregation problem, on which there is a voluminous literature. Rather than add to this inconclusive discussion we simply state as our opinion that of all the errors likely to be made in demand analysis, the aggregation error is the least troublesome. As evidence we cite our lack of success in finding significant demographic variables (see the first edition of this book), most of which would capture distributional effects. A formal discussion of aggregation

---

[6] Per capita relationships have the additional advantage of being more meaningful and stable than relationships between aggregates. This is illustrated by Houthakker and Taylor (1970, p. 29).

in dynamic models would lead us much too far afield, even if it were likely to be fruitful. We therefore proceed to matters of greater practical importance.

4.2. Engel curves

Applied consumption analysis proceeds from two sorts of data, cross-sectional data or time series.[7] As the former are easier to interpret in the light of demand theory, we will take them as the starting point of our discussion of empirical studies.

4.2.1. Household budgets and Engel curves

The cross-sections referred to are collections of household budgets indicating all expenditures on consumer goods and services made by individual families.

These budgets are collected in budget surveys in the following way. The Institutes of Statistics of most countries ask a number of families (at more or less regular intervals) to write down all receipts and all expenses of the household during a short time period (from a week to a year). To take an example, the Belgian National Institute of Statistics has organized a survey over the period extending from the 22d January 1961 to the 20th January 1962.[8] The choice of families was organized by stratified random sampling. In a first stage, all Belgian families were partitioned into strata of two thousand units. Out of the 1513 strata obtained, 225 were chosen at random. In a second stage, 40 households were chosen in each of the 225 strata, in the population registers, with the help of tables of random numbers. These nine thousand families were offered a fee of 3000 Belgian francs (60 dollars) for their collaboration, while the Statistical Institute made it clear that individual responses would be strictly confidential (and in particular, never communicated to the Ministry of Finance ...). 3451 families answered that they were ready to collaborate.

The survey started in fact with the collaboration of 1986 households, of which 1588 filled in their forms until the end of the survey period. Of the final responses, 9 budgets were eliminated. All in all, the survey retained 1579 budgets, classified as follows: 480 budgets of employees, 764 of worker families, and 335 of persons with no professional activity.

---

[7] It may of course happen that time series of cross-sections are available. This opens the way to the use of powerful econometric techniques. See Balestra (1967) and Balestra and Nerlove (1966).

[8] Institut National de Statistique. *Etudes statistiques et économétriques*, nr. 5, 7 and 9. Brussels.

Each household was asked to write down carefully in a special booklet, day after day, all expenses and all receipts and to answer various questionnaires. The information included all consumption and income items, all savings, transfers and capital transactions.

The collected data are of course transformed in different ways. The first objective of a budget survey is to obtain the percentage budget shares of all consumptions items, to be used as weights in the official cost-of-living index (see Chapter V). The data are also classified according to homogeneous social and professional categories (rural versus urban working class, etc.). For each of these categories different income classes are defined. The average expenditure on each consumption good or service is associated with the corresponding income class. This gives a 'cross-section' of average expenditures associated with the different income classes, for a particular social and professional category.

These cross-sections are the sort of data we are interested in here. They give rise to the so-called 'Engel curves', which express the expenditure on a good as a function of income only, or

$$p_i x_i = \phi_i(y). \tag{4.5}$$

These functions are so named in honour of Ernst Engel (1857) who seems to have been the first to formulate empirical laws governing the relation between income and particular categories of expenditure. The following 'laws' can be found in his work:

(1) food is the most important item in household budgets;

(2) the proportion of total expenditures allocated to food decreases as income increases;

(3) the proportion devoted to clothing and housing is approximately constant, while the share of luxury items increases when income increases.

EXERCISE
4.3. Which of these 'laws' is still valid, according to you?

4.2.2. Ceteris paribus

An Engel curve is a relationship between income and the expenditure on a particular commodity, all other things being equal. Let us take a closer look at this 'ceteris paribus' condition, remembering that the Engel curve is a demand function derived by (constrained) utility maximization.

EXERCISE

4.4. Show how an Engel curve can be derived from a diagram representing an indifference field for two goods.

Suppose for example, that a demand equation is specified as

$$x_i = \alpha_i + \beta_i \frac{p_j}{p_i} + \gamma_i \frac{y}{p_i} + \varepsilon_i,$$

and rewritten as

$$p_i x_i = (\alpha_i p_i + \beta_i p_j) + \gamma_i y + \varepsilon_i p_i. \tag{4.6}$$

We then see that, in the regression line

$$p_i x_i = \hat{a}_i + \hat{b}_i y, \tag{4.7}$$

$\hat{a}_i$ is an estimate of $(\alpha_i p_i + \beta_i p_j)$ and $\hat{b}_i$ an estimate of γ_i, on the assumption that prices are constant. Indeed, referring to equations (2.1), it should be clear that Engel curves are demand equations in which all prices are supposed to be constant. That is why cross-section data are appropriate, as they relate to one moment of time, so that prices have no time to change.

EXERCISE

4.5. (a) Qualify the preceding statement and explain why there would be changes in prices, even if a cross-section really related to one moment in time.
(b) What does b_i measure, given price differences within a cross-section of household budgets?
Hint: See Houthakker (1957, p. 538).

In theory, the γ coefficient describes the reaction of one and the same individual whose income is increasing, with given prices and a given utility function. In practice, the data used to estimate γ relate to different families, grouped according to income classes. The relationship between average expenditures per income class and average income is supposed to reflect the behaviour of one family facing an increasing income.

The idea is interesting. Using a cross-section, the investigator exploits the fact that prices are (almost) constant to isolate the influence of income: he thus avoids the difficulties encountered in time series analysis, where prices and income vary simultaneously.

However useful in that respect, a cross-section does not automatically take care of the assumption of a single given utility function. On the contrary, the preference ordering may very well change from family to family, e.g. according to income level, just as it may change over time. To satisfy the ceteris paribus conditions, it is thus necessary to take a collection of families that is as homogeneous as possible. Before estimating a relationship such as (4.7), the families should therefore be classified (as is in fact the case in budget surveys, as explained above)

– in homogeneous social classes;
– in homogeneous geographical areas;
– according to family composition;
– etc.

And the computations should be made on data[9] relating to one homogeneous category (such as urban worker families with two children). We may add at once that perfect homogeneity can never be realized: age differences, differences in social or working habits, in religion, etc. will always be present. The investigator has to decide for himself whether the data set is homogeneous enough to subsume the remaining differences in an error term with known properties.[10] Although it is probably impossible to achieve a perfect correspondence between the theory and the facts, much can be done to satisfy the hypothesis of a given utility function by a careful choice of the data *and* a careful analysis of the error term.

Needless to say the 'ceteris paribus' condition can also be taken care of by introducing additional variables in the estimating function, as is exemplified in the following exercise.

EXERCISE
4.6. Let the Engel curve be $x_i = \phi_i(y, n)$, where n is the number of persons in the family, to take account of a varying household composition in the data. Suppose that large families realize neither economies nor diseconomies of scale. Show that, in this case, luxury goods are characterized by the fact that consumption decreases with increasing family size.

Answer: Euler's theorem on homogeneous functions gives

$$1 - \frac{y}{x_i} \frac{\partial x_i}{\partial y} = \frac{n}{x_i} \frac{\partial x_i}{\partial n}.$$

---

[9] An alternative way to correct the data for family composition is to divide all expenditures by the corresponding 'equivalence scale' which converts these to a needs corrected basis. The basic reference on equivalence scales is Muellbauer (1980).

[10] For example, there may remain differences in tastes related to the level of income. One way of taking account of this is to suppose that the error term is heteroscedastic, i.e. that its variance is increasing with income. This leads to the use of 'generalized least squares'. See Prais and Houthakker (1955).

Therefore, when

$$\frac{y}{x_i}\frac{\partial x_i}{\partial y} > 1, \qquad \frac{n}{x_i}\frac{\partial x_i}{\partial n} < 0. \quad \text{Q.E.D.}$$

4.2.3. General restrictions

To ensure the theoretical plausibility of estimated Engel curves, the investigator has to make sure that the general restrictions of demand theory are satisfied, as emphasized in Houthakker (1960a). The problem simplifies drastically, as all restrictions in terms of price derivatives (homogeneity, symmetry, negativity of the own substitution effect) disappear, given that prices are constant. The only restriction that remains is the adding-up condition, which says that, if

$$q_i = \phi_i(y),$$

where

$$q_i = p_i x_i,$$

$$\sum_i \phi_i(y) = y$$

or

$$\sum_i \frac{dq_i}{dy} = 1. \tag{4.8}$$

The sum of the marginal propensities to consume (or the marginal budget shares) has to be equal to one at all income levels.

4.2.4. Allen and Bowley

The publication, in 1935, of Allen and Bowley's *Family Expenditure*, marks the first major analysis of cross-section data based on a theoretical model.

The main feature of their analysis is the estimation of *linear* Engel curves of the form

$$q_i = a_i + b_i y + \varepsilon_i \quad \text{or} \quad x_i = a_i' + b_i' y + \varepsilon_i' \tag{4.9}$$

where $q_i = p_i x_i$, a_i and b_i are the coefficients to be estimated and y is measured by total expenditures.

A few of the most interesting diagrams, representing the fitted lines, are reproduced below (Figures 4.1 and 4.2). We notice that some intercepts are positive while others are negative. What are the economic implications of a positive or negative sign of a_i?

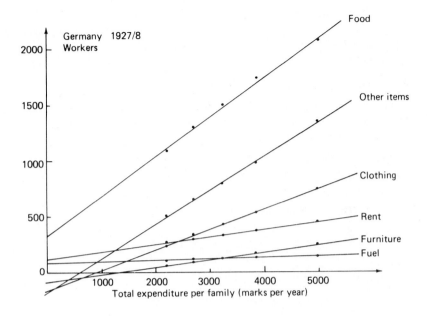

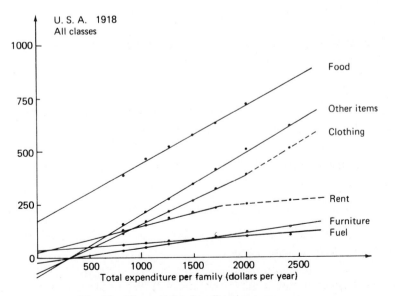

Fig. 4.1. Allen and Bowley: Engel curves.

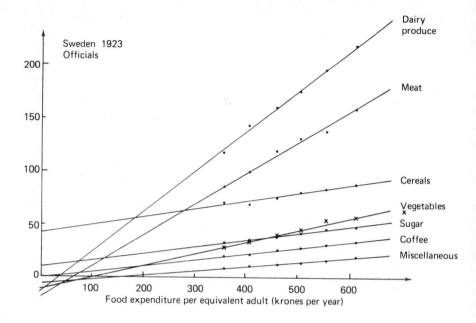

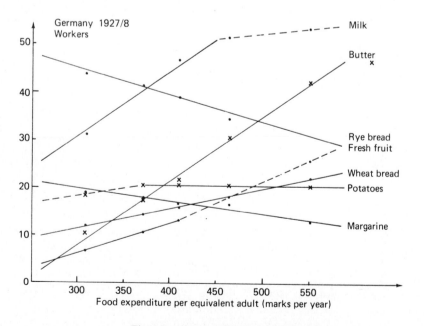

Fig. 4.2. Allen and Bowley: Engel curves.

EXERCISE

4.7. Show that, for linear and positively sloped Engel curves, a positive intercept implies that:
- the average propensities to consume (or average budget shares) q_i/y decrease when y increases;
- the income elasticities are smaller than 1;
- the income elasticities increase as income increases and tend to one.

Goods with a negative intercept have an income elasticity that is greater than one and are – by definition – luxury goods. Linearity implies that the average budget shares of these goods increase with income, while the income elasticities decrease and tend to one.

How far are these linear curves theoretically plausible? First of all, we should notice that the adding-up condition is satisfied, so everything is all right from the point of view of the general restrictions.

EXERCISE

4.8. Allen and Bowley derive the following regression results from a budget survey for 1926, covering 112 families of employers living in large British cities:

$$q_1 = 62.66 + 0.47 \, y \qquad e_{1y} = 0.8$$
$$q_2 = 4.82 + 0.06 \, y \qquad e_{2y} = 0.8$$
$$q_3 = -67.48 + 0.47 \, y \qquad e_{3y} = 1.5$$

where q_1 = expenditures on food, rent and clothing, q_2 = expenditures for heating and lighting, q_3 = other expenditures, and e_{iy} = income elasticity at the mean value of y. Verify that the adding-up condition is satisfied.

It is a property of linear regression equations that they satisfy the adding-up criterion. That is, if a set of linear Engel curves obeying (4.9) are fitted to an additive data set, then the regression estimates will satisfy $\sum_i a_i = 0$, $\sum_i b_i = 1$ and $\sum_i \varepsilon_i = 0$.

However, linearity is not without other theoretical implications. Linearity of the Engel curves implies that the utility function is of a special form. Investigating the class of additive utility functions yielding demand functions which are locally linear in income, or, equivalently, yielding Engel curves which are linear in some region of the commodity space, Pollak (1971b) finds that an additive utility function yields demand functions locally linear in income if and only if it is either of the form

$$u = \sum_i \beta_i \log (x_i - \gamma_i), \qquad \beta_i > 0, \quad (x_i - \gamma_i) > 0, \quad \sum \beta_i = 1, \quad (4.10)$$

which is the familiar Stone-Geary function (see exercise 1.14.), or

$$u = \sum_i \alpha_i (\beta_i + \delta_i x_i)^c \qquad (4.11)$$

which is a generalization of the additive quadratic utility function, or

$$u = -\sum_i \alpha_i e^{-\beta_i x_i}, \qquad \alpha_i > 0, \quad \beta_i > 0, \qquad (4.12)$$

which is an additive function used by Chipman (1965).

EXERCISE

4.9. Allen and Bowley derive their linear Engel curves from the first order conditions, on the assumption that the marginal utility of commodity i is a linear function of x_i. Which of the utility functions (4.10), (4.11) or (4.12) is therefore implied in their analysis? *Hint:* see exercise 3.2.

The origin of the particular restriction of linearity is thus explained, but not justified. Indeed, the implications of linearity in terms of the evolution of the income elasticities with respect to y are unsatisfactory from an economic point of view. We have seen that luxury goods $(a_i < 0)$ have an income elasticity that declines with increasing income, while the reverse in true when $a_i > 0$. This is intuitively unacceptable. One would rather expect the opposite, on intuitive grounds. It is not surprising, then, to discover that the statistical fit of linear Engel curves is very poor. This means that the data reject the linearity restrictions in this context.[11]

4.2.5. Prais and Houthakker

In *The Analysis of Family Budgets* (1955), which has become a classic in the field, Prais and Houthakker have therefore adopted different

---

[11] The same is not true for demand equations which are linear in income *and prices*, i.e. for the linear expenditure system. See Section 4.3.3 below.

non-linear functions in order to obtain a better description of observed facts.

The use of these functions is justified on the following grounds: (a) for many commodities, there exists a level of income below which these commodities are not consumed; (b) in many cases, there is also a saturation level which acts as an upper limit, whatever the level of income; (c) the adding-up criterion implies that all commodities cannot display a saturation level, for otherwise total income would not be entirely allocated above a certain level. If some commodities have a saturation level, some other commodities that do not have it must exist.

On the basis of these considerations, Prais and Houthakker have tried out the following specifications (besides the linear one):

$$\log q_i = a_i + b_i \log y \quad \text{(double-logarithmic)} \tag{4.13}$$

$$q_i = a_i + b_i \log y \quad \text{(semi-logarithmic)} \tag{4.14}$$

$$q_i = a_i - \frac{b_i}{y} \quad \text{(hyperbolic)} \tag{4.15}$$

$$\log q_i = a_i - \frac{b_i}{y} \quad \text{(log-reciprocal)} \tag{4.16}$$

EXERCISE

4.10. Determine for each these specifications:
- (a) the change (with respect to y) of the marginal budget shares;
- (b) the change (with respect to y) of the average budget shares;
- (c) the change (with respect to y) of the income elasticities;
- (d) at which point the curves cut the horizontal axis (measuring y).

Hint: If necessary, consult Johnston (1963, Chapter 2) or Brown and Deaton (1972, p. 1176–1179).

Notice that total expenditures are used to measure y, not disposable income. Why is this? Earlier, Allen and Bowley proceeded in the same way, disposable income not being available in the budget surveys then. Prais and Houthakker (1955, p. 80–81), on the contrary, invoke a theoretical argument. By using budgets from different income classes, one tries to measure the *long-run* reactions of a representative family. The average expenses in an income class may be considered as typical for a family that has adapted itself to the social status associated with the income class. The b coefficient therefore measures the reactions of a family to a variation in y, on the condition that this family has had time to adapt its consumption pattern fully to the new values of y. For consistency, one should thus try to measure the 'normal' values of y, i.e. the values considered as normal given the corresponding social status. Total expenditures, which are under the family's control, are probably a better proxy for this than the actual incomes, which may include all sorts of transitory (positive or negative) components. Furthermore, static demand theory defines y as total expenditure, not as disposable income (which includes savings), as was made clear in Section 1.4.

What are the findings? After a careful comparison of the statistical results, Prais and Houthakker conclude that the semi-logarithmic function gives the best results, as far as food items are concerned. This is understandable: the semi-logarithmic form makes it possible for a commodity to appear as a luxury at low income levels, and as a necessity (income elasticity below one) at higher income levels. For all other goods and services, the double-logarithmic form gives the best statistical results.

Table 4.1 reproduces the estimated income elasticity, at average income of 1938, together with the corresponding standard-error, for a selected number of commodities or services.[12]

TABLE 4.1
Estimates of total expenditure elasticities based on British inquiries

Item	Working Class	Middle Class
Rice	0.34 ± 0.03	0.41 ± 0.08
Condensed milk	-0.22 ± 0.33	-0.08 ± 0.18
Butter	0.39 ± 0.02	0.35 ± 0.04
Margarine	-0.25 ± 0.06	0.02 ± 0.06
Tea	0.37 ± 0.04	0.68 ± 0.08
Coffee	0.74 ± 0.13	1.42 ± 0.20
Drink (alcoholic and soft)	1.63 ± 0.13	0.96 ± 0.16
Carpets	2.36 ± 0.17	2.10 ± 0.26
Theatres	2.02 ± 0.10	1.17 ± 0.09

EXERCISE

4.11. Would you please write down your own intuitive estimates of the income elasticity of the following commodities and services (*before*

---

[12] These results are taken from Table 20, p. 106, 107 in Prais and Houthakker (1955).

looking at the estimates obtained by Prais and Houthakker): rice, condensed milk, butter, margarine, tea, coffee, drinks, carpets and theatres. Which of the estimates in Table 4.1 are acceptable to you? Discuss questions such as: would margarine still appear as an inferior good today? would 'theatres' still appear as 'luxury' services?

Prais and Houthakker's choice among specifications (4.13) to (4.16) is based on the goodness of fit. But what about their theoretical plausibility? Comparing their approach with Allen and Bowley's, we come to realize that while much has been gained in terms of descriptive power, much has been lost in terms of theoretical plausibility. By introducing more realistic changes of the income elasticities, Prais and Houthakker loose contact with the theory of utility maximization. Indeed, there is no longer any reference to a specific utility function. Much more, these specifications are not compatible with utility maximization, as they do not satisfy the adding-up criterion exactly. The approach is entirely pragmatic.

The same can be said about similar realistic specifications, such as the lognormal distribution analysed by Aitchison and Brown (1957), the family of Engel curves introduced by Törnqvist (1941) and used by Wold and Juréen (1952), or the forms suggested by Champernowne (1969). Much work remains to be done to find specifications that are both realistic and theoretically plausible.

4.2.6. Addilog utility functions

In his later work, Houthakker (1960a, b) has given an example of how further progress can be made towards the integration of demand theory and empirical work. One would like to find an analytical form that would combine the advantage of a good statistical fit with the satisfaction of the adding-up restriction. If possible, one would also like to know the form of the utility function to which the said analytical form corresponds.

Houthakker has concentrated his efforts on the double-logarithmic[13] form, whose excellent descriptive properties were confirmed at the international level in his 1957 paper commemorating the centenary of Engel's law.

---

[13] A rationalization of the semi-logarithmic form, written as $w_i = \alpha_i + \beta_i \log y$, where w_i is the budget share, is discussed in Sections 4.3.4 and 4.3.5 below.

He starts from the fact that any non-additive function $\phi_i(y)$ can be made additive by the following transformation

$$g_i(y) = \frac{y\phi_i(y)}{\sum_k \phi_k(y)} \qquad (i, k = 1, \ldots, n) \tag{4.17}$$

as

$$\sum_i g_i(y) = \frac{y\sum_i \phi_i(y)}{\sum_i \phi_i(y)} = y. \tag{4.18}$$

The application of this transformation to the double-logarithmic Engel curve $q_i = A_i y^{b_i}$ gives the additive curve

$$q_i = \frac{yA_i y^{b_i}}{\sum_k A_k y^{b_k}} = \frac{A_i y^{b_i+1}}{\sum_k A_k y^{b_k}} \tag{4.19}$$

Finally, Houthakker (1960a) shows that this function corresponds to the indirect utility function

$$u = \sum_i a_i \left(\frac{y}{p_i}\right)^{b_i} \tag{4.20}$$

which he called 'additive logarithmic' or 'addilog'. The reader who has worked out exercise 1.24 has gone through the converse problem of deriving the demand equations (4.19) from the addilog utility function.

For purposes of empirical implementation, we transform (4.19) into a linear relationship in the following way. Consider two goods i and j, and take the ratio of q_i and q_j, namely

$$\frac{q_i}{q_j} = \frac{A_i y^{b_i+1}}{A_j y^{b_j+1}} = \frac{A_i}{A_j} y^{(b_i-b_j)}$$

or, taking logarithms,

$$\log\left(\frac{q_i}{q_j}\right) = (\log A_i - \log A_j) + (b_i - b_j) \log y. \tag{4.21}$$

The ratio of the expenditures on any two goods has a constant elasticity $(b_i - b_j)$ with respect to y. It suffices therefore to take double-logarithmic paper and to measure q_i/q_j on the vertical axis and y on the horizontal axis: when the points representing the data are located on a straight line, its slope measures $(b_i - b_j)$ and there is an indication that the addilog specification is not in contradiction with facts.

EXERCISE

4.12. The following series, taken from the 1960–1961 survey of American urban households, give, for 17 income classes and for families with two children, the arithmetic means of (1) total expenditures, and expenditures on (2) food, (3) clothing, (4) refrigerators and (5) washing machines:

Income class	(1)	(2)	(3)	(4)	(5)
< 2000	1582	537	82	3.4	1.5
2000– 2499	2264	694	135	8.4	5.4
2500– 2999	2751	810	168	4.2	2.7
3000– 3499	3255	925	251	4.6	9.7
3500– 3999	3738	995	294	16.7	14.1
4000– 4499	4253	1039	359	19.2	11.4
4500– 4999	4746	1148	428	31.1	16.0
5000– 5499	5241	1192	488	30.7	9.0
5500– 5999	5726	1279	509	29.5	18.2
6000– 6499	6227	1341	570	36.3	33.4
6500– 6999	6749	1450	591	38.6	29.7
7000– 7499	7239	1395	638	25.8	10.5
7500– 7999	7763	1532	736	32.1	42
8000– 8999	8433	1552	822	35.1	35
9000– 9999	9431	1771	924	9.8	18
10000–11999	10948	1902	1111	29.6	24.9
> 11999	15695	2511	1588	40.2	27.8

Determine, with the help of double-logarithmic paper, for which series the hypothesis of an indirect addilog utility function seems appropriate.

4.13. Do the same for the 'direct addilog' case, where the utility function is written as

$$u = \sum_i \alpha_i x_i^{\beta_i}.$$

Hint: See Houthakker (1960b, p. 252–253) if you do not manage to derive the corresponding estimating equations from combining the first-order conditions by pairs.

A final remark is in order. When prices are allowed to vary, the indirect addilog utility function leads to the demand equations derived in exercise 1.24, which can be estimated from time series.[14]

4.3. Studies using time series

Over time, prices as well as income vary. This creates a host of new problems. For one thing, all general restrictions are now valid. Furthermore, the ceteris paribus condition creates the additional problems alluded to earlier. To make things even worse, prices and income generally move in the same direction, so that it becomes difficult to separate their individual impacts on consumption. On top of all these, there is the identification problem.

We will try to show how these problems have been tackled and solved, by analyzing the pioneering work of Schultz, Stone, Klein and Rubin.

4.3.1. Schultz

Schultz's monumental book, *The Theory and Measurement of Demand* (1938), is generally considered as the pioneering work in the field of time series analysis. It contains, apart from a theoretical exposition, studies of demand in the U.S. for particular agricultural products such as sugar, wheat, cotton, potatoes, etc.

This choice of products is particularly appropriate from the point of view of the correspondence between theory and empirical work. Indeed, these products have characteristics that make it relatively easy to bridge the gap between theory and facts.

We have seen that an observed relationship between quantities and prices can be identified as a demand equation when the demand curve is stable over time while the supply curve is subject to displacements, because the observed points of intersection are then located on the demand curve. As this is typically the case for agricultural products,

---

[14] The appropriate estimation procedure is to be found in Parks (1969).

Schultz is right in thinking that his computations relate to demand equations, without need for further sophistication.

Schultz gives his full attention to the 'ceteris paribus' question. Here again, the choice of products is fortunate. For these basic agricultural commodities, tastes probably do not change rapidly over time. Furthermore, production typically takes place within a season (or a year) and the crops are sold annually. All economic reactions therefore relate to one and the same period: there are no time lags, and stock building is not too important in most cases. Static demand theory, in which delayed adjustments are ignored, is therefore liable to give a reasonably good description of facts.

More specifically, Schultz tries to satisfy the *ceteris paribus* condition by putting all variables that theory supposes constant in a time trend. This trend shifts the demand curves in a systematic way. It includes the effects of changing tastes, of prices other than the product's price, of income and of changes in the population structure. The impact of this trend is eliminated with the help of the following alternative specifications of the demand equations:

(a) the multiple regression models

$$x_{it} = a_i + b_i p_{it} + c_i t + \varepsilon_{it} \tag{4.22}$$

or

$$x_{it} = A_i p_{it}^{\alpha_i} e^{\beta_i t + \varepsilon_{it}} \tag{4.23}$$

where x_{it} is the per capita consumption of commodity i, p_{it} is a price index of the commodity divided by a general price index and t measures time $(t = 0, 1, 2, 3, \ldots)$;

(b) the simple regression models

$$X_{it} = a_i + b_i P_{it} + \varepsilon_{it} \tag{4.24}$$

or

$$X_{it} = A_{it} P_{it}^{\alpha_i} e^{\varepsilon_{it}} \tag{4.25}$$

where X_{it} and P_{it} are either the ratio of the variable to its time trend or the ratio of the value taken by the variable in one year, and its value in the preceding year.

Schultz also takes care to divide the observation period into sub-periods, and to recompute his regressions for each of these, whenever history suggests that structural breaks may be present.

EXERCISE

4.14. What signs do you expect for the estimates of a_i, b_i, c_i, α_i and β_i?

Here are the multiple regression results for the demand for sugar in the U.S.[15], for the two subperiods 1875–1895 and 1896–1914.

(A) *Subperiod 1875–1895*

$$x_t = 70.6200 - 2.2588p_t + 0.8371t$$
$$\ (0.7322)\quad(0.2152)$$

$$e_{\bar{p}} = -0.3622$$
$$\phantom{e_{\bar{p}} = }\ (0.1553)$$

$$\log x_t = 2.0559 - 0.3828 \log p_t + 0.0156t \log_{10}e.$$
$$\ (0.1224)\quad\quad(0.0044)$$

The first result says that, ceteris paribus, an increase in the relative price index by one point was associated with a decrease of per capita consumption by 2.26 pounds. In fact, other things were not equal. Per capita consumption increased year by year at the average rate of 0.84 pounds per annum, because of a change in tastes and other factors. To obtain the price elasticity e_p (at a point on the demand curve corresponding to the average price $\bar{p} = \sum_{t=1}^{T} (1/T)p_t$, where T is the number of years in the subperiod), one multiplies the derivative -2.2588 by $\bar{p}$ and divides by the average consumption $\bar{x} = \sum_{t=1}^{T} (1/T)x_t$.

The second equations says that the (constant) price elasticity was -0.3828. In other words, if the demand curves had remained stable, a decrease by one per cent of the relative price would have increased per capita consumption by 0.38 per cent. On the other hand, if the relative price of sugar had been maintained constant, per capita consumption would have increased at the average rate of 1.56 per cent per annum.

(B) *Subperiod 1896–1914*

$$x_t = 92.8952 - 3.3408p_t + 0.9197t$$
$$\ (1.0090)\quad(0.1521)$$

---

[15] See Schultz (1938, Chapter 6).

$$e_{\bar{p}} = -0.2578$$
$$(0.0930)$$

$$\log x_t = 2.0701 - 0.2717 \log p_t + 0.0124t \log_{10} e.$$
$$(0.0844) \qquad\qquad (0.0022)$$

EXERCISE

4.15. Compare and interpret the results of the two subperiods, and of the two specifications (within each subperiod). Why are the estimates of the price elasticity so close from one specification to the other?

4.3.2. *Stone's 'Measurement of Consumers' Expenditure and Behaviour'*

The use of a time trend to catch the impact of all variables other than the price of the commodity under study is but a palliative. It is possible to do much better, as is exemplified in another classic, namely Stone's impressive book[16] on *The Measurement of Consumers' Expenditure and Behaviour in the United Kingdom* (1954).

To begin with, Stone has introduced (beside the trend) a number of prices (of complementary and competing goods) and per capita income in his regression equations. But, above all, he has given much greater attention to the theoretical plausibility of his computations.

Homogeneity of degree zero is imposed by specifying double-logarithmic demand functions as follows:

$$\log x_{it} = \log \alpha_i + \gamma_i \log y_t^* + \sum_j \beta_{ij} \log p_{jt} + \delta t + \varepsilon_{it} \qquad (i = 1, \ldots, n)$$
$$(4.26)$$

where y_t^* is the ratio of nominal income to a general price index P_t defined as a geometric mean, that is

$$\log P_t = \sum_j \omega_j \log p_{jt}, \qquad\qquad (4.27)$$

where ω_j is the average budget share $p_j x_j / y$, so that $\sum_j \omega_j = 1$.

---

[16] See especially Chapters 17, 18 and 20.

EXERCISE

4.16. Given that $y_t^* = y_t / \prod_j p_j^{\omega_j}$, does homogeneity of degree zero imply $\sum_j \beta_{ij} = -\gamma_i$ as in exercise 2.4, or rather $\sum_j \beta_{ij} = 0$? Then what is the form of the estimating equation, for $n = 3$?

Answer: Substitute y_t / P_t into (4.26) to find that γ_i drops out from the homogeneity condition. To satisfy $\sum_j \beta_{ij} = 0$, with three commodity prices, the estimating equation can be written as

$$\log x_i = \log \alpha_i + \gamma_i \log y_t^* + \beta_{i1} \log\left(\frac{p_{1t}}{p_{3t}}\right) + \beta_{i2} \log\left(\frac{p_{2t}}{p_{3t}}\right)$$

given that the homogeneity restriction reduces to $\beta_{i1} + \beta_{i2} = -\beta_{i3}$.

Given the double-logarithmic specification, adopted because of its goodness of fit, Stone was of course unable to take the other general restrictions into account. The only thing he could do, was to decompose[17] the cross-price elasticity into a substitution effect and an income effect, using the Slutsky equation rewritten in elasticity terms[18] as

$$\frac{\partial x_i}{\partial p_j} \frac{p_j}{x_i} = \omega_j \sigma - \omega_j \frac{\partial x_i}{\partial y} \frac{y}{x_i} \tag{4.28}$$

where σ is the 'elasticity of substitution' defined as

$$\sigma = \frac{d(x_j/x_i)}{x_j/x_i} \bigg/ \frac{d(f_i/f_j)}{f_i/f_j}$$

and $f_i = \partial u / \partial x_i$. Rewriting (4.26) as

$$\log x_{it} = \log \alpha_i + \gamma_i \log y_t - \gamma_i \sum_j \omega_j \log p_{jt} + \sum_j \beta_{ij} \log p_{jt} + \delta t + \varepsilon_{it}$$

or

$$\log x_{it} = \log \alpha_i + \gamma_i \log y_t + \sum_j (-\omega_j \gamma_i + \beta_{ij}) \log p_{jt} + \delta t + \varepsilon_{it},$$

---

[17] See Stone (1954, p. 262 and 277–278).
[18] See Allen and Hicks (1934, p. 201–202).

we see that $\beta_{ij} = \omega_j \sigma$, while $-\omega_j \gamma_j$ is the income effect in elasticity terms. The coefficients β_{ij} are therefore 'substitution elasticities' (i.e. cross-substitution effects expressed in elasticity terms, and not to be confused with σ). The decomposition is of course based on the somewhat artificial trick of defining the general price index as a geometric mean.

A further feature is worth mentioning. Because of the fact that income and prices tend to move together over time, with the result that it becomes difficult to get statistically significant estimates of both γ_i and the β_{ij}'s, Stone replaces γ_i by estimates of it taken from surveys on British household budgets. This amounts to taking (log $x_{it} - \hat{\gamma}_i$ log y_t), where $\hat{\gamma}_i$ is the cross-section estimate of γ_i (such as the slope of a double-logarithmic Engel curve), as the dependent variable to be regressed on the prices.

This use of extraneous estimates, which can be found in many other analyses (e.g. in Wold and Juréen (1953, Chapter 15)), has been criticized by Kuh and Meyer (1957). On the one hand, the income elasticities derived from budget studies are simple (or total) elasticities, while γ_i is a partial elasticity. On the other hand, budget studies often reveal long-run behaviour, while γ_i is rather short-run. One may therefore think that the information taken from Engel curves is not appropriate.[19]

The estimated substitution elasticities β_{ij} for six food items[20] can be found in Table 4.2. The time series extend over the period 1920–1938. The income elasticities are taken from budget surveys relating to 1937–1939.

EXERCISE

4.17. Which commodities appear, according to the estimates given in Table 4.2, as (a) luxury, (b) necessary and (c) inferior goods, considering the absolute values and the signs of the income elasticity and the own price elasticity? Which goods appear as complements or substitutes according to the Hicksian definitions? *Hint:* See Sections 2.3 and 3.4.

---

[19] Another detail of Stone's approach is that the regressions are run on the first differences of the variables, to reduce serial correlation in the error terms. As a result, an estimate of δ_i (the trend coefficient) is obtained from the intercept of the estimating equation.

[20] Taken from Stone (1954), Table 106.

TABLE 4.2
Income elasticities and substitution elasticities

Commodity	Income elasticity	Substitution elasticity with respect to Own price					Trend coefficient	R^2	d (Durbin-Watson)
			Beef and veal price	Cream price					
Fresh milk	0.50 (0.18)	−0.49 (0.13)	0.73 (0.15)	−0.23 (0.07)	—	—	0.004 (0.004)	0.81	2.01
			Fresh milk price	Margarine price	Tea price	Cheese price			
Condensed milk	−0.53 (0.18)	−1.23 (0.32)	2.25 (0.53)	0.80 (0.23)	1.06 (0.35)	0.43 (0.19)	−0.047 (0.016)	0.82	1.85
			Flour price	Cakes and biscuit price	Carcass meat price				
Butter	0.37 (0.08)	−0.41 (0.13)	−0.21 (0.11)	0.56 (0.26)	0.63 (0.30)	—	0.040 (0.009)	0.61	1.84
			Butter price	Chocolate and confectionary price	Cakes and biscuit price				
Margarine	−0.16 (0.11)	0.01 (0.17)	1.01 (0.17)	1.02 (0.26)	−0.46 (0.31)		0.016 (0.010)	0.77	1.76
			Coffee price	Beer price					
Tea	0.04 (0.04)	−0.26 (0.07)	0.14 (0.08)	0.08 (0.05)	—	—	0.003 (0.003)	0.56	2.15
			Tea price						
Coffee	1.42 (0.30)	0.55 (0.42)	−0.54 (0.39)	—	—	—	−0.010 (0.018)	0.15	1.57

4.3.3. The linear expenditure system

Stone's work, summarized above, remained unsatisfactory from the point of view of its theoretical plausibility: the homogeneity restriction is the only one to be satisfied. He had to do better, and succeeded in 1954, when he published, in the *Economic Journal*, the first empirical estimation of a system of demand equations satisfying all general restrictions.

This system is known as the 'linear expenditure system' and is still widely used in applied work, especially for short-term projections. It was in fact introduced in the literature by Klein and Rubin (1947–1948) in an attempt to construct a true cost-of-living index. Klein and Rubin proceed as follows.

In order to be able to apply linear regression methods, one would like to have linear demand equations. Consider the linear equation

$$x_i = \sum_j \alpha_{ij} p_j + \beta_i y. \tag{4.29}$$

Is this a demand equation? Certainly not, as the general restrictions of demand theory are not satisfied. To transform it into a demand equation, the general restrictions have to be imposed.

Homogeneity is very simply achieved by dividing all independent variables by the price of one good, say p_i:

$$x_i = \sum_j \alpha_{ij} \frac{p_j}{p_i} + \beta_i \frac{y}{p_i}. \tag{4.30}$$

The *symmetry* of the cross-substitution effects implies that

$$\frac{\partial x_i}{\partial p_j} + x_j \frac{\partial x_i}{\partial y} = \frac{\partial x_j}{\partial p_i} + x_i \frac{\partial x_j}{\partial y}, \qquad (i \neq j)$$

which condition demands that in the case of our equations

$$\frac{\alpha_{ij}}{p_i} + x_j \frac{\beta_i}{p_i} = \frac{\alpha_{ji}}{p_j} + x_i \frac{\beta_j}{p_j}, \qquad (i \neq j)$$

or, on multiplying both sides by $p_i p_j$,

$$\alpha_{ij} p_j + \beta_i p_j x_j = \alpha_{ji} p_i + \beta_j p_i x_i. \tag{4.31}$$

Substituting equation (4.30) for x_i and x_j, we obtain

$$\alpha_{ij} p_j + \beta_i \left[\sum_{k=1}^n \alpha_{jk} p_k + \beta_j y \right] = \alpha_{ji} p_i + \beta_j \left[\sum_{k=1}^n \alpha_{ik} p_k + \beta_i y \right]$$

or

$$\alpha_{ij} p_j + \beta_i \sum_k \alpha_{jk} p_k = \alpha_{ji} p_i + \beta_j \sum_k \alpha_{ik} p_k, \qquad (i \neq j)$$

which can be written as

$$(\alpha_{ij} + \beta_i \alpha_{jj}) p_j + \beta_i \alpha_{ji} p_i + \beta_i \sum_k \alpha_{jk} p_k =$$

$$= (\alpha_{ji} + \beta_j \alpha_{ii}) p_i + \beta_j \alpha_{ij} p_j + \beta_j \sum_k \alpha_{ik} p_k$$

for $k \neq i \neq j$. Since this equation must hold for all possible price systems, the coefficients corresponding to p_k $(k = 1, \ldots, n)$ on the two sides of the equality sign must be equal, so that

$$
\begin{aligned}
\alpha_{ij} &= \beta_i[\alpha_{jj}/(\beta_j - 1)] \\
\alpha_{ii} &= \beta_i(\alpha_{ji}/\beta_j) - (\alpha_{ji}/\beta_j) \\
\alpha_{ik} &= \beta_i(\alpha_{jk}/\beta_j)
\end{aligned}
\tag{4.32}
$$

for $i \neq j \neq k$. Defining

$$
\begin{aligned}
\gamma_k &= \alpha_{jk}/\beta_j && \text{for} \quad k \neq j, \\
&= \alpha_{jk}/(\beta_j - 1) && \text{for} \quad k = j,
\end{aligned}
$$

we obtain the following general formulation

$$
\alpha_{ik} = \beta_i\gamma_k - \delta_{ik}\gamma_i \qquad (i = 1, \ldots, n; k = 1, \ldots, n)
\tag{4.33}
$$

where

$$
\begin{aligned}
\delta_{ik} &= 0 && \text{for} \quad i \neq k, \\
&= 1 && \text{for} \quad i = k.
\end{aligned}
$$

Thus imposition of the symmetry restriction implies defining the price coefficients of $(n - 1)$ equations in terms of the price and income coefficients of the jth equation and of its own income coefficient.

EXERCISE
4.18. Make sure that you understand (4.33). Check that (4.31) implies (4.32), e.g. by working out the case where there are three goods in the demand system $(k = 1, 2, 3)$.

Before continuing, it is worth noticing that restriction (4.33) corresponds to the particular restriction derived in Section 3.1, equation (3.12), for a directly additive utility function. The proportionality of the cross-price derivatives to the income derivatives is indeed implied in (4.33), as the reader will easily verify. We would not be surprised, therefore, to discover – as we will in a moment – that the linear expenditure system implies a directly additive preference ordering.

We return to our main argument and consider the *adding-up* restriction. Writing the original equation after imposition of homogeneity as

$$
p_i x_i = \sum_j \alpha_{ij} p_j + \beta_i y
$$

and taking into account the symmetry restriction, we find

$$p_i x_i = \sum_j [\beta_i \gamma_j - \delta_{ij} \gamma_i] p_j + \beta_i y$$

$$= \beta_i \sum_j p_j \gamma_j - p_i \gamma_i + \beta_i y.$$

(4.34)

The adding-up condition demands that

$$y = \sum_i p_i x_i = \sum_i \beta_i \sum_j p_j \gamma_j - \sum_i p_i \gamma_i + \sum_i \beta_i y$$

$$= \sum_j p_j \gamma_j [\sum_i \beta_i - 1] + y \sum_i \beta_i,$$

so that we must have

$$\sum_i \beta_i = 1.$$

Gathering together our information, we can now write equation (4.30) as

$$x_i = -\gamma_i + \frac{\beta_i}{p_i}(y + \sum_j p_j \gamma_j) \quad \text{with} \quad \sum_i \beta_i = 1,$$

using (4.34), or, since γ_i is any constant, as

$$x_i = \gamma_i + \frac{\beta_i}{p_i}[y - \sum_j p_j \gamma_j]$$

(4.35)

with $\sum_i \beta_i = 1$.

We have not yet considered the *negativity* of the direct substitution effect, i.e.

$$k_{ii} = \frac{\partial x_i}{\partial p_i} + x_i \frac{\partial x_i}{\partial y} < 0,$$

which is thus not imposed. But it is easy to find out what it implies. In this system,

$$k_{ii} = -\frac{\beta_i}{p_i^2}[y - \sum_j p_j \gamma_j] - \frac{\beta_i}{p_i}\gamma_i + x_i \frac{\beta_i}{p_i}$$

$$= -\frac{x_i - \gamma_i}{p_i} + \frac{\beta_i}{p_i}(x_i - \gamma_i)$$

$$= \frac{(x_i - \gamma_i)}{p_i}(\beta_i - 1) < 0.$$

Since p_i is positive, this condition will be satisfied only if $(x_i - \gamma_i)$ and $(\beta_i - 1)$ are of opposite sign, for every i. This can only be true if

$$x_i > \gamma_i \quad \text{and} \quad 0 < \beta_i < 1. \tag{4.36}$$

To conclude, we have

$$x_i = \gamma_i + \frac{\beta_i}{p_i}(y - \sum_j p_j \gamma_j)$$

or

$$p_i x_i = p_i \gamma_i + \beta_i [y - \sum_j p_j \gamma_j] \tag{4.37}$$

with $0 < \beta_i < 1$, $\sum_i \beta_i = 1$ and $x_i > \gamma_i$. The original equation has thus been transformed into a theoretically acceptable form without losing its linearity. (4.37) is known as 'the linear expenditure system'. You have obtained the same result in solving exercise 1.14.

Samuelson (1947–1948) has suggested a nice interpretation of equation (4.37). The expenditure on good i, $p_i x_i$, is decomposed into two parts: the first part, $p_i \gamma_i$, is the 'minimum' expenditure to which the consumer commits himself in order to attain a minimal subsistence level. Accordingly, γ_i can be interpreted as the 'minimum required quantity' which the consumer purchases first (on the assumption[21] that γ_i turns out to be positive). At given prices, $\sum_j p_j \gamma_j$ measures 'subsistence income', so that $(y - \sum_j p_j \gamma_j)$ is the 'supernumerary income' which the consumer allocates among the n commodities in the proportions $\beta_1, \ldots, \beta_n$ (which are thus marginal budget shares).

EXERCISE

4.19. Compute the cross-substitution effect between goods i and j and show that it is positive for all pairs of goods.
   Hint: Knowing that direct additivity is implied, you may use equation (3.14).

---

[21] There is no reason why γ_i should in fact be positive. Solari (1971) analyses the case where some γ_i are negative.

Samuelson (1947–1948) and Geary (1950–1951) have worked out the utility function from which the linear expenditure system may be derived by constrained maximization. The reasoning goes as follows.

For any utility function, we have $\partial u/\partial x_i = \lambda p_i$ at equilibrium, and $du = \sum_i (\partial u/\partial x_i)dx_i = 0$, so that

$$du = \sum_i \lambda p_i \, dx_i = 0$$

$$= \sum_i p_i \, dx_i = 0.$$

From (4.37) we have

$$p_i = \frac{\beta_i}{x_i - \gamma_i}(y - \sum_j p_j\gamma_j), \qquad (4.38)$$

so that

$$du = \sum_i \frac{\beta_i}{x_i - \gamma_i} r \, dx_i = 0 \qquad (4.39)$$

where $r = y - \sum_j p_j\gamma_j$. The variable r may be eliminated from (4.39). Then

$$du = \sum_i \frac{\beta_i}{x_i - \gamma_i} \, dx_i = 0$$

and, on integration,

$$u = \int \sum_i \frac{\beta_i}{x_i - \gamma_i} \, dx_i \qquad (4.40)$$

or

$$u = \sum_i \beta_i \log(x_i - \gamma_i)$$

with $0 < \beta_i < 1$, $\sum_i \beta_i = 1$. This function, which we called the Stone-Geary utility function, is defined for $(x_i - \gamma_i) > 0$.

We have thus shown, knowing that the constrained maximization of (4.40) leads to the system (4.37), that the class of utility functions to which the Stone-Geary function belongs is the only one leading to a system of demand equations that are linear in income and prices. Linearity is seen to have very strong implications! All implications of direct additivity show up, and in particular the fact that all goods appear as substitutes according to the Hicksian definitions (as was confirmed in exercise 4.19).

A positive β_i implies that the marginal utility of good i is decreasing. Combined with additivity, this excludes the possibility of having inferior goods in the model, as we saw in exercise 3.5. To the extent that the model can be implemented only for very broad aggregates such as food, clothing, housing, etc., the reader will probably readily consider this as a very reasonable restriction.

There are further restrictions related to the sign of γ_i, which the reader is invited to discover for himself by solving the following exercise.

EXERCISE

4.20. (a) Show that, given $\beta_i > 0$, all income elasticities derived from the linear expenditure system are positive, confirming the absence of inferior goods.

(b) Show that, when $\gamma_i > 0$, the own price elasticity of good i is smaller than one, so that good i is 'price inelastic'.

(c) Show that, when good j is 'price elastic', the cross-price elasticity is positive.

(Goods i and j are then called 'gross-substitutes' by analogy with the Hicksian definition in terms of the sign of the substitution effect).

Hint: (b) You should find that the own price elasticity is

$$-1 + \frac{\gamma_i(1 - \beta_i)}{x_i}$$

(c) You should find a cross-price elasticity equal to

$$-\gamma_j \frac{p_j\beta_i}{x_i p_i}.$$

The linear expenditure system has been extensively applied over the past twenty years. Stone and his colleagues (1964) continued to use the system with British data. For other countries we may give the following references in chronological order: Paelinck (1964) for Belgium, Leoni (1967) for Italy, Parks (1969) for Sweden, Pollak and Wales (1969) for the United States, Yoshihara (1969) for Japan, Goldberger and Gamaletsos (1970) for thirteen O.E.C.D. nations, Van Broekhoven (1971) for

Belgium, Solari (1971) for Denmark, France, Italy, Norway, the United Kingdom and Switzerland, Baschet and Debreu (1971) for Canada, Italy, Great Britain, the Netherlands, Belgium and Norway, Sanz-Ferrer (1972) for Belgium, and Sanz-Ferrer (1973) for Spain.

As an illustration of the model's capability of forecasting the allocation of consumption expenditures, Table 4.3. reproduces the estimates[22] obtained for Belgium by Sanz-Ferrer (1972) for the period 1953–1969, together with forecasts for 1970 (using the observed prices and observed income in 1970). The comparison with the observed expenditures shows that the errors made are relatively small.

TABLE 4.3

The linear expenditure system: estimates over the period 1953–1969, and forecasts for 1970. Private consumption in Belgium, in Belgian Francs per capita

Commodity groups	Estimated parameters		Expenditures in 1970		
	β_i	γ_i	Forecasted	Observed	Differences
(1) Food and drinks	0.185	11,279.43	22,645	23,496	−851
	(0.001)	(151.71)			
(2) Tobacco	0.021	561.32	1,697	1,587	110
	(0.000)	(15.58)			
(3) Clothing	0.086	2,699.23	7,213	7,202	11
	(0.001)	(63.37)			
(4) Housing	0.151	6,795.34	15,559	15,382	177
	(0.001)	(130.17)			
(5) Durables	0.208	819.03	10,448	10,014	434
	(0.002)	(146.18)			
(6) Services	0.194	622.08	9,721	9,540	181
	(0.001)	(176.33)			
(7) Recreation	0.089	1,944.68	6,622	6,829	−207
	(0.001)	(83.88)			
(8) Expenditures abroad	0.066	−526.55	2,261	2,116	145
	(0.002)	(23.96)			
Total	1.000		76,166	76,166	0

Table 4.4 reproduces Sanz-Ferrer's estimates of the compensated own and cross-price elasticities. All compensated own price elasticities are negative, reflecting the general restriction on the sign of the substi-

---

[22] The estimation is based on Solari's maximum likelihood method. For details, see Sanz–Ferrer (1972). During the observation period, the official exchange rate was 1 U.S. dollar = 50 B.F.

tution effect k_{ii}. All compensated cross-price elasticities are positive (so that all commodity groups are substitutes according to the Hicksian definitions) but not symmetric, as the symmetry condition relates to the cross-derivatives, not to the elasticities (why?).

TABLE 4.4
Belgium: compensated own and cross-price elasticities

Commodity groups	1	2	3	4	5	6	7	8
(1) Food and drinks	−0.214	0.005	0.022	0.040	0.055	0.051	0.023	0.017
(2) Tobacco	0.082	−0.436	0.038	0.067	0.093	0.086	0.039	0.030
(3) Clothing	0.076	0.008	−0.375	0.062	0.085	0.079	0.036	0.027
(4) Housing	0.061	0.007	0.028	−0.278	0.068	0.064	0.029	0.022
(5) Durables	0.162	0.018	0.075	0.132	−0.692	0.169	0.077	0.058
(6) Services	0.167	0.019	0.077	0.136	0.187	−0.726	0.080	0.060
(7) Recreation	0.094	0.010	0.043	0.076	0.105	0.098	−0.460	0.034
(8) Expenditures abroad	0.311	0.035	0.144	0.254	0.349	0.326	0.149	−1.568

Table 4.5 reproduces the corresponding uncompensated elasticities. Commodity 8 being price elastic (because its γ is negative), the cross-elasticities with respect to this commodity (column 8) are positive, while all others are negative. The fact that there are no positive 'minimum' or 'committed' expenditures abroad seems quite reasonable. The same can be said about their large sensitivity to price changes.

TABLE 4.5
Belgium: uncompensated own and cross-price elasticities

Commodity groups	1	2	3	4	5	6	7	8
(1) Food and drinks	−0.399	−0.007	−0.032	−0.081	−0.008	−0.006	−0.023	0.007
(2) Tobacco	−0.232	−0.457	−0.055	−0.138	−0.013	−0.010	−0.039	0.012
(3) Clothing	−0.213	−0.011	−0.460	−0.127	−0.012	−0.009	−0.036	0.011
(4) Housing	−0.171	−0.008	−0.040	−0.429	−0.010	−0.007	−0.028	0.009
(5) Durables	−0.455	−0.023	−0.108	−0.271	−0.900	−0.019	−0.076	0.024
(6) Services	−0.469	−0.023	−0.111	−0.279	−0.027	−0.920	−0.078	0.024
(7) Recreation	−0.263	−0.013	−0.062	−0.157	−0.015	−0.011	−0.549	0.014
(8) Expenditures abroad	−0.875	−0.043	−0.207	−0.521	−0.051	−0.036	−0.146	−1.634

Table 4.6 reproduces the estimated income elasticities. These are all positive, as required by the model, given that all β's are positive. Food,

clothing and housing appear as necessities. Journeys abroad are clearly to be considered as luxury expenditures.

TABLE 4.6
Belgium: income elasticities

(1) Food and drinks	0.549
(2) Tobacco	0.931
(3) Clothing	0.857
(4) Housing	0.685
(5) Durables	1.827
(6) Services	1.883
(7) Recreation	1.056
(8) Expenditures abroad	3.513

EXERCISE

4.21. How would you compute the income elasticity of λ, given time series for y and p_i and estimates for γ_i?
   Hint: see exercise 1.14.

In the linear expenditure system, the income elasticity of λ (which we designate as ω) is equal to minus the ratio of income to supernumerary income. The larger are the committed expenditures, in comparison with total expenditures, the smaller is the supernumerary income and the larger is the income elasticity of λ in absolute value.

This absolute value can therefore be interpreted as a welfare indicator: the more a country is developed, the smaller $-\omega$ is likely to be; the same is true for higher income classes.

In Frisch's terminology, ω is called the 'money flexibility'. Frisch (1959, p. 189) suggests the following range of values:

We may, perhaps, assume that in most cases the money flexibility has values of the order of magnitude given below:

$\omega = -10$ for an extremely poor and apathetic part of the population.

$\omega = -4$ for the slightly better off but still poor part of the population with a fairly pronounced desire to become better off.

$\omega = -2$ for the middle income bracket, 'the median part' of the population.

$\omega = -0.7$ for the better-off part of the population.

$\omega = -0.1$ for the rich part of the population with ambitions towards 'conspicious consumption'.

It would be a very promising research project to determine ω for different countries and for different types of populations; a universal 'atlas' of the values of ω should be constructed. It would serve an extremely useful purpose in demand analysis.

The values of ω obtained for Belgium, using the estimates of γ_i reproduced in Table 4.3 are given in Table 4.7, together with per capita total expenditures in constant prices (real income). ω decreases in absolute value as real income increases and vice-versa, which confirms Frisch's suggestion. At the mean value of income and prices, ω is -2.09.

TABLE 4.7
The money flexibility in Belgium, 1953–1969

Year	Per capita y_t in constant prices (B.F.)	ω
1953	36,849	-2.93
1954	37,858	-2.81
1955	39,385	-2.62
1956	40,154	-2.54
1957	41,241	-2.44
1958	41,012	-2.45
1959	41,711	-2.39
1960	43,435	-2.25
1961	44,717	-2.17
1962	46,099	-2.10
1963	47,870	-2.02
1964	48,906	-1.98
1965	50,673	-1.92
1966	51,787	-1.88
1967	53,122	-1.84
1968	55,411	-1.78
1969	58,447	-1.71

The linear expenditure model has been generalized in several directions. Stone (1964) and Nasse (1970), for example, have suggested to make γ_i a function of the prices. Alternatively, the β's may be made price-sensitive. This leads to more general utility functions, of which the Stone-Geary function is a special case, as was shown by Johansen (1969). It is also possible to adapt the system in order to allow for weak separability, as in Brown and Heien (1972) and Heien (1973). Finally, attempts have been made to dynamize the system, e.g. by making γ_i (or β_i) a function of time or of past consumption. More will be said about these in Part II.

4.3.4. Duality and flexible functional forms

Linearity was seen, in the previous section, to carry with it all the implications of directly additive preferences. These implications are often too strong in applied work, especially for the estimation of sub-systems of demand equations for specific commodities. (For example, the linear expenditure system should not be used to estimate the demands for different types of tobacco – cigarettes, cigars, chewing tobacco – since these cannot be said to have independent marginal utilities and may even include an inferior good.) On the other hand, the generalizations of the linear expenditure system do not provide an entirely satisfactory answer, since a number of particular restrictions cannot be avoided.

That is why an alternative approach developed in the seventies, based on the seminal paper by Diewert (1971), which showed the analytical possibilities offered by 'duality'. While originally applied to the theory of production, the methods involved were soon used to generate new demand systems.[23]

The basic idea is to derive input demand functions from the cost function of a firm, using Shephard's lemma according to which these input demand functions are simply the derivatives (with respect to input prices) of the cost function. The latter is the result of cost minimization, given a level of production. Since output maximization, given any input cost, leads to the same input demand functions as cost minimization, the latter is the dual problem to the former. It then suffices to postulate a convenient cost function to be able to obtain the corresponding system of demand equations by simple derivation. (Conversely, given a system of demand equations, the underlying cost function can be found by integration.)

In terms of demand analysis, maximization of the direct utility function $u(x)$ subject to $p'x = y$ (the approach used so far in this book) leads to the system of demand equations $x_i = \phi_i(p_1, \ldots, p_n, y) = \phi_i(p, y)$. Substitution of these into the direct utility function gives the indirect utility function. The dual problem is then to minimize $y = p'x$ subject to $u(x) = \bar{u}$, i.e. to find the minimum total expenditure that suffices to reach a given indifference curve. This minimum is the 'cost function', written as

$$C(p, u) = \min_x [p'x; u(x) = \bar{u}]. \tag{4.41}$$

Shephard's lemma then says that

$$\frac{\partial C(p, u)}{\partial p_i} = h_i(p, u) = x_i = \phi_i(p, y). \tag{4.42}$$

---

[23] See also Diewert (1974a), Caves and Christensen (1980), Cooper and McLaren (1980) and Weymark (1980). Deaton and Muellbauer (1980) use duality throughout their book *Economics and Consumer Behavior*. Duality also facilitates the analysis of 'inverse' demand functions expressing price as a function of quantities and total expenditure: see Theil (1976), Barnett (1977b), Christensen and Manser (1977), Salvas-Bronsard et al. (1977), Laitinen and Theil (1979) and especially the handy survey by Anderson (1980).

Notice that, although $h_i = \phi_i$, h_i expresses x_i as a function of p and u, *not y*. It is, as the notation suggests, a constant utility demand function (also called 'compensated' demand function, since u is constant). To find $\phi_i(p, y)$, it suffices to 'invert' the cost function to obtain

$$u = f^*(p, C) = f^*(p, y) \tag{4.43}$$

and to substitute this into $h_i(p, u)$. (In order to make the distinction more obvious, ϕ_i is often called the 'Marshallian' demand function, while h_i is called the 'Hicksian' demand function).

Notice also that $f^*(p, C)$ *is* the indirect utility function, since u is the maximum attainable utility with a given total expenditure. It should thus be clear that duality provides a supplementary and handy way to generate utility functions (indirect ones, of course).

Notice finally that the cost function can be used to define a true index of the cost of living. It suffices, obviously, to choose a reference value for u and then to compute the ratio of $C(p^1, u)$ to $C(p^0, u)$ where p^0 are the prices in a base year and p^1 the prices in the current period, say. This idea will be worked out in the next chapter.

Deaton (1978) provides a simple illustration of the possibilities offered by the duality approach, in addition to a passionate apology for it. Remember from Section 4.2.5 that the semi-log Engel curve fits particularly well for food items. But suppose you want to use the budget share $w_i = p_i x_i / y$ as the dependent variable, following H. Working (1943) and Leser (1963), and to include prices among the independent variables. You thus want to make

$$w_{it} = \alpha_i + \beta_i \log y_t + \sum_j \gamma_{ij} \log p_{jt} \tag{4.44}$$

compatible with demand theory and find the underlying (indirect) utility function. Since

$$\frac{\partial \log C}{\partial \log p_i} = \frac{\partial C}{\partial p_i} \cdot \frac{p_i}{C}$$

and

$$\frac{\partial C}{\partial p_i} = x_i,$$

it so happens that

$$\frac{\partial \log C}{\partial \log p_i} = w_i$$

for a utility maximizing (or cost minimizing) consumer.

Why not, then, rewrite (4.44) as

$$\frac{\partial \log C}{\partial \log p_i} = \alpha_i + \beta_i \log y_t + \sum_j \gamma_{ij} \log p_{jt}, \tag{4.45}$$

(a system of partial differential equations)? Its solution is

$$\log C(p, u) = \alpha_0^* + \sum_j \alpha_j^* \log p_j + u \prod_j p_j^{\beta_j}, \tag{4.46}$$

where $\alpha_0^* = -\theta$ and $\alpha_i^* = \alpha_i - \theta\beta_i$, subject to the restriction that, for some θ,

$$\gamma_{ij} = \beta_i(\theta\beta_j - \alpha_j).$$

The (logarithm of the) cost function is thus found and (4.44) is shown to be compatible with demand theory. Inverting the cost function, the indirect utility function appears to be

$$u = \left(\log C - \alpha_0^* - \sum_j \alpha_j^* \log p_j\right) \Big/ \prod_j p_j^{\beta_j}. \tag{4.47}$$

To check that (4.46) is indeed the solution to (4.45) – and to show how Hicksian and Marshallian demands are derived from a cost function – compute $\partial C/\partial p_i = h_i$ from (4.46) written as

$$C(p, u) = e^{\alpha_0^*} \prod_j p_j^{\alpha_j^*} \exp\left[u \prod_j p_j^{\beta_j}\right].$$

You should find

$$\frac{\partial C(p, u)}{\partial p_i} \equiv h_i(p, u) = \frac{C}{p_i}\left(\alpha_i^* + u\beta_i \prod_j p_j^{\beta_j}\right),$$

the constant utility demand functions. Next substitute (4.47), to obtain the Marshallian demands (using $C = y$)

$$\phi_i(p, y) = \frac{y}{p_i}\left[\alpha_i^* + \beta_i\left(\log y - \alpha_0^* - \sum_j \alpha_j^* \log p_j\right)\right].$$

Finally, multiply by p_i/y and use the restrictions on the parameters to find the demand system (4.45) you started with. (Though logically simple, the procedure obviously requires some skills!)

EXERCISES

4.22. Check that the cost function of a consumer who has a Stone–Geary function is

$$y = \sum_j p_j \gamma_j + u\beta_0 \prod_j p_j^{\beta_j}$$

so that his indirect utility function is

$$u = \left(y - \sum_j p_j \gamma_j\right)\Bigg/ \beta_0 \prod_j p_j^{\beta_j},$$

where β_0 is a function of the parameters only. (Hint: see exercise 1.20 and compare with equations (5.6) to (5.10) below.) Note the similarity of this cost function with (4.46) and of this indirect utility function with (4.47).

4.23. Show that, in system (4.44), commodity i is a luxury when $\beta_i > 0$ and a necessity or an inferior good when $\beta_i < 0$.

In addition to (4.42), the cost function has a number of properties which are worth remembering: (1) it is of course homogeneous of degree one in prices, since doubling all prices will double the outlay required to stay on the same indifference curve; (2) it is increasing in u, non-decreasing in p, and increasing in at least one price (because of the axiom of dominance); (3) it is concave in prices, because the consumer will rearrange purchases when relative prices change, with the result that cost rises no more than linearly; (4) it follows from (3) that the cost function is continuous in p and that the first and second derivatives with respect to p exist almost everywhere.[24]

Following the methodology outlined above, a number of authors[25] have generated particular cost functions (and the corresponding indirect and direct utility functions) using some specific functional form. They have called these 'flexible functional forms' to emphasize that by adding enough parameters these forms can approximate whatever the true unknown function may be. For example, a quadratic function of the logarithms of x or of y and p, called the 'translog' utility function, is interpreted as a second-order Taylor expansion to the true utility function. Such a statement, while promising at first sight, is in fact an overstatement: the approximation can be accurate only in the locality of some point, i.e. at a particular value of x_i or y or p, not over an entire sampling period.[26]

4.3.5. *An almost ideal demand system*

Deaton and Muellbauer (1980b) have continued the exploration of the semi-logarithmic model (4.44) by slightly complicating its cost function

---

[24] For further details, see Deaton and Muellbauer (1980a, pp. 39–40).
[25] See Christensen et al. (1975) and Jorgenson and Lau (1975).
[26] Simmons and Weiserbs (1979) have developed this idea.

(4.46). They write it as

$$\log C(p, u) = \alpha_0 + \sum_j \alpha_j \log p_j + \frac{1}{2} \sum_i \sum_j \gamma_{ij}^* \log p_i \log p_j + u\beta_0 \prod_j p_j^{\beta_j},$$

$$(4.48)$$

adding a quadratic form to allow for interaction between prices. Using (4.42) and substituting for u, they find

$$w_i = \alpha_i + \sum_j \gamma_{ij} \log p_j + \beta_i \log(y/P), \qquad (4.49)$$

where P is a price index defined by

$$\log P = \alpha_0 + \sum_j \alpha_j \log p_j + \frac{1}{2} \sum_i \sum_j \gamma_{ij} \log p_i \log p_j$$

and $\gamma_{ij} = \frac{1}{2}(\gamma_{ij}^* + \gamma_{ji}^*) = \gamma_{ji}$. They called system (4.49) an 'almost ideal demand system' (AIDS).

This system has indeed its advantages: it is easier to estimate than the linear expenditure system and the translog model; as the Rotterdam system, it can be used to test homogeneity and symmetry through linear restrictions on fixed parameters, yet it has the advantage of being derived explicitly from utility maximization.

Notice first that all general restrictions (except the negativity condition) are satisfied provided that

$$\sum_i \alpha_i = 1,$$

$$(4.50)$$

$$\sum_j \gamma_{ij}^* = \sum_i \gamma_{ij}^* = \sum_j \beta_j = 0.$$

EXERCISE
4.24. Convince yourself that these restrictions imply that
   (a) the cost function (4.48) is linearly homogeneous in p, as it should be;
   (b) $\sum_i \gamma_{ij} = \sum_j \gamma_{ij} = 0$;
   (c) system (4.49) satisfies the adding-up condition, the homogeneity condition and the symmetry condition.

In the absence of changes in relative prices and real expenditure (y/P), the budget shares are constant. Changes in relative prices work through the

γ_{ij}'s. Changes in real expenditure operate through the β_i coefficients, which are positive for luxuries and negative for necessities (see exercise 4.23 above).

Since the cost function is defined as a *flexible* functional form, i.e. is general enough to act as a second order approximation to any arbitrary cost function, the AIDS is a first order approximation to any set of demand functions (as is the Rotterdam system). Yet, additional restrictions can easily be put on the parameters, e.g. by making γ_{ij} zero for some pairs of goods.

EXERCISE

4.25. Write the first difference form of (4.49), on the assumption that P is defined as Stone's index (4.27), and compare it with the Rotterdam system as defined in (2.43). The latter is not derived from utility maximization, while the AIDS is.

Our discussion of duality and flexible forms started with the remark that duality raised hopes that it would be possible to get rid of the assumption of additive preferences in the construction of operational demand systems. Did these hopes materialize? The answer is: yes, of course. From this point of view, duality led to an important breakthrough.

EXERCISE

4.26. Convince yourself that this conclusion is correct. (Hint: are the specific substitution effects zero in the AIDS?)

V

Cost-of-living indices

In his classical survey of index number theory, Frisch (1936) classifies index numbers into two categories: 'statistical' index numbers and 'functional' index numbers. The former are purely descriptive statistics, measuring the variations in a set of comparable phenomena (prices, quantities, etc.) along an axis of observation (e.g. time, space, etc.), without any direct theoretical underpinning.[1] The latter are based on a formal theory, and have therefore a precise theoretical interpretation.

The official cost-of-living indices, published by the National Statistical Institutes in most countries, belong to the first category. We want to investigate whether these indices can be considered as good approximations to the functional or 'true' cost-of-living index derived from demand theory. We also want to discuss the possibility of computing the true index itself.

5.1. Statistical price indices

The statistical indices that interest us here belong to the class of *weighted price indices*, i.e. averages of a number of price ratios, where each price ratio is properly weighted before summation.

Consider any two situations, indexed 0 and 1, selected at will from a set of situations, each characterized by a price vector. For each commodity entering the index, we can compute the ratio p_i^1/p_i^0. Each ratio can be given a weight w_i measuring the share of commodity i in total expenditures, i.e. its average budget share, in

---

[1] For an exhaustive analysis of statistical index numbers, see Fisher (1923).

a given situation. At the prices prevailing in situation 0, we have

$$w_i = \frac{p_i^0 x_i}{\sum_j p_j^0 x_j} \quad \text{and} \quad \sum w_i = 1. \tag{5.1}$$

The weighted price index is

$$\sum_i \left(\frac{p_i^1}{p_i^0}\right) w_i = \frac{\sum_i p_i^1 x_i}{\sum_i p_i^0 x_i}. \tag{5.2}$$

It remains to specify to which situation the quantities x_i refer. On taking the quantities consumed in situation 0, we obtain the *Laspeyres index*

$$L = \frac{\sum p_i^1 x_i^0}{\sum p_i^0 x_i^0}. \tag{5.3}$$

If, on the contrary, we use $x^1 = (x_1^1, \ldots, x_n^1)$, we get the *Paasche index*

$$P = \frac{\sum p_i^1 x_i^1}{\sum p_i^0 x_i^1}. \tag{5.4}$$

Notice that, when these indices are computed for successive time periods, the quantities x^0 are those consumed in the period chosen as the base period and remain constant in the Laspeyres index. In the Paasche index, the quantities x^1 are those consumed in the current period and change from period to period. Notice also that if all commodities were included in the computations, the denominator of L would be equal to total expenditures in situation 0 (income y^0), while the numerator of P would be equal to total expenditures in situation 1 (income y^1).

Most official cost-of-living indices are Laspeyres indices. They use as weights the average budget shares of some base period. These weights are taken from the family budget surveys, organized at regular intervals. (In Belgium, for example, they are organized every ten years.) As explained in Section 4.2.1, the computation of w_i is in fact the first objective of budget surveys. The use of the Paasche formula would imply the necessity of a continuing budget survey, the cost of which would be prohibitive.

5.2. The true cost-of-living index[2]

The *functional price index* can be defined as follows. Suppose that we employ some criterion by which it is possible to determine whether or not a given income will allow a person to be just as 'well off' in situation 1 as he was in situation 0 with the prices of that situation and an arbitrary but determined income. The income which realizes this we shall call an income equivalent to the arbitrarily chosen income. The functional price index is the ratio of the equivalent income to the arbitrarily defined income. The latter income together with the prices characterizing situation 0 serve as base for the index, whereas the prices characterizing situation 1 serve for comparison.

The criterion which leads to the *true cost-of-living index* is taken from the theory of consumer demand. Two incomes, each associated with a price regime, are equivalent if they allow the consumer to attain optimally the same indifference curve under their respective price regimes. Given this criterion, we shall lift the quality of arbitrariness from the base income and transfer it to the indifference class; in other words, we shall define as base income that which allows the consumer to attain optimally an arbitrarily chosen indifference curve, given base prices. We shall call the indifference curve the reference curve, and qualify as 'reference' all the factors that lead to its choice.

The true cost-of-living index can now be defined, with Pollak (1971c), as the ratio of the minimum cost of attaining a reference indifference curve under comparison prices to that of attaining it under base prices. In symbols,

$$I(p^0, p^1, u, R) = \frac{C(p^1; u, R)}{C(p^0; u, R)}, \tag{5.5}$$

where u is the reference indifference curve and R the relevant preference ordering.

There exist two spaces from which the indifference curve (or surface) may be chosen: the commodity space and the price-income space. These

---

[2] This section draws heavily on de Souza (1972).

lead to two parallel but equivalent definitions of the static cost-of-living index. The definition given above is that corresponding to the commodity space. When the reference indifference class is chosen with respect to the price-income space, the true cost-of-living index is the ratio of that income which places the consumer in the reference indifference surface given comparison prices to that income which does the same given base prices.

It remains for us to choose the relevant preference ordering R and the reference indifference curve (or surface). As to the former, there is no problem when the index measures prices over time and when the approach is static: the possibility of a temporal variation of preferences is excluded. In a static context, spatial differences are still possible, however, and will be considered in the final section of this chapter. In a dynamic approach, where preferences are changing over time, the choice of the relevant preference ordering raises problems which will be discussed in Chapter IX.

The indifference curve is determined with reference to a chosen reference price-income vector, with the help of the direct or the indirect utility function. In the commodity space, maximization of the direct utility function subject to the budget constraint determined by the reference price-income vector will yield the relevant indifference curve (more precisely, the utility level indicating or representing the indifference curve). In the price-income space, the indirect utility function will directly yield the relevant indifference surface by mere substitution therein of the reference price-income vector.

Finally, we have to be specific about the choice of the reference price-income vector. Certain price-income vectors appear as natural or obvious ones on which to base the index. First, there is the price vector serving as base for the index together with the income actually available during the base period. The use of these as the reference price-income vector leads to what can be called a Laspeyres type true cost-of-living index. Secondly, there is the price vector serving for comparison in the index together with the income actually available during the comparison period. This yields a Paasche type true cost-of-living index.

5.3. The true index in the linear expenditure system

The true index can be computed if one is willing to specify the utility function algebraically. The Stone-Geary utility function is a natural candidate, the more so as the associated linear expenditure system came to life as an illustration of the computation of a true cost-of-living index in Klein and Rubin (1947–1948). We will consider a Laspeyres type index, choosing (p^0, y^0) as the reference price-income vector.

Remembering that the indirect Stone-Geary utility function is[3]

$$\sum_i \beta_i \log \beta_i - (\sum_i \beta_i) \log (\sum_i \beta_i) + (\sum_i \beta_i) \log (y - \sum_j p_j \gamma_j) - \sum_i \beta_i \log p_i$$

the reference utility level can be determined (in the price-income space) as

$$u^0 = \sum_i \beta_i \log \beta_i - (\sum_i \beta_i) \log (\sum_i \beta_i) +$$
$$+ (\sum_i \beta_i) \log (y^0 - \sum_j p_j^0 \gamma_j) - \sum_i \beta_i \log p_i^0. \tag{5.6}$$

We first proceed in the commodity space and want to minimize the cost of attaining u^0 under comparison prices p^1. Minimizing

$$\sum_i p_i^1 x_i \quad \text{subject to} \quad \sum_i \beta_i \log (x_i - \gamma_i) = u^0 \tag{5.7}$$

we find the first order conditions

$$p_i^1 - \lambda \beta_i/(x_i - \gamma_i) = 0 \qquad (i = 1, \ldots, n)$$
$$\sum_i \beta_i \log (x_i - \gamma_i) - u^0 = 0. \tag{5.8}$$

Their resolution yields the constant utility demand functions

$$x_i^{**} = \gamma_i + \frac{\beta_i}{p_i^1}\left(\text{antilog}\left[\frac{u^0}{\sum_j \beta_j}\right]\right)\left(\prod_j \left[\frac{p_j^1}{\beta_j}\right]^{\beta_j/\sum \beta_j}\right) \tag{5.9}$$

so that the cost function is

$$C^1 = \sum_i p_i^1 \gamma_i + (\sum_i \beta_i)\left(\text{antilog}\left[\frac{u^0}{\sum_j \beta_j}\right]\right)\left(\prod_j \left[\frac{p_j^1}{\beta_j}\right]^{\beta_j/\sum \beta_j}\right) \tag{5.10}$$
$$= y^{**}$$

where y^{**} is the equivalent or 'true' income that leaves the consumer as 'well off' as in situation 0.

---

[3] See exercise 1.20.

The true index is, on the assumption that $\sum_i \beta_i = 1$,

$$I(p^0, p^1, u^0, R) = \frac{C^1}{C^0} = \frac{y^{**}}{y^0}$$

$$= \frac{\sum_j p^1_j \gamma_j}{y^0} + \left(\frac{y^0 - \sum_j p^0_j \gamma_j}{y^0}\right) \prod_j \left[\frac{p^1_j}{p^0_j}\right]^{\beta_j} \quad (5.11)$$

$$= \frac{\sum_j p^1_j \gamma_j}{y^0} + \left(1 - \frac{\sum_j p^0_j \gamma_j}{y^0}\right) \prod_j \left[\frac{p^1_j}{p^0_j}\right]^{\beta_j}$$

using (5.6). It can be computed from the observations on the prices and total expenditure, using estimates of γ_i and β_i.

An alternative procedure is to work in the price-income space, to equate the indirect utility function for the comparison period

$$u^1 = (\sum_i \beta_i) \log (y^{**} - \sum_j p^1_j \gamma_j) - \sum_i \beta_i \log p^1_i$$

with the reference utility function (5.6) and to solve for the true income y^{**}. From

$$(\sum_i \beta_i) \log (y^{**} - \sum_j p^1_j \gamma_j) - \sum_i \beta_i \log p^1_i =$$

$$= (\sum_i \beta_i) \log (y^0 - \sum_j p^0_j \gamma_j) - \sum_i \beta_i \log p^0_i$$

we derive, for $\sum_i \beta_i = 1$,

$$\log\left[\frac{y^{**} - \sum_j p^1_j \gamma_j}{y^0 - \sum_j p^0_j \gamma_j}\right] = \sum_j \beta_j \log\left(\frac{p^1_j}{p^0_j}\right)$$

or

$$\frac{y^{**} - \sum_j p^1_j \gamma_j}{y^0 - \sum_j p^0_j \gamma_j} = \prod_j \left(\frac{p^1_j}{p^0_j}\right)^{\beta_j}$$

$$y^{**} = \sum_j p^1_j \gamma_j + (y^0 - \sum_j p^0_j \gamma_j) \prod_j \left[\frac{p^1_j}{p^0_j}\right]^{\beta_j}$$

so that $I(p^0, p^1, u^0, R)$ is equal to the expression found in (5.11).

From the Belgian data[4] for the period 1953–1969 and the estimates of γ_i and β_i given in Table 4.3, $n = 8$ and 1963 $= 100$, we can compute the true index reproduced in Table 5.1.

TABLE 5.1
The true cost-of-living index in Belgium

Year	True index	L
1953	85.446	85.515
1954	86.662	86.715
1955	86.587	86.612
1956	89.255	89.292
1957	91.943	91.986
1958	93.032	93.061
1959	94.532	94.536
1960	94.802	94.804
1961	95.978	95.982
1962	97.695	97.696
1963	100.000	100.000
1964	103.618	103.631
1965	107.844	107.880
1966	112.291	112.351
1967	114.976	115.091
1968	117.553	117.720
1969	120.754	120.926

As the utility level was chosen with reference to the base year price-income vector, one may wonder how this index compares to the Laspeyres index. A comparison with the official Belgian cost-of-living index is of course out of question, as the official index is computed from a very different (and much more disaggregated) set of data. The Laspeyres index should be computed on the same data set. But even this is not sufficient to insure its comparability with the true index, given that the latter is based on a particular utility function. To stay within the same theoretical framework, L should be computed utilizing not only the same data but also the same estimates of γ_i and β_i. This can be done as follows.

Assume that the quantities consumed are determined as in the linear expenditure system, so that

$$x_i^0 = \gamma_i + \frac{\beta_i}{p_i^0} \left[y^0 - \sum_j p_j^0 \gamma_j \right] \tag{5.12}$$

---

[4] Estimates for Australia and the United Kingdom can be found in Hoa (1969a, b).

Inserting (5.12) into (5.3):

$$L = \frac{\sum p_i^1(\gamma_i + [\beta_i/p_i^0] [y^0 - \sum p_j^0\gamma_j])}{\sum p_i^0(\gamma_i + [\beta_i/p_i^0] [y^0 - \sum p_j^0\gamma_j])}$$

or

$$L = \frac{\sum p_i^1\gamma_i}{y^0} + \left(1 - \frac{\sum p_i^0\gamma_i}{y^0}\right) \sum_i \left(\frac{p_i^1\beta_i}{p_i^0}\right). \tag{5.13}$$

The only difference between (5.13) and the true index (5.11) is the presence, in the second term to the right, of an arithmetic mean in L and a geometric mean in I. As an arithmetic mean is superior to a geometric mean, $L > I$ (except if all prices were to change in the same proportion) in the linear expenditure system. In Table 5.1, L is slightly larger than I.

5.4. The true index and the Laspeyres index

It is of interest to analyse the relationship between I and L in some detail, as it can be shown that, in general,[5]

$$L \geqslant I \tag{5.14}$$

when L is computed with the parameters from the model on which I is based.

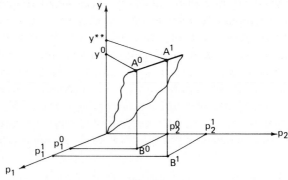

Fig. 5.1.

Consider Figure 5.1, in which one indifference surface is represented in the price–income space for $n = 2$. (Figure 5.1 corresponds to Figure

---

[5] Haberler (1927) seems to have been the first to show this, while Konus (1924) was the first to introduce the true index concept.

1.3.) In situation 0, the reference price–income vector is (p_1^0, p_2^0, y^0) and determines the reference surface which is represented in the diagram. Suppose relative prices change, so that the economy moves from point B^0 to point B^1.

What is the equivalent income y^{**} that allows the consumer to be just as 'well off' as with the reference price–income vector? It is the income corresponding to A^1, that is

$$y^{**} = \sum p_i^1 x_i^{**}$$

where x_i^{**} are the optimal quantities that leave the consumer as well off as in situation 0. The true index is

$$I(p^0, p^1, u^0, R) = \frac{y^{**}}{y^0} = \frac{\sum p_i^1 x_i^{**}}{\sum p_i^0 x_i^0} \tag{5.15}$$

If, in situation 1, the consumer were given an income equal to $y^0 I$, that is his income in situation 0 times the true index, his utility level would remain unchanged. The only difference with the Laspeyres formula (5.3) is the presence of x_i^{**} instead of x_i^0 in the numerator.

Suppose, then, the consumer were given, in situation 1, an income equal to $y^0 L$. By definition, this income would allow him to consume the same quantities as in situation 0. In fact, however, he will not continue to consume x^0. From the Slutsky equation, we know that a change in relative prices induces a change in the quantities consumed. There is an income effect and a substitution effect. The income $y^0 L$ gives a compensation for the former effect, not for the latter. Furthermore, as he could have consumed the 'old' quantities x^0, the very fact that the consumer does not do so *reveals* that from his income $y^0 L$ he can derive a utility that is larger than the one associated with y^0 or y^{**}.

According to the indirect utility function, a higher utility associated with a given price regime implies a higher income. Therefore, at prices p^1, we have

$$y^0 L > y^{**}$$

or

$$L > \frac{y^{**}}{y^0},$$

Q.E.D.

EXERCISES

5.1. Explain why $L = I(p^0, p^1, u^0, R)$ in the limiting case where relative prices do not change, that is when all prices move in the same proportion.

5.2. Illustrate our finding that L is an upper bound to $I(p^0, p^1, u^0, R)$ with the help of a diagram in the commodity space, for $n = 2$.
   Hint: Have a look at diagram 9.1 in Chapter IX if necessary. Show that $y^0 L$ leads to a utility level that lies above u^0.

In these days of rapid inflation, the fact that the Laspeyres index is an upper bound[6] to the true index makes it possible to give an economic interpretation to, and to judge the effectiveness of practices such as the 'indexing' of wages, rents, mortgage interests, etc., that is the linkage of these prices to the official index.

EXERCISE

5.3. Would you conclude that the indexing of wages leaves the wage-earners better off than they were in the base year?

As should be clear from exercice 5.2, it is the neglect of the substitution effect that biases L upwards. Whether this bias is, in fact, important is an empirical question. The computations reported in Table 5.1 suggest that it is rather small.[7]

It should be emphasized that the above analysis is based on the assumption of an unchanged preference ordering (R is supposed to be the same in situations 0 and 1). One may question the relevance of this sort of analysis for periods in which tastes are changing. How should one define the true index when R has changed between situation 0 and situation 1? Is L still an upper bound in that case? These are questions to be taken up in Part II, Chapter IX.

---

[6] Pollak (1971c) shows that the smallest of the price ratios p_i^1/p_i^0 is a lower bound of $I(p^0, p^1, u^0, R)$. He also show that both this ratio and L are the closest possible bounds.

[7] For a discussion of the upward bias in the official U.S. consumer price index, see Stigler (1961, p. 35, 52, 53), Heien (1969), Noe and van Furstenberg (1972) and especially Triplett (1973).

EXERCISE

5.4. Show that the Paasche index is a lower bound[8] to the true index $I(p^0, p^1, u^1, R)$. Illustrate with a diagram drawn in the commodity space.

5.5. International comparisons of purchasing power

Even in a static framework, there is a class of problems for which the use of cost-of-living index numbers implies a choice of the relevant preference ordering, because it may differ between situation 0 and situation 1. This happens when prices and incomes are compared between two different points in space and when spatial differences in tastes are present. A discussion of these comparisons is interesting in itself and can also serve as an introduction to the difficulties we shall encounter when we allow for a temporal variation in preferences.

Take the following problem. The Belgian government, considering how much to pay its diplomats in London, would have to determine the salary equivalent to their Belgian salary, given the structure of consumer prices in London (and in Belgium). But to do this, it would also have to choose between Belgian and English tastes. The preference ordering of the representative Belgian consumer would be a normal criterion. Suppose, moreover, that the Belgian government wants to compare prices in London with those in Ottawa to decide on appropriate salary differentials for its diplomats. Again, the comparison would normally be based on Belgian tastes. This example shows that the reference preference ordering need not be one associated with either base or comparison prices.

Statistical indices, obeying the Laspeyres or Paasche formulae, can again be used as approximations to the relevant true indices. p^1 would be the vector of prices in the foreign country, p^0 the prices in the home country, while the weights would describe the structure of consumption in the base country, or in the comparison country or in any third country, according to the preference ordering chosen as a reference. The reference indifference class would be determined by the choice of a particular consumption pattern (in a particular year, that is) in the reference country.

---

[8] In general, it is *not* true that $P < (p^0. p^1. u^0. R) < L$. For the very special circumstances in which it is true, see Staehle (1934–1935) and Schultz (1939).

EXERCISES

5.5. In a letter written in Leipzig, in which he applies for a new job in Thüringen, Johan Sebastian Bach says the following: 'My present job yields about seven hundred crowns and when the number of funerals is somewhat above normal, the number of premiums increases proportionaly; but when the weather is good, the number of deaths falls. This was the case last year: I lost more than one hundred crowns in supplementary fees, only because the number of usual funerals decreased. In Thüringen I could live more easily with four hundred crowns than here with twice as much, because of the cost of living'. If you were an economic historian, asked to verify the last statement, what sort of empirical data would you try to collect? What sort of computations would you make? What would be the order of magnitude of L if Bach had correctly evaluated the situation in Leipzig and in Thüringen?

   Hint: Remember that Bach's wife, Anna-Magdalena Bach, carefully kept her household budget, which is still available.

5.6. A Belgian diplomat joins his new post in London. His Belgian salary has been multiplied by a Laspeyres index, comparing prices in London and in Belgium, based on the Belgian consumption pattern. Why would he be better off than in Belgium?

   Answer: His wife would adjust the household expenditures to the structure of consumer prices in London, in accordance with the Slutsky equation. In so doing, a higher indifference curve will be reached.

The emphasis on equivalent incomes should not make us forget that cost-of-living indices are *price* indices. Their first objective is and remains to measure changes in price levels. In a spatial context, they allow us to determine in which of two countries prices are higher. However, the discussion above makes us realize that this sort of international price comparison makes sense only if we choose a reference preference ordering. We always have to make it clear for whom prices are higher in London than in Belgium: is it for the Belgian diplomat in London, or for the British diplomat joining the Common Market Authorities in Brussels? Absolute statements make no sense. And one cannot exclude the possibility that prices appear as higher in London, given Belgian tastes, while simultaneously prices appear as higher in Brussels, given British tastes.

The computations to approximate the true spatial index with the help of Laspeyres and Paasche indexes can be illustrated from an impressive study made by the Statistical Office of the European Communities (1960) to determine purchasing power parities in Europe.[9]

Suppose, to begin with, that French and German families consume only one product, coffee. In 1958, 1 kg coffee was sold at the average price of 17.13 D.M. in Germany and 912.2 F.F. in France. This gives the following 'economic parities':

France/Germany 100 F.F. = 1.878 D.M.
Germany/France 1 D.M. = 53.25 F.F.

In 1958, the official exchange rate was 100 F.F. = 0.9935 D.M. Coffee was thus cheaper in France. To buy, in Germany, the quantity of coffee you could buy in France for 100 F.F., more than 0.9935 D.M. was needed.

There is an economic parity for each good in the consumer's 'basket'. These parities differ from commodity to commodity. To compute one global economic parity (called 'purchasing power parity in consumption') one has to choose a reference 'basket', i.e. a consumption pattern typical for one country.

The Statistical Office of the European Communities chose one homogeneous group, the group of workers employed in the European Coal and Steel Community, to come as close as possible to the assumption of one single preference ordering (per country). It organized a special budget survey to determine the average basket in each country.

Using the average basket for Belgian workers (x^B), the Statistical office finds the global Belgium/Germany parity to be, in 1958:

$$\frac{\sum p_i^G x_i^B}{\sum p_i^B x_i^B} = 9.143 \quad \text{or} \quad 100 \text{ B.F.} = 9.143 \text{ D.M.}$$

As the official exchange rate was 100 B.F. = 8.404 D.M., the cost of living was seen to be higher in Germany, *for a Belgian worker*. A Belgian miner, taking a job in a German mine, would need a salary (in D.M.) equal to his Belgian salary times 9.143 to be as well off as before – if the Laspeyres index did not ignore the substitution effect. In fact, he

---

[9] This study has led to further computations by Houthakker (1961a), Kloek and Theil (1965) and Kloek (1966).

would not continue to buy his Belgian basket but adjust to German consumption patterns, so that he would be soon slightly better off.

EXERCISES

5.7. Would it be possible to answer the question whether the Belgian basket is equivalent to the German basket in terms of the satisfaction derived from it?

Answer: No. Interpersonal comparisons of utility are impossible[10] and have been carefully avoided in the analysis above.

5.8. The study of the Statistical Office of the E.E.C. (1960, p. 33) we referred to publishes, for Belgium and Germany, the following parities:

(1) Belgium/Germany based on the Belgian basket;
(2) Germany/Belgium based on the German basket;
(3) Belgium/Germany based on the German basket;
(4) Germany/Belgium based on the Belgian basket.

  (a) Write down the corresponding formulae and compare (1) and (4) and (2) and (3) respectively.

  (b) What may be the use of parities (3) and (4)?

Answer: (b) The pair of parities (1) and (3) may give an upper and a lower bound for the 'true' Belgium/Germany parity. The same is true for the parities (2) and (4) with respect to the 'true' Germany/Belgium parity.

---

[10] Notice, however, that one could test the equality of tastes among countries for a similar social class of consumers. On this, see Houthakker (1961a).

Part II

Dynamics

VI

Dynamic single-equation models

6.1. Introduction

The theory exposed in Part I leads to a system of demand equations describing the equilibrium values which x_i will take in any price and income situation. This theory is static in that it assumes an instantaneous adjustment to the new equilibrium values when prices or income change. More precisely, if p_i increases in period t, the quantity demanded for any good is supposed to react immediately and to take its new equilibrium value during the same period t.

It should be obvious that a static approach does not provide a realistic description of how consumers behave in real life. In fact, consumers very often react with some delay to price and income changes, with the implication that the adjustment towards a new equilibrium situation is spread over several time periods. In each time period, the adjustment is then partial. If this is the case, the new equilibrium values implied by a price or income change are reached only after a number of time periods, on the condition that prices and income do not change again during the adaptation process. And if they change again, which is most likely to happen, a new adaptation to still different equilibrium values is started, with the implication that equilibrium may never be realized.

What is the origin of these lags? As far as consumers are concerned, two main sources of explanation may be given.

On the one hand, *habit formation* seems to be a predominant characteristic of consumer behaviour. It leads to the well-known phenomenon of 'inertia'. After a price increase for a good for which he developed buying habits, the consumer may appear to buy quantities which are larger than the equilibrium values indicated by his static demand equation.

At first sight, he is out of equilibrium. One may then imagine a slow adaptation process by which he gradually reduces his consumption to the 'correct' level. But one may also consider the possibility that the static approach does not do justice to the situation involved. By sticking to the static equilibrium values, we implicitly assume the presence of 'frictions' (inertia!) which lead to an 'irrational' behaviour. It may be more correct to hypothesize that the consumer has good reasons to behave in the way he does, to try to explain his behaviour in a maximizing framework, and to suppose for example, that his preferences have changed as a result of his developing habits.

The durability of some consumption goods is the other main source of delays. Suppose the consumer has acquired a small car in period $t - 1$, in accordance with his price and income situation. In period t, he gets a promotion with a concomitant salary increase. According to his static demand equation for automobiles, he should now spend much more on that item. As he had just bought his small car, he would prefer to wait and stay for some time 'below' the new equilibrium value of his demand for automobiles.

The example just given furthermore suggests the need for a distinction between the demand for a stock of durable goods, the purchase of a durable and the demand for the services it renders. In static theory, x_{it} is a commodity flow consumed during period t. When commodity i is a durable, one does not escape the necessity of specifying whether x_{it} represents a stock or a flow. If it is a stock of durables, one has to indicate with precision at what point in time it is measured (at the end of period t, for example). If it is a flow of purchases, the consumer may be thought of as adapting his stock to its equilibrium level by an increase or a decrease of this flow of purchases. But these flows may also be replacement purchases corresponding to depreciation of the existing stock. (In any case, the assumption of divisibility of x_i is not abandoned in this sort of analysis, with a possible resulting lack of realism.) Finally, x_{it} may the flow of services rendered by a given stock.

As in the case of habit formation, it would be desirable not simply to postulate some sort of adjustment to a static equilibrium level of stocks, but to derive the optimal adjustment path from maximizing behaviour. Indeed, there are good reasons to suppose that it may be in the consumer's interest *not* to move immediately to the static equilibrium position, if only because of the (psychological or other) costs involved.

In this chapter, we will introduce the reader to the by now traditional ways in which the phenomenon of a delayed response has been analysed in the literature. These approaches have been typically limited to single equation models, i.e. attempts to dynamize the demand equation for one particular commodity. In the pioneering days, it was simply assumed that the reaction predicted by the static theory is distributed over several time periods according to some *ad hoc* scheme. In later developments, partial adjustment models were set up, to provide some economic rationale for the hypothesized lag distribution.

These developments are important improvements with respect to the static approach. They remain unsatisfactory, however, in that they have no theoretical standing. What we really would like to do, is to build a theoretical model in which the maximization of utility *implies* a partial adjustment to some equilibrium value. We will make some steps in that direction in Chapter VII, with the introduction of 'dynamic' utility functions, i.e. utility functions that are changing over time. As a further advantage, we will then be able to derive a dynamic complete set of demand equations, allowing for both habit formation and the presence of durable goods.

6.2. Distributed lag models

6.2.1. Empirical distributed lag models

The simplest way to introduce a delayed response in the analysis is to suppose a fixed lag, of say θ time periods. It is then assumed that a change in an independent variable in period $t - \theta$ affects the dependent variable in period t only: after $t - \theta$ periods, the dependent variable suddenly jumps to its new equilibrium value.

However, we want to represent a process in which a change in the independent variable X, ΔX, in period 0, will induce a response of the dependent variable Y that is distributed over a number of periods. The new equilibrium position may be reached after k periods or approached asymptotically, in which case the responses of Y form the infinite series: $\Delta Y_0, \Delta Y_1, \Delta Y_2, \ldots$.

Considering the value taken by Y in period t, Y_t, we come to realize that it results from the influences of present and past X's. If the new equilibrium value of Y, resulting from a change in X, is approached asymptotically, we have

$$Y_t = a + b_0 X_t + b_1 X_{t-1} + b_2 X_{t-2} + \ldots + \varepsilon_t$$

$$= a + \sum_{i=0}^{\infty} b_i X_{t-i} + \varepsilon_t \tag{6.1}$$

where ε_t is a stochastic error term. The sum of the b_i's is supposed to be finite and all b_i have the same sign. Equation (6.1) then defines a 'distributed lag model'.[1]

$\sum_i b_i$ describes the total or 'long-run' reaction of Y with respect to X, each b_i defining the part of the total response that is being realized in a particular time period. The successive values of b_i describe the time shape of the reaction. To formalize this idea, we rewrite (6.1) as

$$Y_t = a + b(\omega_0 X_t + \omega_1 X_{t-1} + \omega_2 X_{t-2} + \ldots) + \varepsilon_t$$

$$= a + b \sum_{i=0}^{\infty} \omega_i X_{t-i} + \varepsilon_t, \tag{6.2}$$

where b is now the total or long-run effect ($b = \sum_i b_i$), while the ω_i indicate the percentage realized in each time period ($b_i = \omega_i b$). $\omega_i \geq 0$ for any i and $\sum_i \omega_i = 1$.

We can now make some assumptions about the distribution of ω_i, and try to specify it in such a way that the entire distribution can be computed with the help of one or two parameters characterizing it. (It suffices then to estimate these parameters by some regression method to be able to derive the entire time shape.) Fisher (1937) suggested the use of the lognormal distribution, while Solow (1960) introduced the Pascal distribution, which has been generalized by Jorgenson (1966). But the distribution that interests us most – because it can be derived from a theoretical model (as we shall see in the next section) – is the geometric distribution.

This distribution has the advantage of being described by one single parameter. It is written as

$$\omega_i = \kappa(1 - \kappa)^i, \qquad \lim \sum_i \omega_i = 1, \tag{6.3}$$

---

[1] The basic reference on distributed lags is Dhrymes (1970b). A useful survey is given in Griliches (1967).

where κ is the parameter to be estimated, and implies that the reactions decrease as time elapses: the influence of X_{t-i} on Y_t is the smaller, the larger is i. The largest reaction κb is attributed to the current period. Substitution of (6.3) into (6.2) gives

$$Y_t = a + b\kappa \sum_{i=0}^{\infty} (1 - \kappa)^i X_{t-i} + \varepsilon_t \qquad (6.4)$$

in which the parameters b and κ are of interest. To make the estimation of these parameters possible, Koyck (1954) suggests the use of the following transformation: substract $(1 - \kappa) Y_{t-1}$ from Y_t, using (6.4), to eliminate the infinite sum. The result is

$$Y_t = a\kappa + b\kappa X_t + (1 - \kappa)Y_{t-1} + [\varepsilon_t - (1 - \kappa)\varepsilon_{t-1}], \qquad (6.5)$$

which is an autoregressive[2] estimating equation (where Y_t is a linear function of Y_{t-1}). The regression coefficient associated with Y_{t-1} gives an estimate of κ. An estimate of b can be derived from the regression coefficient of X_t, given the estimate of κ.

EXERCISES

6.1. Verify in detail that (6.5) is the result of applying the Koyck transformation to (6.4).

6.2. (a) Suppose Y_t measures consumption in constant prices and X_t disposable real income, so that (6.5) is a consumption function. Let the estimated regression coefficients be:

$a\kappa \quad = 20$
$b\kappa \quad = 0.7$
$(1 - \kappa) = 0.25$

By definition, the short-term propensity to consume is 0.7. What is your estimate of the long-run propensity to consume?
(b) Given the regression coefficients obtained in (a), what are the values of b_0, b_1, b_2, b_3 and b_4 in equation (6.1)?

---

[2] Problems of estimation are discussed in Orcutt and Winokur (1969). An elementary discussion can be found in Phlips, Blomme and Vanden Berghe (1981, Chapter V).

6.2.2. The partial adjustment model[3]

The distributed lag model described above is entirely empirical, in that the form of the lag has no theoretical underpinning. An approach in which the form of the lag is the result of some behavioral assumption is presented here. The assumption is still rather crude, and we shall have to wait until Chapter VII before we shall be able to present a distributed lag model based on a rationality assumption, i.e. derived from a maximization hypothesis.

It is assumed here that the economic agent partially adjusts to the equilibrium values determined by static maximum (or minimum) conditions. In the case of a consumer, for example, the equilibrium values are the quantities defined by a static demand equation. The adjustment is partial because of some frictions, such as inertia, earlier commitments, lack of information, etc.

The equation defining the equilibrium values may be written as

$$Y_t^* = a + bX_t + \varepsilon_t \tag{6.6}$$

where the star indicates equilibrium or 'desired' values, and X_t represents the variables that determine these values. The current value of Y is supposed to adjust to its equilibrium value according to

$$Y_t - Y_{t-1} = \kappa(Y_t^* - Y_{t-1}), \qquad 0 < \kappa < 1 \tag{6.7}$$

where κ, the 'adjustment coefficient', measures the proportion by which the difference between the equilibrium value Y_t^* and the realized value Y_{t-1} is reduced during period t. When $\kappa = 1$, the current value of Y is equal to its equilibrium value ($Y_t = Y_t^*$), the adjustment is total and immediate, and we are back in the static case. The model implies that $0 < \kappa < 1$. The smaller is κ, the smaller is the adjustment.

On combining (6.6) and (6.7), we rediscover the distributed lag model based on a geometric distribution. Indeed,

$$Y_t - Y_{t-1} = \kappa(a + bX_t + \varepsilon_t - Y_{t-1})$$
$$= \kappa a + \kappa b X_t - \kappa Y_{t-1} + \kappa \varepsilon_t$$

or

$$Y_t = \kappa a + \kappa b X_t + (1 - \kappa)Y_{t-1} + \kappa \varepsilon_t \tag{6.8}$$

---

[3] The partial adjustment model was introduced in the literature by Nerlove (1958).

which is observationally equivalent to (6.5): the equation to be estimated is the same.[4] The static coefficient b appears as the 'long-run' coefficient, while the product κb measures the short-run reaction. If (6.6) were a consumption function, b would be the long-run marginal propensity to consume, and κb the short-run propensity.

The partial adjustment model has been widely used in the analysis of the demand for and the supply of particular commodities. We might mention, among the most typical studies, the work of Nerlove (1956) on the supply of selected agricultural commodities, Griliches (1958 and 1960) on the demand for fertilizers and the demand for tractors respectively, Brechling (1960) on the demand for labour, Chow (1960 and 1967) on the demand for automobiles and for computers respectively, Stone and Rowe (1960) on household durables. This short and highly selective list suggests that the partial adjustment model is particularly appropriate for the analysis of durable goods. In the next two sections, we will show why this is so, by considering in some detail the demand for automobiles and for some household durables. The stage will then be set for a generalization of the approach to all sorts of commodities, both durable and non-durable.

6.2.3. *The demand for automobiles*

This section reproduces the main results of Chow's book[5] *Demand for Automobiles in the U.S.: A Study in Consumer Durables* (1957) and its further development in Chow (1960).

The variables in the model are defined as follows:

x_t = annual purchases of automobiles per capita (measured as the number of new automobiles per annum, divided by total population);

p_t = annual price index of automobiles (computed as a weighted average of the prices of several brands) divided by the general index of consumer prices;

y_t^d = disposable income in constant prices, divided by total population;

s_t = stock of automobiles per capita, at the end of year t (computed

---

[4] Notice, however, that the error term is different. In (6.5), the error term is a moving average, and therefore autocorrelated. In (6.8), there is no autocorrelation, if ε_t is not autocorrelated. The estimation problems are greatly simplified in (6.8), which is a further advantage of the partial adjustment model.

[5] Earlier pioneering studies of the demand for automobiles include De Wolff (1938), Roos and Von Szelinski (1947) and Farrell (1954).

as a weighted sum of the registrations at the end of year t, divided by total population, the weights being proportional to the prices of used cars of different ages to take account of the age structure of the stock).

Equilibrium values have to be determined for the stock. The desired stock of automobiles s_t^* is taken to be a linear function of the relative price of automobiles and real disposable income:

$$s_t^* = a_0 + a_1 p_t + a_2 y_t^d + \varepsilon_t. \tag{6.9}$$

If the demand for annual purchase were to adjust instantaneously to the desired level of s_t, it would be equal in each time period to

$$x_t = s_t^* - (1 - \delta)s_{t-1} \tag{6.10}$$

where δ is the constant annual rate of depreciation of the stock. That is, purchase per capita during a year would simply be the difference between desired stock per capita at the end of the year and the depreciated old stock per capita from the preceding year. (6.10) Can alternatively be written as

$$x_t = (s_t^* - s_{t-1}) + \delta s_{t-1}, \tag{6.11}$$

breaking up annual purchase into two parts. The first, $s_t^* - s_{t-1}$, is the demand for the desired change in stock during the year; the second, δs_{t-1}, is the demand for replacement of old stock.

EXERCISE

6.3. Suppose $\delta = 0.25$. Let $s_t = 100$ and $x_t = 25$ in Year 1, and suppose population is constant. Let desired stock in Year 2 be shifted to 110, and let it stay at that level during the following years. Compute the series of annual purchases, using (6.11), to show that the 10 per cent change in desired stock would generate a 40 per cent change in purchase in Year 2, and a 10 per cent change in all subsequent years as long as the stock stays at its equilibrium level of 110.

The time path of purchases obtained in exercise 6.3. shows a sharp jump in the year of the shift in desired stock and a large drop in the year immediately afterward. This appears as unrealistic. Chow (1960, p. 154) remarks:

Why does the adjustment of existing stock to the desired level have to be accomplished in one year? As a matter of fact, there are reasons to the contrary, the most important one being the cost of buying and selling automobiles. If this model of the individual consumer were valid, he would be observed to buy and sell automobiles frequently in response to any change in price and income. With a positive cost of transaction, the individual may not change his automobile stock at once even if it is somewhat different from his desired ownership.

It is more realistic to assume that only a fraction κ of the desired change in ownership will take place in one year, and to modify (6.11) accordingly. The demand for purchases becomes

$$x_t = \kappa(s_t^* - s_{t-1}) + \delta s_{t-1}, \tag{6.12}$$

which is the partial adjustment model, if one assumes that

$$x_t - \delta s_{t-1} = s_t - s_{t-1}. \tag{6.13}$$

EXERCISE

6.4. Compute the time path of x_t, using (6.12) and the assumptions of exercise 6.3, for $\kappa = 0.50$. Show that the 10 per cent change in desired stock now generates a 20 per cent change in purchase in Year 2 and tends towards a 10 per cent change as $t \to \infty$.

The estimating equation is obtained by substituting (6.9) into (6.12):

$$\begin{aligned} x_t &= \kappa(a_0 + a_1 p_t + a_2 y_t^d + \varepsilon_t) - \kappa s_{t-1} + \delta s_{t-1} \\ &= a_0 \kappa + a_1 \kappa p_t + a_2 \kappa y_t^d + (\delta - \kappa)s_{t-1} + \kappa \varepsilon_t. \end{aligned} \tag{6.14}$$

Besides price and income, ownership at the beginning of the year (i.e. s_{t-1}) influences purchase during the year.

The statistical findings, for U.S. time-series covering the years 1921–1953, are:

$$x_t = 0.07791 - 0.020127 \, p_t + 0.011699 \, y_t^d - 0.23104 \, s_{t-1}$$
$$ (0.002648) \quad (0.001070) \quad (0.04719) \tag{6.15}$$

$$R^2 = 0.858.$$

The stock at the beginning of the year has a *negative* influence on purchase during the year. On the assumption that the rate of depreciation is 0.25 (which is confirmed by a comparison of the prices of cars of different ages), we find

$$-0.23 = \delta - \kappa = 0.25 - \kappa$$

or

$$\kappa = 0.25 + 0.23 = 0.48$$

as an estimate of the adjustment coefficient.

On dividing the regression coefficient of p_t by the estimated value of κ, and multiplying by $\bar{p}_t/\bar{x}_t$, Chow gets an estimate of the long-run price elasticity of -0.63, which is very close to the estimate obtained by fitting the static equation for the desired stock (6.9). By a similar procedure, Chow gets an estimate of the long-run income elasticity of 1.70, which is again very close to the static elasticity estimated from (6.9). In this sort of models, the long-run relations indeed correspond to the static relationships, as we have already remarked when commenting on equation (6.8).

6.2.4. The demand for household durables

In the analysis described above, the rate of depreciation was supposed to be known, because there was no way to estimate it consistently with the other parameters of the model. In the present section, we present a study by Garcia dos Santos (1972) which extends the Stone and Rowe (1960) model of consumers' durables. This model is itself a modified version, based on a suggestion by Nerlove (1960), of an earlier model by Stone and Rowe (1957).

The first equation of the model is a definition. It translates the fact that the quantities of a durable good bought during a period of time are composed of replacement purchases (corresponding to depreciation) and of net investment:

$$x_t = d_t + v_t \tag{6.16}$$

where d_t is depreciation and v_t is net investment. Given that $v_t = s_t - s_{t-1}$, equation (6.16) conveys the same message as equation (6.13).

Depreciation, however, is supposed to affect not only the stock existing at the beginning of the year (s_{t-1}), but also the purchases made during the year. That is

$$d_t = \frac{1}{m}x_t + \frac{1}{n}s_{t-1}, \tag{6.17}$$

where $1/m$ and $1/n$ are constant rates of depreciation, and $m > n$ since purchases are not concentrated at the very beginning of the year. For goods that are not 'very' durable, it seems important to allow for a depreciation during the current year. In Chow's model for automobiles, the current purchases were not allowed to depreciate, but the error involved is perhaps not too serious, given that cars have a rather long life. On the contrary, specification (6.17) is to be preferred for less durable goods such as electrical appliances and other goods used in the household. In any case, (6.17) is more general than Chow's specification of d_t as $d_t = \delta s_{t-1}$ and is to be preferred in principle.

Remembering that $v_t = s_t - s_{t-1}$, equations (6.16) and (6.17) lead to:

$$
\begin{aligned}
x_t &= \frac{1}{m}x_t + \frac{1}{n}s_{t-1} + s_t - s_{t-1} \\
&= k[ns_t + (1-n)s_{t-1}] \\
&= k\Psi s_t
\end{aligned}
\tag{6.18}
$$

where $k = m/n\,(m-1)$, $\Psi = [1 + (n-1)\Delta]$, and Δ is the first difference operator such that $\Delta X_t = X_t - X_{t-1}$.

Consider the existence of a desired level of stock, s_t^*, which corresponds to the equilibrium flow of services rendered by the durable good which is the object of the analysis. The consumer is supposed to approach this optimal stock according to

$$
s_t - s_{t-1} = \kappa(s_t^* - s_{t-1}) + u_t,
\tag{6.19}
$$

which is the partial adjustment equation, to which a normally distributed error term is added.

When the desired level of stock is reached, $v_t = 0$, and from (6.16) and (6.17) we have

$$
x_t^* = d_t^* = \frac{1}{m}x_t^* + \frac{1}{n}s_t^*
$$
$$
= ks_t^*,
\tag{6.20}
$$

where x_t^* represents the equilibrium purchases. This variable is a function of income and prices. It is assumed that x_t^* is a linear function of the commodity's relative price and real income:

$$
x_t^* = a_0 + a_1 p_t + a_2 y_t + \eta_t
\tag{6.21}
$$

where y_t is measured as total consumers' expenditures at constant prices and η_t is a normally distributed error term.

Equations (6.18) through (6.21) lead to the estimating equation

$$
x_t = \kappa a_0 + \kappa a_1 \Psi p_t + \kappa a_2 \Psi y_t + (1-\kappa)x_{t-1} + \varepsilon_t
\tag{6.22}
$$

where $\varepsilon_t = \kappa \Psi \eta_t + k \Psi u_t$ is a normally distributed and autocorrelated error term.

Notice that the stock variable does not appear in (6.22), so that there is no need to estimate the stock of the durable good. In applied work, this is an important improvement, as it is very difficult – and in most cases impossible – to measure stocks. Whenever estimates of s_t are provided, as in Chow's study of automobiles, these are but very rough calculations based on a series of simplifying assumptions.

EXERCISE

6.5. Please find out, by going through the derivation of (6.22) from equations (6.18) to (6.21), how the stock variable is eliminated from the model.

Another advantage of this model is that it permits the estimation of the depreciation rate $1/n$. (Remember that in Chow's approach δ is supposed to be known.) Indeed, the parameter n appears in the error term ε_t which has a known structure, based on the properties of u_t (in 6.19) and η_t (in 6.21). Indeed

$$
\begin{aligned}
\varepsilon_t &= \kappa\Psi\eta_t + k\Psi u_t \\
&= n(\kappa\eta_t + ku_t) - (n-1)(\kappa\eta_{t-1} + ku_{t-1}) \\
&= n\xi_t - (n-1)\xi_{t-1}
\end{aligned}
\tag{6.23}
$$

where $\xi_t = \kappa\eta_t + ku_t$ is normally distributed since it is a linear function of normal variables. ξ_t has zero mean and constant variance and is not autocorrelated. However, ε_t is autocorrelated, since it is a moving average of two successive ξ's. The variance-covariance matrix of ε_t is therefore:

$$
\Sigma = \sigma_\varepsilon^2 \, \Omega = \sigma_\varepsilon^2
\begin{bmatrix}
1 & \rho & 0 & \cdot & \cdot & \cdot & 0 \\
\rho & 1 & \rho & \cdot & \cdot & \cdot & 0 \\
0 & \rho & 1 & \cdot & \cdot & \cdot & 0 \\
\cdot & & & & & & \cdot \\
\cdot & & & & & & \cdot \\
0 & \cdot & \cdot & 0 & \rho & 1 & \rho \\
0 & \cdot & \cdot & \cdot & 0 & \rho & 1
\end{bmatrix}
\tag{6.24}
$$

with

$$
\rho = \frac{-n(n-1)}{n^2 + (n-1)^2}
\tag{6.25}
$$

Garcia dos Santos uses this information on the structure of the error term to estimate n by generalized least squares. To do this, he takes a series of values of ρ between -0.5 and 0.5, and retains as his best estimate the regression results obtained with the value of ρ – and therefore of n – that maximizes the likelihood function.[6] These results are reproduced in Tables 6.1 and 6.2, and are based on quarterly data (covering the period 1955, first quarter, to 1968, third quarter) taken from the British *Monthly Digest of Statistics*. Two types of household durables, namely 'radio and electrical goods' on the one hand, and 'furniture and floor coverings' on the other hand, are considered.

TABLE 6.1
Household durables: estimated coefficients

Radio and electrical goods				Furniture and floor coverings			
$\kappa a_0 =$	0.1749 (0.0832)	$a_0 =$	0.830	$\kappa a_0 =$	0.130 (0.052)	$a_0 =$	0.929
$\kappa a_1 =$	-0.0027 (0.0005)	$a_1 =$	-0.013	$\kappa a_1 =$	-0.0003 (0.0004)	$a_1 =$	-0.0021
$\kappa a_2 =$	0.0061 (0.0009)	$a_2 =$	0.029	$\kappa a_2 =$	0.0017 (0.0003)	$a_2 =$	0.0121
$1-\kappa =$	0.7892 (0.0223)	$\kappa =$	0.211	$1-\kappa =$	0.860 (0.037)	$\kappa =$	0.140

'Furniture and floor coverings' appear to have a smaller adjustment coefficient (κ) than 'radio and electrical goods', which is what intuition suggests.

TABLE 6.2
Household durables: estimated elasticities (at mean values)

Elasticities	Radio and electrical goods	Furniture and floor coverings
long-run elasticity ro relative price	-0.589	-0.126
long-run elasticity to real income	1.175	0.579
short-run elasticity to relative price	-0.113	-0.016
short-run elasticity to real income	0.228	0.074

---

[6] For details on this estimation procedure, see Garcia dos Santos (1972, Appendices A and B).

EXERCISE

6.6. (a) Write down the formulas used to compute the elasticities listed in Table 6.2.

(b) Compare the values of the short-and long-run elasticites.

Garcia's best estimates for n are $n = 14$ for 'radio and electrical goods' and $n = 26$ for 'furniture and floor coverings'. This means that the durability, defined as the time required for the depreciation of 90 per cent of the initial value[7], of 'radio and electrical goods' is of about 7.8 years and that of 'furniture and floor coverings' is about 14.6 years. These estimates are much more reasonable than those of Stone and Rowe (1960) who obtained $n = 2$ and $n = 3$ respectively, corresponding to durabilities of 0.83 and 1.42 years! The improvement is due to the fact that the autocorrelation of the error term, as expressed in (6.24) and (6.25), has been taken into account during estimation.

6.3. Habit formation and stock adjustment: a generalization to all commodities

In the preceding section, the distributed lag model (and in particular the partial adjustment version of it) was found to be particularly useful for the analysis of durable goods. To summarize in a few words what was done above, we could say that one has simply to distinguish between purchases and stocks, define desired stock with the help of static demand theory and assume a partial adjustment towards desired stock, to derive an estimating equation from which short- and long-run elasticities can be derived. When the stock variable is not eliminated, the estimating equation typically takes the form of equation (6.14). Otherwise it becomes autoregressive as in (6.22).

Equation (6.14) is characterized by the fact that purchases appear as a function not only of price and income, but also of the stock variable.

---

[7] Let h be the number of periods necessary for a commodity to reduce to a certain proportion of its initial value X_0. With a depreciation rate of $1/n$, one has

$$X_h = X_0\left(1 - \frac{1}{n}\right)^h.$$

Consider a proportion of 10% of the initial value. Then $X_h = 0.1\, X_0$. Solving for h:

$$h = \frac{-1}{\log_{10}\left(\dfrac{n-1}{n}\right)} \quad \text{for} \quad n \neq 1.$$

And the latter turns out to have a regression coefficient whose sign is negative for durables. There is thus a negative 'stock effect', reflecting a simple fact: the larger stocks are at the beginning of a year, the less is bought during that year. This effect, often verified in time series analysis, has been confirmed by cross-section analysis, as in Houthakker and Haldi (1960).

A natural question is to ask what sort of dynamic behaviour, if any, is typical for non-durable goods. The answer is: habit formation. How can it be formalized, possibly in terms of the distributed lag models discussed in this chapter?

A first hint on how to introduce habits in demand theory was given by Marshall (1920, Appendix H, §3) in his discussion of the limitations of the use of static assumptions. He says:

Whether a commodity conforms to the law of diminishing or increasing return, the increase in consumption arising from a fall in price is gradual: and, further, habits which have once grown up around the use of a commodity while its price is low, are not quickly abandoned when its price rises again. If therefore after the supply has gradually increased, some of the sources from which it is derived should be closed, or any other cause should occur to make the commodity scarce, many consumers will be reluctant to depart from their wonted ways. For instance, the price of cotton during the American war was higher than it would have been if the previous low price had not brought cotton into common use to meet wants, many of which had been created by the low price. Thus then the list of demand prices which holds for the forward movement of the production of a commodity will seldom hold for the return movement, but will in general require to be raised.

In this quotation, Marshall introduces three ideas: (a) adaptation to a change in price is gradual: there is a partial adjustment; (b) the movement along a demand curve is irreversible, when habits have developed in the meantime; (c) the effect of habits is positive.

Some thirty years later Marshall's suggestion was taken up[8] by Farrell in his paper on 'Irreversible demand functions' (1952), in which he tried to specify and estimate demand functions for particular commodities subject to habit formation, such as tobacco, beer and spirits.

His basic idea is the following:

The most general form of irreversible demand function would make the individual's demand a function of all his past price-income-consumption positions, but it would obviously be impossible to estimate such a function statistically from the data available. A simpler form,

$$C_t = f(Y_t, P_t, C_{t-1}, Y_{t-1}, P_{t-1}),$$

---

[8] Haavelmo (1944) discussed the problem theoretically, while Duesenberry (1949) and Modigliani (1949) introduced irreversible consumption functions.

would make current demand depend only on current price and income and on the individual's price-income-consumption position in the previous period. This involves some loss of generality, although it should be noted that, since C_{t-1} depends on C_{t-2}, and so on, the individual's history in the more distant past is allowed some influence on current consumption (Farrell, 1952, p. 175).

EXERCISE

6.7. Given your knowledge of the partial adjustment model, would you agree with Farrell that to write C_t as a function of C_{t-1} only, involves a loss of generality?

The partial adjustment model clearly enables one to take advantage of the ideas put forward by both Marshall and Farrell, and to develop a first-order autoregressive estimating equation that implies no loss of generality. To see this, it suffices to redefine the variable s_t as a 'psychological stock of habits' and to proceed as in the case of durable goods. All goods can thus be formally treated in the same way. It was Houthakker and Taylor's merit to have exploited this idea in Chapter 1 of their book *Consumer Demand in the United States: Analyses and Projections* (1st ed., 1966, or 2nd enlarged ed., 1970). Houthakker and Taylor proceed as follows.

Let $s(t)$ be the current value[9] of a 'state variable' in continuous time. In the case of a durable good, $s(t)$ represents its physical stock at time t. But $s(t)$ may also be interpreted as a 'psychological stock of habits'. In both cases, $s(t)$ represents a measure of accumulated purchases in the past, discounted or depreciated at the constant rate δ. That is

$$s(t) = \int_{-\infty}^{t} x(u)e^{\delta(u-t)}\,du. \tag{6.26}$$

The consumer's past purchases, and therefore his past price-income situations, are thus taken into account. Equation (6.26) is the solution of

$$\dot{s}(t) = x(t) - \delta s(t) \tag{6.27}$$

(which is the continuous analogue to (6.16) and (6.17) combined).

EXERCISE

6.8. It is often rather incorrectly assumed that the discrete counterpart of (6.27) is $s_t - s_{t-1} = x_t - \delta s_{t-1}$. This is incorrect in that goods

---

[9] The subscript i is deleted in what follows to simplify the notation.

purchased in the beginning of year t cannot depreciate during the year (compare with equations 6.16 and 6.17). Show that δ can take values between 0 and 2. Does this make sense?

Hint: Solve the difference equation to find the stability condition $|1 - \delta| < 1$. Then insert $\delta = 2$ into the discrete counterpart of (6.27).

On the assumption that purchases gradually bring $s(t)$ to its desired level $s^*(t)$, the demand function can be written as

$$x(t) = \theta + \alpha s(t) + \gamma y(t), \qquad (6.28)$$

ignoring prices to simplify the exposition. Equation (6.28) corresponds to Chow's equation (6.14), ignoring the error term. When commodity i is a durable, α_i should be negative to reflect the 'stock effect' discussed earlier. When commodity i is habit forming, α_i has to be positive. Notice in passing that α plays the role of $(\delta - \kappa)$ in (6.14).

The state variables are very difficult to measure, so that for most commodities there are no statistical observations available. Using (6.27) and assuming a value for δ, a rough estimation of $s(t)$ could be computed, using statistical data on purchases, (as is done in the National Accounts to compute the capital stock in an economy, using investment data). But why not try to eliminate the stock variable from the estimating equation *and* to estimate δ together with the other coefficients?

In fact, this can easily be done. Write (6.28) as

$$s(t) = \frac{1}{\alpha} [x(t) - \theta - \gamma y(t)]$$

and use (6.27) to obtain

$$\dot{s}(t) = x(t) - \frac{\delta}{\alpha} [x(t) - \theta - \gamma y(t)]. \qquad (6.29)$$

Differentiate (6.28) and use (6.29) to get

$$\dot{x}(t) = \theta\delta + (\alpha - \delta)x(t) + \gamma\dot{y}(t) + \gamma\delta y(t), \qquad (6.30)$$

so that $s(t)$ is eliminated.

All these results describe short-run behaviour, as there is a partial adjustment towards 'long-run' or 'desired' levels going on as long as the state variable changes independently of income and prices. What are the corresponding long-run results?

Suppose that $y(t)$ changes at some point in time and remains constant afterwards. The resulting variation in $x(t)$ leads to a variation in $s(t)$ which in turn is going to affect purchases. Concurrently, depreciation affects $s(t)$ and therefore purchases. Long-run equilibrium is realized (on the unrealistic assumption that income and prices do not change any more) when the interplay of x and s comes to an end so that s and x stabilize, that is when $\dot{s}(t) = 0$.

Using stars to denote long-run values, we have in the long-run

$$x^*(t) = \delta s^*(t)$$

or

$$s^*(t) = \frac{1}{\delta} x^*(t) \tag{6.31}$$

from (6.27). Substitution in (6.28) gives

$$x^*(t) = \theta + \frac{\alpha}{\delta} x^*(t) + \gamma y^*(t)$$

or

$$x^*(t) = \frac{\delta\theta}{\delta - \alpha} + \frac{\delta\gamma}{\delta - \alpha} y^*(t). \tag{6.32}$$

The ratio $\delta/(\delta - \alpha)$ is the factor by which the short-run coefficient γ has to be multiplied to find its long-run value.

EXERCISES

6.9.   Show that equation (6.28) implies a partial adjustment of $s(t)$ to its long-run value $s^*(t)$, with the implication that $\alpha = \delta - \kappa$, where κ is the adjustment coefficient, so that an estimate of κ can be derived from the estimates of δ and α.

6.10. For the commodity group 'food', Houthakker and Taylor computed the following estimates:

$$\theta = 59.28 \qquad \alpha = 0.118 \qquad \gamma = 0.108 \qquad \delta = 0.614.$$

(a) Give the economic interpretation of α, γ and δ.
(b) Check that the long-run income derivative is larger than the short-run derivative (γ) and interpret this result.

(c) Suppose that y stabilizes at an equilibrium level of \$ 1657. What would be the equilibrium level of food expenditure? *Hint:* Use equation 6.32.

You will have noticed that up to now the analysis has been conducted in continuous time. This has the advantage of allowing for a continuous depreciation. In later chapters, we will discover that it has the additional advantage of making the use of powerful techniques (such as optimal control theory) possible. However, all statistical data are in discrete time (i.e. for discrete periods such as a year, a quarter or a month). One therefore has to derive a finite approximation to the equations derived above, which necessarily involves some approximation error.

To minimize this error, it is advisable *not* to replace, say, $\dot{s}(t)$ by $s_t - s_{t-1}$ or $s(t)$ by s_{t-1} (see exercise 6.8). One should rather work by interpolation, as in the following procedure which allows for continuous depreciation. The approximation presented here is due to Winder (1971) and is itself a drastic simplification of the original procedure worked out by Houthakker and Taylor (1966, Chapter 1 or 1970, Chapter 1) and leading to the same result.

Assume that the rate of change of stock is a linear function of time over the finite interval chosen for unit time. Equation (6.28) can then be written as

$$x_t = \theta + \alpha \left(\frac{s_t + s_{t-1}}{2} \right) + \gamma y_t; \tag{6.33}$$

where s_t is the level of stock at the end of period t, x_t is the flow of purchases during period t and y_t is the income flow. Similarly, equation (6.27) can be written as

$$\Delta s_t = s_t - s_{t-1} = x_t - \delta \left(\frac{s_t + s_{t-1}}{2} \right). \tag{6.34}$$

Notice that δ can take values between 0 and 2, as in the approximation discussed in exercise 6.8. But now $s_t = \frac{1}{2}x_t$, for $\delta = 2$, which makes sense. Substituting from (6.33) into (6.34):

$$\Delta s_t = x_t - \frac{\delta}{\alpha}(x_t - \theta - \gamma y_t). \tag{6.35}$$

First-differencing (6.33):

$$\Delta x_t = \alpha\left(\frac{\Delta s_t}{2} + \frac{\Delta s_{t-1}}{2}\right) + \gamma \Delta y_t. \tag{6.36}$$

Substituting from (6.35) into (6.36):

$$\Delta x_t = \theta\delta + \frac{(\alpha - \delta)}{2}(x_t + x_{t-1}) + \gamma\left(1 + \frac{\delta}{2}\right)y_t - \gamma\left(1 - \frac{\delta}{2}\right)y_{t-1},$$

from which one derives the Houthakker and Taylor estimating equation

$$x_t = \frac{\delta\theta}{1 - (\alpha - \delta)/2} + \frac{1 + (\alpha - \delta)/2}{1 - (\alpha - \delta)/2}x_{t-1} + \frac{\gamma(1 + \delta/2)}{1 - (\alpha - \delta)/2}y_t$$
$$- \frac{\gamma(1 - \delta/2)}{1 - (\alpha - \delta)/2}y_{t-1}. \tag{6.37}$$

As $y_t \equiv (y_t - y_{t-1}) + y_{t-1} \equiv \Delta y_t + y_{t-1}$, (6.37) can be rewritten as

$$x_t = \frac{\delta\theta}{1 - (\alpha - \delta)/2} + \frac{1 + (\alpha - \delta)/2}{1 - (\alpha - \delta)/2}x_{t-1} + \frac{\gamma(1 + \delta/2)}{1 - (\alpha - \delta)/2}\Delta y_t$$
$$+ \frac{\delta\gamma}{1 - (\alpha - \delta)/2}y_{t-1}. \tag{6.38}$$

This gives the regression equation

$$x_t = K_0 + K_1 x_{t-1} + K_2 \Delta y_t + K_3 y_{t-1}. \tag{6.39}$$

EXERCISE

6.11. Show how you would compute the estimates θ, α, γ *and* δ from the estimated regression coefficients K_0, K_1, K_2 and K_3.

6.12. For 'clothing', Houthakker and Taylor obtain the following regression results:

$$x_t = 17.595 + 0.6243 x_{t-1} + 0.0763 \Delta y_t + 0.0173 y_{t-1}.$$

From these, they derive:

$$\theta = 84.5902 \qquad \alpha = -0.2065 \qquad \gamma = 0.0833 \qquad \delta = 0.2561$$

(a) Show that the long-run income coefficient is about half of the short-run effect and interpret this result.

(b) Show that, in 1961, clothing expenditures (of $ 164) were above their equilibrium level but that they would have tended gradually, from 1962 to 1970, to the equilibrium level if y_t had stayed over this period at the equilibrium level of $ 1657.

Prices have been left out of this analysis to simplify the presentation. They can (and should) of course be introduced. When this is done, the long-run price coefficient turns out to be $\delta\eta/(\delta - \alpha)$, where η is the short-run coefficient. The estimating equation becomes

$$x_t = K_0 + K_1 x_{t-1} + K_2 \Delta y_t + K_3 y_{t-1} + K_4 \Delta p_t + K_5 p_{t-1}. \quad (6.40)$$

EXERCISES

6.13. The data used by Houthakker and Taylor are series of annual expenditures (on 84 commodity groups) in current dollars and in constant dollars (in prices of 1958) covering the period 1929–1964. There are no official price indices available for these 84 commodity groups. How would you compute (a) the p_t series, (b) the x_t series, and (c) the y_t series?

Answer: (a) p_t is a price index obtained by dividing the constant-dollar expenditures into the current-dollar expenditures, for each commodity group, *and* by deflating the resulting index (called 'implicit deflator') in turn by the price index for *total* consumption expenditures. The latter is derived by dividing total expenditures in constant dollars into total expenditures in current dollars. p_t is thus a relative price index.

(b) x_t is measured as the constant-dollar expenditure for a particular item (per capita).

(c) y_t is total expenditures in constant dollars (per capita).

6.14. Interpret the results obtained by Houthakker and Taylor for the selected list of commodities, reproduced in Table 6.3, p. 176. (You might want to compare your comments with those given by Houthakker and Taylor in Chapter 3 of their book.)

Dynamic single-equation models

TABLE 6.3
Houthakker and Taylor's single equation results

Commodities	θ	α	γ	δ
Food	51.56	0.2365	0.0942	0.7851
	(18.09)	(0.2774)	(0.0251)	(0.4780)
Tobacco	16.11	0.8958	0.0045	1.1800
	(15.20)	(1.1345)	(0.0039)	(1.1587)
Furniture	36.73	−0.1435	0.0402	0.0366
	(52.54)	(0.0876)	(0.0041)	(0.0464)
Water	5.52	−0.2133	0.0038	0.4335
	(6.63)	(0.4182)	(0.0027)	(0.9080)
Drug preparations	−4.45	0.2732	0.0056	0.3434
	(1.49)	(0.2343)	(0.0018)	(0.3092)
Cars	0	−0.6408	0.2610	0.1569
		(0.1566)	(0.0436)	(0.0402)

VII

Dynamic demand systems

7.1.* Dynamic utility functions

In Chapter VI demand functions for particular products were dynamized with the help of distributed lag formulations, allowing for partial adjustments to long-run equilibria. In this chapter, we shall try to dynamize the utility function, to take account of the phenomenon of changing tastes.

A preliminary question is: why dynamize the utility function rather than the demand function? A first advantage is that the maximization of the former will provide a complete system of demand functions, which will have the property of being theoretically plausible. In other words, all 'general' restrictions will be automatically satisfied. When one starts from dynamic demand functions that are specified a priori, one has to impose these restrictions. Even in a static world, this is a very difficult task. In a dynamic setting, it seems hard to know how to proceed.

A second possible advantage is that, after maximizing a dynamized utility function, one might end up with demand functions characterized by a distributed lag scheme. A theoretical foundation of the existence of lags would thus be obtained, in the sense that lagged responses would appear as being *implied* by utility maximization[1], rather than as a result of inertia or frictions or other apparently 'irrational' circumstances. In fact, we will be able to show, in the case of the dynamic utility functions analysed in Sections 7.5 and 7.6, that the short-run demand functions (derived from these) obey a partial adjustment model.

---

[1] See Lucas (1967) for an analogous argument in terms of profit maximization in the theory of supply.

Our problem is to incorporate the phenomenon of taste changes in the analysis. Let us begin by trying to enumerate a number of reasons why tastes may change, it being understood that our list could not pretend to be complete: some reasons are so mysterious to the economist that he is unlikely to offer much in the way of a systematic understanding, as is emphasized by Fisher and Shell (1969).

As a first approximation, I would suggest that taste changes may be of two sorts: they either result from better outside information due to external influences on a consumer, or they are of the 'built-in' type, being related to past decisions.

Instances of changes of the first type are easily found. A consumer may learn about the usefulness of a durable good which he has not yet purchased (an electric appliance, say) or of a perishable good which he has already consumed (he learns how to use fuel more efficiently or discovers that a particular food is dangerous to his health). In these examples, a taste change results from social contacts: the consumer may talk with his neighbours, be influenced by a demonstration effect or impressed by advertising.

The influence of past decisions on current tastes is perhaps even more striking and was already introduced in Chapter VI. Habit formation clearly falls in this class. Smoking habits are a positive function of past consumption: the more you smoke, the more you want to smoke. The phenomenon is 'auto-regressive' and obeys a 'built-in' mechanism, which is typical for non-durable goods.

The corresponding phenomenon for durables has been described as a 'stock effect'. Past purchases of durables affect current needs for the same durables, but here the influence has the opposite sign: the better your library is furnished, the fewer books you have to buy per year (ignoring the replacement of books that become outdated or got damaged).

Needless to say, interdependencies have to be taken into account. For example, social contacts most certainly interfere with smoking habits: the more cocktail parties I attend, the more cigarettes I smoke. Interdependencies among different goods should not be ignored either: the more books you buy, the greater will be your demand for book-shelves.

How should one proceed to formalize the ideas expressed above? One possibility is to assume that the taste changes are translated in each period by the consumer into new exponents in his utility function, following a suggestion made by Peston (1967). Examples are easily constructed by analogy with the modern theory of technical progress. Formally speaking, taste changes indeed play the same role as changes in production techniques in the theory of production.

Suppose, for purposes of illustration, that the consumer has, in each period, a utility function belonging to the class of homothetic functions we analysed extensively in Part I (see Section 3.5):

$$u_t = A x_{1t}^{\beta_1} x_{2t}^{\beta_2}.$$

To introduce taste changes, we make the exponents functions of time and write:

$$u_t = A x_{1t}^{\beta_{1t}} x_{2t}^{\beta_{2t}}. \tag{7.1}$$

We can be even more explicit and explain the evolution of β_{1t} and β_{2t}. If we regard the consumer as experimenting or learning from past experiences, we may adopt Peston's specification and write the learning functions as

$$\beta_{1t} = f\left(\frac{x_{1t-1}}{x_{2t-1}}\right) \tag{7.2}$$

$$\beta_{2t} = g\left(\frac{x_{1t-1}}{x_{2t-1}}\right) \tag{7.3}$$

for example. These functions are homogeneous of degree zero in x_1 and x_2 and are also assumed to be single valued, continuous and positive and finite for x_1/x_2 non-negative. It follows that β_1/β_2 is a continuous, positive, single-valued function of x_1/x_2.

Assuming that utility is maximized, in every period, relative to the constraint $p_{1t}x_{1t} + p_{2t}x_{2t} = y_t$, the first-order condition for a maximum is

$$\frac{\beta_{1t}}{\beta_{2t}} = \frac{x_{1t}p_{1t}}{x_{2t}p_{2t}}. \tag{7.4}$$

EXERCISE

7.1. In applied work in the field of production, 'neutral' technical change is often introduced making the coefficient A a function of time, with constant exponents β_1 and β_2. The change is 'neutral' in the sense that it leaves the marginal rate of substitution unaffected.

Would it make sense of define a neutral taste change in a similar way? And to specify a dynamic utility function as

$$u_t = A_t x_{1t}^{\beta_1} x_{2t}^{\beta_2}$$

where β_1 and β_2 are constants?

Answer: To make the coefficient A a function of time amounts to adopting a series of linear homogeneous transformation of the utility functions, which do not affect the marginal rate of substitution. The underlying preference ordering remains therefore unchanged. In my opinion, this does not imply that 'neutral' taste changes are without interest. They may be interpreted as changes in the efficiency of the consumer as a 'pleasure machine'. And it may be important to make it clear whether this sort of change is included in the analysis or not. (This matter will be taken up again in the discussion of dynamic cost-of-living indices.)

Peston's formulation (7.2)–(7.3) has the advantage of taking the possible relationship between two goods into account. But there is at least one drawback: it would be difficult indeed to derive from (7.4) a system of demand equations that could be estimated with the usual regression techniques. And as homotheticity implies unitary income elasticities, it is of interest to look for other specifications.

EXERCISE

7.2. What are the first-order conditions when Peston's procedure is applied to the Stone-Geary utility function

$$u = \beta_1 \log (x_1 - \gamma_1) + \beta_2 \log (x_2 - \gamma_2)?$$

An alternative and apparently more fruitful approach, suggested by Fisher and Shell (1969), defines quantity augmenting (or diminishing) taste changes by analogy with factor augmenting (or diminishing) technical progress. This approach is thought to be more fruitful because it leads to specifications that can be verified empirically without great difficulties, as will become clear in later sections.

A taste change is said to be good augmenting if and only if the preference maps can be represented by a utility function whose ith argument is a function of the amount of purchases of the ith good and of the level of some taste change parameter. If the taste change is independent of any change in the qualities of the goods, it is called a disembodied taste change, following the terminology employed in capital theory.

Assuming for convenience that only one good, say the first, experiences an own-augmenting disembodied taste change, the utility function can be written as

$$u = u(bx_1, x_2, \ldots, x_n) \tag{7.5}$$

where b is the parameter representing the first good augmenting taste change.

There is a large number of possibilities to specify the change parameter. It can be specified as a function of time, or of any variable that determines the taste change.

When the taste change is determined by past decisions, we can introduce lagged consumption. The number of possible lags is unlimited in principle. We can also introduce a variable s_i, summarizing past decisions. This variable is called a 'state variable' because it describes the state of a system as the result of past behaviour. In particular, we will define s_i as measuring stocks of durables or stocks of habits as in Chapter VI.

EXERCISE
7.3. The Stone-Geary utility function has $(x_i - \gamma_i)$ as arguments (rather than x_i). How would you proceed to dynamize it along the lines suggested by Fisher and Shell?

One answer is that one should work with γ_i, transform it into a variable and relate it to 'time', to $x_{it-1}, x_{it-2}, \ldots$ (in discrete time), or to s_i. To stay within the framework of linear expenditure models, the relation should be linear, i.e.

$$\gamma_i = \theta_i + \alpha_i s_i \tag{7.6}$$

leading to

$$u = \sum_i \beta_i \log (x_i - \theta_i - \alpha_i s_i) \tag{7.7}$$

When $\alpha_i > 0$, the taste change is quantity diminishing; when $\alpha_i < 0$, the change is quantity augmenting (verify your understanding, please).

It is important to realize that different decisions in the past lead to different preference orderings in the present according to (7.7). The implication is that a commodity bundle x_t may be preferred to x_t' with yesterday's consumption equal to the bundle x_{t-1}, while x_t' may be preferred to x_1 when yesterday's consumption was different, say equal to x_{t-1}'.

EXERCISE

7.4. The reader is requested to construct a numerical example to illustrate our last statement.

Hint: Suppose $i = 1, 2$, $\gamma_{it} = \alpha_i x_{it-1}$; imagine a set of values for x_t and x_t', x_{t-1} and x_{t-1}' and a value for α; compute $u(x_t)$ and $u(x_t')$ when past consumption is x_{t-1} to discover that $u(x_t) > u(x_t')$; do the same with past consumption equal to x_{t-1}' to discover that now $u(x_t') > u(x_t)$.

The exercise above is presented in a forthcoming book by Houthakker and Pollak on *The Theory of Consumer's Choice*. These authors take the following sets of numbers:

$$x_t = x_{t-1} = (6, 4)$$
$$x_t' = x_{t-1}' = (4, 7)$$
$$\alpha_i = 0, 5.$$

You might want to use these numbers if you get into difficulties.

A model based on specification (7.6) will be worked out and estimated in a later Section. A specification of γ_{it} as a linear function of x_{it-1} is at the core of a paper by Pollak (1970) that led to the estimations given in Pollak and Wales (1969).

7.2.* Short-run and long-run utility functions

The 'dynamic' utility functions introduced in the preceding section belong to the class of what we will call short-run utility functions. In a dynamic context, the short-run is indeed defined as a framework of analysis in which the variables under study have no time to adjust fully so as to attain a steady state. The long-run is then, by definition, such that the variables may reach a position of rest at an equilibrium point. (These definitions imply that models based on a 'partial adjustment' process or a distributed lag scheme are *ipso facto* short-run.)

In this context, the important variables are x_{it} and s_{it}. The 'steady state' or long-run equilibrium will be characterized by the fact that

$x_{it} = x_{it-1}$ for all t, or $x_{it} - x_{it-1} = 0$ or $\dot{x}_i = 0$ in continuous time. The same is true for s_i, for which $\dot{s}_i = x_i - \delta_i s_i = 0$ implies

$$x_i = \delta_i s_i$$

in continuous time.

Given the short-run demand functions derived from a short-run utility function, we can obtain the long-run demand functions by imposing $x_{it} = x_{it-1}$ or $\dot{s}_i = 0$.

EXERCISE
7.4a. Derive the long-run demand functions corresponding to the dynamic Stone-Geary function $u = \sum_i \beta_i \log (x_i - \theta_i - \alpha_i s_i)$.

The answer to exercise 7.4a is somewhat complicated by the fact that, when s_i is replaced by x_i/δ_i, the budget constraint is not necessarily satisfied and has therefore to be imposed again.

One procedure is to rewrite the short-run demand functions

$$x_i = \theta_i + \alpha_i s_i + \frac{\beta_i}{p_i}\left[y - \sum_j p_j(\theta_j + \alpha_j s_j)\right] \tag{7.8}$$

as

$$x_i = \theta_i + \frac{\alpha_i}{\delta_i}x_i + \frac{\beta_i}{p_i}\left[y - \sum_j p_j\left(\theta_j + \frac{\alpha_j}{\delta_j}x_j\right)\right]$$

or

$$x_i = \frac{\delta_i\theta_i}{\delta_i - \alpha_i} + \frac{\delta_i\beta_i}{(\delta_i - \alpha_i)p_i}\left[y - \sum_j p_j\left(\theta_j + \frac{\alpha_j}{\delta_j}x_j\right)\right]$$

and to impose $\sum_i p_i x_i = y$, which gives:

$$y = \sum_i p_i\left(\frac{\delta_i\theta_i}{\delta_i - \alpha_i}\right) + \sum_i \frac{\delta_i\beta_i}{(\delta_i - \alpha_i)}\tilde{y}$$

where

$$\tilde{y} = y - \sum_j p_j\left(\theta_j + \frac{\alpha_j}{\delta_j}x_j\right).$$

Therefore, the budget constraint implies

$$\tilde{y} = \left[y - \sum_i p_i \left(\frac{\delta_i \theta_i}{\delta_i - \alpha_i} \right) \right] \bigg/ \sum_i \frac{\delta_i \beta_i}{(\delta_i - \alpha_i)}$$

and finally

$$x_i = \frac{\delta_i \theta_i}{\delta_i - \alpha_i} + \frac{\delta_i \beta_i/(\delta_i - \alpha_i)}{p_i \sum_j \delta_j \beta_j/(\delta_j - \alpha_j)} \left[y - \sum_j p_j \left(\frac{\delta_j \theta_j}{\delta_j - \alpha_j} \right) \right].$$

These long-run demand functions are of the same form as the static linear demand system, as they can be written as

$$x_i = \gamma_i^* + \frac{\beta_i^*}{p_i} \left[y - \sum_j p_j \gamma_j^* \right] \tag{7.9}$$

with

$$\gamma_i^* = \frac{\delta_i \theta_i}{\delta_i - \alpha_i} \quad \text{and} \quad \beta_i^* = \frac{\delta_i \beta_i/(\delta_i - \alpha_i)}{\sum_j \delta_j \beta_j/(\delta_j - \alpha_j)}.$$

An alternative and perhaps simpler procedure would be to impose $s_i = x_i/\delta_i$ in the $(n + 1)$ first-order conditions

$$x_i = \theta_i + \alpha_i s_i + \frac{\beta_i}{\lambda p_i}$$

$$\sum_i p_i x_i = y.$$

EXERCISE

7.5. The reader should verify that the long-run demand functions obtained are the same, by solving the system of first-order conditions.

The derivation of long-run demand functions is interesting in itself, because it provides a means to define and possibly compute long-run elasticities. For the moment, however, we are interested in the existence and significance of long-run utility functions and the derivation of long-run demand functions was meant to give us some insight in that respect.

A first point to be made is that it is technically possible to write down a long-run utility function that rationalizes the long-run first-order conditions (or demand functions) in the examples given in this and the preceding section.

Take the case analyzed by Peston. When x_{1t} and x_{2t} stabilize over time, such that $x_{1t} = x_{1t-1}$ and $x_{2t} = x_{2t-1}$, there exists at least one stable ratio β_1^*/β_2^* compatible with (7.2) and (7.3) on the one hand and the first-order conditions (7.4) on the other hand. In other words, one can write the long-run utility function:

$$u = Ax_{1t}^{\beta_1^*}x_{2t}^{\beta_2^*}.$$

Similarly, nothing prevents us from considering the long-run linear expenditure system (7.9) as being obtained by maximizing the long-run utility function

$$u = \sum_i \beta_i^* \log (x_i - \gamma_i^*). \tag{7.10}$$

A second point is that these long-run utility functions are of the same form as the corresponding static functions. This is not at all surprising, given that the 'long-run' implies full adjustment just as in static theory: it suffices to add the assumption of *immediate* adjustment to be back in a static framework. The reader should recall that the partial adjustment model analysed in Chapter VI is based on exactly the same idea, although applied in reverse order, so to speak: there, a function taken from static theory was supposed to describe the desired long-run equilibrium state, and combined with a partial adjustment process implying lagged adjustments that are distributed over time. Here, the short-run utility functions are seen to move towards a long-run utility function under the impact of endogenous taste changes.[2]

A third point is that long-run demand functions can be rationalized by a long-run utility function under special conditions only. These conditions were examined by Gorman (1967) and happen to be satisfied in the examples given above.

A final point is that long-run utility functions, when they can be written down, are *not* obtained by imposing the steady state conditions in short-run *utility* functions. If we were to do so, we would end up with demand functions different from the long-run demand functions.

---

[2] A revealed preference interpretation of long-run indifference curves is given in von Weizsäcker (1971). For a critical discussion of this interpretation, see Pollak (1976a).

EXERCISE

7.6. The reader should verify that if the short-run $u = \sum_i \beta_i \log (x_i - \theta_i - \alpha_i s_i)$ is transformed into

$$u = \sum_i \beta_i \log \left[\left(\frac{\delta_i - \alpha_i}{\delta_i} \right) x_i - \theta_i \right],$$

maximization of the latter does *not* lead to the long-run demand functions (7.9).

Hint: carefully distinguish β_i and β_i^*.

At first sight, this is a surprising situation. On second thoughts, it is not surprising at all. To suppose a stationary state is to suppose full adjustment. It does make sense to impose a full adjustment to quantity demanded, to find out what the properties of the demand functions will be in terms of price and income elasticites, and to find out what sort of utility function could explain this behaviour. This utility function *has* to have a static form and to represent a static preference ordering, as the adjustment is supposed to have taken place. It does not make sense to impose stationary state conditions to a short-run utility function in which tastes are changing under the impact of past decisions.

We conclude that whereas short-run utility functions represent changing tastes (or preference orderings), long-run utility functions represent an unchanging and therefore static preference ordering.

7.3.* The general restrictions again

Whenever long-run demand equations can be interpreted as resulting from the maximization of a static utility function, they must satisfy all the general restrictions derived in Chapter III. Do short-run demand equations also satisfy the general restrictions? This is a general question we have to answer before deriving dynamic demand systems from particular utility functions.

The answer is: yes. In each period, the consumer is supposed to maximize his short-run utility function as it appears during that period: the past decisions, which cause the taste changes, take on fixed values. In each period, the current (or instantaneous) utility function is maximized as if it were a static function, without consideration of future changes. Given the current values of the taste change parameters, the general restrictions have to show up again.

It is nevertheless of some interest to consider the case where the short-run utility function is specified as

$$u = f(x, s), \tag{7.11}$$

and to work out the fundamental equation again. s represents a vector of state variables, while x is a vector of quantities purchased. We are interested in deriving analytical expressions describing not only the effects of changes in prices and income, but also the impact of the additional variable s.

Maximization of (7.11) with respect to x, i.e. with given s, under the usual budget constraint gives the first order conditions

$$\begin{align} u_x &= \lambda p \\ p'x &= y. \end{align} \tag{7.12}$$

On solving (7.12) we get the system of $n + 1$ equations:

$$\begin{align} x &= x(y, p, s) \\ \lambda &= \lambda(y, p, s). \end{align} \tag{7.13}$$

The total differential of the vector of marginal utilities is $du_x = U\,dx + V\,ds$, where V is the matrix of partial derivatives of the marginal utilities with respect to the state variables, that is

$$V = \left[\frac{\partial^2 u}{\partial x_i\, \partial s_j} \right].$$

Total differentiation of the first order conditions (7.12) gives

$$\begin{align} U\,dx &= p\,d\lambda + \lambda\,dp - V\,ds \\ dy &= p'\,dx + x'\,dp \end{align}$$

or

$$\begin{bmatrix} U & p \\ p' & 0 \end{bmatrix} \begin{bmatrix} dx \\ -d\lambda \end{bmatrix} = \begin{bmatrix} 0 & \lambda I & -V \\ 1 & -x' & 0 \end{bmatrix} \begin{bmatrix} dy \\ dp \\ ds \end{bmatrix} \tag{7.14}$$

which is the 'fundamental equation' with state variables. (Compare with equation (2.14).)

On the other hand, total differentiation of (7.13) shows that

$$\begin{align} dx &= x_y\,dy + X_p\,dp + X_s\,ds \\ d\lambda &= \lambda_y\,dy + \lambda_p'\,dp + \lambda_s'\,ds \end{align}$$

or

$$\begin{bmatrix} dx \\ -d\lambda \end{bmatrix} = \begin{bmatrix} x_y & X_p & X_s \\ -\lambda_y & -\lambda_p' & -\lambda_s' \end{bmatrix} \begin{bmatrix} dy \\ dp \\ ds \end{bmatrix} \tag{7.15}$$

where

$$X_s = \begin{bmatrix} \dfrac{\partial x_i}{\partial s_j} \end{bmatrix} \quad \text{and} \quad \lambda_s = \begin{bmatrix} \dfrac{\partial \lambda}{\partial s} \end{bmatrix}.$$

Substitution from (7.15) into (7.14) shows that the fundamental equation can be written in terms of partial derivatives as

$$\begin{bmatrix} U & p \\ p' & 0 \end{bmatrix} \begin{bmatrix} x_y & X_p & X_s \\ -\lambda_y & -\lambda_p' & -\lambda_s' \end{bmatrix} = \begin{bmatrix} 0 & \lambda I & -V \\ 1 & -x' & 0 \end{bmatrix}. \tag{7.16}$$

To solve (7.16), we suppose that

$$\begin{bmatrix} U & p \\ p' & 0 \end{bmatrix}^{-1} = \begin{bmatrix} Z & z \\ z' & \xi \end{bmatrix} \tag{7.17}$$

so that

$$\begin{bmatrix} x_y & X_p & X_s \\ -\lambda_y & -\lambda_p' & -\lambda_s' \end{bmatrix} = \begin{bmatrix} Z & z \\ z' & \xi \end{bmatrix} \begin{bmatrix} 0 & \lambda I & -V \\ 1 & -x' & 0 \end{bmatrix}$$

or

$$\lambda_y = -\xi \tag{7.18}$$

$$\lambda_p = \xi x - \lambda z \tag{7.19}$$

$$x_y = z \tag{7.20}$$

$$X_p = Z\lambda - zx' \tag{7.21}$$

$$\lambda_s = V'z \tag{7.22}$$

$$X_s = -ZV. \tag{7.23}$$

From (2.17), we know that

$$Z = U^{-1} - (p'U^{-1}p)^{-1}U^{-1}pp'U^{-1} \tag{7.24}$$

$$z = (p'U^{-1}p)^{-1}U^{-1}p \tag{7.25}$$

$$\xi = -(p'U^{-1}p)^{-1}. \tag{7.26}$$

Substitution of these values into (7.18)–(7.21) leads us back to equations (2.18)–(2.21) from which the general restrictions were derived in Section 2.4.

Two additional results are to be considered here. From equation (7.22) we see that

$$\frac{\partial \lambda}{\partial s_i} = \sum_j \frac{\partial^2 u}{\partial x_j \partial s_i} \frac{\partial x_j}{\partial y} \tag{7.27}$$

given that $z = x_y$. As for (7.23), we can rewrite it considering that

$$
\begin{aligned}
Z &= U^{-1} - z(p'U^{-1}p)z' && \text{using (7.25)} \\
&= U^{-1} - x_y(p'U^{-1}p)x'_y && \text{using (7.20)} \\
&= U^{-1} + \xi^{-1}x_y x'_y && \text{using (7.26)} \\
&= U^{-1} - \lambda_y^{-1}x_y x'_y && \text{using (7.18).}
\end{aligned}
$$

Premultiplication by λ gives

$$\lambda Z = \lambda U^{-1} - \lambda \lambda_y^{-1} x_y x'_y = K \tag{7.28}$$

so that

$$X_s = -\frac{1}{\lambda}KV. \tag{7.29}$$

This is a fundamental result, showing that whenever an additional variable is introduced in the utility function as a parameter, the matrix of derivatives of x with respect to this variable is equal to the substitution matrix K times $-1/\lambda$ times the matrix of second order partial derivatives of the utility function with respect to the additional variable. When $V = I$, we end up with the substitution matrix except for sign and the positive constant $1/\lambda$. This result will be further exploited in Chapter VIII.

7.4.* Derivation of a dynamic linear system

We now proceed to the derivation[3] of a system of linear demand equations in which the state variables appear among the independent variables. Start from

$$\hat{p}x = \beta y + Bp + A\hat{p}s \tag{7.30}$$

---

[3] This derivation is due to P. Balestra.

where the 'hats' denote diagonal matrices which matricize[4] the corresponding vectors. B and A are square matrices of constants and β is a vector of constants.

Proceeding along the lines suggested by Klein and Rubin (see Section 4.3.3), we notice first that the adding-up restriction implies

$$\begin{aligned} \iota'\beta &= 1 \\ \iota'B &= 0 \\ \iota'A &= 0. \end{aligned} \qquad (7.31)$$

where ι is a vector whose elements are all equal to unity.

The homogeneity condition is satisfied already by the unrestricted system (7.30), which can indeed be rewritten as

$$x = \hat{p}^{-1}\beta y + \hat{p}^{-1}Bp + \hat{p}^{-1}A\hat{p}s. \qquad (7.32)$$

We thus have

$$\begin{aligned} X_p &= \hat{p}^{-1}\{B - \hat{p}^{-1}[\hat{\beta}y + \hat{B}p] + A\hat{s} - \widehat{\hat{p}^{-1}A\hat{p}s}\} \\ x_y &= \hat{p}^{-1}\beta. \end{aligned} \qquad (7.33)$$

The substitution matrix $K = X_p + x_y x'$ is equal to

$$K = \hat{p}^{-1}\{\beta\iota' + [B - \hat{p}^{-1}(\hat{\beta}y + \widehat{Bp}) + A\hat{s} - \widehat{\hat{p}^{-1}A\hat{p}s}]\hat{x}^{-1}\}\hat{x} \qquad (7.34)$$

and its non diagonal part K^* is

$$K^* = \beta\iota' + B\hat{x}^{-1} + A\hat{s}\hat{x}^{-1}. \qquad (7.35)$$

K^* can be transformed into

$$K^{**} = K^*\hat{x}\hat{p} = \beta x'\hat{p} + B\hat{p} + A\hat{s}\hat{p}. \qquad (7.36)$$

Substitution of (7.32) into (7.36) gives

$$K^{**} = \beta\beta'y + \beta p'B' + \beta s'\hat{p}A' + B\hat{p} + A\hat{s}\hat{p}$$

of which only the non-symmetric part

$$K^{***} = \beta\iota'\hat{p}B' + \beta\iota'\hat{s}\hat{p}A' + B\hat{p} + A\hat{s}\hat{p}$$

---

[4] Let $p = [p_1, p_2, \ldots, p_n]'$. Then

$$\hat{p} = \begin{bmatrix} p_1 & & & 0 \\ & p_2 & & \\ & & \cdot & \\ & & & \cdot \\ 0 & & & p_n \end{bmatrix}$$

is relevant here. Indeed we want to impose symmetry, which implies

$$(K^{***})' = K^{***}$$

or

$$B\hat{p}[I - \iota\beta'] + [\beta\iota' - I]\hat{p}B' = A\hat{p}\hat{s}[\iota\beta' - I] + [I - \beta\iota']\hat{p}\hat{s}A'$$

or

$$
\begin{aligned}
B &= -[\beta\iota' - I]\hat{\theta} \\
A &= -[\beta\iota' - I]\hat{\alpha}
\end{aligned}
\tag{7.37}
$$

where θ_i and α_i are arbitrary constants. Substituting back into (7.32) one finds

$$x = (\theta + \hat{\alpha}s) + \hat{p}^{-1}\beta[y - p'(\theta + \hat{\alpha}s)] \tag{7.38a}$$

or

$$x_i = \theta_i + \alpha_i s_i + \frac{\beta_i}{p_i}[y - \sum_j p_j(\theta_j + \alpha_j s_j)]. \tag{7.38b}$$

This is the linear expenditure system (see equation (4.38)) with γ_i redefined as $\gamma_i = \theta_i + \alpha_i s_i$. The underlying utility function obviously is

$$u = \sum_i \beta_i \log(x_i - \theta_i - \alpha_i s_i), \tag{7.39}$$

which is the dynamic utility function introduced in equation (7.7) above. It follows that this is the only utility function that leads to a system of linear demand equations in which state variables are included.

7.5.* A dynamic version of the linear expenditure system[5]

We now have to take a closer look at this generalized Stone-Geary utility function, analyse the properties of the demand equations that are generated from it and try to derive estimating equations, knowing that the state variables are not observable.

First of all, we should notice that x_i is defined as measuring flows of quantities *purchased*, as in Chapter VI. This seems reasonable enough, given that purchases will be shown to adjust partially to the long-run level of stocks s_i^*, proportional to long-run consumption $x_i^* = \delta_i s_i^*$.

---

[5] This section is based on Phlips (1972).

The long-run model is therefore in terms of consumption, while the short-run model is in terms of purchases.

Needless to say (7.39) is directly additive ($\partial^2 u/\partial x_i \, \partial x_j = 0$, $i \neq j$). Marginal utilities are decreasing, as

$$\frac{\partial^2 u}{\partial x_i^2} = -\frac{\beta_i}{(x_i - \theta_i - \alpha_i s_i)^2}$$

is negative (with $\beta_i > 0$). The marginal utility of good i is influenced by its stock according to

$$\frac{\partial^2 u}{\partial x_i \, \partial s_i} = \frac{\beta_i \alpha_i}{(x_i - \theta_i - \alpha_i s_i)^2}$$

We see that an increase in s_i raises the marginal utility of x_i when α_i is positive. This confirms that positive α's indicate habit formation, while negative α's characterize stocks of durable goods. Notice also that

$$\frac{\partial^2 u}{\partial x_i \, \partial s_j} = 0 \qquad (i \neq j).$$

7.5.1. 'Myopic' maximization

Maximizing (7.39) with respect to x_i subject to the budget constraint

$$\sum_i p_i x_i = y \tag{7.40}$$

we obtain the first order conditions

$$\frac{\beta_i}{(x_i - \theta_i - \alpha_i s_i)} = \lambda p_i \tag{7.41}$$

where λ is the marginal utility of money. Solving for x_i,

$$x_i = \theta_i + \alpha_i s_i + \frac{\beta_i}{\lambda p_i}. \tag{7.42}$$

We now proceed to eliminate the unobservable state variables. Replacing λp_i by p_i^* and differentiating (7.42) with respect to time, we find

$$\dot{x}_i = \alpha_i \dot{s}_i - \frac{\beta_i \dot{p}_i^*}{(p_i^*)^2}$$

or, using the assumption $\dot{s}_i = x_i - \delta_i s_i$,

$$\dot{x}_i = \alpha_i x_i - \alpha_i \delta_i s_i - \frac{\beta_i \dot{p}_i^*}{(p_i^*)^2}.$$

But, according to (7.42)

$$\alpha_i s_i = -\theta_i + x_i - \frac{\beta_i}{p_i^*}$$

so that

$$\dot{x}_i = \delta_i \theta_i + (\alpha_i - \delta_i)x_i + \frac{\delta_i \beta_i}{p_i^*} - \frac{\beta_i \dot{p}_i^*}{(p_i^*)^2}. \tag{7.43}$$

To introduce income, use (7.40) which, applied to (7.42), gives

$$\lambda = \frac{\sum_i \beta_i}{y - \sum_i p_i(\theta_i + \alpha_i s_i)}. \tag{7.44}$$

The marginal utility of money appears as a function of income, all prices and all state variables.

What are the restrictions on our parameters? The axiom of dominance implies $\beta_i > 0$. $(x_i - \theta_i - \alpha_i s_i) > 0$ is necessary for the utility function to be defined. θ_i and α_i might be either positive or negative and δ_i is normally positive. We decided not to normalize the β's, i.e. not to impose $\sum_i \beta_i = 1$.

It is readily admitted that the equilibrium conditions (7.40) and (7.41) answer but half of the problem. They refer to a consumer who only takes past choices into account. With durable goods and habit formation in the model, the consumer should also be allowed to look into the future, to take account of the future effects of his present decisions, and to proceed to intertemporal utility maximization. In the final chapter we will make some efforts in that direction. For the time being, the 'myopic' maximization described in equations (7.40) to (7.44) creates problems enough.

7.5.2. *Long-run effects*

In long-run equilibrium $\dot{s}_i = 0$. Quantities purchased are then equal to consumption or depreciation $(\delta_i s_i)$. Replacing s_i by x_i/δ_i in the first order conditions and taking account of the budget constraint, we find the system of long-run demand equations (7.9) and the corresponding long-run utility function (7.10).

We notice that $\gamma_i^* = \delta_i \theta_i / (\delta_i - \alpha_i)$ is larger than θ_i when $\alpha_i > 0$, i.e. for habit forming commodities and smaller for $\alpha_i < 0$. There is no need to restate the long-run income and price elasticities, as they obviously obey the static formulae with β_i and γ_i replaced by β_i^* and γ_i^* respectively. Notice only that β_i^* is negative if $\alpha_i > \delta_i$. The influence of habits is then stronger than that of depreciation.

EXERCISE

7.7. Show that, when $\alpha_i > \delta_i$, the long-run own substitution effect may become positive (as is the income effect), while the long-run cross substitution effect may become negative.

7.5.3. Short-run effects

Equations (7.40) to (7.44) describe short-run behaviour. Indeed, our model is a short-run model in the traditional sense: it can be seen to incorporate a partial adjustment process to long-run demand. To show this, let us use matrix notation again (hats designate diagonal matrices) and suppose that

$$\dot{s} = \kappa(s^* - s) \tag{7.45}$$

where κ is an $n \times n$ matrix of adjustment coefficients. Replace s^* by $\hat{\delta}^{-1} x^*$, define x^* from the first order conditions (7.42) with s replaced by $\hat{\delta}^{-1} x$, and recall that $\dot{s} = x - \hat{\delta} s$. A little manipulation then leads to

$$x = \kappa(\hat{\delta} - \hat{\alpha})^{-1}\theta + (\hat{\delta} - \kappa)s + \kappa[(\hat{\delta} - \hat{\alpha})\lambda\hat{p}]^{-1}\beta \tag{7.46}$$

which is simply equation (7.42) with

$$\kappa = \hat{\delta} - \hat{\alpha}.$$

This little exercise is also useful to show that once we have estimates of $\hat{\delta}$ and $\hat{\alpha}$, their difference gives an estimate of the adjustment coefficients (as was already the case in the Chow model and in the Houthakker-Taylor model above). Our model implies that all κ_{ij} are zero, for $i \neq j$.

EXERCISE

7.8. How should equation (7.39) be modified to allow for interaction between commodities, i.e. for s_j to affect γ_i $(i \neq j)$?

Answer: Redefine γ_i as $\gamma_i = \theta_i + \sum_j \alpha_{ij} s_j$ and work out the first order conditions.

To say that $\kappa_{ii} = \delta_i - \alpha_i$ makes sense. The greater is the rate of depreciation δ_i, for a given α_i, the faster habits wear off and the faster habits can adjust to their equilibrium level s^*. The same is true for stocks of durable goods, of course. The greater is the influence (α_i) of habits, for a given δ_i, the smaller is the reaction coefficient. And conversely for durables, i.e. when α_i is negative.

In discrete time, the partial adjustment model implies

$$\frac{\partial s_{t-1}}{\partial y_t} = 0 \quad \text{and} \quad \frac{\partial s_{t-1}}{\partial p_t} = 0.$$

In continuous time, it implies

$$\frac{\partial s}{\partial y} = 0 \quad \text{and} \quad \frac{\partial s}{\partial p} = 0.$$

It is an easy matter then to derive the short-run elasticities.

Differentiating (7.42) and (7.40) with respect to income, with $\partial s / \partial y = 0$, we obtain

$$x_y = (\iota'\beta)\hat{p}^{-1}\beta. \tag{7.47}$$

Differentiation with respect to prices, imposing $\partial s / \partial p = 0$, leads to

$$X_p = -\lambda^{-1}\hat{p}^{-1}\hat{\beta}\hat{p}^{-1} + \lambda^{-1}(\hat{p}^{-1}\beta)(\iota'\beta)^{-1}(\hat{\beta}\hat{p}^{-1}) - \hat{p}^{-1}\beta(\iota'\beta)^{-1}x'. \tag{7.48}$$

This is the matrix of short-run uncompensated price derivatives, decomposed in a diagonal matrix of specific substitution effects, a matrix of general substitution effects and a matrix of income effects.

EXERCISE

7.9. Convince yourself that (7.47) and (7.48) are exactly the formulas one obtains from the static linear expenditure model, so that these formulas show up in both the long and the short-run. (Needless to say, in both 'runs' the estimated values derived from the dynamic model are different from those one would get by estimating the static model!)

7.5.4. A finite approximation

We now proceed to the derivation of a system of estimating equations in discrete time. The state variables have to be eliminated, as they are not observable, and a finite approximation describing their evolution within a discrete time period has to be chosen. For the reasons given in Chapter VI, we put

$$\bar{s}_{it} = \tfrac{1}{2}(s_{it} + s_{it-1}) \tag{7.49}$$

where s_t is the stock at the end of period t, so that s_{t-1} is the stock at the beginning of period t. We can then write the first order conditions (7.42) as

$$x_{it} = \theta_i + \alpha_i \bar{s}_{it} + \beta_i \pi_{it} \tag{7.50}$$

where $\pi_{it} = 1/\lambda_t p_{it}$. On the other hand, $\dot{s}_i = x_i - \delta_i s_i$ becomes

$$s_{it} - s_{it-1} = x_{it} - \delta_i \bar{s}_{it}.$$

Furthermore,

$$
\begin{aligned}
2(\bar{s}_{it} - \bar{s}_{it-1}) &= (s_{it} + s_{it-1}) - (s_{it-1} + s_{it-2}) \\
&= (s_{it} - s_{it-1}) + (s_{it-1} - s_{it-2}) \\
&= (x_{it} + x_{it-1}) - \delta_i(\bar{s}_{it} + \bar{s}_{it-1}).
\end{aligned}
$$

From (7.50)

$$
\begin{aligned}
2(x_{it} - x_{it-1}) &= 2\alpha_i(\bar{s}_{it} - \bar{s}_{it-1}) + 2\beta_i(\pi_{it} - \pi_{it-1}) \\
&= \alpha_i(x_{it} + x_{it-1}) - \alpha_i \delta_i(\bar{s}_{it} + \bar{s}_{it-1}) + 2\beta_i(\pi_{it} - \pi_{it-1})
\end{aligned}
$$

while

$$-\alpha_i \delta_i \bar{s}_{it} = \delta_i \theta_i + \delta_i \beta_i \pi_{it} - \delta_i x_{it},$$

so that

$$
\begin{aligned}
2(x_{it} - x_{it-1}) &= (\alpha_i - \delta_i)(x_{it} + x_{it-1}) + 2\delta_i \theta_i \\
&\quad + \delta_i \beta_i(\pi_{it} + \pi_{it-1}) + 2\beta_i(\pi_{it} - \pi_{it-1})
\end{aligned}
$$

or, finally,

$$x_{it} = K_{i0} + K_{i1}x_{it-1} + K_{i2}\frac{1}{\lambda_t p_{it}} + K_{i3}\frac{1}{\lambda_{t-1} p_{it-1}} \tag{7.51}$$

where

$$K_{i0} = \frac{2\delta_i \theta_i}{2 - \alpha_i + \delta_i} \qquad K_{i2} = \frac{\beta_i(\delta_i + 2)}{2 - \alpha_i + \delta_i}$$

$$K_{i1} = \frac{2 + \alpha_i - \delta_i}{2 - \alpha_i + \delta_i} \qquad K_{i3} = \frac{\beta_i(\delta_i - 2)}{2 - \alpha_i + \delta_i}. \tag{7.52}$$

On solving this set of regression coefficients in terms of the four structural coefficients, we find

$$\delta_i = \frac{2(K_{i2} + K_{i3})}{K_{i2} - K_{i3}} \qquad \alpha_i = \frac{2(K_{i2} + K_{i3})}{K_{i2} - K_{i3}} - \frac{2(1 - K_{i1})}{1 + K_{i1}}$$

$$\beta_i = \frac{K_{i2} - K_{i3}}{1 + K_{i1}} \qquad \theta_i = \frac{K_{i0}(K_{i2} - K_{i3})}{(1 + K_{i1})(K_{i2} + K_{i3})}. \tag{7.53}$$

For each commodity, the four structural coefficients can thus be computed from the regression coefficients.[6]

7.5.5. Empirical results

It should be emphasized that the n estimating equations (7.51) are finite approximations to the first n equilibrium conditions (7.41). The $(n + 1)$th equilibrium condition, which is the budget constraint (7.40), has not been taken into account. The usual procedure to transform the estimating equations (7.51) into demand equations would be to proceed analytically, i.e. by solving the $n + 1$ first order conditions for λ_t and inserting this solution back into (7.51). Substituting (7.51) into the budget constraint, written in discrete time as

$$\sum_i p_{it} x_{it} = y_t, \tag{7.54}$$

one finds

$$y_t = \sum_i p_{it} \left(K_{i0} + K_{i1} x_{it-1} + K_{i2} \frac{1}{\lambda_t p_{it}} + K_{i3} \frac{1}{\lambda_{t-1} p_{it-1}} \right)$$

---

[6] A different finite approximation, in which $s(t)$ is simply replaced by s_{t-1}, leads to the same estimating equations, but with other solutions for the structural coefficients. Attempts in this direction by Rossier (1972) led to estimates which are not statistically significant for a large number of coefficients. My impression is that this is because commodities purchased in period t are not allowed to depreciate during that same period.

or

$$\lambda_t = \frac{\sum K_{i2}}{y_t - \sum p_{it} K_{i0} - \sum p_{it} K_{i1} x_{it-1} - \dfrac{1}{\lambda_{t-1}} \sum \dfrac{K_{i3} p_{it}}{p_{it-1}}} \qquad (7.55)$$

where the summations are over all commodities. Inserting this result back into (7.51), one would end up with terribly complicated and highly non-linear regression equations, which could not be estimated in the present state of the art. We have to proceed differently.

In Chapter V of the second edition of *Consumer Demand in the United States*, Houthakker and Taylor (1970) have proposed a numerical method that amounts essentially to the same, but without modification of equations (7.51). The idea is to obtain values for λ_t (and λ_{t-1}), such that the estimates satisfy the budget constraint, by iteration.

First, set λ_t equal to some convenient starting value[7] and estimate the system of equations (7.51). Use the estimates for $K_{i0}, \ldots, K_{i3}$ (and the data) to compute a first set of λ_t's according to (7.55) and use this set of λ_t's to reestimate (7.51). This gives a second set of K's and a new set of λ's. Use the latter to estimate a third set of K's, etc., etc., until the estimated expenditures add up to observed total expenditure for each time period. When this condition is satisfied, the estimating equations have become demand equations.

According to (7.55), λ_t is a function of λ_{t-1}. An initial value of λ_t for $t = 0$, (i.e. the first period for which statistical data are available), is therefore needed. For lack of any better value, this λ_0 may be kept equal to one at all iteration steps, given that the absolute value of λ is not determined (see exercises 1.15 and 1.16). To put λ_0 equal to one amounts to dividing the 'true' unknown value of λ_0 by itself, which in turn implies that a linear transformation is applied to the utility function. We have seen that such a transformation affects neither the demand equations nor the additive character of the utility function nor the specific and general substitution effects.[8]

At each step of the iteration, the system of equations has to be estimated by an appropriate regression technique. Given that the system has to be additive, in the sense that the sum of the estimated expenditures has to be equal to the sum of the observed expenditures in each time

---

[7] Knowing that λ_t is inversely related to y_t, it is natural to start with $\lambda_t = 1/y_t$.

[8] See exercise 1.15 and Section 3.1.

period, the error terms of the equations are not independent: the equations are but 'seemingly unrelated'. Zellner's method for 'seemingly unrelated regressions' (1962) is therefore appropriate.[9] The estimates given below, obtained by Weiserbs (1972 or 1973), are based on this method.[10]

For data, Weiserbs utilizes the eleven United States consumption series published in the *Survey of Current Business*, for the period 1929–1970. Quantities purchased (x_{it}) are measured by expenditures in constant (1958) prices. Prices are obtained by dividing constant-dollar into current-dollar expenditures. Income (y_t) is defined as total personal consumption expenditures at current prices, i.e. the sum of the eleven series at current prices. All expenditures are per capita.

EXERCISE

7.10. Please notice that the price deflators for the different commodities are *not* divided by a general price index. Why is this correct here, while it is not in a single equation model, such as the Houthakker-Taylor model discussed in Chapter VI?

Answer: Constrained utility maximization implies that the homogeneity restriction is satisfied. In this model, λ_t is homogeneous of degree minus one in income and prices in any period t according to (7.55), so that x_{it} is homogeneous of degree zero according to (7.51).

Table 7.1 reproduces the estimated coefficients, with standard errors between brackets as usual. In general the statistical fit is excellent. The global R^2 for the entire system is 0.999979, while the regression coefficients are significantly different from zero except for a few K_{i0} and K_{63}.

All depreciation rates are positive and in general lower than in Phlips (1972), which may be due to the use of a more efficient estimation procedure. In particular, a rate of 0.43 for automobiles is close to what may be expected. For some nondurables, δ_i is on the low side, but this

---

[9] The budget constraint implies $\iota' \varepsilon_t = 0$. As a result, there must be some correlation between the error terms of different equations. Zellner's method takes exactly this phenomenon into account. For details, see Zellner (1962).

[10] An additional reason for reproducing these estimates is that they are comparable with Weiserbs' estimates of the quadratic model in Section 7.6. However, the possible serial correlation of the error terms is ignored.

probably reflects the persistence of habits, given that δ is then the rate at which habits wear off.

TABLE 7.1
Coefficients of the dynamic linear expenditure system

Commodity	K_{i0}	K_{i1}	K_{i2}	K_{i3}	δ_i	β_i	α_i	θ_i
(1) Automobiles	−29.3	0.128	116.0	−74.3	0.434	168.0	−1.110	−120.0
and parts	(6.2)	(0.061)	(7.6)	(8.5)	(0.060)	(15.6)	(0.159)	(19.8)
(2) Furniture and	1.2	0.883	56.8	−53.3	0.063	58.4	−0.061	20.2
household	(2.3)	(0.070)	(6.7)	(7.7)	(0.053)	(7.2)	(0.035)	(43.2)
equipment								
(3) Other durable	−2.3	0.800	10.8	−7.0	0.426	9.9	0.203	−7.5
goods	(0.6)	(0.046)	(1.4)	(1.6)	(0.121)	(1.5)	(0.085)	(1.7)
(4) Food and	38.0	0.827	58.3	−44.6	0.266	56.3	0.076	157.0
beverages	(7.2)	(0.024)	(5.9)	(6.2)	(0.052)	(6.5)	(0.040)	(34.1)
(5) Clothing and	0.6	0.882	44.2	−38.0	0.152	43.7	0.026	4.4
shoes	(4.3)	(0.040)	(5.0)	(5.4)	(0.041)	(5.2)	(0.029)	(29.4)
(6) Gasoline and	−1.1	0.877	6.6	−2.8	0.819	5.0	0.687	−1.5
oil	(0.6)	(0.033)	(1.7)	(1.7)	(0.331)	(1.8)	(0.318)	(0.8)
(7) Other non-	1.5	0.889	31.7	−24.9	0.241	29.9	0.124	6.7
durable goods	(1.9)	(0.062)	(3.2)	(3.8)	(0.123)	(3.3)	(0.059)	(6.8)
(8) Housing	−3.7	0.976	16.3	−10.2	0.460	13.4	0.435	−8.1
	(0.8)	(0.011)	(2.6)	(2.7)	(0.124)	(2.6)	(0.117)	(2.4)
(9) Household	−1.7	0.954	14.5	−11.4	0.235	13.2	0.188	−7.4
operation	(0.8)	(0.028)	(1.8)	(2.0)	(0.095)	(1.8)	(0.070)	(3.6)
(10) Trans-	1.2	0.807	10.9	−7.6	0.355	10.3	0.141	3.8
portation	(1.2)	(0.054)	(1.4)	(1.8)	(0.127)	(1.6)	(0.078)	(3.6)
(11) Other services	−19.3	1.05	39.3	−35.2	0.110	36.3	0.158	−171.0
	(5.3)	(0.02)	(6.3)	(6.6)	(0.072)	(6.1)	(0.063)	(84.1)

All the β's are positive, thereby indicating the marginal utility of each good to be decreasing in the short-run. Two durable goods (automobiles and furniture) have a negative α, while most other commodities are characterized by habit formation. For 'clothing and shoes', an α equal to zero suggests that the stock effect is neutralized by habit formation. This interpretation is confirmed by the values taken by $\partial x_i/\partial s_i$ in Table 7.2.

The coefficients θ are the highest for food, beverages, furniture and household equipment, which one can view as necessities. On the other hand, θ_i is negative for 'other services', which includes medical care, cleaning, funeral expenses, movies, television and higher education, and for automobiles, housing and other durables.

Subtracting α_i from δ_i, we get an estimate of κ_{ii}, which turns out to be higher than 1 for automobiles, contradicting the assumption of a partial adjustment. For the item 'other services', the adjustment coefficient is negative, with the implication that the long-run coefficient β_i^* is negative (habit formation is too strong). The other adjustment coefficients seem to make sense.

EXERCISE

7.11. What are the consequences of $(\delta_i - \alpha_i) < 0$ for the long-run income and price derivatives? Can you pinpoint these in Table 7.2?

TABLE 7.2
Dynamic linear expenditure system: derivatives and elasticities

Commodities	Run	Income elasticity	Compensated price elasticity	Uncompensated price elasticity	$\dfrac{\partial x_i}{\partial s_i}$
(1) Automobiles and	short	7.57	−1.75	−2.13	−0.887
parts	long	1.65	−1.26	−1.35	
(2) Furniture and	short	2.35	−0.76	−0.89	−0.068
household equipment	long	0.92	−0.84	−0.90	
(3) Other durable goods	short	1.27	−0.46	−0.48	0.255
	long	1.88	−1.47	−1.50	
(4) Food and beverages	short	0.53	−0.17	−0.30	0.085
	long	0.58	−0.39	−0.53	
(5) Clothing and shoes	short	1.11	−0.37	−0.47	0.035
	long	1.04	−0.88	−0.97	
(6) Gasoline and oil	short	0.36	−0.13	−0.15	0.872
	long	1.76	−1.12	−1.17	
(7) Other nondurable	short	0.76	−0.26	−0.33	0.149
goods	long	1.21	−0.81	−0.92	
(8) Housing	short	0.24	−0.09	−0.12	0.543
	long	3.49	−0.99	−1.43	
(9) Household operation	short	0.58	−0.21	−0.24	0.235
	long	2.23	−1.26	−1.38	
(10) Transportation	short	0.80	−0.29	−0.31	0.176
	long	1.03	−0.84	−0.87	
(11) Other services	short	0.56	−0.19	−0.27	0.186
	long	−0.99	0.70	0.85	

Turning to Table 7.2, we note, to begin with, that the relation between long-run and short-run income elasticities does not depend uniquely on the sign of α: income elasticities may be higher in the short-run than in the long-run, even if α is positive (why?). We feel authorized, therefore, following Houthakker and Taylor (1970, p. 208), to characterize durable goods, or inventory adjustment, by the fact that the short-run income elasticity exceeds its value in the long-run, and conversely for habit formation. According to this criterion, inventory adjustment appears to be typical for automobiles, furniture and household equipment and clothing and shoes. Habit formation appears to dominate the purchase of gasoline and oil, other nondurables (tobacco, toilet articles, cleaning, drugs, magazines, newspapers, nondurable toys, flowers), housing and household operation, while transportation does not show any dynamic behaviour at all.

All direct price elasticities have the right sign, and all (direct) compensated price elasticities are, of course, smaller than the corresponding uncompensated elasticities. But all short-run price elasticities are *not* smaller than the corresponding long-run elasticities.

At the final iteration step, λ_t took the values reported in Table 7.3. When we compare its evolution over time with that of real income, we see that it increases when income falls and decreases when income goes up. Should it be pointed out again that λ_t is defined up to a monotonic transformation? While the (positive) sign of λ is invariant under any such transformation, its absolute value is not. The reader should thus be careful not to attach any particular meaning to the absolute values of λ_t reported. Recall also that the derivative of λ with respect to y is not invariant. However, the income elasticity of λ is invariant under *linear* transformations.

TABLE 7.3
The marginal utility of money in the dynamic linear expenditures system

Year	Per capita y_t at constant prices (\$)	λ_t	ω	ω^*
1929	1,146	1.000	−1.43	−1.27
1930	1,058	1.210	−1.54	−1.30
1931	1,016	1.470	−1.61	−1.29
1932	920	2.000	−1.75	−1.29
1933	900	2.163	−1.77	−1.34
1934	934	1.855	−1.69	−1.42
1935	988	1.673	−1.65	−1.41
1936	1,080	1.430	−1.55	−1.36
1937	1,111	1.323	−1.54	−1.36
1938	1,080	1.403	−1.55	−1.34
1939	1,131	1.334	−1.53	−1.32
1940	1,171	1.261	−1.51	−1.31
1941	1,235	1.075	−1.45	−1.30

TABLE 7.3 (*continued*)

Year	Per capita y_t at constant prices ($)	λ_t	ω	ω^*
1942	1,194	1.025	−1.51	−1.34
1943	1,206	0.966	−1.57	−1.36
1944	1,236	0.896	−1.57	−1.36
1945	1,302	0.806	−1.54	−1.33
1946	1,436	0.661	−1.50	−1.32
1947	1,425	0.622	−1.55	−1.36
1948	1,433	0.581	−1.54	−1.36
1949	1,445	0.569	−1.51	−1.34
1950	1,513	0.513	−1.45	−1.32
1951	1,504	0.477	−1.43	−1.33
1952	1,519	0.461	−1.42	−1.33
1953	1,566	0.441	−1.42	−1.32
1954	1,569	0.440	−1.43	−1.32
1955	1,652	0.407	−1.40	−1.30
1956	1,665	0.388	−1.38	−1.31
1957	1,675	0.374	−1.38	−1.31
1958	1,659	0.373	−1.39	−1.32
1959	1,729	0.352	−1.38	−1.30
1960	1,750	0.346	−1.40	−1.31
1961	1,755	0.346	−1.42	−1.31
1962	1,814	0.332	−1.42	−1.30
1963	1,868	0.319	−1.42	−1.30
1964	1,948	0.299	−1.41	−1.29
1965	2,048	0.279	−1.40	−1.28
1966	2,128	0.263	−1.40	−1.28
1967	2,165	0.254	−1.41	−1.28
1968	2,257	0.235	−1.41	−1.27
1969	2,317	0.220	−1.42	−1.27
1970	2,324	0.212	−1.44	−1.28

EXERCISE

7.12. Derive the formulae from which the short-run and the long-run income elasticity of λ (or money flexibility) can be computed, for our dynamic version of the linear expenditure system.

Answer: Differentiate the short-run and the long-run first-order conditions with respect to y, solve for the income derivative and multiply by y/λ or y/λ^* respectively, where λ^* is the long-run marginal utility of income. You should find

$$\omega = -\frac{\lambda y}{\sum_i \beta_i}$$

for the short-run elasticity, and

$$\omega^* = -\frac{y}{y - \sum_i p_i \gamma_i^*}$$

for the long-run elasticity.

The latter is the same formula as for the static linear expenditure system, with γ_i replaced by γ_i^*. See exercise 4.21.

Returning to Table 7.3, we see that the 'money flexibility' (ω) is around -1.4 in the short-run and -1.3 in the long run since the war. Its absolute value, which we interpreted as a welfare indicator, decreases when real income increases. These results seem plausible in view of the comments made in Section 4.3.3.

7.6.* A dynamic quadratic model

The model developed in Section 7.5 is very largely inspired by the path-breaking work presented in Chapter V of the second edition of Houthakker and Taylor's book on *Consumer Demand in the United States*. Strangely enough, although their dynamic single equation model was based on a linear demand equation (see equation (6.28)), Houthakker and Taylor (HT for short) did not try to dynamize the Stone-Geary utility function, which is the only utility function consistent with linear demand equations (as we have shown in Section 7.4). Instead, they choose to work with the quadratic utility function, probably because its first order partial derivatives are linear, so that the equilibrium conditions are linear in the variables.

The 'dynamic' quadratic utility function is written as

$$x'a + s'b + \tfrac{1}{2}x'Ax + x'Bs + \tfrac{1}{2}s'Cs \tag{7.56}$$

where x and s are $(n \times 1)$ vectors, a and b constant vectors, and A, B and C are constant nonsingular and diagonal matrices; x and s are functions of time, which is treated as continuous. The vector Bs measures the influence of habit formation or inventory adjustment on marginal utilities.

HT assume the state variables to be related to the flows of purchases through

$$\dot{s} = x - Ds \tag{7.57}$$

where $D = \hat{\delta}$ is a diagonal and nonsingular matrix, with δ_i on the main diagonal. The third and final equation in the model is the budget constraint

$$p'x = y. \tag{7.58}$$

EXERCISES

7.13. Maximize (7.56) subject to (7.58) and eliminate the state variables, as was done in equations (7.41) to (7.43).

Answer: You should find

$$\dot{x} = -A^{-1}Da - (A^{-1}B + D)x + A^{-1}\dot{p}^* + A^{-1}Dp^*.$$

7.14. Derive a finite approximation of the result just obtained using (7.49).

Hint: Proceed as in equations (7.50) to (7.52).

The finite approximation to the first order condition gives the estimating equations

$$x_t = K_0 + K_1 x_{t-1} + K_2 \lambda_t p_t + K_3 \lambda_{t-1} p_{t-1} \tag{7.59}$$

where[11]

$$\begin{aligned}
K_0 &= -[I + \tfrac{1}{2}(A^{-1}B + D)]^{-1}A^{-1}Da \\
K_1 &= [I + \tfrac{1}{2}(A^{-1}B + D)]^{-1}[I - \tfrac{1}{2}(A^{-1}B + D)] \\
K_2 &= [I + \tfrac{1}{2}(A^{-1}B + D)]^{-1}A^{-1}(I + \tfrac{1}{2}D) \\
K_3 &= -[I + \tfrac{1}{2}(A^{-1}B + D)]^{-1}A^{-1}(I - \tfrac{1}{2}D).
\end{aligned} \tag{7.60}$$

Given the diagonality of A, B and D, equation (7.59) is seen as the equation for the ith good, all matrices being treated as scalars, and the equations (7.60) can be solved for the structural coefficients a, A, B and D. The diagonal elements of B, b_{ii}, play the same role as α_i in the dynamic linear expenditure system.

Comparing (7.59) with the estimating equation (7.51) for the linear expenditure system, we see that the only difference is that λp is replaced by its reciprocal.

---

[11] A slightly different discrete model was estimated by Mattei (1971) using Swiss data.

EXERCISES

7.15. Show that, in the short-run, i.e. for $\partial s/\partial y = 0$ and $\partial s/\partial p = 0$,

$$\lambda_y = (p'A^{-1}p)^{-1}$$
$$x_y = (p'A^{-1}p)^{-1}A^{-1}p$$
$$X_p = \lambda A^{-1} - \lambda(p'A^{-1}p)^{-1}A^{-1}pp'A^{-1} - x_y x'$$

where λA^{-1} is the matrix of specific substitution effects.

7.16. Show that the formulae obtained in the preceding exercise are the same as those obtained after maximizing the static quadratic utility function.

7.17. Show that the long-run derivatives, i.e. for $\dot{s} = 0$, obey the same formulae as in exercise 7.15., with A replaced by $W = A + BD^{-1}$.

TABLE 7.4
Coefficients of the dynamic quadratic model

Commodity	K_{i0}	K_{i1}	K_{i2}	K_{i3}	a_i	a_{ii}	b_{ii}	δ_i
(1) Automobiles	146.0	0.416	−486.0	265.0	0.660	−0.002	−0.0004	0.588
and parts	(13.0)	(0.050)	(32.0)	(37.3)	(0.018)	(0.000)	(0.0002)	(0.124)
(2) Furniture and	66.7	0.709	−157.0	74.3	0.802	−0.007	0.003	0.718
household	(13.7)	(0.066)	(20.5)	(26.1)	(0.027)	(0.001)	(0.001)	(0.242)
equipment								
(3) Other durable	2.0	1.020	−23.8	20.2	0.567	−0.046	0.008	0.162
goods	(2.0)	(0.035)	(4.9)	(5.5)	(0.246)	(0.010)	(0.003)	(0.421)
(4) Food and	96.5	0.854	−201.0	120.0	1.190	−0.006	0.002	0.504
beverages	(13.7)	(0.023)	(21.5)	(23.4)	(0.090)	(0.001)	(0.000)	(0.203)
(5) Clothing	45.9	0.826	−132.0	84.5	0.972	−0.008	0.002	0.437
and shoes	(9.1)	(0.040)	(13.8)	(16.2)	(0.075)	(0.001)	(0.000)	(0.210)
(6) Gasoline	5.1	0.994	−10.4	4.7	0.891	−0.132	0.099	0.757
and oil	(2.3)	(0.023)	(5.1)	(4.9)	(0.106)	(0.085)	(0.007)	(0.800)
(7) Other non-	7.2	0.999	−89.3	79.0	0.706	−0.012	0.001	0.122
durables	(9.9)	(0.036)	(9.9)	(11.6)	(0.288)	(0.001)	(0.001)	(0.213)
goods								
(8) Housing	11.5	1.010	−29.5	14.8	0.788	−0.045	0.030	0.660
	(2.3)	(0.006)	(5.3)	(5.6)	(0.064)	(0.011)	(0.001)	(0.322)
(9) Household	10.0	0.985	−43.9	29.1	0.674	−0.027	0.011	0.405
operation	(3.0)	(0.017)	(5.8)	(6.3)	(0.061)	(0.004)	(0.001)	(0.252)
(10) Trans-	15.7	0.825	−40.7	24.1	0.942	−0.028	0.009	0.513
portation	(4.1)	(0.050)	(5.3)	(6.7)	(0.071)	(0.005)	(0.001)	(0.263)
(11) Other	−1.4	1.050	−119.0	100.0	−0.071	−0.009	0.002	0.174
services	(11.0)	(0.022)	(20.5)	(20.9)	(0.629)	(0.002)	(0.001)	(0.321)

7.18. Convince yourself that

$$X_s = -\frac{1}{\lambda} KB.$$

Hint: see equation (7.29).

7.19. Show that the HT model also incorporates a partial adjustment process to long-run demand, so that the matrix of reaction coefficients κ can be estimated from $\kappa = D + A^{-1}B$.
Hint: proceed as in equations (7.45) and (7.46).

7.20. Convince yourself that the general restriction $k_{ii} < 0$ implies $a_{ii} < 0$, where a_{ii} is an element on the main diagonal of matrix A.

The empirical results obtained by Weiserbs (1972 or 1973) are reproduced in Tables 7.4 and 7.5. These are directly comparable to Tables 7.1 and 7.2 as the estimation method and the data are the same.

TABLE 7.5
Dynamic quadratic model: derivatives and elasticities

Commodity	Run	Income elasticity	Compensated price elasticity	Uncompensated price elasticity	$\frac{\partial x_i}{\partial s_i}$
(1) Automobiles and	short	7.56	−1.94	−2.32	−0.146
parts	long	0.73	−3.18	−3.14	
(2) Furniture and	short	1.96	−0.72	−0.84	0.335
household equipment	long	0.56	−2.44	−2.41	
(3) Other durable goods	short	1.12	−0.46	−0.48	0.176
	long	−1.37	6.37	6.34	
(4) Food and beverages	short	0.57	−0.20	−0.34	0.298
	long	0.25	−1.05	−0.99	
(5) Clothing and shoes	short	1.11	−0.42	−0.52	0.222
	long	0.35	−1.51	−1.48	
(6) Gasoline and oil	short	0.22	−0.09	−0.10	0.746
	long	3.61	−14.50	−14.40	
(7) Other nondurable	short	0.79	−0.31	−0.38	0.112
goods	long	9.48	−6.20	−5.34	
(8) Housing	short	0.16	−0.07	−0.09	0.657
	long	−1.39	7.45	7.27	
(9) Household operation	short	0.58	−0.23	−0.26	0.378
	long	2.04	−8.24	−8.14	
(10) Transportation	short	0.98	−0.40	−0.43	0.312
	long	0.04	−1.59	−1.58	
(11) Other services	short	0.59	−0.22	−0.31	0.204
	long	−0.29	1.35	1.31	

The results obtained for the dynamic linear expenditure system are better in many respects. First of all, three equations (nrs. 3, 8 and 11) of Table 7.4 do not satisfy the stability conditions of the quadratic model. Indeed, HT (1970, Appendix to Chapter 5) have shown that a set of sufficient conditions for the system of differential equations, describing the law of motion for x to converge to a long-run solution, when income and prices are held constant, is for the matrices A and $(AD + B)$ both to be negative definite. On the other hand, Taylor and Weiserbs (1972) notice that these conditions translate to

$$\frac{1 + K_{i1}}{K_{i2} - K_{i3}} < 0 \quad \text{and} \quad (K_{i2} - K_{i3})(1 - K_{i1}) < 0 \qquad (7.61)$$

in terms of regression coefficients. Given that empirically $K_{i2} - K_{i3}$ has never been found to be positive, while K_{i1} is rarely found to be negative, let alone less than -1, these conditions can be reduced to one, namely,

$$K_{i1} < 1.$$

Three of the eleven estimating equations for the quadratic model have $K_{i1} > 1$.

EXERCISE

7.21. Verify (7.61), knowing that the solution of (7.60) in terms of the structural coefficients is

$$a = -[K_2 + K_3]^{-1}K_0;$$
$$A = [K_2 - K_3]^{-1}[I + K_1];$$
$$B = -4[K_2 - K_3]^{-1}[K_1K_2 + K_3];$$
$$D = 2[K_2 - K_3]^{-1}[K_2 + K_3].$$

7.22. Show that the stability conditions, together with $a > 0$, are both necessary and sufficient for the dynamic quadratic model to possess a point of satiation.
Hint: Satiation implies $\partial u/\partial x_i = 0$ for all i, together with $\dot{s} = 0$ and $\partial^2 u/\partial x_i^2 < 0$. Show that these conditions imply that A and $(AD + B)$ are negative definite.

In the dynamic linear expenditure system, we can analyse the stability conditions in the following way. Start from $\dot{s}_i = x_i - \delta_i s_i$ and use the first-order conditions (7.42) to obtain

$$\dot{s} = \theta_i + (\alpha_i - \delta_i)s_i + \frac{\beta_i}{\lambda p_i}. \tag{7.62}$$

Substitute expression (7.44) into (7.62) to find

$$\dot{s}_i = \theta_i + (\alpha_i - \delta_i)s_i + \frac{\beta_i}{\sum_j \beta_j p_i}\left[y - \sum_j p_j(\theta_j + \alpha_j s_j)\right]$$

or

$$\dot{s}_i = \theta_i + \frac{\beta_i}{\sum_j \beta_j p_i}(y - \sum_j p_j\theta_j - \sum_{j\neq i} p_j\alpha_j s_j) + \left(\alpha_i - \delta_i - \frac{\beta_i\alpha_i}{\sum_j \beta_j}\right)s_i. \tag{7.63}$$

For constant prices, income *and* s_j $(j \neq i)$, stability of equation i requires

$$\alpha_i - \delta_i - \frac{\beta_i\alpha_i}{\sum_j \beta_j} < 0. \tag{7.64}$$

This condition is not satisfied in equation nr. 11, namely for 'other services', in Table 7.1. (We have already emphasized that habit formation is stronger than depreciation in that item.) In the quadratic model, the corresponding condition was $a_{ii}\delta_i + b_{ii} < 0$.

Whenever the stability conditions are not satisfied, the long-run elasticities turn out to have the wrong sign, as can be seen in Table 7.5. This table also displays many implausible elasticities.

Looking at the time shape of λ_t for the quadratic model (Table 7.6), we see that it is similar to the time shape observed in the linear expenditure system (Table 7.3), except for a drop during the period 1965–1970. More disturbing is the fact that the absolute value of the short-run money flexibility increases very rapidly, while real income is increasing, to attain implausibly high values. The long-run money flexibility ω^* also moves in the wrong direction, while taking extremely small values.

TABLE 7.6

The marginal utility of money in the dynamic quadratic model

Year	Per capita y_t at constant prices ($)	λ_t	ω	ω^*
1929	1,146	1.000	−1.79	−0.20
1930	1,058	1.187	−1.46	−0.18
1931	1,016	1.364	−1.32	−0.17
1932	920	1.656	−1.06	−0.14
1933	900	1.720	−1.06	−0.13
1934	934	1.505	−1.18	−0.14
1935	988	1.397	−1.38	−0.15
1936	1,080	1.240	−1.71	−0.17
1937	1,111	1.185	−1.79	−0.18
1938	1,080	1.281	−1.57	−0.17
1939	1.131	1.228	−1.74	−0.18
1940	1,171	1.178	−1.84	−0.19
1941	1,235	1.015	−2.07	−0.21
1942	1,194	1.005	−1.86	−0.20
1943	1,206	0.936	−1.82	−0.20
1944	1,236	0.857	−1.82	−0.21
1945	1,302	0.763	−1.99	−0.22
1946	1,436	0.606	−2.59	−0.26
1947	1,425	0.602	−2.40	−0.25
1948	1,433	0.573	−2.38	−0.24
1949	1,445	0.569	−2.37	−0.25
1950	1,513	0.504	−2.78	−0.26
1951	1,504	0.488	−2.66	−0.26
1952	1,519	0.480	−2.68	−0.27
1953	1,566	0.458	−2.95	−0.28
1954	1,569	0.472	−2.93	−0.29
1955	1,652	0.416	−3.50	−0.31
1956	1,665	0.409	−3.45	−0.31
1957	1,675	0.406	−3.32	−0.31
1958	1,659	0.424	−3.08	−0.31
1959	1,729	0.382	−3.47	−0.33
1960	1,750	0.383	−3.56	−0.33
1961	1,755	0.394	−3.48	−0.34
1962	1,814	0.366	−3.85	−0.36
1963	1,868	0.343	−4.24	−0.37
1964	1,948	0.303	−4.99	−0.40
1965	2,048	0.257	−6.21	−0.43
1966	2,128	0.228	−7.29	−0.46
1967	2,165	0.231	−7.18	−0.47
1968	2,257	0.195	−8.52	−0.50
1969	2,317	0.178	−9.26	−0.53
1970	2,324	0.192	−8.29	−0.53

Finally, the quadratic model is inferior in terms of forecasting performance, as can be seen from the forecasts made for the 1963–1968 period by Taylor and Weiserbs (1972). We conclude with these authors that 'the empirical results leave little question but that the linear expenditure system is a better vehicle of analysis than the additive quadratic model'.

VIII

Substitution, complementarity and the utility tree

8.1.* Introduction

The dynamic versions of both the linear expenditure system and the quadratic model, presented in Chapter VII, are based on an additive utility function. Strong separability has been assumed between commodities, between stocks and between commodities and stocks. The reader is entitled to think that this is an oversimplified view of the structure of preferences and that one should allow for all sorts of interdependencies.

To do this, use can be made of some of the particular restrictions (derived in Chapter III) resulting from weak separability. An obvious starting point would be to pick up one particular branch of the utility function and to write down a set of demand equations such that the demand for each commodity in the branch is a function of the prices in and the budget allotment to that branch, using restriction (3.29). A step further would be to construct a branch utility function allowing for weak separability, as was done in Brown and Heien (1972).

However, the use in applied work of the restrictions derived from weak separability implies that the 'correct' grouping of the commodities is known. Indeed, the theory of separability presupposes that the commodities are partitioned in such a way that there is (weak or strong) separability. The grouping itself is treated as an empirical question, to be answered by intuition or by facts. It is therefore of some interest to develop a procedure that gives insight in the grouping of commodities and answers questions such as: what are the branches of the utility function?; which branches, if any, are strongly separable?

This chapter presents a procedure[1] based on the idea that some

---

[1] This Chapter is based on Phlips (1971a) and Phlips and Rouzier (1972).

information can be gathered from an analysis of the residuals obtained after fitting a system of demand equations based on an additive utility function. To the extent that the utility function is misspecified, in that it ignores interdependencies between commodities, these interdependencies may show up in the residuals, more precisely in the correlations between the residuals belonging to different equations.

8.2.* Random shocks

Before proceeding, we should recall a number of results obtained earlier. First of all, the relationships we are interested in are to be found in the off-diagonal elements of the substitution matrix K. The sign of these elements determines whether two commodities are substitutes or complements according to the Hicksian definitions. Subtraction of the 'general' substitution effect from these elements gives the 'specific' substitution effect, which provides information on the structure of preferences in terms of the second order partial derivatives of the utility function.

On the other hand, we know that any additional variable introduced in the utility function has an impact on the quantities demanded equal to

$$-\frac{1}{\lambda} K V$$

where V is the matrix of the derivatives of the marginal utilities with respect to that additional variable.[2]

It is tempting, then, to proceed as follows. Define the error term ε_i (of which the corresponding residual is an estimate) as the impact on x_i of random shocks. And assume that these random shocks affect the marginal utilities.

A number of random events affect the satisfaction derived from consuming a commodity: ceteris paribus, ice cream tastes better when the sun shines than when it does not. These random events can be introduced in the utility function and treated as additional variables.

The quadratic utility function has the advantage of having linear first-order derivatives. It is therefore an easy matter to introduce random shocks in it. The simplest way is to locate these in the linear

---

[2] See equation (7.29).

part $a'x$ and to interpret the vector a as being subject to random shocks (Δa_t). We accordingly define the vector of error terms ε_t as

$$\varepsilon_t = \Delta x_t = X_a \Delta a_t \qquad (8.1)$$

and want to determine $X_a = [\partial x_i/\partial a_j]$ on the assumption that the consumer continues to act rationally, i.e. to maximize utility within the budget constraint.[3]

Starting from the first order conditions

$$a + Ax + Bs = \lambda p \qquad (8.2)$$

and

$$p'x = y \qquad (8.3)$$

we differentiate with respect to a, treating p and y as constant and λ and x as variable.

In the short run, $\partial s/\partial a = 0$. Differentiation of (8.2) and (8.3) gives

$$I + AX_a = p\lambda_a \qquad (8.4)$$

where $\lambda_a = [\partial\lambda/\partial a_i]$, and

$$p'X_a = 0. \qquad (8.5)$$

This leads to

$$\begin{aligned} X_a &= A^{-1}(p\lambda_a - I) \\ p'X_a &= p'A^{-1}p\lambda_a - p'A^{-1} = 0 \\ \lambda_a &= (p'A^{-1}p)^{-1}p'A^{-1} \end{aligned} \qquad (8.6)$$

and

$$X_a = -[A^{-1} - (p'A^{-1}p)^{-1}A^{-1}pp'A^{-1}]. \qquad (8.7)$$

EXERCISES

8.1. Show that equation (8.7) may be rewritten as

$$X_a = -[A^{-1} - (1/\lambda_y)x_y x_y']$$

---

[3] This reasoning is entirely in line with the approach outlined by Theil and Neudecker (1958) for the static quadratic utility function and further developed by Barten (1966, Chapter 3) and Theil (1967, Chapter 7). See O'Brien (1974) for an application to financial assets.

or as

$$X_a = -\frac{1}{\lambda}KV$$

where

$$V = \left[\frac{\partial^2 u}{\partial x_i \partial a_j}\right].$$

Hint: See exercise 7.15 and notice that here $V = I$.

8.2. Show that, in the long run, one has

$$X_a^* = -[W^{-1} - (1/\lambda_y^*)x_y^* x_y^{*\prime}]$$

where $W = A + BD^{-1}$.
Hint: See exercise 7.17.

In both the long and the short run, the random shocks influence the quantities demanded in the same way as the substitution effect of price changes, except for sign and a positive constant. We conclude that the error term of the estimating equations (7.59) for the quadratic model, which are short-run, is

$$\varepsilon_{it} = -\sum_j \left[a^{ij} - (1/\lambda_y)\frac{\partial x_i}{\partial y}\frac{\partial x_j}{\partial y}\right]\Delta a_{jt} \tag{8.8}$$

where a^{ij} indicates an element of A^{-1}.

8.3.* The residual variation and the structure of preferences

We now introduce a probability distribution for the random shocks and for the error terms, at each t and for each j, and proceed to derive the moments. Following Barten (1966, par. 3.3), we suppose $E(\Delta a_{jt}) = 0$ such that $E(\varepsilon_{it}) = 0$, and also that the 'contemporaneous' variance-covariance matrix of the random shocks can be specified for any t as

$$E[(\Delta a_t)(\Delta a_t)'] = -k_t^2 U = -k_t^2 A \tag{8.9}$$

where k is a non-zero scalar. As A is negative definite by assumption, the minus sign is needed to insure positive variances.

The specification says that the variances are proportional to the absolute value of the second order direct partial derivatives of the utility function: if the marginal utility of good i is much affected by a change in its quantity, then the variance of the random shock Δa_{it} is large. As for the covariances, these are zero in the case of want independence. Otherwise, they are proportional to the cross-partial derivatives of the utility function, a negative derivative implying a positive covariance.

Barten (1966, p. 49) justifies his specification as follows:

Consider (...) two commodities, say beef and pork, which have much in common with respect to the satisfaction of wants. The marginal utility of pork then decreases almost as much when one buys more beef than when the same additional quantity of pork is bought. The corresponding off-diagonal element of U is thus negative and not very different in magnitude from the diagonal element for pork. According to [(8.9)] a stochastic increase in the need for pork then implies on the average a stochastic increase in the need for beef. This amounts to a stochastic increase of the need for meat in general, which can be satisfied by either beef or pork.

It follows from (8.9) that the variance-covariance matrix of the ε's is

$$E(\varepsilon_t \varepsilon_t') = -k_t^2 [A^{-1} - (1/\lambda_y) x_y x_y'] A [A^{-1} - (1/\lambda_y) x_y x_y']$$

as $[A^{-1} - (1/\lambda_y) x_y x_y']$ is symmetric, or

$$E(\varepsilon_t \varepsilon_t') = -k_t^2 [A^{-1} - (1/\lambda_y) x_y x_y'] [I - (1/\lambda_y) A x_y x_y']. \tag{8.10}$$

However,

$$(1/\lambda_y) A x_y = (p'A^{-1}p) A (p'A^{-1}p)^{-1} A^{-1} p = p. \tag{8.11}$$

Therefore

$$E(\varepsilon_t \varepsilon_t') = -k_t^2 [A^{-1} - (1/\lambda_y) x_y x_y'] [I - p x_y']. \tag{8.12}$$

But, as the reader will verify,

$$[A^{-1} - (1/\lambda_y) x_y x_y'] [-p x_y'] = 0. \tag{8.13}$$

Finally,

$$E(\varepsilon_t \varepsilon_t') = -k_t^2 [A^{-1} - (1/\lambda_y) x_y x_y']. \tag{8.14}$$

The contemporaneous covariances of the error terms are seen to be equal to the total cross substitution effects except for sign and a positive constant. The structure of preferences can now be described in the following terms.

When two goods are substitutes in the Hicksian sense, the total cross substitution effect is positive and the correlation of the corresponding error terms is negative. When two goods are complements in the

Hicksian sense; the correlation is positive. And when *all* goods are independent.

$$\text{cov}(\varepsilon_{it}, \varepsilon_{jt}) = (k_t^2/\lambda_y)\frac{\partial x_i}{\partial y}\frac{\partial x_j}{\partial y} \qquad (i \neq j) \tag{8.15}$$

which are all negative (as $\partial\lambda/\partial y$ is negative) in the absence of inferior goods. These are the general substitution effects except for sign and a positive constant.

These findings imply that, if good estimates of the ε's can be obtained, the correlation matrix of these estimates gives valuable information on the structure of preferences. If all correlations turn out to be negative, we are not allowed to reject the hypothesis that the utility function is additive, i.e. that A is diagonal. If the signs differ, we may interpret a negative correlation between ε_{it} and ε_{jt} to indicate that goods i and j are substitutes, and a positive that they are complements. But then we have to admit a misspecification of the utility function.

Notice, however, that the above test is biased in favour of additivity. Indeed, as $\varepsilon_t = K^*\Delta a_t$, where K^* is proportional to the substitution matrix K, and Δa_t is the vector of random shocks, the correlation matrix R is equal to $K^*E\left[(\Delta a_t)(\Delta a_t)'\right]K^*$ after normalization. As the homogeneity condition implies $K^*p = 0$, we have also $Rp = 0$. Therefore R is singular, so that at least one correlation must be negative in each row of R. If nevertheless some correlations turn out to be positive, the point that this indicates absence of additivity is reinforced. Conversely, the singularity of R weakens the interpretation to be given to the signs in terms of substitutability and complementarity.

It is the more important, therefore, to find a way to shift from Hicksian concepts to cardinal concepts, apart from the fact that the latter are intuitively more appealing to work with. To do this, it suffices to subtract the correlation due to the general substitution effect from the 'total' correlation coefficients.[4] The difference is the correlation due to the specific effect, which informs directly about the structure of preferences in terms of the Hessian matrix of the utility function. The argument runs as follows.

Under independence, the covariance between ε_i and ε_j can be written as

$$\text{cov}(\varepsilon_i, \varepsilon_j) = -k'\frac{\partial x_i}{\partial y}\frac{\partial x_j}{\partial y}, \qquad (i \neq j) \tag{8.16}$$

---

[4] This procedure was suggested by A.P. Barten.

where $k' = -k^2/\lambda_y > 0$. The variance of ε_i can be written as

$$\text{var}(\varepsilon_i) = k' \frac{1}{p_i} \frac{\partial x_i}{\partial y} \left(1 - p_i \frac{\partial x_i}{\partial y}\right). \tag{8.17}$$

The correlation between ε_i and ε_j is therefore, under independence,

$$-\sqrt{\frac{p_i \dfrac{\partial x_i}{\partial y} p_j \dfrac{\partial x_j}{\partial y}}{\left(1 - p_i \dfrac{\partial x_i}{\partial y}\right)\left(1 - p_j \dfrac{\partial x_j}{\partial y}\right)}}. \tag{8.18}$$

Using estimates of the income derivatives one can compute (8.18) and subtract it from the corresponding total correlation. This amounts to adding a positive number to each total correlation coefficient, and therefore to increasing specific complementarity.

EXERCISE
8.3. Verify equations (8.17) and (8.18) using (8.14) and the results obtained in exercise 7.15 for λ_y and x_y.

8.4.* Principal components

The findings of the preceding section are in terms of the signs of the elements of the residual correlation matrix R. This matrix contains more information, however: from the magnitude of the correlation coefficients, it is possible to determine which commodities are strongly related to each other. The grouping of commodities into 'branches' or 'blocks' can thus be ascertained.

In principle, an examination of the elements of R is sufficient for this purpose. In fact, this is a difficult task whenever R has many entries. It is the more difficult when the grouping is not clearcut, as is generally the case. A method that clarifies the picture, isolating the commodities that are strongly related to each other, would be welcome. Furthermore, such a method should be purely descriptive, in the sense that the grouping should be revealed by the data without any a priori assumption as to their structure. Indeed, the partition of the commodities, as emphasized earlier, is treated in the theory of the utility tree as an empirical question.

Principal component analysis[5] is a natural proceeding, as it allows us to factorize the residual correlation matrix without any a priori hypothesis[6] as to its structure and without loss of information. It can be briefly described[7] as follows.

Consider a $(T \times n)$ matrix of observations X. (In the application made below, the observations are the residuals of the $n = 11$ equations fitted to estimate the dynamic quadratic model.) The observations are standardized, so that $R = X'X$. The total variance of the observations is thus equal to n, i.e. the trace of R.

The principal components are defined as the n linear transformations $z_{1t}, \ldots, z_{nt}$ $(t = 1, \ldots, T)$, such that

$$Z = XF \tag{8.19}$$

where Z is $(T \times n)$ and F is $(n \times n)$. Furthermore, these transformations are required to be orthogonal, i.e.

$$F'F = I, \tag{8.20}$$

so that $Z'Z$ is diagonal and $ZF' = X$. Finally, the components have to be constructed in such a way that each *successive* component contributes most to the total variance of the observations, i.e. 'explains' the largest part of the total variance not explained by the preceding components.

The computations are greatly simplified by the fact that each column f_i of the matrix F (called 'matrix of factor loadings') turns out to be the eigenvector associated with an eigenvalue (or latent root) of R.

Indeed, let us compute the first component $z_1 = Xf_1$, which is a $(T \times 1)$ vector. By definition, its variance $z_1'z_1 = \sum_t z_{1t}^2$ must be maximum, subject to the constraint $f_1'f_1 = 1$. Differentiation of the Lagrangean

$$L_1 = f_1'X'Xf_1 + \lambda_1(1 - f_1'f_1) \tag{8.21}$$

gives

$$\frac{\partial L_1}{\partial f_1} = 2X'Xf_1 - 2\lambda_1 f_1 \tag{8.22}$$

---

[5] Alternatively, one could use cluster analysis. See W. Fisher (1969).

[6] The absence of an a priori hypothesis on the structure of R is what distinguishes principal component from factor analysis. See Harman (1960).

[7] Its first application in economics is probably due to Stone (1947). For more details, see e.g. Dhrymes (1970a, Chapter 2).

and

$$\frac{\partial L_1}{\partial \lambda_1} = 1 - f_1'f_1. \tag{8.23}$$

Putting the derivatives equal to zero, we find

$$(X'X)f_1 = \lambda_1 f_1$$

or

$$f_1'(X'X)f_1 = \lambda_1$$

so that λ_1 is seen to be the variance of z_1, and λ_1/n is the contribution of the first component to the total variance of the observations. We also have

$$(X'X - \lambda_1 I)f_1 = 0$$

or

$$(R - \lambda_1 I)f_1 = 0.$$

To find f_1, we simply have to find the eigenvector associated with the first latent root of R.

To find f_2, maximize $f_2'X'Xf_2$ subject to $f_2'f_2 = 1$ and $f_1'f_2 = 0$. The Lagrangean is now

$$L_2 = f_2'X'Xf_2 + \lambda_2(1 - f_2'f_2) + \mu(f_1'f_2) \tag{8.24}$$

and leads to $(R - \lambda_2 I)f_2 = 0$. The successive columns of F are seen to be associated with the successive latent roots of R.

EXERCISE
8.4. Show that $\mu = 0$ and $\lambda_2 = f_2'X'Xf_2 = z_2'z_2$, so that

$$Z'Z = \begin{bmatrix} \lambda_1 & & & & 0 \\ & \lambda_2 & & & \\ & & \cdot & & \\ & & & \cdot & \\ & & & & \cdot \\ 0 & & & & \lambda_n \end{bmatrix}$$

The different steps in the computations are therefore:
Compute the roots of the polynomial of degree n you obtain by

putting the determinant $|R - \lambda I|$ equal to zero. These roots will be real and positive or zero, as R is a correlation matrix, and therefore symmetric and positive semi-definite.

Insert the appropriate λ_i in the system $(R - \lambda_i I)f_i = 0$ and solve for f_i. If f_i had not been normalized, you would have had an infinity of solutions, as the system is homogeneous. Fortunately, right from the start we imposed $f_i'f_i = 1$, or $\sum_j (f_{ij})^2 = 1$. The solution is therefore unique.

Compute the components $z_i = Xf_i$, if you wish to have time series of·principal components at your disposal. For example, you might want to relate these components to observed variables, as was done in Stone (1947). In many applications, as in the one below, it is not necessary to compute the z's, as all the relevant information can be found in F.

8.5.* Some empirical results

Table 8.1 reproduces[8] the correlations between the residuals obtained after fitting the dynamic quadratic model (equations (7.59) by ordinary least squares and iterating on λ to impose the budget constraint, as explained in Chapter VII. For data, we took the eleven U.S. commodity series of the *Survey of Current Business* over the period 1949–1969.

First of all, we notice that the correlations between commodities are not all negative, as would have been expected with an additive preference ordering. Almost half (23 out of 55) are positive.

The sign of the correlation between two commodities indicates whether these are (Hicksian) substitutes or complements. Cars (1) are complementary to gasoline, household operation and transportation, while furniture (2) is complementary to other non-durables and other durables (which include jewelry, watches, books, toys, etc.) as is clothing. Food (4) is negatively correlated with household operation and gasoline, which appears itself as a substitute for other services.

Our main interest goes to Table 8.2. There we find the 'specific' correlations obtained after subtracting the correlation due to the general substitution effect. As this amounts to adding a positive number to each total correlation coefficient, specific complementarity is increased. The basic relationships of Table 8.1 are maintained.

---

[8] Tables 8.1, 8.2 and 8.3 are taken from Phlips and Rouzier (1972), to which the reader is referred for further details.

TABLE 8.1

Matrix of 'total' correlations (R), eleven U.S. commodity series

	1	2	3	4	5	6	7	8	9	10
(1) Auto and parts	1.000									
(2) Furniture and equipment	-0.345	1.000								
(3) Other durables	-0.629	0.366	1.000							
(4) Food and beverages	-0.649	-0.287	0.252	1.000						
(5) Clothing and shoes	-0.475	0.305	0.805	-0.076	1.000					
(6) Gasoline and oil	0.451	-0.155	-0.034	-0.553	0.193	1.000				
(7) Other nondurables	-0.453	0.326	0.195	0.005	0.470	-0.029	1.000			
(8) Housing	-0.041	0.164	-0.010	-0.338	0.206	0.314	0.049	1.000		
(9) Household operation	0.365	0.149	-0.238	-0.564	-0.005	0.361	-0.086	0.060	1.000	
(10) Transportation	0.347	-0.439	-0.240	0.037	-0.354	0.069	-0.417	-0.206	-0.008	1.000
(11) Other services	-0.511	0.066	-0.070	0.500	-0.279	-0.688	-0.035	-0.147	-0.348	-0.177

TABLE 8.2

Matrix of 'specific' correlations

	1	2	3	4	5	6	7	8	9	10
(1) Auto and parts	1.000									
(2) Furniture and equipment	-0.018	1.000								
(3) Other durables	-0.500	0.434	1.000							
(4) Food and beverages	-0.266	-0.086	0.331	1.000						
(5) Clothing and shoes	-0.222	0.438	0.857	0.080	1.000					
(6) Gasoline and oil	0.519	-0.120	-0.020	-0.511	0.220	1.000				
(7) Other nondurables	-0.264	0.425	0.234	0.121	0.547	-0.009	1.000			
(8) Housing	0.046	0.209	0.008	-0.285	0.241	0.323	0.075	1.000		
(9) Household operation	0.462	0.200	-0.218	-0.504	0.034	0.372	-0.057	0.074	1.000	
(10) Transportation	0.436	-0.392	-0.222	0.092	-0.318	0.079	-0.390	-0.194	0.006	1.000
(11) Other services	-0.313	0.170	-0.029	0.622	-0.199	-0.667	0.025	-0.119	-0.317	-0.149

To get an idea of the grouping implied in these interrelations, we might rearrange Table 8.2, putting together the commodities with the highest correlations. A better picture is obtained by principal components analysis.

Table 8.3 reproduces the six first columns (f_1 to f_6) of the matrix F, which suffice to obtain a partitioning of all commodities. Together, the corresponding six latent roots account for 89.8 per cent of the total variance. (We thus cut off four columns of (very low) factor loadings, the last latent root being zero).

TABLE 8.3
Specific correlations: factor loadings (F)

	1	2	3	4	5	6
(1) Auto and parts	0.385	−0.316	0.278	*0.757*	0.106	−0.002
(2) Furniture and household equipment	*0.701*	0.410	−0.261	−0.172	0.214	0.265
(3) Other durables	−0.049	*0.991*	−0.068	−0.172	−0.034	0.012
(4) Food and beverages	−0.396	0.280	*−0.734*	0.232	−0.178	0.150
(5) Clothing and shoes	0.087	*0.862*	0.176	−0.090	0.143	0.372
(6) Gasoline and oil	0.065	0.069	*0.797*	0.323	0.282	0.102
(7) Other nondurables	0.043	0.207	−0.024	−0.198	0.009	*0.939*
(8) Housing	0.041	0.055	0.152	−0.070	*0.962*	0.019
(9) Household operation	*0.776*	−0.126	0.392	0.133	−0.066	−0.047
(10) Transportation	−0.199	−0.090	0.031	*0.789*	−0.182	−0.310
(11) Other services	0.002	−0.112	*−0.927*	−0.103	0.048	0.025

The grouping is very clear. The six groups include respectively: furniture and household equipment and household operation; clothing and other durables; food and beverages, gasoline and oil and other services; automobiles and parts and transportation; housing; other nondurables. These branches are not strongly separable. On the assumption that they are weakly separable, the demand for particular commodities in each of these branches may be written as a function of the prices in and the budget allotment to their branch, possibly with the help of nonadditive branch utility functions. It would be a promising research project to derive branch utility functions suitable for the derivation of 'branch' systems of demand equations allowing for substitutability and complementarity.

IX

Dynamic cost-of-living indices

9.1.* Introduction

In the static context of Chapter V, the true cost-of-living index could be unambiguously defined on account of the invariable nature of the indifference maps. With the introduction of dynamic preference orderings, we entered a situation of everchanging indifference maps. To define a dynamic true cost-of-living index, we must take account of the fact that the preference orderings of a consumer are different at each point in time, so that there is a close analogy with the spatial index discussed in the final section of Chapter V.

Before proceeding, we wish to recall what sort of taste changes we are considering. First of all, 'neutral' taste changes are excluded from the analysis. These are the changes in the efficiency of the consumer as a 'pleasure machine' we briefly referred to in exercise 7.1, and which seem to be totally unexplored up to now. Secondly, we exclude quality changes embodied in consumption goods, on which there is a rapidly growing literature.[1] We are thus left with the disembodied quantity augmenting or diminishing taste changes as specified in Chapter VII.

In a static context, the relevant indifference class is mostly chosen with reference to a price-income vector which is itself arbitrarily chosen. (For example, prices and income may be those prevailing during the base period or those prevailing during the period of comparison.) But the indifference class can also be made subject to the choice of a commodity vector, there being a one-to-one correspondence between the two vectors. In a dynamic world with continuous and systematic taste changes, on the contrary, the two vectors will not lead to the identifi-

---

[1] This literature is mainly concerned with quality changes in particular commodities. See Griliches (1971). Muellbauer (1975a) presents an extension to a group of commodities.

cation of the same indifference class other than in the reference period, as was pointed out by de Souza (1972).

Furthermore, the indifference class chosen is indicated by a corresponding utility level in a static model, while the utility function is time dependent in a dynamic model. A reference year is then needed to 'fix' the time dependent parameters of the dynamic utility function. This opens the way to using the utility level not only as an indicator representative of an indifference class but also as determining of itself a level of satisfaction in a cardinal sense. A correspondence has then to be established between indifference curves of one map at one moment of time and those of a map at another moment (i.e. after a change in tastes). And this correspondence has to be interpreted as representing equal welfare.

All in all, three reference points, the utility level, the price–income vector and the commodity vector, lead to three different kinds of dynamic cost-of-living indices. Moreover, as de Souza (1972) emphasizes, for each reference point we can define a 'simultaneous' index as well as a 'temporal' index. In the case of a simultaneous index, a simultaneous comparison of two price vectors is realized, employing only one preference map. It then appears as normal to consider as reference year, the moment at which the two price vectors are compared, so that the comparison is based on current tastes. In the case of a 'temporal' index, on the contrary, the fact that tastes have changed between the moments to which the two price vectors refer can be taken into account, with the result that a 'temporal' index can vary when tastes change even if prices happened to be constant.

These different possibilities (six in fact) are far from being all explored. In what follows, we concentrate on two lines of approach for which results are available. One is the index developed by Fisher and Shell (1969), which belongs to the class of 'simultaneous price-income' indices, the comparison being based on current tastes while the indifference class is chosen (in the current preference map) with reference to the base period price-income vector. The other index, called the 'cardinal' index, belongs to the class of 'temporal' indices. It takes the base year utility level as a reference point and determines the income that together with comparison period prices and tastes will allow the consumer to attain the base-year utility level.

9.2.* The Fisher-Shell index [2]

Fisher and Shell (F–S for short) formalize as follows the question which their true cost-of-living index is designed to answer. Given base period prices of goods p_1^0, p_2^0, ..., p_n^0, base period income y^0, current (comparison) prices of goods p_1^1, p_2^1, ..., p_n^1, the problem is to find that income y^{**} such that the representative consumer is *currently* indifferent between facing current prices with income y^{**} and facing base period prices with base period income. The true cost-of-living index is then (y^{**}/y^0).

F–S only determine the manner of choosing the comparison income. It is clear that the index is of a 'price–income' nature. Moreover, the reference triplet is (p^0, y^0, u^1): the authors exclude the right of recourse to past or future preference orderings.[3] Therefore, the index is of a simultaneous nature. F–S are not concerned with the derivation of base income (the denominator of the index) which is taken as base period income. The F–S index is therefore of the Laspeyres type.

F–S choose to derive the reference utility level in the commodity space. Let $(p_1^0, \ldots, p_n^0, y^0)$ be the base period (and reference) price-income vector and $(p_1^1, \ldots, p_n^1)$ the current (comparison period) price vector. The *current* utility function is written as

$$u(bx_1, x_2, \ldots, x_n) \tag{9.1}$$

where b is a taste change parameter interpreted as in (8.5). For concreteness, the taste change is affecting the first commodity only, and is either good augmenting or good diminishing. Maximize

$$L = u(bx_1, x_2, \ldots, x_n) - \lambda(\sum_i p_i^0 x_i - y^0) \tag{9.2}$$

with respect to the variables $(x_1, \ldots, x_n, \lambda)$. The solution $\hat{x}$, $\hat{\lambda}$ is found by solving the system of first order conditions

$$\sum_i p_i^0 x_i - y^0 = 0$$

$$b\frac{\partial u}{\partial(bx_1)} - \lambda p_1^0 = 0 \tag{9.3}$$

$$\frac{\partial u}{\partial x_i} - \lambda p_i^0 = 0 \quad \text{for} \quad i = 2, \ldots, n.$$

---

[2] This presentation and interpretation of the Fisher-Shell index is taken from de Souza (1972).

[3] As will be further explained and discussed in Section 9.3.

The reference utility level is given by $\hat{u} = u(b\hat{x}_1, \ldots, \hat{x}_n)$. $\hat{x}$ is the reference commodity vector, $\hat{x}_i$ being the amount of the ith good the consumer would have purchased if he had faced the base period constraints with current tastes.

To find the equivalent income y^{**}, F–S minimize the cost of attaining the indifference curve indicated by $\hat{u}$ under comparison period prices. Define

$$L' = \sum_i p_i^1 x_i - \lambda'(u(bx_1, \ldots, x_n) - \hat{u}). \tag{9.4}$$

Minimization of L' with respect to $(x_1, \ldots, x_n, \lambda')$ implies that

$$u - \hat{u} = 0$$

$$b\frac{\partial u}{\partial(bx_1)} - (1/\lambda')p_1 = 0 \tag{9.5}$$

$$\frac{\partial u}{\partial x_i} - (1/\lambda')p_i = 0 \quad \text{for} \quad i = 2, \ldots, n.$$

This system can be solved for the vector x^{**} and for $\lambda^{**} = (1/\lambda')$. The equivalent income is given by $\sum_i p_i^1 x_i^{**}$.

It should be noted that when b is equated to unity so that taste change is excluded, the F–S equivalent income reduces to the static index equivalent income. Therefore, in order to analyse the relation between the two, it seems only natural to examine the derivative $(\partial y^{**}/\partial b)$.

Suppose that the taste change parameter were to vary without p^0, p^1 or y^0 changing. Our results would be affected at each of the two steps:

(i) the level of reference utility would change

(a) on account of the direct variation of the parameter, b, which intervenes as such in the utility function;

(b) on account of the variation of the reference commodity vector, $\hat{x}$;

(ii) the equivalent income would change even if the reference utility level were to remain constant on account of the influence of b on the constant utility demand functions, x_i^{**}.

In formula

$$\frac{\partial y^{**}}{\partial b} = \left(\frac{\partial y^{**}}{\partial b}\right)_{u = \hat{u} \text{ constant}} + \left(\frac{\partial y^{**}}{\partial \hat{u}}\right)\left(\frac{\partial \hat{u}}{\partial b}\right) + \frac{\partial y^{**}}{\partial \hat{u}}\left(\frac{\partial \hat{u}}{\partial \hat{x}}\right)'\left(\frac{\partial \hat{x}}{\partial b}\right) \tag{9.6}$$

where

$$\left(\frac{\partial y^{**}}{\partial \hat{u}}\right)\left(\frac{\partial \hat{u}}{\partial b}\right)$$

is impact (a) on the reference utility level,

$$\frac{\partial y^{**}}{\partial \hat{u}}\left(\frac{\partial \hat{u}}{\partial \hat{x}}\right)'\left(\frac{\partial \hat{x}}{\partial b}\right)$$

is impact (b), and

$$\left(\frac{\partial y^{**}}{\partial b}\right)_{u=\hat{u}\text{ constant}}$$

is the direct influence on the equivalent income.

The elaboration of each of the derivatives intervening in the equation is the subject of 3 lemmas which are given in the following exercise.

EXERCISE

9.1. Show that:

$$\left(\frac{\partial y^{**}}{\partial b}\right)_{u=\hat{u}\text{ constant}} = -\frac{p_1^1 x_1^{**}}{b} \qquad \text{(Lemma 1)}$$

$$\left(\frac{\partial \hat{u}}{\partial \hat{x}}\right)'\left(\frac{\partial \hat{x}}{\partial b}\right) = \sum_i \frac{\partial \hat{u}}{\partial \hat{x}_i}\frac{\partial \hat{x}_i}{\partial b} = 0 \qquad \text{(Lemma 2)}$$

$$\frac{\partial y^{**}}{\partial \hat{u}} = \frac{1}{\lambda^{**}}. \qquad \text{(Lemma 3)}$$

Hint: see Fisher and Shell (1969).

The difference between the F–S index and the static index is of course equal to

$$\frac{(\partial y^{**}/\partial b)\mathrm{d}b}{y^0}. \qquad (9.7)$$

9.3.* The cardinal index

F–S argue that their approach is the only correct one in a dynamic framework. In saying this, they probably do not want to exclude the (totally unexplored) possibility of using a quantity vector as a reference instead of a price-income vector. What they do want to exclude is the possibility of using the base year utility level as the reference utility level, as would seem natural when the true index is meant to leave the consumer as well off today as he was in the base year.

The following quotation from F–S (1969, p. 98–99) is revealing:

As indicated, a frequently encountered view of the true cost-of-living index is that it is designed to answer the question: 'What income would be required to make a consumer faced with today's prices just as well off as he was yesterday when he faced yesterday's income and yesterday's prices?' The difficulty that is presented by taste changes for the answer to this question is immediately apparent. What is meant by 'just as well off as he was yesterday' if the indifference map has shifted?

Yet reflection on this issue shows that the same difficulty appears even if tastes do not change. While it is apparently natural to say that a man whose tastes have remained constant is just as well off today as he was yesterday if he is on the same indifference curve in both periods, the appeal of that proposition is no more than apparent. In both periods, the man's utility function is determined only up to a monotonic transformation; how can we possibly know whether the level of true utility (whatever that may mean) corresponding to a given indifference curve is the same in both periods? The man's efficiency as a pleasure-machine may have changed without changing his tastes.

Indeed, we have no more justification for saying that a man on the same indifference curve at two different times is equally well off at both than we do for saying that two men who happen to have the same indifference map are equally well off if they have the same possessions. Both statements are attractive for reasons of simplicity and both are completely without any operational content whatsoever. One never steps into the same river twice and the comparison between a man's utility now and his utility yesterday stands on precisely the same lack of footing as the comparison of the utilities of two different men.

Thus, a consideration of the problem of taste change in this interpretation of the theory of the true cost-of-living index merely makes explicit a problem that is apparently there all the time. If that theory were really founded upon intertemporal comparisons of utility of the type described, then theory would be without foundation.

My feeling is that F–S push ordinalist purity too far. To put it bluntly, their argument is that a consumer can never compare his utility level between two points in time, even if his indifference map has not shifted, because his 'efficiency as a pleasure machine' may have changed. Even the static true index should thus be redefined as establishing indifference between yesterday's budget constraint and today's constraint defined in terms of today's prices and y^{**}.

In the absence of any information on possible changes in my 'efficiency as a pleasure-machine', I prefer to exclude this sort of change. As emphasized earlier[4], this amounts to excluding the right of recourse to

---

[4] See exercise 7.1.

time dependent monotonic transformations of the utility function, i.e. to exclude neutral taste changes from the analysis. Otherwise, it would be impossible to construct 'temporal' price indices.

Indeed, if one were to adopt the F–S point of view, all true indices would have to be 'simultaneous', in the sense of being based on one single preference map (the current one). In particular, these indices would remain unchanged whenever prices remain unchanged.[5] This means that they would cease to be dynamic in the full sense of the word. It seems worthwhile to try to construct truly dynamic indices, such that they are affected by taste change even if all prices remain constant. As we shall see, however, such indices may not be invariant under monotonic transformations of the utility function that are time dependent.

In such a 'cardinal' approach, one would typically take the utility level u^0, determined by inserting base period prices and income in the indirect utility function, as the reference utility level, equate u^0 and u^1, where u^1 is the current indirect utility function with current prices and y^{**} as arguments, and solve for y^{**}.

In the F–S terminology, this amounts to supposing that in the calculation of the reference utility level the parameter b is assigned its base period value and that in the calculation of y^{**} it assume its comparison period value. The value of b in the base period is unity and serves as reference for the static index also. Hence, the difference between the 'cardinal' equivalent income and the static equivalent income lies not in the calculation of the reference utility level, but only in the calculation of y^{**}. Therefore, the difference between the cardinal and the static index is simply

$$\frac{[(\partial y^{**}/\partial b)_{u=\hat{u}\text{ constant}}]db}{y^0}. \tag{9.8}$$

Equation (9.7) defines the difference between the F–S and the static index. Subtracting (9.8) from (9.7), using (9.6), we find the difference between the F–S and the cardinal index to be

$$\left(\frac{\partial y^{**}}{\partial \hat{u}}\frac{\partial \hat{u}}{\partial b}db\right)/y^0. \tag{9.9}$$

---

[5] F–S prove that $\partial y^{**}/\partial b = 0$ if $p^1 = p^0$ in their corollary 3.1.

9.4.* A dynamic specification[6]

To obtain computable results we have to work with a specified utility function. The dynamic Stone-Geary function

$$u = \sum_i \beta_i \log (x_i - \theta_i - \alpha_i s_i), \qquad (9.10)$$

which is at the heart of our dynamic linear expenditure system, is obviously a good candidate to start with. In this specification, taste changes are incorporated in the utility function through the alleged influence of past purchases as measured by $\alpha_i s_i$. These taste changes are due to habit formation or to stock effects (or both), and are thus of the 'built-in' type. This class of taste changes was not considered explicitly by F–S, who give examples referring to cases where the consumer is learning about the usefulness (a) of a durable good which he has not yet purchased (an electric appliance, say) or (b) of a nondurable good which he has already consumed (he learns how to use fuel more efficiently or discovers that a particular food is dangerous to his health). According to the F–S examples, a taste change results from outside information due to external influences on a consumer. He may talk to his neighbours, be influenced by a demonstration effect or impressed by advertising. Our specification highlights the impact of past decisions, but is of course compatible with the F–S emphasis on extraneous information which may affect (or even create) the formation of habits or the building-up of stocks.

In case of habit formation, $\alpha_i > 0$ and the taste change is *quantity diminishing*. More of x_i is needed in the current year to get the same satisfaction as last year: to obtain the satisfaction derived from smoking 10 cigarettes a day last year, the consumer who develops smoking habits now needs 20 cigarettes a day.

Remember that $\alpha_i > 0$ implies that γ_i increases with s_i: cigarettes become more 'necessary' or 'basic', given the interpretation of γ_i as the minimum required quantity. Simultaneously the marginal utility $\beta_i/(x_i - \theta_i - \alpha_i s_i)$ increases with s_i, so that good i becomes more desirable, although the taste change is quantity diminishing. This is an interesting case, not considered by F–S, in which a quantity diminishing taste change implies an increase in 'desirability'.

---

[6] This and the following sections are taken from Phlips and Sanz-Ferrer (1972).

If good i is a durable (and in the absence of habit formation), $\alpha_i < 0$ and the taste change is *quantity augmenting*. Less of x_i is needed now to get the same satisfaction as yesterday. To the extent that your library is well furnished, additional books appear to you as luxuries (ignoring the replacement of books that become outdated or were not returned to you by their borrower). Here, a quantity augmenting change is coupled with a reduction in γ_i and a concomitant decrease in marginal utility.

Figure 9.1 describes a case of quantity augmenting taste change, typical for durable goods, affecting goods 1 and 2. The dotted curve describes the indifference map in the base year t_0, while the dotted line (AK) represents the base year constraints. P is the equilibrium point in t_0.

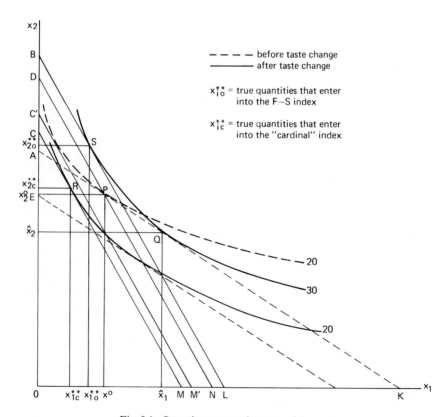

Fig. 9.1. Quantity augmenting taste change.

In t_1, there is a taste change (leading to a new indifference map) *and* a change in prices, reflected in the slope of a new budget line. The position of this line, determined by total expenditures in t_1 is of no interest here. Following F–S, we want to know the position which this line takes if the consumer is to be indifferent, *given his tastes in* t_1, between the old budget constraint (line) *AK* and this new line.

In t_1, the old budget line (*AK*) determines the equilibrium point *Q*, to which correspond the quantities $\hat{x}_1$ and $\hat{x}_2$, i.e. the quantities the consumer would choose if, given his *current* tastes, he were confronted with last year's constraints. The consumer is indifferent between *AK* and the new line *BL*, as the latter is tangent to the indifference curve on which he found *Q*. We assume that p_2, the price of good 2 in period t_1, is equal to one. The income y^{**} that appears in the F–S true index (y^{**}/y^0) is equal to *OB*, while the numerator of the static true index is *OC′*.

Following F–S, we now want to decompose *C′B*, which corresponds to $\partial y^{**}/\partial b$, and to find a discrete counterpart for $(\partial y^{**}/\partial b)_{u = \hat{u} \text{constant}}$. What is $\hat{u}$ constant? This must be the utility obtained with the old budget constraint, before the taste change, say 20. A parallel displacement of *BL* gives a tangency point *R* on the new indifference curve to which the number 20 is associated. The discrete counterpart we are looking for is *C′C*, which is a negative number.

Suppose now we were to take the cardinal view that, what is to be compared, is utility in time zero and utility in t_1. We would then define the numerator of the true index as measuring the income in today's prices that would make the consumer just as well off as he was yesterday. Looking at Figure 9.1, that income is *OC*. The difference with the static index is *C′C*, which we identified as measuring $(\partial y^{**}/\partial b)_{u = \hat{u} \text{constant}}$.

The other component of $\partial y^{**}/\partial b$ is

$$\frac{\partial y^{**}}{\partial \hat{u}} \frac{\partial \hat{u}}{\partial b} + \frac{\partial y}{\partial \hat{u}} \left(\frac{\partial \hat{u}}{\partial \hat{x}}\right)' \left(\frac{\partial \hat{x}}{\partial b}\right).$$

This is of course equal to *CB*, which is the difference between the F–S and the cardinal index. We conclude that a given quantity augmenting taste change leads to a cardinal index that is below the static index and to a F–S index that is above the cardinal index.

EXERCISES

9.2. Construct a diagram for the case of a quantity diminishing taste change (typical for habit formation) using the same symbols, so that all curves, lines and points have the same interpretation as in Figure 9.1.

9.3. Use the diagram just constructed to show that the cardinal approach leads to the conclusion that (a) the cost of living is higher than indicated by the static index, (b) the F–S index is now below the cardinal index.

9.5.* A computational algorithm

In this section, we will first derive an algorithm for the computation of the change in y^{**} with $u = \hat{u}$ constant, using our dynamic specification (9.10). As was mentioned at the end of the preceding section, the assumption $\hat{u}$ constant allows us to take the traditional 'cardinal' viewpoint, i.e. to start from $\Delta u = 0$. Next, we will derive an algorithm for the computation of the 'ordinal' F–S index, measuring the total impact of taste changes when y^{**} is evaluated in current tastes.

With a dynamic utility function, the computations are somewhat more complicated than in the static case. One has to fall back on the first order conditions, because of the nonlinearity of the demand equations. Indeed, in the estimation of the model obtained by maximizing (9.10), the n conditions $\partial u/\partial x_i = \lambda p_i$ (where λ is the Lagrangian multiplier) were used as estimating[7] equations (after suitable transformations to take account of the side conditions $\dot{s}_i = x_i - \delta_i s_i$ and to eliminate the unobservable state variables s_i).

Given this estimation procedure, we derive the 'cardinal' true index corresponding to the generalized Stone-Geary function as follows. The conditions $\partial u/\partial x_i = \lambda p_i$ can be written as

$$\alpha_i s_i = -\theta_i + x_i - \frac{\beta_i}{\lambda p_i}. \tag{9.11}$$

Insert (9.11) in (9.10) to obtain the indirect utility functions

$$u^1 = \sum_i \beta_i \log\left(\frac{\beta_i}{\lambda^{**} p_i^1}\right)$$

---

[7] See equations (7.51).

and

$$u^0 = \sum_i \beta_i \log\left(\frac{\beta_i}{\lambda^0 p_i^0}\right).$$

Putting $\Delta u = u^1 - u^0 = 0$ leads to

$$\sum_i \beta_i \log \lambda^{**} p_i^1 = \sum_i \beta_i \log \lambda^0 p_i^0$$

or

$$(\sum_i \beta_i) \log \lambda^{**} - (\sum_i \beta_i) \log \lambda^0 = \sum_i \beta_i \log\left(\frac{p_i^0}{p_i^1}\right).$$

Taking antilogs:

$$\lambda^{**} = \lambda^0 \prod_i \left(\frac{p_i^0}{p_i^1}\right)^{\beta_i/\Sigma \beta_i} \tag{9.12}$$

From λ_t^{**} compute x_{it}^{**}, using (7.51), as

$$x_{it}^{**} = K_{i0} + K_{i1} x_{it-1} + K_{i2} \frac{1}{\lambda_t^{**} p_{it}} + K_{i3} \frac{1}{\lambda_{t-1} p_{it-1}} \tag{9.13}$$

where x_{it-1}, p_{it} and p_{it-1} are observed and K_{i0} to K_{i3} and λ_{t-1} are the known estimates obtained in the estimation of the model.
Finally, compute y_t^{**} as

$$y_t^{**} = \sum_i p_{it} x_{it}^{**}. \tag{9.14}$$

Going back to the diagram in Figure 9.1, we note that the quantities x_i^{**} correspond to point R. On the other hand, λ^{**} is such that $\lambda^{**} = \lambda^0$ when the prices do not change. However, on the same assumption of constant prices, $y^{**} \neq y^0$ (i.e. $OE \neq OA$) because of the taste change, which is reflected in (9.13) in the variables x_{it-1} and λ_{t-1}, both functions of the state variables (which determine the change in tastes).
The cardinal true index is $I = y^{**}/y^0$.

EXERCISES
9.4. Show that the cardinal true index I is invariant under monotonic increasing transformations of the utility function that are not time dependent.

9.5. Show that I is not invariant under time dependent transformations. Consider the case of 'neutral' taste change where

$$v = \sum_i \beta_i \log \gamma_{it}(x_{it} - \gamma_{it})$$

9.6. Compute the true long-run index I^* (on the assumption that $\dot{s}_i = 0$ for all i) using our dynamic linear expenditure system. Compare with the static true index obtained in Chapter V.

We now turn to the computation of the ordinal F–S true index corresponding to the same generalized Geary function (specified in equation 9.10)). Now u^0 drops out of the picture. We are left with $u^1 = \sum_i \beta_i \log (x_i^1 - \theta_i - \alpha_i s_i^1)$ only. This function is to be maximized, first under the old constraint, then with respect to the new prices and the income that would leave the consumer indifferent between the old constraint and the new one, defined in terms of current prices and that income. This income, and the Lagrangian multiplier that is associated with it, will be designated again by y^{**} and λ^{**} to simplify the notation.

Given the old constraint (and current tastes), the first order conditions are:

$$\alpha_i s_i^1 = -\theta_i + \hat{x}_i - \frac{\beta_i}{\hat{\lambda} p_i^0}.$$

These are to be inserted in $\hat{u} = \sum_i \beta_i \log (\hat{x}_i - \theta_i - \alpha_i s_i^1)$. The resulting indirect utility function is

$$\hat{u} = \sum_i \beta_i \log\left(\frac{\beta_i}{\hat{\lambda} p_i^0}\right)$$

while

$$u^1 = \sum_i \beta_i \log\left(\frac{\beta_i}{\lambda^{**} p_i^1}\right).$$

The ordinal F–S true index is such that $u^1 = \hat{u}$, or

$$\left(\sum_i \beta_i\right) \log \lambda^{**} - \left(\sum_i \beta_i\right) \log \hat{\lambda} = \sum_i \beta_i \log\left(\frac{p_i^0}{p_i^1}\right)$$

or

$$\lambda^{**} = \hat{\lambda} \prod_i \left(\frac{p_i^0}{p_i^1}\right)^{\beta_i/\Sigma\beta_i} \tag{9.15}$$

As before, $y_t^{**} = \sum_i p_{it} x_{it}^{**}$.

EXERCISE

9.7. Is the F–S index invariant under time dependent transformations?

From the computational viewpoint, the only difference between the ordinal and the cardinal index stems from the fact that λ^{**} is proportional to the *current* $\hat{\lambda}$ in the former, while λ^{**} is proportional to the base year λ^0 in the latter. The higher the rise in prices, the higher is y^{**} (in both cases) and the smaller is λ^{**}. The weights $\beta_i/\sum_i \beta_i$ in the proportionality factor are the marginal propensities to consume.

But what is $\hat{\lambda}$? Recall that it is the Lagrangian multiplier associated with point Q in Figure 9.1. How to compute $\hat{\lambda}$? Remember that $\hat{x}_{it}$ represents the quantities the consumer would purchase if, with his current tastes, he were confronted with the base year budget constraint. Therefore, $\hat{x}_{it}$ must obey

$$\hat{x}_{it} = K_{i0} + K_{i1}x_{it-1} + K_{i2}\frac{1}{\hat{\lambda}_t p_i^0} + K_{i3}\frac{1}{\lambda_{t-1}p_{it-1}}$$

where the K's are the known estimated regression coefficients, once again, λ_{t-1} is estimated through the iteration procedure described above, x_{it-1}, p_{it-1} and p_i^0 are observed and λ_t has to satisfy $\sum_i p_i^0 x_{it} = y^0$. Substituting,

$$y^0 = \sum_i p_i^0 \left[K_{i0} + K_{i1}x_{it-1} + K_{i2}\frac{1}{\hat{\lambda}_t p_i^0} + K_{i3}\frac{1}{\lambda_{t-1}p_{it-1}} \right]$$

and

$$\hat{\lambda}_t = \frac{\sum_i K_{i2}}{y^0 - \sum_i p_i^0 K_{i0} - \sum_i p_i^0 K_{i1}x_{it-1} - \sum_i K_{i3}\frac{p_i^0}{\lambda_{t-1}p_{it-1}}}. \tag{9.16}$$

It remains to check whether this algorithm guarantees that the F–S true index does not change when prices remain constant, i.e. whether

$y_t^{**} = y^0$ when all $p_i^1 = p_{it}$ are equal to p_i^0. It is easy to see that this is indeed the case:

$$y_t^{**} = \sum_i p_{it} \left[K_{i0} + K_{i1}x_{it-1} + K_{i2}\frac{1}{\lambda_t^{**}p_{it}} + K_{i3}\frac{1}{\lambda_{t-1}p_{it-1}} \right]$$

$$= \sum_i p_i^0 \left[K_{i0} + K_{i1}x_{it-1} + K_{i2}\frac{1}{\hat{\lambda}_t p_i^0} + K_{i3}\frac{1}{\hat{\lambda}_{t-1}p_i^0} \right]$$

$$= y^0$$

when $p_{it} = p_{it-1} = p_i^0$ for all i and $\lambda_t^{**} = \hat{\lambda}_t$.

Summing up: to compute our 'cardinal' true index (I), insert (9.12) in (9.13) and (9.13) in (9.14); to compute the F–S index (I_{FS}), substitute (9.16) in (9.15), (9.15) in (9.13) and (9.13) in (9.14). The following data are needed:

(1) observations on x_{it} and p_{it}
(2) estimates of λ_t
(3) estimates of K_{i0}, K_{i1}, K_{i2} and K_{i3}
(4) estimates of β_i.

9.6.* Comparing different indices

In static theory, the Laspeyres index is an upper bound for the true index, and biased upwards whenever all prices do not change proportionally. In dynamic theory (with taste change) as F–S emphasize in (1969, p. 102):

a Laspeyres index loses much of its meaning. That index is a relevant upper bound for a true cost-of-living index with base year tastes; it need not be such a bound for a true cost-of-living index with current tastes. A Paasche index, on the other hand, retains its property of being a lower bound on the current-tastes index (but may lose it for the base-year-taste index). When tastes change, a Laspeyres and Paasche index cease to become approximations to the same thing and become approximations to different things. As we have just seen, it is the Paasche index which approximates the relevant magnitude; the Laspeyres index becomes less relevant.

The above quotation can be illustrated fairly easily in the framework of the present model.

Our comparisons are based on estimates obtained from the eleven U.S. consumption series published in the *Survey of Current Business* for the period 1929–1970. These estimates are taken from Table 7.1 and from the column (λ_t) in Table 7.3.

TABLE 9.1
Indices (1958 = 100), U.S.A., 1929–1970

Year	L	I	I_{FS}	I^*	L^*	P
1929	—	—	—	59.6747	60.3891	—
1930	55.4436	47.2636	52.4668	57.5066	58.3842	53.6351
1931	49.7256	42.8888	47.1595	51.6639	52.8169	47.8772
1932	44.2552	38.2679	41.8650	45.8940	47.1367	42.1266
1933	42.0825	36.5172	40.0065	43.6253	44.1895	40.4109
1934	44.6342	39.0523	42.9152	45.8244	46.0172	43.3796
1935	45.5020	39.4833	43.4008	46.6948	46.8415	44.3583
1936	46.0032	39.7416	43.6990	47.2139	47.4389	44.6730
1937	47.6943	41.3041	45.3164	48.9481	49.2245	46.3565
1938	46.9538	40.9944	44.8766	48.3569	48.7665	45.5584
1939	46.5002	40.8730	44.4021	47.9115	48.3606	45.0136
1940	46.8719	41.4800	44.9070	48.2921	48.7026	45.4529
1941	49.8681	44.6882	48.2852	51.2423	51.4750	48.6527
1942	55.3071	50.0276	53.8656	56.4478	56.4671	54.6257
1943	60.0793	56.0415	59.1137	60.8993	60.7732	59.8541
1944	63.4086	60.7024	62.8909	63.8630	63.7585	63.0655
1945	65.7159	64.3357	65.5162	65.9465	65.8571	65.2380
1946	70.2443	70.3958	70.4926	69.9360	69.9937	70.3241
1947	77.3855	78.3635	77.7371	76.3248	76.5564	77.7663
1948	81.9205	82.9165	82.3059	80.8298	81.0452	82.2869
1949	81.5505	82.4708	81.9542	80.9126	80.9918	81.7092
1950	82.7322	82.8925	82.9859	82.3038	82.3263	82.8387
1951	88.3462	87.7162	88.7175	87.5523	87.6389	88.5247
1952	90.3268	89.7360	90.6800	89.8067	89.8312	90.4884
1953	91.6697	91.1269	91.5883	91.5467	91.5354	91.7310
1954	92.5193	91.5242	92.1188	92.6418	92.6348	92.5083
1955	92.8916	92.0547	92.4301	93.1033	93.1147	92.8059
1956	94.8123	93.6645	94.5640	94.9605	94.9735	94.7941
1957	97.6831	97.2802	97.6193	97.7104	97.7172	97.6864
1958	100.0000	100.0000	100.0000	100.0000	100.0000	100.0000
1959	101.2546	102.5812	101.3270	101.2931	101.2953	101.2700
1960	102.8448	104.6211	102.7324	102.9099	102.9093	102.8387
1961	103.9024	106.3118	103.7890	103.9997	103.9950	103.9279
1962	104.9099	108.5481	104.8529	105.0613	105.0517	104.9213
1963	106.1497	110.4929	106.1301	106.3161	106.2886	106.1231
1964	107.4460	112.4730	107.5225	107.6130	107.5549	107.3570
1965	109.1020	115.1671	109.2748	109.2519	109.1809	108.8120
1966	112.0986	118.9164	112.4101	112.1171	112.0160	111.4871
1967	114.8304	123.3706	115.4956	114.8213	114.6629	114.3176
1968	119.0806	129.9073	120.1078	118.9594	118.7154	118.4991
1969	124.3111	136.8501	125.7294	124.1123	123.7688	123.5128
1970	130.2492	144.8532	132.2071	129.9862	129.5674	129.3993

L = Laspeyres index, using the (short-run) estimates of x_i^0.
I = Cardinal true index.
I_{FS} = Fisher-Shell true index.
I^* = Long-run true index (see exercise 9.6).
L^* = Laspeyres index, using the parameters of the long-run model (see exercise 9.8).
P = Paasche index, using the (short-run) estimates of x_i^1.

All indices mentioned in the text and in the exercises were computed and put together in Table 9.1. The reader will be easily convinced that the Laspeyres index L is not an upper bound to I (the 'cardinal' true index) or I_{FS} (the F–S true index) any longer. But the Paasche index P still approximates I_{FS}.

EXERCISE

9.8. Show that the Laspeyres index remains an upper bound to the long-run dynamic true index I^* derived in exercise 9.6.

Answer:

$$L^* = \frac{\sum p_i^1 \gamma_i^*}{y^0} + \left(1 - \frac{\sum p_i^0 \gamma_i^*}{y^0}\right) \sum_i \left(\frac{p_i^1 \beta_i^*}{p_i^0}\right)$$

while

$$I^* = \frac{\sum p_i^1 \gamma_i^*}{y^0} + \left(1 - \frac{\sum p_i^0 \gamma_i^*}{y^0}\right) \prod_i \left(\frac{p_i^1}{p_i^0}\right)^{\beta_i^*}$$

On the other hand, I lies well above I_{FS}, because of the predominance of quantity diminishing taste changes (most α_i are positive). From a practical point of view, it is very important therefore to know whether one should define dynamic indices in current tastes or in base year tastes. The final section is devoted to this question.

9.7.* Final remarks

Suppose now that wages and salaries follow an official index corrected to take account of the F–S recommendations. Then durable goods will get higher weights in the index and those consumers who accumulate durables will push the index upwards, while reaching higher and higher levels of 'satisfaction'. On the contrary, those who develop (good or bad) habits push the index downwards, while getting less and less satisfaction. This is not a satisfactory state of affairs.

Why not admit that utility in some base year remains the yardstick, and correct the official index to approximate as closely as possible our cardinal index? In other words, why not keep everybody on some pre-assigned utility level? This is, indeed, necessary if we want to let the consumer free to displace his indifference map in the direction he prefers. The concept of consumer sovereignty should apply not only to his current preference ordering but also to the changes in what *he* considers as his basic needs.

A practical suggestion in this direction would be to recommend adapting the weights in the cost-of-living index using our estimates of α_i. It may be argued, indeed, that these estimates indicate the direction of the taste changes as they measure the net combined effect of habit formation and inventory adjustment.

Needless to say, the approach developed above is limited by the assumption of independent utilities. It should be made more flexible, and applicable to more disaggregated commodity groups, on the basis of a utility-tree maximization hypothesis allowing for interdependent utilities within separable branches of the utility function. Substitution and complementarity could then be explored. But that is another problem.

X

The demand for leisure and money

10.1. * Introduction[1]

A long tradition in microeconomic theory analyses the demand for leisure (and the related supply of labour) by considering leisure time as one of the arguments of the consumer's utility function. Another venerable tradition, in monetary theory, associated with the name of Patinkin, recognizes that money, or at least cash holdings for transactions purposes, may be treated as another argument of the same utility function. Nevertheless the two approaches were developed along separate lines, possibly because of a specialization of research interests. Efforts to bring these different strands together were reported only recently, as far as we know: Dutton and Gramm (1973), for example, argue that the demand for money is a function of the wage rate, i.e. the market price for leisure time, because the use of money saves time, while Barzel and McDonald (1973) insist on the fact that the supply of labour is a function of wealth, of which money is the most common element.

In this chapter, the demand for leisure and the transactions demand for money are imbedded in a demand system derived from a specified utility function. It is hoped that the theory of consumer demand will thus be fully integrated with both the utility approach to the demand for money and the traditional analysis of the supply of labour. Before entering into a detailed exposition of the model, it may be of some interest to discuss the specific reasons for building a system of equations and for choosing a particular specification.

To construct a demand system amounts to putting on a straitjacket voluntarily. All restrictions resulting from utility maximization (except the nega-

---

[1] Sections 10.1 to 10.5 are based on Phlips (1978a).

tivity of the own substitution effects) are imposed on the data, together with any additional restriction implied in the assumptions made about the preference ordering. This makes a rejection of the model by the data more likely: if it does fit the data, then our confidence in the results should be increased. Furthermore, the use of the information (i.e. the restrictions) given by economic theory implies a gain in efficiency as an additional bonus, in comparison with an ad hoc equation-by-equation approach.[2]

The inclusion of money and leisure leads to an augmented budget constraint, according to which it is 'full income', to use a concept coined by Becker (1963), that has to be allocated. Full income includes, besides total consumption expenditures, the income lost by keeping some cash liquid for transactions purposes (rather than investing it) and by enjoying hours of leisure (instead of working day and night). The prices of leisure and of the use of money appear in each equation, but with cross substitution effects constrained to be symmetric. And all equations are homogeneous of degree zero in full income and prices (including the 'price of money' and the wage rate).

Demand theory thus provides useful a priori information. But it does so at a cost which may be high. For one thing, all equations have to have the same functional form. With respect to the demand for leisure, for example, this means that we cannot take special features into account, such as the impact of the unemployment rate (analyzed by Owen, 1969), the simultaneity bias (Hall, 1973), the selectivity bias due to the fact that data on wages are available only for those who effectively participate in the labour force (Heckman, 1974b), discontinuities at the point of entry into the market, and the specific properties of the supply of labour in terms of weeks and in terms of hours worked, as in work by Hanoch (1975a and b).

The specification of the demand system presented below is an extension of the dynamic version of the linear expenditure system constructed in Chapter VII. This system has the advantage of introducing minimum required quantities for each consumption good, for leisure and for money. The underlying assumption of additive preferences implies that neither cash holdings nor leisure time are supposed to affect the marginal utility of any particular consumption good, and that the time saved through increased transaction balances is not necessarily leisure time, because there are no special links

---

[2] The improvement in the precision of the parameter estimates has been verified by Ashenfelter and Heckman (1974) for a model of family labour supply. This led to the construction of a complete system of demand equations, including leisure, by Abbott and Ashenfelter (1974).

between leisure and money in the preference ordering. This additivity assumption is obviously too strong for a detailed breakdown of consumption, but may be acceptable as a first approximation for large commodity groups such as those considered here.

The Stone–Geary utility function is dynamized by the introduction of state variables as parameters. This is thought to have many advantages, in particular when leisure and money are brought into the picture. Indeed, it makes it possible to distinguish between short-run and long-run behaviour, which in turn allows for a reversal of the signs of the elasticities. For example, the labour supply curve may appear as backward bending in the short run and as positively sloped in the long run. On the other hand, the use of state variables such as stocks of durables *and* the stock of wealth makes it possible to insert money as an argument in the utility function without explicitly introducing prices in it. The Slutsky equation will thus remain valid, even for the money equation, without further breakdowns (in contradiction with the complications arising in what has become the traditional approach in monetary theory[3]). Furthermore, real balance effects will be present, simply through the working of the system, thanks to the presence of a wealth constraint. Finally, the use of a dynamized utility function gives a theoretical foundation to the resulting lag structure of the estimating equations.

It is realized that a fully satisfactory treatment of durables, money and wealth would require an intertemporal approach such as the one developed in Chapter XI rather than the myopic instantaneous maximization behaviour assumed here[4]. The same is true for leisure, as was emphasized by Lewis (1975) and Stephan (1975). The empirical implementation of a dynamic intertemporal system, taking advantage of the state variable approach, has to wait until the myopic exercise presented here has been carried out. In this sense, some of the empirical results reported here are an approximation to those presented in Chapter XI.

10.2.* A demand system including leisure and money

Let the consumer's preference ordering be represented by an extended Stone–Geary utility function

---

[3] See Lloyd (1964 and 1971), Dusansky and Kalman (1972 and 1974), and Berglas and Razin (1974).

[4] See also Diewert (1974b). Blinder (1974, Chapter 3) and Heckman (1974a) analyse the labour–leisure choices over a life-time. Phlips (1976) gives an intertemporal treatment of the demand for money.

$$u = \sum_i \beta_i \log(x_i - \gamma_i) + \beta_1 \log(l - \gamma_1) + \beta_m \log(m - \gamma_m), \qquad (10.1)$$

in which $x_i = x_i(t)$ represents purchases of consumption good i $(i = 1, \ldots, n)$, $l = l(t)$ represents hours of leisure time and $m = m(t)$ is the stock of money in real terms held for transactions purposes. Nominal cash balances are defined as $M(t) = p_m(t)m(t)$, where p_m is the 'price of money compared to the prices of other things' as in Samuelson (1947, p. 120). $\gamma_i = \gamma_i(t)$, $\gamma_1 = \gamma_1(t)$ and $\gamma_m = \gamma_m(t)$ are the 'minimum required quantities', defined as linear functions of the state variables s_i, s_1 and w respectively:

$$\gamma_i = \theta_i + \alpha_i s_i, \qquad (i = 1, \ldots, n),$$

$$\gamma_1 = \theta_1 + \alpha_1 s_1,$$

$$\gamma_m = \theta_m + \alpha_m w. \qquad (10.2)$$

The state variables $s_i = s_i(t)$ are physical stocks of durables or stocks of habits, while $s_1 = s_1(t)$ is the stock of habits with respect to leisure and $w = w(t)$ is non-human wealth in real terms. Nominal non-human wealth is defined as $W(t) = p_m(t)w(t)$. The state variables s_i, s_1 and w are defined respectively as the solution of the following differential equations which constrain their time paths:

$$ds_i/dt = x_i - \delta_i s_i, \qquad (10.3)$$

$$ds_1/dt = l - \delta_1 s_1, \qquad (10.4)$$

$$dW/dt = r(W - M) + p_1(T - l) - \sum_i p_i x_i. \qquad (10.5)$$

The coefficient δ appearing in (10.3) and (10.4) is the rate at which durables depreciate (radioactive decay) or the rate at which habits disappear. The wealth equation (10.5) defines nominal savings (dW/dt) as the sum of non-labour income $r(W - M)$ – where $r = r(t)$ represents 'the' (nominal) rate of interest – and labour income $p_1(T - l)$ minus total expenditures. The constant T is the maximum amount of time available and $p_1 = p_1(t)$ is the (nominal) wage rate. Equation (10.5) can be rewritten as

$$dW/dt = (p_1 T - y) + rW, \qquad (10.6)$$

where

$$y = \sum_i p_i x_i + p_1 l + r p_m m. \qquad (10.7)$$

Capital gains (or losses) are ignored.

Equation (10.7) defines the budget constraint subject to which the consumer is supposed to maximize (10.1) instantaneously, while (10.3) to (10.5) define the time paths of the state variables. The prices p_i, p_1, p_m and r are given, as well as T and '*full income*' y. In static theory, full income is defined as non-labour income plus maximum labour income, i.e. as

$$y = rW + p_1 T, \tag{10.8}$$

on the assumption that $dW/dt = 0$ (no savings). In the present model, y will obey (10.8) in the long run, in which $dW/dt = 0$ by definition.

Before deriving results, it may be worthwhile to briefly discuss the model just outlined. First, it may be noticed that the state variables are introduced in (10.2) in an asymmetric way. Instead of defining a stock (say s_m such that $\dot{s}_m = m$) for money, wealth is used as the corresponding state variable. While it is doubtful that a symmetric use of s_m would add anything, the introduction of w in the utility function provides a handy way of introducing prices into the utility function in the long run, while avoiding to do the same in the short-run utility function. This simplifies computations a lot, as the estimating equations will be derived from the short-run model. By the same token, the parameter α_m provides an empirical test of the impact of prices on utility. Second, the utility function is written in terms of purchases rather than services. From an analytical point of view, this leads to an unsatisfactory treatment of the demand for durable goods in the presence of markets for used durables and for renting durables. On the other hand, it provides a satisfactory explanation of the available time series. Third, money is handled as a consumer durable which enters the consumer's utility function to take advantage of the systems approach, although this may not be the most desirable way of treating a transaction demand, as pointed out by Diewert (1974b, note 25).

The first-order conditions can be written as

$$x_i = \theta_i + \alpha_i s_i + \beta_i/\lambda p_i,$$
$$l = \theta_1 + \alpha_1 s_1 + \beta_1/\lambda p_1,$$
$$m = \theta_m + \alpha_m w + \beta_m/\lambda r p_m, \tag{10.9}$$

together with the budget equation (10.7) and the state equations (10.3) to (10.5). The Lagrangian multiplier λ is the marginal utility of full income.

Differentiating (10.9) with respect to time, and using (10.3), (10.4) and (10.5) to eliminate all state variables, we end up with the system

$$\dot{x}_i = \theta_i \delta_i + (\alpha_i - \delta_i)x_i + \beta_i \left(\frac{\delta_i}{\pi_i} - \frac{\dot{\pi}_i}{\pi_i^2} \right),$$

$$\dot{l} = \theta_1 \delta_1 + (\alpha_1 - \delta_1)l + \beta_1 \left(\frac{\delta_1}{\pi_1} - \frac{\dot{\pi}_1}{\pi_1^2} \right),$$

$$\dot{M} = \theta_m(\dot{p}_m - rp_m) + rM - \beta_m \left(\frac{r}{\pi_m} + \frac{\dot{\pi}_m}{\pi_m^2} \right) + \alpha_m(p_1 T - y), \qquad (10.10)$$

in which $\pi_i = \lambda p_i$, $\pi_1 = \lambda p_1$, $\pi_m = \lambda r$, and the dots represent derivatives with respect to time.

The differential equation for money shows that it has a special feature. It is a function of all (individual) prices in the system not only because of the budget constraint – as are all other commodities in the system – but because its rate of change over time depends *directly* upon all elements of full income through the wealth equation. We see no need, therefore, to insert prices as arguments in the utility function. To say (quite correctly of course) that 'the amount of money which is needed depends upon the work that is to be done, which in turn depends upon the prices of all goods in terms of gold' (Samuelson, 1947, p. 119) does not necessarily imply that all prices have to appear together with the level of m in the utility function, nor a fortiori that all marginal utilities have to be functions of all prices. A number of complications can thus be avoided by using the state variable approach: given that the state variables have no time to adjust to price changes in the short run (by definition), marginal utilities are defined in the short run by functions in which prices do not appear as arguments. As a result, the Slutsky conditions of demand theory remain unaltered[5] (except for the inclusion of p_1 and $p_m r$ in the price vector and an additional income effect for these variables as noted below).

The substitution of the first-order conditions (10.9) into the budget equation (10.7) leads to

$$\lambda = \frac{\sum \beta_i + \beta_1 + \beta_m}{y - \left(\sum_i p_i(\theta_i + \alpha_i s_i) + p_1(\theta_1 + \alpha_1 s_1) + rp_m(\theta_m + \alpha_m w) \right)}, \qquad (10.11)$$

which establishes that λ, and therefore each quantity in the system, is a function of all prices, all state variables and full income. Each variable depends upon λ: the demand for leisure, for example, or equivalently the supply of labour, can thus be said to be determined by past consumption decisions.

---

[5] For a formal demonstration, see Phlips (1976).

And as the supply of labour determines labour income, there is a feedback between past consumption and present income. However vague, this idea should be sympathetic to sociologists and anthropologists and may be suitable for further refinement (e.g. by redefining the state variable s_1 associated with leisure in terms of environmental variables).

The negativity restriction on the own substitution effect implies $\beta_i > 0, \beta_1 > 0, \beta_m > 0$ and

$$0 < (x_i - \theta_i - \alpha_i s_i),$$

$$0 < (l - \theta_1 - \alpha_1 s_1),$$

$$0 < (m - \theta_m - \alpha_m w).$$

The θ and α coefficients can be positive or negative. The depreciation rate δ has to be positive, but its range of variation depends upon the technique chosen to derive results in discrete time, as shown by Weiserbs (1975). The coefficients α_i are expected to be positive when habit formation dominates, and negative when the stock effect is predominant. The signs of α_1 and α_m are to be determined by the sample. On intuitive grounds, α_1 is expected to be positive.

10.3.* Short-run and long-run effects

Short-run effects are derived using the first-order conditions (10.9) together with the budget constraint (10.7) and the state equations (10.3) to (10.5). In this sense, the model of Section 10.2 is a short-run model.

Long-run equilibrium is defined by the conditions

$$ds_i/dt = 0 \quad \text{or} \quad s_i^* = x_i^*/\delta_i,$$

$$ds_1/dt = 0 \quad \text{or} \quad s_1^* = l^*/\delta_1,$$

$$dW/dt = 0 \quad \text{or} \quad W^* = (y^* - p_1 T)/r \quad \text{or} \quad y^*/r = W^* + p_1 T/r,$$

$$(10.12)$$

where stars denote long-run values. In a stationary state, the present value of the constant stream of full income (y^*/r) is equal to maximum wealth $(W^* + p_1 T/r)$. The corresponding statement in static theory is that full income is equal to nonlabour income plus maximum labour income (equation (10.8) above). Alternatively, we can write (10.12) as

$$W^* + p_1(T - l^*)/r = M^* + \sum_i p_i x_i^*/r, \qquad (10.12a)$$

which says that, in a stationary state, total wealth (i.e. non-human wealth W^* plus human wealth $p_1(T - l^*)/r$) is equal to initial cash balances plus the present value of future consumption.

Long-run demand equations are obtained by substituting the conditions (10.12) into the first-order conditions (10.9) and imposing the budget constraint (10.7). After reparametrizing all coefficients, one finds the system of demand equations

$$p_i x_i^* = p_i \gamma_i^* + \beta_i^* \left\{ y - \left(\sum_j p_j \gamma_j^* + r p_m \gamma_m^* + p_1 \gamma_1^* \right) \right\},$$

$$p_1 l^* = p_1 \gamma_1^* + \beta_1^* \left\{ y - \left(\sum_j p_j \gamma_j^* + r p_m \gamma_m^* + p_1 \gamma_1^* \right) \right\},$$

$$r p_m m^* = r p_m \gamma_m^* + \beta_m^* \left\{ y - \left\{ \sum_j p_j \gamma_j^* + r p_m \gamma_m^* + p_1 \gamma_1^* \right) \right\}, \qquad (10.13)$$

which is the familiar static linear expenditure system extended to $n + 2$ commodities. The reparametrization is as follows:

$$\beta_i^* = \frac{\delta_i \beta_i / (\delta_i - \alpha_i)}{\sum_j \delta_j \beta_j / (\delta_j - \alpha_j) + \delta_1 \beta_1 / (\delta_1 - \alpha_1) + \beta_m / (1 - \alpha_m)},$$

$$\beta_1^* = \frac{\delta_1 \beta_1 / (\delta_1 - \alpha_1)}{\sum_j \delta_j \beta_j / (\delta_j - \alpha_j) + \delta_1 \beta_1 / (\delta_1 - \alpha_1) + \beta_m / (1 - \alpha_m)},$$

$$\beta_m^* = \frac{\beta_m / (1 - \alpha_m)}{\sum_j \delta_j \beta_j / (\delta_j - \alpha_j) + \delta_1 \beta_1 / (\delta_1 - \alpha_1) + \beta_m / (1 - \alpha_m)}, \qquad (10.14)$$

for $j = 1, \ldots, n$, and

$$\gamma_i^* = \delta_i \theta_i / (\delta_i - \alpha_i), \qquad (10.15a)$$

$$\gamma_1^* = \delta_1 \theta_1 / (\delta_1 - \alpha_1), \qquad (10.15b)$$

$$\gamma_m^* = \theta_m / (1 - \alpha_m) - \left(\alpha_m / (1 - \alpha) r p_m \right) \left(p_1 (T - l^*) - \sum_i p_i x_i^* \right). \qquad (10.15c)$$

The implicit long-run utility function is

$$u^* = \sum_i \beta_i^* \log(x_i - \gamma_i^*) + \beta_1^* \log(l - \gamma_1^*) + \beta_m^* \log(m - \gamma_m^*).$$

It has the same form as the static Stone–Geary utility function. But now all prices appear explicitly in it, through γ_m^*, as is required by traditional monetary theory (which is static). However, for prices to have an impact on γ_m^*, α_m has to be non-zero. On the other hand, the marginal utilities of consumer goods and of leisure remain independent of prices, in the preference ordering.

Equation (10.15c) has to be taken into account in the computation of long-run elasticities when $\alpha_m \neq 0$. Otherwise, use can be made of the well-known static formulas which are valid in both the short run and the long run with one alteration only: one should be aware of the fact that a change in r or p_l induces a change in full income, because of equation (10.8). An element respectively equal to

$$\frac{\partial x_i^*}{\partial y} \cdot \frac{\partial y}{\partial r} \quad \text{or} \quad \frac{\partial x_i^*}{\partial y} \cdot \frac{\partial y}{\partial p_l} \tag{10.16}$$

should therefore be added to the static expressions for the derivatives $\partial x_i^*/\partial r$ and $\partial x_i^*/\partial p_l$. And similarly for the derivatives of l^* and m^* with respect to r and p_l. For example, $\partial l^*/\partial p_l$ becomes

$$\frac{\partial l^*}{\partial p_l} = k_{11}^* - \frac{\partial l^*}{\partial y} l + \frac{\partial l^*}{\partial y} T = k_{11}^* + \frac{\partial l^*}{\partial y}(T - l). \tag{10.17}$$

As $T > l$, we may end up with a positive elasticity of leisure with respect to the wage rate, even if the own substitution effect k_{11}^* is negative and the income derivative positive. Cross-derivatives with respect to p_l are always positive: an increase in the wage rate always increases demand. We also notice that a derivative of leisure is transformed into a derivative of the supply of labour simply by a change in sign, given that $l = T - h$, where h represents the number of hours worked. A positive elasticity of leisure with respect to the wage rate implies a negative elasticity of the supply of labour ('backward bending' supply curve).

As for the demand for money, one would expect $1 - \alpha_m$ to be positive, so that β_m^* (and $\partial m^*/\partial y$) should be positive too. On the assumption that $\alpha_m = 0$ (which will turn out to be the case in the sample analyzed below) we then see that

$$\frac{\partial m^*}{\partial r} = p_m k_{mm}^* + p_m(w^* - m^*)\frac{\partial m^*}{\partial y} \tag{10.18}$$

is negative when $w^* = m^*$, but its chances of becoming positive increase with w. The impact of an increase of the rate of interest on transactions balances is thus a function of the level of non-human wealth in both the short run and the long run[6]. Its impact on consumption goods and leisure is positive, as, e.g.,

$$\frac{\partial x_i}{\partial r} = p_m \left\{ \frac{\beta_i^*}{p_i}(m^* - \gamma_m^*) + \frac{\beta_i^*}{p_i}(w^* - m^*) \right\} = \frac{\beta_i^*}{p_i} p_m(w^* - \gamma_m^*), \quad (10.19)$$

and $w^* \geqslant m^* > \gamma_m^*$, on the assumption (again) that $\alpha_m = 0$.

The price of money in this system is (rp_m). A change in p_m will therefore have the same effect, with r constant, as a change in r with p_m constant. We can thus identify the term $\beta_i^* w_i^*/p_i$, i.e. $w^* \partial x_i^*/\partial y$, which is added to the traditional substitution and income effects, as the (long-run) real balance effect, and conclude that it is this real balance effect which guarantees that money is a gross substitute for all other goods (including leisure).

10.4.* Estimation procedures

For estimation purposes, the model is rewritten in discrete time, using the Houthakker–Taylor approximation, which has the advantage of allowing purchases made in year t to depreciate during that year, (see equation (6.34)). That is, state variables are measured as the simple average of their value at the end of period $t - 1$ and period t, or $\bar{s}_{it} = \frac{1}{2}(s_{it-1} + s_{it})$ and $\bar{W}_t = \frac{1}{2}(W_{t-1} + W_t)$. After elimination of the state variables, the estimating equations derived from the first-order conditions (10.9) appear to be

$$p_{it}x_{it} = p_{it}\left(K_{i0} + K_{i1}x_{it-1} + K_{i2}\frac{1}{\lambda_t p_{it}} + K_{i3}\frac{1}{\lambda_{t-1}p_{it-1}} \right) \quad (10.20)$$

for the consumption goods. For leisure we have

$$p_{1t}l_t = p_{1t}\left(K_{10} + K_{11}l_{t-1} + K_{12}\frac{1}{\lambda_t p_{1t}} + K_{13}\frac{1}{\lambda_{t-1}p_{1t-1}} \right). \quad (10.21)$$

The relationships between the regression coefficients K_{ij} and K_{1j} ($j = 0, 1, 2, 3$) and the structural parameters are of course the same as in Chapter

---

[6] In Diewert (1974b), the interest elasticity of transaction balances is also a function of human wealth, as a result of the intertemporal set-up.

VII. The elimination of $\bar{W}_t$ from the equation for money leads to

$$r_t((2 - r_t)\bar{M}_t - (2 + r_{t-1})\bar{M}_{t-1}) = \theta_m((2 - r_t)p_{mt} - (2 + r_{t-1})p_{mt-1})r_t$$
$$+ \alpha((p_{1t} + p_{1t-1})T - (y_t + y_{t-1}))r_t$$
$$+ \beta_m\left(2\left(\frac{1}{\lambda_t r_t} - \frac{1}{\lambda_{t-1}r_{t-1}}\right)\right.$$
$$\left. - \left(\frac{1}{\lambda_t} + \frac{1}{\lambda_{t-1}}\right)\right)r_t, \qquad (10.22)$$

where $\bar{M}_t = \frac{1}{2}(M_{t-1} + M_t)$.

The elimination of the state variables is necessary not only because s_i and s_1 are not observable: it is the simplest way to make sure that the state equations are satisfied. Although data are available on private net worth, which could be used as observations on W_t, it is necessary to impose the wealth equation and therefore preferable to estimate (10.22) rather than

$$\bar{M}_t = \theta_m p_{mt} + \alpha_m \bar{W}_t + \beta_m \frac{1}{\lambda_t r_t}. \qquad (10.23)$$

λ_t is defined by the condition that

$$y_t = \sum_i p_i x_{it} + p_{1t}l_t + r_t\bar{M}_t. \qquad (10.24)$$

This condition is imposed using the Houthakker–Taylor iteration on λ_t, pushing to the point where the difference between observed full income and estimated full income is smaller than 0.0005 for all t. At each step of the iteration, Zellner's method for the estimation of 'seemingly unrelated regressions' is used, so that the estimates are consistent and asymptotically efficient, on the assumption[7] that the errors are not autocorrelated.

For data we use the eleven yearly U.S. consumption series (in nominal terms) published by the *Survey of Current Business*. The rate of interest r_t is measured using the Aaa series (corporate bonds), while the implicit price deflator for total consumption expenditures measures p_{mt}. The stock of money (currency plus demand deposits) of American households at the end of the year is taken from the flow of funds data of the Federal Reserve (starting in 1938). Leisure is defined as $l = T - h$, where h is the number of hours worked. As an estimate of the latter, and of the price p_{1t}, we use Abbott

---

[7] This assumption seems to be satisfied for all items but one (money), as can be seen from Table 10.1, where the last column gives the estimated first-order autocorrelation coefficients.

and Ashenfelter's series, which end in 1967. (Efforts to extend these series for recent years proved unsuccessful.) All in all, then, we are able to cover the period 1938–1967. Wages are *after taxes*. The observations on h_t are given in Table 10.3 below.

Two problems arise in connection with this sort of data: first, one has to realize that T, the maximum number of hours available for work and leisure, is unknown, and either find a way to estimate T or to eliminate it; second, one has to determine whether the data are to be expressed per capita or per employee.

The numerical value of T is arbitrary to the extent that the notion of leisure is not defined with precision. Should one include hours of sleep, travel to work, time spent in household production, etc.? Owen (1969) uses a wide definition of leisure, which leads to $T = 150$ hours per week. Lewis (1975) puts T equal to 100 per week, while Diewert (1974b) takes it to be equal to 60 hours per week.

In a static single-equation approach, the matter is not terribly important, because there any error made in estimating T amounts to adding an (unknown) constant to the dependent variable (l_t), which affects only the estimate of the intercept in a linear regression. For our approach, the matter is important. First, because l_{t-1} appears among the independent variables. Secondly, because any error in T makes itself felt throughout the system, because of its impact on the value of y_t, and therefore on λ_t, λ_{t-1}, etc.

In a static system, the difficulty can be circumvented by using h instead of l as dependent variable, as in Abbott and Ashenfelter (1976) and Ashenfelter and Heckman (1974). The same is true in a dynamic system such as ours.

Define γ_h, the *maximum* number of hours one is ready to work, as

$$\gamma_h = T - \gamma_1, \tag{10.25}$$

and the stock of hours worked in the past, s_h, as

$$s_h(t) = \int_{-\infty}^{t} \left[T - l(u) \right] e^{\delta_1(u - t)} \, du$$

$$= \frac{T}{\delta_1} - s_l(t). \tag{10.26}$$

Equation (10.26) assumes that the habit of working wears off at the same rate as the habit of not working $(\delta_h = \delta_1)$, and that s_h decreases when s_l increases. (This restriction is not essential and can be dropped at a cost which is indicated below.) Equations (10.25), (10.2) and (10.26) together imply

$T - \theta_1 = \theta_\mathrm{h} + \alpha_1 T/\delta_1$ and $\alpha_1 = \alpha_\mathrm{h}$. Under these assumptions the branch utility function for leisure, u_1, can be written as

$$u_1 = \beta_1 \log(l - \gamma_1)$$

$$= \beta_1 \log(-h + \gamma_\mathrm{h})$$

$$= \beta_1 \log\left(-h + \theta_\mathrm{h} + \alpha_1 \frac{T}{\delta_1} - \alpha_1 s_1\right). \tag{10.27}$$

Proceeding in discrete time as before, the maximization of u under the constraint

$$\sum_i p_{it} x_{it} + p_{1t}(-h_t) + r_t \bar{M}_t = \tilde{y}_t, \tag{10.28}$$

where $\tilde{y}_t$ is now non-labour income available for consumption, i.e. non-labour income minus savings, leads to the estimating equation

$$p_{1t}(-h_t) = p_{1t}\left(K_{\mathrm{h}0} + K_{\mathrm{h}1}(-h_{t-1}) + K_{\mathrm{h}2} \frac{1}{\lambda_t p_{1t}} + K_{\mathrm{h}3} \frac{1}{\lambda_{t-1} p_{1t-1}}\right).$$

$$\tag{10.21a}$$

T has dropped out. The structural parameters δ_1, α_1 and θ_h (not θ_1) can be computed from

$$K_{\mathrm{h}0} = -\frac{2\delta_1\theta_\mathrm{h}}{2 - \alpha_1 + \delta_1}, \qquad K_{\mathrm{h}2} = \frac{\beta_1(\delta_1 + 2)}{2 - \alpha_1 + \delta_1},$$

$$K_{\mathrm{h}1} = \frac{2 + \alpha_1 - \delta_1}{2 - \alpha_1 + \delta_1}, \qquad K_{\mathrm{h}3} = \frac{\beta_1(\delta_1 - 2)}{2 - \alpha_1 + \delta_1}. \tag{10.29}$$

It is impossible to solve for θ_1 or T. These parameters are of no direct interest, anyway, as they are not needed for the computation of the elasticities and as we are not interested, here, in a 'deeper economics of sleeping', on which the reader is referred to Bergstrom (1976). When assumption (10.26) is dropped, θ_h cannot be estimated either, e.g. replacing (10.26) by the assumption $\theta_\mathrm{h} = T - \theta_1$ does not suffice to identify θ_h. But the other structural coefficients (δ_1, β_1 and α_1) are unaffected, since the regression coefficients $K_{\mathrm{h}1}$, $K_{\mathrm{h}2}$ and $K_{\mathrm{h}3}$ remain unchanged.

The second problem is to express the data per capita in a correct way. System estimation implies that all expenditure series should be divided by the same population series. And as the underlying theory refers to the choice between leisure and work, everything should be expressed per worker. But what sort of average worker? If the possibility of a rationed supply of labour had been explicitly allowed for in the model, one would have chosen total active population (including the unemployed). Since rationing[8] is not taken into account – while it is certainly present in the data to some degree, i.e. for some workers and for some time periods – one should use a series of employees *engaged in production* (i.e. excluding the unemployed), to come as close as possible to the theoretical assumptions. Following Abbott and Ashenfelter, all expenditure series were therefore divided by the (total) number of 'persons engaged in production' as given in the National Income and Product Accounts of the U.S. (for all industries).

The results reported in the next section were obtained after 28 iterations, when convergence, as defined above, was reached.

10.5.* Empirical results

The regression results (Table 10.1) are encouraging, two blemishes not-withstanding. First, the equation for 'other services' is unstable ($K_1 > 1$), as was the case in earlier work[9] (in the same system without leisure and money). This item includes medical care, cleaning, funeral expenses, movies, television and higher education. $K_1 > 1$ leads to $\delta < \alpha$, so that β^* is negative (see Table 10.2) while γ^* is larger than the observed quantities: the interpretation of equation (10.11) in terms of utility theory breaks down. Second, K_3 has the wrong sign for 'automobiles and parts'. As a consequence, the rate of depreciation is larger than its maximum (i.e. $\delta = 2$) and α is implausibly large. These defects, and their consequences, have to be kept in mind when interpreting Tables 10.2 to 10.4.

Turning to the structural coefficients (Table 10.2), we are glad to discover that all marginal propensities to consume (including β_1) are positive and highly significant. Habit formation ($\alpha > 0$) is predominant except for food and transportation. In particular, leisure appears as a habit forming commodity, which is in accordance with common experience. As for the demand for transactions balances, accumulated wealth does not seem to have any impact at all.

Large positive θ coefficients show up for money, leisure and food, which can thus be viewed as necessities. In the long run, minimum cash balances are slightly below 550 dollars, while the maximum number of hours one is

---

[8] On rationing, see Tobin and Houthakker (1951), Tobin (1952), Ashenfelter (1980), Barnett (1979b) and Deaton (1981).

[9] See Table 7.1 above.

TABLE 10.1
Regression coefficients

Commodity	K_{i0}	K_{i1}	K_{i2}	K_{i3}	ρ
(1) Automobiles and parts	−56.07	0.4216	72.37	17.93	−0.20
	(11.30)	(0.0181)	(6.57)	(6.76)	(0.19)
(2) Furniture and household	11.84	0.6050	55.08	−10.69	0.35
equipment	(6.77)	(0.0329)	(7.96)	(8.39)	(0.18)
(3) Other durable goods	−1.67	0.9639	14.29	−10.75	−0.01
	(1.61)	(0.0391)	(2.28)	(2.46)	(0.19)
(4) Food and beverages	292.60	0.6084	157.71	−88.06	0.16
	(17.14)	(0.0218)	(5.48)	(6.82)	(0.19)
(5) Clothing and shoes	2.59	0.9415	48.87	−36.11	−0.22
	(10.52)	(0.0356)	(5.52)	(6.20)	(0.19)
(6) Gasoline and oil	−3.87	0.7493	27.06	−7.53	0.26
	(2.48)	(0.0323)	(2.82)	(3.22)	(0.18)
(7) Other non-durable goods	10.44	0.9320	34.71	−22.79	0.10
	(5.09)	(0.0255)	(4.28)	(4.45)	(0.19)
(8) Housing	−0.35	0.9330	55.18	−29.96	−0.13
	(4.31)	(0.0122)	(5.39)	(5.84)	(0.19)
(9) Household operation	−0.64	0.8820	24.30	−8.39	0.02
	(2.68)	(0.0199)	(2.98)	(3.10)	(0.19)
(10) Transportation	25.41	0.7279	16.92	−10.84	−0.05
	(5.60)	(0.0592)	(3.05)	(3.04)	(0.19)
(11) Other services	−34.26	1.0273	77.45	−64.48	−0.14
	(10.60)	(0.0130)	(7.22)	(6.93)	(0.19)
(12) Leisure ($-h$)	−442.04	0.8306	92.47	−41.18	0.05
	(34.12)	(0.0163)	(11.27)	(9.09)	(0.19)
(13) Money	816.32	−0.0075	3.54		0.71
	(241.77)	(0.0065)	(0.68)		(0.13)

ready to work (γ_h^*) is around 2,600 (or 50 hours a week). This number is to be compared with the number of hours actually worked and the short-run γ_{ht}'s reported in Table 10.3. It can be seen that, although γ_h^* is a parameter of the long-run utility function which rationalizes the long-run demand functions, it has a value to which the short-run γ_h does *not* converge.[10]

In the short run, employees would in fact refuse to work more than a number of hours which is markedly lower than 50 hours a week. In 1939, γ_h was around 46 hours a week. In 1967, it was down to about 41 hours, as it decreases with h_t reflecting an increase in the minimum required hours of leisure (γ_{lt}). It is of some interest to notice that observed working hours were very close to the psychologically admissible maximum during the second

---

[10] See Pollak (1976a) for a discussion of habit formation and long-run utility functions. The numbers reported illustrate Pollak's point that, although the long-run solution seems to be on a higher indifference curve, the average worker nevertheless prefers to work less under the impact of leisure enjoyed in the past. It is difficult, therefore, to interpret the long-run utility function as representing a 'long-run preference structure'. See also p. 185.

TABLE 10.2
Structural coefficients

	β	$\beta/\sum_{1}^{13}\beta$	θ	α	δ	β^*	γ^*	Annual rate of depreciation[a]
(1) Automobiles and parts	38.30 (8.61)	0.068	−23.78 (6.07)	2.504 (0.775)	3.317 (0.776)	0.116	−96.94	1.248
(2) Furniture and household equipment	40.98 (9.84)	0.073	10.92 (7.25)	0.858 (0.348)	1.350 (0.361)	0.083	29.97	0.806
(3) Other durable goods	12.75 (2.29)	0.022	−6.03 (5.76)	0.246 (0.105)	0.283 (0.135)	0.073	−46.40	0.248
(4) Food and beverage	152.81 (6.52)	0.271	641.93 (48.66)	0.080 (0.034)	0.567 (0.054)	0.132	747.12	0.442
(5) Clothing and shoes	44.80 (5.60)	0.080	10.77 (42.73)	0.187 (0.063)	0.247 (0.085)	0.137	44.23	0.220
(6) Gasoline and oil	19.77 (3.13)	0.035	−3.92 (2.41)	0.842 (0.223)	1.129 (0.248)	0.058	−15.43	0.722
(7) Other non-durable goods	29.76 (4.14)	0.053	26.04 (12.66)	0.344 (0.115)	0.415 (0.137)	0.130	153.50	0.344
(8) Housing services	44.04 (5.54)	0.078	−0.62 (7.49)	0.523 (0.107)	0.593 (0.114)	0.280	−5.30	0.457
(9) Household operation	17.37 (3.02)	0.031	−0.99 (2.92)	0.848 (0.208)	0.973 (0.220)	0.100	−5.42	0.655
(10) Transportation	16.07 (3.30)	0.029	67.19 (28.88)	0.123 (0.143)	0.438 (0.186)	0.017	93.36	0.359
(11) Other services	70.01 (6.65)	0.124	−184.92 (55.43)	0.210 (0.058)	0.183 (0.062)	−0.354	1 256.93	0.168
(12) Leisure (or supply of labour when indicated)	73.01 (10.67)	0.130	$629.2(\theta_h)$ (109.15)	0.582 (0.118)	0.768 (0.114)	0.225	$2\,609.4(\gamma_h^*)$	0.555
(13) Money	3.54 (0.68)	0.006	816.32 (241.77)	−0.007 (0.007)	—	0.003	548.41[b]	—

[a] Equal to $2\delta(\delta + 2)^{-1}$. See Weiserbs (1975).
[b] On the assumption that $\alpha_m = 0$.

TABLE 10.3
Maximum working hours (per year)

Year	h_t	γ_{ht}	$\gamma_{ht} - h_t$
1939	2334	2431	97
1940	2340	2416	76
1941	2361	2416	55
1942	2416	2432	16
1943	2465	2466	1
1944	2489	2503	14
1945	2427	2478	51
1946	2308	2427	119
1947	2252	2350	98
1948	2228	2309	81
1949	2223	2313	90
1950	2197	2290	93
1951	2185	2252	67
1952	2187	2254	67
1953	2159	2231	72
1954	2139	2224	85
1955	2161	2245	84
1956	2151	2224	73
1957	2121	2190	69
1958	2099	2173	74
1959	2122	2184	62
1960	2126	2184	58
1961	2110	2169	59
1962	2117	2175	58
1963	2117	2179	62
1964	2122	2182	60
1965	2134	2192	58
1966	2126	2174	48
1967	2126	2165	39

world war. Since then, the discrepancy fluctuates slightly over the business cycle.

The reader may wonder where our estimates of γ_{ht} come from, given that s_{ht} is not observable. They are, in fact, derived from the estimated price and income elasticities reported in Table 10.4. Indeed, for the demand for leisure, these elasticities turn out to be

$$(\partial h/\partial p_1)(p_1/h) = \beta_1(\bar{y} - \sum_j^m p_j \gamma_j + \gamma_h p_1)/hp_1 \tag{10.30}$$

and

$$(\partial h/\partial \bar{y})(\bar{y}/h) = -\beta_1 \bar{y}/p_1 h, \tag{10.31}$$

where $m = n + 2 = 13$.

The ratio of these two elasticities is equal to

$$-1 + \sum_{j}^{m} p_j \gamma_j / \tilde{y} - p_1 \gamma_h / \tilde{y}, \tag{10.32}$$

so that the sum, over all equations, of the ratios of the estimated uncompensated price and income elasticities is equal to

$$(m - 1) \sum_{j}^{m} p_j \gamma_j / \tilde{y} - m. \tag{10.33}$$

It is thus possible to compute $\sum_{j}^{m} p_j \gamma_j / \tilde{y}$ (from the estimated price and income elasticities) and γ_h (using (10.32) and observations on p_1 and $\tilde{y}$) for each t.[11]

It may be worth noticing that the uncompensated price elasticity of the demand for leisure is

$$(\partial l / \partial p_1)(p_1 / l) = -\beta_1 \left(y - \sum_{j}^{m} p_j \gamma_j - p_1 T + p_1 \gamma_1 \right) \bigg/ l p_1$$

$$= -\beta_1 \left(y - \sum_{j}^{m} p_j \gamma_j - p_1 \gamma_h \right) \bigg/ l p_1, \tag{10.30a}$$

where y is full income. If this elasticity turns out to be positive (backward bending supply of labour), this result is compatible with $\gamma_1 > 0$ and $\gamma_h > 0$ thanks to the presence of the term $(-p_1 T)$ which appears because full income is a function of the price of labour.

Table 10.4 suggests that the supply of labour is indeed slightly backward bending in both the short run and the long run: the uncompensated price elasticity of the supply of labour is around -0.085, which is almost identical to the estimate of Abbott and Ashenfelter. Ashenfelter and Heckman (1974) report an elasticity of -0.15, while Kiefer (1977) finds -0.18 and Diewert (1974b) an even higher -0.25 (possibly due to a wealth effect which is absent here).

The demand for transactions balances appears to be rather insensitive to changes in the rate of interest if we compare our own interest elasticities with the values of -0.78 and -0.74 obtained by Meltzer (1963) and Chow (1966) in a single-equation approach. Notice, however, that the interest elasticity of money is still negative although the income effect is positive (because of the influence of non-human wealth). To turn it into a positive number, it may be necessary to make money a function of human and non-human wealth, as in Diewert (1974).

---

[11] I am grateful to J. Drèze for pointing this out to me.

TABLE 10.4
Elasticities[a] (simple averages)

	Run	Compensated price	Uncompensated price	$\bar{y}$	Compensated wage	Uncompensated wage	Uncompensated interest
(1) Automobiles and parts	Short	−0.46	−0.53	0.54	0.06	1.85	0.35
	Long	−1.72	−1.84	0.91	1.44	3.41	0.61
(2) Furniture and household equipment	Short	−0.31	−0.38	0.36	0.04	0.95	0.21
	Long	−0.78	−0.87	0.41	0.44	1.21	0.25
(3) Other durable goods	Short	−0.32	−0.34	0.36	0.04	0.89	0.20
	Long	−1.59	−1.67	1.15	1.16	3.22	0.66
(4) Food and beverage	Short	−0.20	−0.47	0.30	0.04	0.74	0.18
	Long	−0.27	−0.41	0.14	0.14	0.40	0.09
(5) Clothing and shoes	Short	−0.21	−0.29	0.24	0.03	0.60	0.15
	Long	−0.76	−0.90	0.42	0.39	1.17	0.25
(6) Gasoline and oil	Short	−0.31	−0.34	0.35	0.04	0.95	0.20
	Long	−1.09	−1.15	0.57	0.65	1.73	0.34
(7) Other non-durable goods	Short	−0.14	−0.19	0.16	0.02	0.40	0.09
	Long	−0.52	−0.65	0.39	0.38	1.10	0.23
(8) Housing services	Short	−0.15	−0.23	0.18	0.02	0.46	0.10
	Long	−0.73	−1.01	0.66	0.67	1.85	0.38
(9) Household operation	Short	−0.15	−0.18	0.17	0.02	0.42	0.10
	Long	−0.92	−1.02	0.54	0.54	1.53	0.31
(10) Transportation	Short	−0.24	−0.27	0.27	0.03	0.67	0.16
	Long	−0.29	−0.31	0.16	0.15	0.44	0.09
(11) Other services	Short	−0.20	−0.33	0.25	0.03	0.63	0.14
	Long	1.43	1.78	−0.71	−0.72	−2.01	−0.41
(12) Supply of labour	Short	0.04	−0.09	−0.06	0.04	−0.09	−0.03
	Long	0.14	−0.09	−0.10	0.14	−0.09	−0.06
(13) Money	Short	−0.20	−0.08	0.22	0.03	0.54	−0.08
	Long	−0.21	−0.16	0.09	0.09	0.25	−0.16

[a] Computed on the assumption that $\alpha_m = 0$.

The elasticities with respect to $\bar{y}$ are reported for the sake of completeness: they are not to be confused with traditional income elasticities. On the other hand, the cross wage elasticities reported do measure reactions to a change in labour income, and may come closer to the intuitive concept of an 'income' elasticity than the usual elasticities with respect to total expenditures. An increase in the wage rate is likely to have a very large impact on the demand for durables, especially in the long run. In the short run, the uncompensated wage elasticity of money turns out to be identical (0.54) with the one reported by Diewert.

We emphasized earlier that the model constrains both money and leisure to be gross as well as net substitutes (in the Hicksian sense) to all other commodities. That is why all cross wage and interested elasticities are positive. In the case of the demand for cars, for example, this may be too strong a restriction as far as money is concerned. It may also help to explain why the equation for 'automobiles and parts' did not perform as well as it does in a demand system without leisure and money. Similarly, items like 'housing', 'transportation' and especially 'other services' may, in fact, be complementary to leisure time, so that the use of less restrictive specifications is certainly to be welcomed.

Finally, Table 10.4 includes *compensated* cross wage elasticities, which are of some interest in view of a theorem by Diamond and Mirrlees (1971) relating the optimal tax structure to these compensated elasticities of demand with respect to the price of labour. Looking at the long-run values (which should be close to the static values), we see that durables display the largest reactions and food and transportation the smallest reactions.

10.6.* True indices of real wages

This section[12] aims at measuring the evolution over time of real hourly wages with reference to a 'true' or functional wage index, defined in a way analogous to the well-known constant-utility index of the cost of living. We elaborate on an idea put forward by Pencavel (1977), who suggests to solve the true index problem, not for the 'income' that leaves the consumer indifferent w.r.t. base period utility, but directly for the constant-utility wage rate.

In standard practice, movements in real wages are measured by comparing changes in nominal earnings with changes in a price index. Attempts to

---

[12] This section is based on Phlips (1978b).

construct a constant-utility price index are meant, in fact, to provide the correct price index to use in this context, or at least to provide a better index than the currently used empirical Laspeyres-type consumer price index.

It should be clear, however, that the constant-utility price index, as defined in the framework of standard demand analysis, presents a number of deficiencies when used to measure changes in real earnings. First of all, it is based on a model in which the length of work time (or leisure time) is ignored, although the consumer is probably not indifferent between an increase in earnings through a wage increase, with constant (or reduced) work time, and the same increase obtained after a longer working day, with a constant hourly wage rate.

Secondly, the true index problem ignores *current* income: only base year income (together with base year and current prices) appears in the analysis as it is usually set up, although the consumer's present situation obviously depends not only on today's prices but also on today's income. This deficiency is inevitable as long as 'income' is defined as the sum of total expenditures on consumption goods.

We are thus led to a third criticism: to talk about 'income' when what is meant is 'total consumption expenditures' is a source of confusion. There is a real need for a theory of demand in which the word 'income' designates what it suggests, i.e. the sum of labour and non-labour income, and in which labour income depends both on the wage rate and on the number of hours worked (or not worked). If such a theory can be used to define a true index, it provides a natural way of introducing the length of work time into the measurement of real wages, as requested above.

Pencavel (1977) has successfully remedied each of these deficiencies, by defining the true wage index in the framework of a model of the allocation of time and implementing it within the (enlarged) linear expenditure system, as worked out by Abbott and Ashenfelter (1976). Further improvements are possible, though.

Indeed, given the static character of his approach, savings (out of labour and non-labour income) are simply supposed to be zero, while earnings foregone by holding cash balances are ignored. There is thus a need for enlarging the budget constraint (recoined the 'full income' constraint to allow for the allocation of time between work and leisure) even further and embedding it in a wealth constraint defining savings. Simultaneously, one may want to allow tastes to change over time, especially since this may destroy the familiar inequalities between the true index and empirical indexes (in particular the Laspeyres and the Paasche index), as emphasized in Chapter IX. It may indeed reveal losses in welfare which outweigh the gains resulting from the celebrated substitution effect which true indexes try to capture.

The enlargement of the budget constraint, coupled with the 'dynamization' of the utility function, is precisely what characterizes the approach presented in the preceding sections. The taste-dependent true wage index may be defined as follows. Suppose the average consumer maximizes the 'dynamized' instantaneous utility function

$$u = u(x, l, m; R). \tag{10.34}$$

R designates the preference ordering represented by u, and is a function of the current values of the $n + 2$ state variables whose movements determine taste changes, i.e.

$$R = R(s, s_1, w). \tag{10.35}$$

These $n + 2$ states are defined as the solutions of (10.5).

The utility function (10.34) is maximized subject to the enlarged 'full income' constraint (10.7), which is part of the wealth constraint (10.5) or (10.6). Note that savings $(\dot{W})$, although present in the model, are unexplained, i.e. exogenous.

Insertion of the demand equations

$$x = x(p, p_1, rp_m, y; R),$$

$$l = l(p, p_1, rp_m, y; R),$$

$$m = m(p, p_1, rp_m, y; R), \tag{10.36}$$

into the utility function gives the indirect utility function

$$u^* = u^*(p, p_1, rp_m, y; R).$$

The true or constant-utility wage rate p_{1t}^* is then the solution of

$$u^*(p_0, p_{10}, r_0 p_{m0}, y_0; R_0) = u^*(p_t, p_{1t}^*, r_t p_{mt}, y_t; R_t), \tag{10.37}$$

and the *true wage index* is p_{1t}^*/p_{10}, where the subscript 0 designates the base year, while what we shall call the *real wage index* is p_{1t}/p_{1t}^*, i.e. the ratio of the current wage over the true wage, and measures the change in real wages between period t and the base year. When the real wage index is larger than one, the consumer is better off than in the base year.

The numbers derived by solving (10.37) will henceforth be called 'cardinal'

– to be consistent with the terminology used in Chapter IX – because a comparison of utility levels over time is involved. Alternatively, one can define the true wage rate p_{1t}^{**} as a solution of

$$u^*(p_0, p_{10}, r_0p_{m0}, y_0; R_t) = u^*(p_t, p_{1t}^{**}, r_tp_{mt}, y_t; R_t), \qquad (10.38)$$

i.e. with reference to the *current* preference ordering only, to follow the recommendations made by Fisher and Shell (F–S). The corresponding indexes may then be called F–S true and real wage indexes.

Once so far, there seems to be no reason not to redefine the true index of the cost of living, in the framework of the model sketched above, as the ratio of the true full income to base year full income. The 'cardinal' true full income is then the value y^* that minimizes (10.7) subject to the condition $u_t = u_0$. The corresponding F–S constant-utility full income is the value y_t^{**} that minimizes (10.7) subject to $u_t = \hat{u}_t$, where $\hat{u}$ is the maximum current (direct) utility obtainable under the base year constraint. These indexes do take past and current wage rates, leisure time, rates of interest and cash holdings into account.

For empirical purposes we specify (10.34) as the generalized Stone–Geary utility function (10.1) and dynamize it by supposing that the minimum required quantities change over time according to (10.2). The cardinal constant-utility wage rate p_{1t}^* turns out to be the solution of

$$1 = \frac{\tilde{y}_0 + p_{10}\gamma_{h0} - \sum_i p_{io}{}' - r_0p_{m0}\gamma_{m0}}{\tilde{y}_t + p_{1t}^*\gamma_{ht} - \sum_i p_{it}\gamma_{it} - r_tp_{mt}\gamma_{mt}} \prod_{i=1}^{n} \left(\frac{p_{it}}{p_{io}}\right)^{\beta_i}\left(\frac{p_{1t}^*}{p_{10}}\right)^{\beta_1}\left(\frac{r_tp_{mt}}{r_0p_{m0}}\right)^{\beta_m}$$

$$(10.39)$$

for each t. This solution can easily be computed by the Gauss–Seidel method, once estimates of γ_{it}, γ_{ht} and γ_{mt} are available.

To compute the Fisher–Shell constant-utility wage rate p_{1t}^{**}, one simply replaces γ_{h0}, γ_{io} and γ_{m0} by γ_{ht}, γ_{it} and γ_{mt} respectively in (10.39). Both the cardinal and the F–S results are invariant under monotonic transformations of the utility function.

The empirical results presented here are based on the data used and the estimates obtained in Section 10.5. Table 10.5 gives observed wage rates and true wage rates for selected years. (The complete series are given in Phlips (1978b, Appendix A). The year 1939 was chosen as the base year, so that the results can be compared directly with Pencavel's.

Looking at the cardinal constant-utility wages first, we see that they are slightly below the observed wages, except for the war years, during which the war effort led to working hours that came very close to the maximum number

TABLE 10.5
Wage rates after taxes (U.S. dollars per hour)

	Observed p_{1t}	Cardinal p_{1t}^{*}	F–S p_{1t}^{**}
1939	0.370	0.370	0.370
1943	0.570	0.791	0.780
1946	0.700	0.676	0.630
1950	0.970	0.958	0.690
1955	1.280	1.229	0.720
1960	1.600	1.466	0.570
1965	1.980	1.705	0.500
1967	2.180	1.876	0.430

TABLE 10.6
Wage index numbers (1939 = 100)

	Cardinal p_{1t}^{*}/p_{10}	F–S p_{1t}^{**}/p_{10}	Cardinal p_{1t}/p_{1t}^{*}	F–S p_{1t}/p_{1t}^{**}
1939	100	100	100	100
1943	187	211	72	73
1946	160	170	104	111
1950	227	186	101	141
1955	291	195	104	178
1960	347	154	109	281
1965	403	135	117	396
1967	444	116	116	507

of hours the average worker was ready to work, and to constraints on wage rates. Otherwise, real wages, as measured by the real wage index p_{1t}/p_{1t}^{*} (see Table 10.6) increased slightly. In 1967, the improvement was about 16% only. This is much below the improvement of about 148% reported by Pencavel on the basis of the static linear expenditure system. The only possible explanation seems to be that taste changes have had a systematic influence. Taste changes due to habit formation seem to have been dominating, so that the consumer needs systematically 'more' to obtain the same utility. This phenomenon is reflected in the positive α-coefficients, and especially in the positive α_1 for the demand for leisure. With an ever increasing minimum amount of leisure, the wage rate that keeps utility constant is continuously increased with the result that the gain in real wages is reduced.

Our estimated rise in real wages is even lower than the one recorded by the Bureau of Labor Statistics (BLS) on the basis of measurements which tend to ignore not only substitution effects but also changes in tastes. While the inclusion of the former tend to indicate greater gains, (as illustrated in Pencavel's approach based on static utility theory), the latter bring us below the descriptive BLS measurements. All in all then, the neglect of dynamic phenomena may bias measurements of real wages as much – and probably more, in fact – as the neglect of substitution phenomena.

The Fisher–Shell cost-of-living index is known to reduce the impact of habit formation in comparison with the cardinal cost-of-living index. One therefore expects the F–S constant-utility wage rate to be below the cardinal p_{lt}^*, and therefore to indicate a greater rise in real wages when compared to the observed wage rate. This is exactly what happens in Tables 10.5 and 10.6. Rather surprisingly, the F–S constant-utility wage rate p_{lt}^{**} even starts to decline in the sixties.

At this point, a word of warning is in order: to the extent that the estimates of the α-coefficients may be biased upwards (which may be the case for a number of items in the system, and is certainly true for the α-coefficient of the item 'automobiles and parts'), the evolutions of both p_{lt}^* and p_{lt}^{**} may be exaggerated, especially in the sixties. Nevertheless, the numbers reported convey three messages which are very clear: (a) a static utility maximization approach exaggerates the gain in real wages; (b) the same is even more true in a dynamic approach, when the Fisher–Shell index, focusing on current tastes, is used; (c) to the extent that habit formation is properly taken into account, the gain in real wages appears as small, and smaller than indicated by the Laspeyres-type index numbers used by the Bureau of Labor Statistics.

To conclude, our numerical exercises tend to corroborate the general feeling that the increases in nominal wages, however impressive, do not more than catch up with our ever increasing needs. In other words, to end in a philosophical mood: while our incomes are higher than those of our parents, this does not imply that we enjoy life more.

XI

An intertemporal approach

In this chapter we analyse the behaviour of a consumer who looks into the future. We want to explain the allocation of his budget among n commodities, when due attention is given to the fact that he is not maximizing an instantaneous 'static' or an instantaneous 'dynamic' utility function (in which the influence of past behaviour is incorporated) as in previous chapters, but is maximizing an 'intertemporal' utility function, defined on sequences over time (from now to some future date) of commodity bundles. The objective is to correct the myopic character of the approach followed until now, by incorporating into the analysis information about the effects on present allocation of future satisfactions linked with a continuing building-up of habits or stocks.

Implicit in the preceding statement is the idea that it seems worthwhile – as a matter of research strategy – to try to define an 'intertemporal' utility function in which the static or dynamic 'instantaneous' utility functions utilized in earlier chapters would be imbedded. Section 11.1 determines at what cost an *ordinal* intertemporal utility function of that sort can be set up. This cost will appear to be high, as it will be necessary to accept a set of rather restrictive postulates.

It turns out that the existence of a utility function satisfying these postulates permits one to conclude that 'impatience', i.e. preference for an advanced timing of consumption, prevails in general. A brief discussion of this and of the related concept of 'time perspective' is offered in Section 11.2.

Our objective is to derive results that can be tested empirically. Section 11.3 is therefore devoted to the additional cost involved in defining an intertemporal utility function as the sum of present and future instantaneous utilities. This sum or integral (called a 'utility functional') is indeed the starting point of most empirical work in the field. The

267

consumer will be supposed to maximize this sum (or integral) in each period (or at each point in time) to determine the optimal sequence over time of commodity bundles. A problem of consistency arises as the future sequence, which appears as optimal today, may turn out (and will in fact turn out) to be different from the sequence that is optimal as of tomorrow (when the consumer proceeds to a new maximization). Section 11.4 is devoted to this difficult problem.

The traditional budget constraint ceases to be appropriate in an intertemporal framework, in which savings and the rate of interest have to play a role. In Section 11.5, the budget constraint is therefore replaced by what we shall call a 'wealth constraint', defined in terms of savings, wealth, the rate of interest, disposable income and total expenditures.

In the remaining sections, systems of demand equations derived by maximizing duly specified utility functionals under an intertemporal budget constraint are constructed. The functionals will be defined as the integral of one of the dynamic instantaneous utility functions discussed in Chapter VII. As a result, the intertemporal analysis presented here will appear as a generalization of the myopic approach followed in earlier chapters, which was itself a generalization of the traditional static analysis.

Our interest is in intertemporal models with taste changes and durables. By definition, such models view the consumer as being conscious of the implications, for the development of future preferences, of past and current consumption decisions. In this sense, 'rational habit formation' is involved and the models (or the consumers) under analysis are said to be rational.

Before entering these (complicated) matters, Section 11.8 discusses the static intertemporal allocation model. Indeed, we want to analyze the relations between the consumption–savings decision and the allocation of a given consumption budget among n commodities. In particular, we want to know under which conditions the two problems can be separated. These conditions have been extensively analyzed in the static case without taste changes.

A natural question will then be to ask, in Section 11.9, whether they extend to the dynamic case with myopic and/or rational habit formation. Once this question is answered, we will move to the practical problem of the estimation of demand systems derived under the assumption of rational habit formation. Many a reader will be surprised, with us, to discover – in Sections 11.10 and 11.11 – that the myopic dynamic demand systems presented in Chapter VII above are observationally equivalent with the corresponding rational dynamic systems.

We abstract throughout from the uncertainty that naturally arises in an intertemporal framework and therefore assume that the consumer has either perfect information or deterministic expectations.

11.1.* Ordinal intertemporal utility functions

We want a utility function representing an ordering of sequences over time of particular commodity bundles. In order to arrive at precise statements, some additional notation is needed. It is convenient to adopt the notation introduced by Koopmans in his pioneering 1960 article and adopted by subsequent writers.

A sequence over time of particular commodity bundles will be called a program and denoted

$$_1x = (x_1, x_2, x_3, \ldots, x_t, \ldots) = (x_1, _2x) = \text{etc.} \tag{11.1}$$

Two things should be noticed. First, the subscripts 1, 2, ... now refer to discrete subsequent time periods. No confusion with our earlier notation should arise, it being understood that each symbol x_t, $t = 1$, 2, ..., represents a bundle (vector)

$$x_t = (x_{t1}, x_{t2}, \ldots, x_{tn}) \tag{11.2}$$

of the non-negative amounts of n listed commodities to be consumed in period t.

Second, each program extends over an infinite future. The (perhaps surprising) implication is that the consumer's horizon is supposed to extend to infinity. In fact, this assumption simplifies matters, as it avoids the difficulties connected with the finite life span of the individual, such as (see Yaari, 1964): should his bequests be included in the program or not?; if they are, what is the utility to be assigned to these bequests?; if they are not included, does this mean that the consumer is obliged to run down his stocks of durables with advancing age? etc.[1] The infinite horizon hypothesis greatly simplifies the presentation of the problem, although it introduces technical complications as we will see later on. (For example, the techniques of optimal control theory to be used will have to be adapted to it.) The scrupulous economist may notice that one could resort to the fiction of an immortal decision unit, the family, say, including the present and all future

---

[1] Furthermore, the consumer does not know how long he will live. See Yaari (1965) for an analysis of the implications of uncertain lifetime.

generations. He may also notice that a bequest, after all, represents the collection of consumption programs (beyond the life time horizon) that it makes possible.

A bundle x_t is a point selected from the (single period) commodity set X (on which the static preference ordering was defined in Chapter I). The utility function we are looking for has to be defined *for all possible programs*, i.e. for all $_1x$, and will be written $U(_1x)$. (The reader is requested to check his understanding of this statement.) We would like $U(_1x)$ to be a (simple) ordinal function of $u_1(x_1)$, $u_2(x_2)$, $u_3(x_3)$, $\ldots$, i.e. of the instantaneous utility functions.

For this to be possible, at least four postulates are to be accepted (a fifth postulate being introduced to allow a scaling of U between 0 and 1). These postulates are directly in terms of U, rather than in terms of an underlying preference ordering, to avoid mathematical difficulties. More recent work by Mantel (1970) for the continuous time case, shows that it is possible to work out corresponding postulates as properties of a preference ordering over time.

P1 (EXISTENCE AND CONTINUITY): *There exists a continuous utility function $U(_1x)$, which is defined for all $_1x = (x_1, x_2, \ldots,)$ such that, for all t, x_t is a point of a bounded convex subset X of the n dimensional commodity space.* A discussion of the concept of continuity to be used in a infinite-dimensional space is to be found in Koopmans (1960).

P2 (SENSITIVITY): *There exist first-period consumption vectors x_1, x_1' and a program $_2x$ from-the-second-period-on, such that*

$$U(x_1, {}_2x) > U(x_1', {}_2x).$$

This postulate requires that utility can be changed by changing the consumption vector in some designated period. It excludes the case, for example, where a decision-maker attaches utility only to a consumption level exceeding some minimum level, no matter how long he has to wait for it: a change in a particular period might then leave U unaffected.

P1 and P2 are not likely to raise objections. The two following postulates are much more restrictive and play in fact the key role.

P3 (LIMITED NONCOMPLEMENTARITY): *For all x_1, x_1', $_2x$, $_2x'$,*
(P3a) $U(x_1, {}_2x) \geqq U(x_1', {}_2x)$ *implies* $U(x_1, {}_2x') \geqq U(x_1', {}_2x')$,
(P3b) $U(x_1, {}_2x) \geqq U(x_1, {}_2x')$ *implies* $U(x_1', {}_2x) \geqq U(x_1', {}_2x')$.

(P3b) says that the particular bundle to be consumed in the first period has no effect on the preference between alternative sequences of bundles in the remaining future. The converse is true according to (P3a). In Koopmans' words: 'One cannot claim a high degree of realism for such a postulate, because there is no clear reason why complementarity of goods could not extend over more than one time period' (Koopmans, 1960, p. 292).

P3 is going to be accepted, because it allows us to write the intertemporal utility function as

$$U(_1x) = V(u_1(x_1), U_2(_2x)),\tag{11.3}$$

where $V(u_1, U_2)$ is a continuous and increasing function of u_1, the instantaneous utility function (at time $t = 1$) and $U_2(_2x)$, the intertemporal utility function associated *in period* 2 with all sequences starting from time $t = 2$.

The form (11.3) is a step forward but not entirely satisfactory. What we are looking for is an intertemporal function of the form

$$U(_1x) = V(u(x_1), U(_2x)),\tag{11.4}$$

where $u_1(x_1)$ is replaced by $u(x_1)$ and $U_2(_2x)$ is replaced by $U(_2x)$. The dropping of the time subscripts is crucial. Indeed, when (11.4) is true, $U(_2x)$ is, in turn, equal to

$$U(_2x) = V(u(x_2), U(_3x))$$

and similarly for $U(_3x)$ and so on. The introduction of U_2 in (11.3) is thus an intermediate step which prepares its replacement by $U(_2x)$ to obtain the *recurrent* relation (11.4). This property will then allow to write $U(_1x)$ as a function of $u(x_1)$, $u(x_2)$, $u(x_3)$, etc., i.e. the *immediate* utility levels associated with the successive vectors x_t of a program $_1x$.

The replacement in (11.3) of $U_2(_2x)$ by $U(_2x)$ is possible if one accepts an additional postulate. A correct interpretation of that postulate will also permit a better understanding of the meaning of the notation $U(_2x)$.

P4 (STATIONARITY): *For a given x_1 and all $_2x$, $_2x'$,*
$U(x_1, _2x) \geqq U(x_1, _2x')$ *if and only if* $U(_2x) \geqq U(_2x')$

The idea is that the passage of time is not allowed to have an effect on preferences. An equivalent statement of P4, given by Koopmans et al. (1964) clarifies matters a lot. Suppose four programmes A, B, C and D, *each starting in period* 1, contain the following bundles:

Program	1	2	3	4	
A	x_1	x_2	x_3	x_4	...
B	x_1	x_2'	x_3'	x_4'	...
C	x_2	x_3	x_4	...	...
D	x_2'	x_3'	x_4'	...	...

P4 says that, *for a given x_1 and all $_2x, _2x'$, program A is at least as good as program B if and only if program C is at least as good as program D.* In other words, the ordering of two programs that differ only from the second period on is supposed to be the same as that of corresponding programs obtained by *advancing* the timing of every future consumption vector by one period. Conversely, *postponement* of entire programs does not affect the *present* ordering, provided gaps created by such post-ponement are filled in the same way (see (P3b)) for all programs compared.

It is worth emphasizing that P4 does not imply the absence or the constancy of a preference for advanced timing of consumption ('impatience'). P4 also 'does *not* imply that, after one period has elapsed, the ordering then applicable to the 'then' future will necessarily be the same as that now applicable to the 'present' future. All postulates are concerned with only one ordering, namely that guiding decisions to be taken in the present. Any question of change or constancy of preferences as the time of choice changes is therefore extraneous to the present study' (Koopmans et al., 1964, p. 85–86). To be even more explicit, P4 does not prevent us from defining the instantaneous utility functions that are going to appear in (11.4) as being dynamic in the sense of Chapter VII.

It remains to show why P4 allows us to go from (11.3) to (11.4). The proof is rather simple. Notice first that $V(u_1, U_2)$ increases with U_2. P4 implies therefore that

$$U_2(_2x) \geqq U_2(_2x') \quad \text{if and only} \quad \text{if } U(_2x) \geqq U(_2x').$$

It follows that $U_2(_2x) = G(U(_2x))$, where G is a continuous increasing function, or $U(_2x) = G^{-1}U_2(_2x)$. As the intertemporal utility function $U(_1x)$ is ordinal, we can replace it by a monotonic transformation of it. The same is true for its arguments u_1 and U_2. It suffices then to choose the transformation

$$U^*(_1x) = U(_1x)$$
$$u_1^* = u_1$$
$$U_2^* = G^{-1}U_2$$
$$V^*(u_1^*, U_2^*) = V(u_1^*, G(U_2^*)).$$

EXERCISE

11.1. (a) Show that the monotonic transformation above makes the functions $U_2^*(_2x)$ and $U^*(_2x)$ identical;

(b) convince yourself that we can therefore drop the time subscripts from the symbols u_1^* and U_2^* and thus write (11.3) as (11.4), dropping all the asterisks.

Koopmans finally introduces a postulate P5 of monotonicity, insuring that $V(0, 0) = 0$ and $V(1, 1) = 1$ when the interval for the values of u and U is defined as the unit interval.

We will not enter into further technical details, but rather emphasize again the recursive nature of the ordinal intertemporal utility function (11.4). Its iterated application leads to

$$U(_1x) = V(u(x_1), u(x_2), \ldots, u(x_\tau), U(_{\tau+1}x)) \tag{11.5}$$

for all τ, where the functions $u(x_1), u(x_2), \ldots$ represent the *immediate* utility levels associated with the successive vectors x_t of a program $_1x$.

At what cost, then, have we been able to derive the desired utility function? Clearly, the problems which the decision-unit analysed here is supposed to be faced with are drastic simplifications of real-world problems: the programs to be ordered by the utility functions are assumed available with certainty; the number of commodities is supposed to be fixed from now to infinity (no new goods are allowed to appear!); we assume that there is a lower and an upper bound to the feasible rates of consumption of any commodity (as the commodity set X is bounded); the stationarity and the limited noncomplementarity postulates are restrictive. Obviously, these simplifications were introduced to isolate the significance of timing in relation to preference from other equally significant aspects of economic choice.

11.2.* Impatience and time perspective

Once the utility function (11.4) or (11.5) and the underlying postulates are accepted, it becomes an easy matter to formulate a sharp definition of *impatience*, the short term Fisher (1930) has introduced for preference for advanced timing of satisfaction. The concept itself goes back to Böhm-Bawerk's *Positive Theorie des Kapitals* (1912), but the definition given here, which is in terms of the intertemporal utility function, is due to Koopmans (1960).

DEFINITION: *A program* $_1x$ *with first-and-second-period utility levels* $u_1 = u(x_1)$, $u_2 = u(x_2)$ *and prospective utility* $U_3 = U(_3x)$ *from-the-third-period-on will be said to meet the impatience condition if*

$$V(u_1, V(u_2, U_3)) \gtreqless V(u_2, V(u_1, U_3)) \quad when \quad u_1 \gtreqless u_2.$$

In other words, if in any given year the consumption of a bundle x of commodities is preferred over that of a bundle x', then the consumption in two successive years of x, x', in that order, is preferred to the consumption of x', x. Impatience so defined is a property of the underlying preference ordering and is therefore invariant under any continuous increasing transformation of the utility scale.

The surprising thing is that the postulates set up to derive an intertemporal utility function imply impatience, at least in certain parts of the programme space, in the sense that impatience is a necessary logical consequence of the postulated properties of the utility function. The reader interested in the proof of this assertion is referred to Koopmans' original article (1960). The surprise stems from the fact that impatience used to be presented as an irrational preference, as exemplified in the quotation form Pigou's *The Economics of Welfare* (1952, Chapter II, § 3) which follows, whereas impatience appears now as implied in a perfectly rational preference ordering. Pigou says:

Generally speaking, everybody prefers present pleasures or satisfactions of given magnitude to future pleasures or satisfactions of equal magnitude, even when the latter are perfectly certain to occur.
... if we set out a series of exactly equal satisfactions – *satisfactions*, not objects that yield satisfactions – all of them absolutely certain to occur over a series of years beginning now, the desires which a man will entertain for these several satisfactions will not be equal, but will be represented by a scale of magnitudes continually diminishing as the years to which the satisfactions are allocated become more remote. This reveals a far-reaching economic disharmony. For it implies that people distribute their resources between the present, the near future and the remote future on the basis of a wholly irrational preference.

Subsequently, a deeper property of the preference ordering in question, called *time perspective*, was found by Koopmans et al. (1964) and used to derive the previous result regarding impatience, and to extend it to a larger part of the program space. In their own words:

To define it, consider two consumption programs, $(x, x', x'', \ldots)$ and $(y, y', y'', \ldots)$ of which the first is preferred to the second. Now postpone each entire program by one time unit, and insert a common consumption bundle z in the gap so created in both programs, to make $(z, x, x', \ldots)$ and $(z, y, y', \ldots)$ respectively. Then, by postulates 3 and 4 of the previous study, the postponed first program is still preferred to the postponed second program. We shall say that a utility function chosen to represent the preference ordering has the property of time perspective if, for all programs $(x, x', x'', \ldots)$ and $(y, y', y'', \ldots)$ and for all inserts z that one may choose in the above description, the *difference* of the utilities of the postponed programs is smaller than the differences of the utilities of the original programs. Since utility differences enter into this definition, time perspective, as a property of a utility function, is not invariant for continuous increasing transformation of the utility scale. We say, however, that a preference ordering of consumption programs itself has the property of time perspective if it can be represented by at least one utility function having that property.

The term 'time perspective' is derived from an analogy with perspective in space. As the timing of the differences between any two programs is made to recede into a more distant future, the utility difference between the programs diminishes, in an appropriate representation of the ordering. (Koopmans et al., 1964, p. 83.)

11.3.* Utility functionals

In applied work, the function (11.5) is generally specified as

$$U(_1x) = \sum_{t=1}^{\infty} a^{t-1} u_t(x_t), \qquad 0 < a < 1, a = \frac{1}{1+\gamma}, \tag{11.6a}$$

in discrete time, or as

$$U(_1x) = \int_0^{\infty} e^{-\gamma t} u_t(x(t)) \, dt, \tag{11.6b}$$

in continuous time. Obviously, this procedure implies a drastic additional restriction of 'additivity' over time, as the intertemporal utility function is defined as a (discounted) *sum* of all future one-period utilities, i.e. as a sum of instantaneous utility functions, or as a functional taking the form of an integral.

In fact, to be able to write (11.6) one has to accept the following independence postulate:

P3′ (INDEPENDENCE): *For all* $x_1, x_2, {}_3x, x_1', x_2', {}_3x',$
(3′a) $U(x_1, x_2, {}_3x) \geqq U(x_1', x_2', {}_3x)$ *implies* $U(x_1, x_2, {}_3x') \geqq U(x_1', x_2', {}_3x')$
(3′b) $U(x_1, x_2, {}_3x) \geqq U(x_1', x_2, {}_3x)$ *implies* $U(x_1, x_2', {}_3x) \geqq U(x_1', x_2', {}_3x).$

Indeed, postulates 1–5 and 3′ together satisfy the premises of a theorem by Debreu (1960) which says that one can find a monotonic transformations of $U(_1x)$ such that

$$U(_1x) = u_1(x_1) + u_2(x_2) + U_3(_3x) \tag{11.7}$$

from which one derives (11.6). Independence implies that the marginal rate of substitution between two adjacent periods is independent of what happens in future periods.

The additive form of (11.6) is *cardinal*, i.e. defined up to a linear increasing transformation, as additivity over time is not invariant under nonlinear transformations (exactly as in the case of additivity over commodities). The reader who has doubts should read Appendix I of Hadley and Kemp's book on *Variational Methods in Economics* (1971).

Cardinality is an unhappy restriction, which one adopts to the extent that it is necessary in view of the objective to be attained. In what follows, we will only use utility functionals, because they make the use of powerful analytical techniques possible. This is not to say that an ordinal approach to intertemporal problems would be impossible. All we claim is that the cardinal approach is the most fruitful in the present state of the art and in the field we are interested in. In saying this we depart from the extreme position taken by Ragnar Frisch, who thinks that in the dynamic part of economic theory, 'it is absolutely *necessary* to consider the concept of cardinal utility if we want to develop a sensible sort of analysis' (1964, p. 418). Indeed, the particular example set up by Frisch to illustrate his statement was shown by Morishima (1965) to be but a particular case of a more general ordinal result.

The discount function appearing in (11.6) expresses the 'impatience', i.e. the preference for advanced timing of consumption. As the present date, at which $U(_1x)$ is defined, is regarded as fixed, the discounting depends on the time distance of a future date from the present moment.

The assumption that the discount function takes the particular form $e^{-\gamma t}$ with a constant factor γ has interesting implications about which more will be said in the next section.

11.4.* Consistency in intertemporal utility maximization

In the set-up of Chapter VII, the consumer was supposed to maximize in each period (or at each moment of time) the instantaneous dynamic utility function of that period (or moment). This behaviour was described

---

[2] See also Morishima (1969, Chapter XII).

as 'myopic' because the consumer is ignoring that he is going to continue to build up habits and stocks and even to purchase and ... consume. We now have concepts at our disposal that permit us to drop the assumption of myopia.

In the meantime, we came across another sort of myopia, namely the phenomenon of impatience and the related 'time perspective', which leads to the introduction of a discount function inside the utility functional. If then the consumer is supposed to maximize his utility functional at each time period, a difficult problem of consistency cannot be avoided, as was pointed out by Strotz (1956).

Today, the consumer maximizes his utility functional. That means that he determines an optimal program of commodity bundles x_t for the present period *and* for all subsequent periods. Tomorrow, he does his computations again, and so on. Whenever new information becomes available, the new optimal program is different from the optimal program determined yesterday. But even if all information about present and future utilities, prices and incomes, etc., remains unaltered, the program that appears as optimal tomorrow will generally be different from the program when viewed at an earlier date, because the discount function in the functional will take on a different value (for a particular time period) for the simple reason that time has evolved! For example, the instantaneous utility function u_2 to which, when viewed at time $t = 1$, a weight smaller than one is associated, appears in period $t = 2$ with a weight equal to one: the old discount function shifted in time. Accordingly, observed consumption in any period is the initial vector of an optimal sequence, the sequence being in general different from period to period as the result of a 'continuous replanning'.

Observed behaviour is therefore seen, not as following one single optimal path over time, but as a sequence of points or segments on successive optimal paths. The presence of impatience is a sufficient reason for the consumer to find himself continuously repudiating his past plans and be apparently inconsistent with himself. This is the problem of consistency raised by Strotz.

As such, continuous replanning is entirely rational. Therefore, the resulting repudiating of past plans is entirely rational also, given that impatience is consistent with out postulates. The consumer may nevertheless want to do something about it.

Two kinds of action are possible. (1) He may try to commit his future activities in advance either irrevocably or by contriving a penalty for his future self if he should misbehave. Joining the army, or marriage for the sake of 'settling down', or adhering to a savings plan[3] are good examples of this *strategy of precommitment*. (2) The consumer may also resign himself to the fact of intertemporal conflict and convince himself that his optimal program at any date is a will-o'-the-wisp, and try to select the present action which will be best in the light of future disobedience. He may decide to reject any plan that will not follow through. This is what Strotz calls the *strategy of consistent planning*.

How is this consistency to be achieved? It turns out, as will be shown in a moment, that the consumer should give his discount function a particular shape. In fact the particular form to be taken by the discount function is the one introduced in (11.6), namely $e^{-\gamma t}$, where γ is a constant.

The proof runs as follows. Consider the simple case where the consumer has to maximize

$$\int_0^T \mu(t) u[C(t), t]\, dt \tag{11.8}$$

with respect to $C(t)$ (given 0 and T) and subject to the constraint that the total consumption $\int_0^T C(t)\, dt$ to be allocated over time is a constant, i.e.

$$\int_0^T C(t)\, dt = K(0).$$

$\mu(t)$ is an unspecified discount function and $C(t)$ is consumption in year t. Define

$$y(t) = \int_0^t C(t)\, dt$$

so that

$$
\begin{aligned}
y(0) &= 0, \\
y(T) &= K(0), \\
\dot{y} &= C(t).
\end{aligned}
$$

Replacing $C(t)$ by $\dot{y}$ in the utility functional, we have an elementary problem of the calculus of variations. The solution is given by the Euler equation (see Hadley and Kemp, 1971, Chapter 2), which is particularly simple here, given that we have to maximize the integral $\int_0^T \mu(t)\, u[\dot{y}(t), t]\, dt$

---

[3] Another way of achieving commitment is to have a preference inheritance mechanism such as the one implied in the state variable approach. On this, see Section 11.12* below.

in which y does not appear. The Euler equation reduces to

$$\frac{\mathrm{d}}{\mathrm{d}t}\left[\frac{\partial}{\partial \dot{y}}\mu(t)u[\dot{y}(t), t]\right] = \frac{\mathrm{d}}{\mathrm{d}t}[\mu(t)u_C] = 0$$

or

$$\mu(t)\dot{u}_C + u_C\dot{\mu} = 0$$

i.e.

$$\dot{\mu}/\mu = -\dot{u}_C/u_C$$

where $u_C = \partial u/\partial C = \partial u/\partial \dot{y}$. Consequently $\mu(t) u_C$ has to be constant over time, which means that the 'stock of consumption' $K(0)$ must be distributed over the interval 0 to T so that the discounted marginal utility of consumption $(\mu(t)u_C)$ is the same for all dates. However, continuous replanning may imply that any program selected according to this criterion today has to be repudiated tomorrow according to the *same* criterion.

Suppose now that this consumer wants to follow the strategy of consistent planning. His problem is then to find a plan which he will follow through. In the narrow framework of the case just described, this consistent plan $\dot{z}(t)$ must have the property that at the limit where $\Delta\tau \to 0$

$$\int_0^\tau \mu(t-\tau)u[\dot{z}(t), t]\mathrm{d}t + \int_\tau^{\tau+\Delta\tau} \mu(t-\tau)u[\dot{z}(t), t]\mathrm{d}t + \int_{\tau+\Delta\tau}^T \mu(t-\tau)u[\dot{z}(t), t]\mathrm{d}t$$

is a maximum of

$$\int_0^\tau \mu(t-\tau)u[\dot{z}(t), t]\mathrm{d}t + \int_\tau^{\tau+\Delta\tau} \mu(t-\tau)u[\dot{y}(t), t]\mathrm{d}t + \int_{\tau+\Delta\tau}^T \mu(t-\tau)u[\dot{z}(t), t]\mathrm{d}t$$

with respect to $\dot{y}(t)$ subject to the constraint defined above. To find this maximum, it suffices to maximize the middle term. The solution has to hold for all τ and is, again according to the Euler equation,

$$\dot{\mu}(t-\tau)/\mu(t-\tau) = -\dot{u}_C/u_C.$$

Since this must hold for every τ, $\dot{\mu}/\mu$ or $\mathrm{d}\log\mu/\mathrm{d}t$ must be a constant. At $\tau = 0$, i.e. at the present moment, we have

$$\dot{\mu}(t)/\mu(t) = \text{a constant}, \tag{11.9}$$

or, using the constant $-\gamma$

$$\mu(t) = e^{-\gamma t}. \tag{11.10}$$

The consistent planner must, therefore, first substitute for his 'true' discount function (which may take any form) one whose relative rate of change over time is a constant and then maximize. Q.E.D.

The rate at which future satisfactions are discounted at any moment has to be a constant, for consistency.[4] In other words, the same rate γ has to be applied, today, to all future utilities (which, by the way, implies a regular decline in the discount function $e^{-\gamma t}$). But γ has also to be a constant over time, i.e. at each re-evaluation of the optimal plan, if one wants to achieve consistency. If, in fact, γ is a variable, there is indication that the strategy of consistent planning has *not* been followed.

We conjecture that the strategy of consistent planning is never entirely successful. In general, expectations of future satisfactions and means of consumption are not verified, so that another strategy has to be worked out.[5] And even if all expectations were verified, impatience may change over time, with the result that γ varies.

Fisher (1930) has analyzed the forces that may influence γ and make it vary, both from individual to individual and over time. The level of income is probably an important factor: the smaller is total consumption, the greater is the preference for advanced timing of consumption. Expectations of future incomes also play a role: the greater is an expected rise in income, the greater is the impatience to spend now rather than tomorrow. Riskiness of future events has a similar effect: during the war, γ was probably higher than after the war; during the Korean crisis, γ probably jumped upwards suddenly, leading to a tremendous increase in purchases.

11.5.* The wealth constraint

In the special case imagined above to prove that consistency requires subjective discounting at a constant rate, the consumer was supposed to face the constraint of a given 'consumption stock' to be allocated over

---

[4] See Pollak (1968) for a further discussion of the strategy of consistent planning.

[5] We have nothing to say about that 'other' strategy that might be 'best' in the face of uncertain events. The techniques of stochastic control (or stochastic programming) may be useful to handle this difficult problem of consistency in an uncertain world.

time. A constraint of this sort clearly has a very limited applicability. It refers to a man who must ration fresh water to himself during a safari, for example, or to other similar extreme situations. We want to introduce prices and income.

The usual static constraint $\sum_i p_i x_i = y$ would not do in this inter-

temporal framework, in which savings, wealth and the rate of interest have to appear. Let $w = w(t)$ represent either total wealth (human and non-human) or non-human only. Non-human wealth is defined here as identical with financial wealth, to simplify the analysis. The consumer is supposed to have no need to hold money. Changes in the value of durables are also excluded from the analysis. Human wealth is defined as the discounted value of future labour income. With $Y = Y(t)$ representing disposable labour income, and $r = r(t)$ the rate of interest

$$Y + r w_F = y + \dot{w}_F \tag{11.11}$$

by definition, if w_F stands for *financial* wealth. Indeed, disposable personal income ($Y + r w_F$) is equal to expenditures ($y = \sum_i p_i x_i$) plus

savings ($\dot{w}_F$). Rearranging (11.11), we see that $\dot{w}$ evolves according to

$$\dot{w}_F = r w_F + Y - y \tag{11.12}$$

which we call the (financial) wealth constraint.

When the problem to be handled is the allocation of disposable income among total consumption (y) and savings ($\dot{w}_F$), Y, p and r are exogenously given and y is the unknown sequence of total consumption expenditures to be determined. This is the typical lifetime allocation process analysed by a number of authors, among which we will cite Fisher (1930), Duesenberry (1949), Friedman (1957), Modigliani and Brumberg (1955) and Yaari (1964).

We are interested in determining the optimal program x describing the optimal vector of purchases x_t in each year. However, with given prices, in each year, total expenditures are determined as soon as the quantity vector is determined. To the extent that the consumer is following a policy of consistent planning, this implies the existence of one optimal path for y that is followed through over the planning period. Otherwise, total expenditures are the initial point (or segment) of an optimal path that may be different from period to period as a result of the strategy of continuous replanning. In any case, total expenditures are also endogenous in our problem, so that there is no need any longer to treat the intertemporal allocation of total expenditures as an independent problem and to consider total expenditures as given.[6]

It is worth noticing that this wealth constraint is *instantaneous*, i.e. valid at each point in time. While the consumer has to know with certainty the future satisfactions he is going to derive from his future consumptions, in order to define his intertemporal utility function, he does *not* have to know future prices or future labour income in the exposition given above. If we can manage to solve our problem in the set-up given, without use of future prices and income, we will have avoided a difficulty that besets investment theory in general, and in particular the theory of the intertemporal allocation of total expenditures referred to above. In our opinion, the main advantage of optimal control theory, which we are going to use to solve our problem, is that it reduces an intertemporal problem to an instantaneous one. As a result, we shall be able to utilize the instantaneous wealth constraint as defined in (11.12): there will be no need to solve the differential equation, so that future prices and incomes will not enter the picture. (The same will be true, as we shall see in the next section, for future satisfactions, as the intertemporal maximization problem will be redefined as an instantaneous one.)

A final comment on the wealth constraint is in order. The feasibility constraint behind (11.12) seems to be that financial wealth should not eventually become and remain negative. At first sight, this seems reasonable enough. In fact, the condition is too strong, as it excludes the possibility that the consumer may wish to accumulate debt that eventually converges to the value of his human wealth. Arrow and Kurz (1969) therefore insist that in a correct setting of the problem w should be defined as representing *total* wealth, i.e. financial plus human wealth.

To take account of this objection, it suffices to redefine (11.12) as

$$\dot{w} = rw - \sum_i p_i x_i \tag{11.13}$$

where w is now financial *plus* human wealth. Indeed, human wealth (w_H) obeys the condition

$$\dot{w}_H = rw_H - Y$$

---

[6] Lluch (1973) has derived the aggregate consumption function implied in this sort of intertemporal maximization, for the case of an instantaneous static Stone-Geary function.

so that

$$\dot{w} = \dot{w}_F + \dot{w}_H = r(w_F + w_H) + Y - y - Y = rw - \sum_i p_i x_i.$$

Now the feasibility condition becomes $w(t) > 0$ for all $t > 0$. In applied work, we shall have to ignore this theoretical refinement and stick to the financial wealth constraint as defined in (11.12), as statistical data measuring the human wealth of the average consumer are of course not available.

We are ready now to solve the problem of finding the optimal program (or path) x that maximizes a utility functional under the wealth constraint (11.12).

11.6.* Dynamic demand systems and the maximum principle

The solution to our problem is given by the conditions which Pontryagin et al. (1964) baptized as 'the Maximum Principle'. As we shall see in a moment, our problem has indeed been set up in such a way that optimal control theory[7] is directly applicable.[8]

The Maximum Principle has been successfully applied to problems of growth and investment by Cass (1965), Arrow and Kurz (1970) and others, and is becoming a popular tool in that area, as can by seen from the symposium edited by Shell (1967). It has been presented to the general economist by Dorfman (1969). New fields of application are being explored every day.

Let the dynamic short-run utility function

$$u = f(x, s) \tag{11.14}$$

which we introduced in Chapter VII, be the consumer's instantaneous time-invariant and strictly concave utility function. In the terminology of control theory, $x = x(t)$ is an n vector of 'decision variables' or 'controls' while $s = s(t)$ is an n vector of 'state variables'. The latter describe the 'state of the system' and are interpreted as before.

The law of motion of the state of the system is described by a set of differential equations (or 'transformation functions')

$$\dot{s}_i = x_i - \delta_i s_i \tag{11.15}$$

---

[7] See Hadley and Kemp (1971) or Intriligator (1973) for excellent introductions to optimal control theory.

[8] This section is based on Phlips (1971b).

with which the reader is already familiar.[9] δ_i is a constant depreciation ratio.

Up to now, we have n decision variables x_i and n state variables s_i related pairwise by n transformation functions. These describe a transitive system, as the whole past is described by the state s attained at time t. The wealth constraint (11.12) provides an additional transformation, function, describing the law of motion of the additional state variable w.

At each moment of time, the consumer is supposed to maximize

$$U = \int_0^\infty e^{-\gamma t} u(x, s)\,\mathrm{d}t \tag{11.16}$$

with respect to the decision variables, subject to (11.12) and (11.15). For simplicity, we ignore possible other constraints, such as the non-negativity of x_i.

If an optimal program exists[10] and if all functions satisfy sufficiently strong smoothness conditions, the Maximum Principle gives the following necessity conditions.[11] Let $x^* = x^*(t)$ be a choice of purchases ($t \geqslant 0$) which maximizes (11.16), subject to (11.12) and (11.15) and initial conditions on the state variables. Then there exist $n + 1$ 'dual' or 'auxiliary' variables, an n vector of auxiliary variables $\psi = \psi(t)$ and a variable $\lambda = \lambda(t)$, such that, for each t:

x^* maximizes the current value Hamiltonian
$$H(x, s, \psi, \lambda) = u(x, s) + \psi' s + \lambda \dot{w}_F \tag{11.17}$$

and

$$\dot{\psi}_i = \gamma \psi_i - \frac{\partial H}{\partial s_i}$$
$$\dot{\lambda} = \gamma \lambda - \frac{\partial H}{\partial w_F} \tag{11.18}$$

evaluated at $s = s(t)$, $x = x^*(t)$, $\psi = \psi(t)$, $\lambda = \lambda(t)$ and $w_F = w_F(t)$.

However, if max H is concave in s for given ψ, λ and t, then any consumption policy satisfying the conditions (11.12), (11.15), (11.17) and (11.18) and the 'transversality conditions'

---

[9] See Chapter VI, equation (6.27).
[10] An existence theorem for this class of problems can be found in Thisse and Weiserbs (1973).
[11] See Arrow and Kurz (1970, Section II.6, 'Continuous time, infinite horizon').

$$\lim_{t \to \infty} \psi_i s_i e^{-\gamma t} = \lim_{t \to \infty} \psi_i e^{-\gamma t} = 0$$

$$\lim_{t \to \infty} \lambda w_F e^{-\gamma t} = \lim_{t \to \infty} \lambda e^{-\gamma t} = 0 \tag{11.19}$$

is optimal.

In economic terms, a very nice interpretation can be given to condition (11.17), which determines equilibrium purchases, and to condition (11.18), which governs optimal stocks (or habits).

The consumer is told by (11.17) to reduce his intertemporal problem to the maximization, in each period, of the Hamiltonian H. Clearly, this Hamiltonian is simply the current flow of utility from all sources, both enjoyed immediately (u) and anticipated for enjoyment ($\psi' \dot{s} + \lambda \dot{w}$). Indeed

$$e^{-\gamma t} \psi_i = \frac{\partial V}{\partial s_i} \quad \text{and} \quad e^{-\gamma t} \lambda = \frac{\partial V}{\partial w}$$

by definition, where

$$V = \max_x \left\{ \int_0^\infty e^{-\gamma t} u(x, s) \, dt \right\}.$$

ψ_i Is thus defined as the marginal contribution of the corresponding state variable to the utility functional, given that the consumer intends to follow the optimal path. In other words, ψ_i is the implicit value attached to a marginal unit of s_i, and λ is the implicit value attached to a marginal unit of wealth. ($\psi_i \dot{s}_i$) is therefore the rate of increase of utility due to the current rate of increase of state variable s_i, and $\psi' \dot{s}$ is the sum over all goods. In a similar way, ($\lambda \dot{w}$) is the rate of increase of utility due to the current rate of increase of wealth.

Purchases are optimal for all t, according to (11.17), when

$$\frac{\partial u}{\partial x_i} + \psi_i = \lambda p_i \tag{11.20}$$

given that $\partial \dot{s}_i / \partial x_i = 1$ and $\partial \dot{s}_j / \partial x_i = 0$ for $j \neq i$.

We turn now to condition (11.18). For optimal stocks (or habits) we have

$$\dot{\psi}_i = \gamma \psi_i - \left(\frac{\partial u}{\partial s_i} + \psi_i \frac{\partial \dot{s}_i}{\partial s_i} \right)$$

$$= (\gamma + \delta_i) \psi_i - \frac{\partial u}{\partial s_i}, \tag{11.21}$$

i.e. the sum of net contributions to utility $[(\partial u/\partial s_i) - (\delta_i + \gamma)\psi_i]$ plus the change in implicit price $(\dot{\psi}_i)$ is zero. In other words, the implicit value of a marginal unit of s_i must change such as to reward the consumer for 'waiting' $(\gamma\psi_i)$ less the value of net satisfaction $[(\partial u/\partial s_i) - \delta_i\psi_i]$ received. Condition (11.18) also gives

$$\frac{\dot{\lambda}}{\lambda} = \gamma - r. \tag{11.22}$$

On the optimal path, the relative rate of change of the implicit value of wealth must be equal to the difference between the rate of time preference (γ) and the rate of interest (r) associated with w_F.

EXERCISES

11.2. (a) Derive conditions (11.17) and (11.18) – or, equivalently, (11.10) to (11.22) – for the case where

$$u(x, s) = \sum_i \beta_i \log (x_i - \theta_i - \alpha_i s_i).$$

(b) Show that these conditions are also sufficient, by verifiing that max H is strictly concave, which itself implies (see Arrow and Kurz, 1970, p. 36) that $\partial^2 H/\partial s_i^2 < 0$.

11.3. Do the same for the case where

$$u(x, s) = a'x + b's + \tfrac{1}{2}x'Ax + x'Bs + \tfrac{1}{2}s'Cs.$$

11.7.* Alternative estimation procedures

From here on, a method for estimating systems of intertemporal demand equations has to be worked out. Several routes can be followed.

In the first edition of this book (Chapter X, pp. 225–263) a first and rather obvious strategy was adopted, namely to try to use the conditions derived from the Maximum Principle as estimating equations. This amounts to supposing that the consumption data observed for period t are the result of planning decisions made in t such that (11.20), (11.21), (11.22), (11.15) and (11.12) are satisfied (except for a random error term). Only the quadratic model, with its linear first order conditions, turned out to be tractable this way. The non-linear character of the first order derivatives of the Stone–Geary utility function makes the elimination of ψ_i very difficult, if not impossible.[12] In addition, it was necessary to use linear approximations to trans-

---

[12] Efforts in that direction are reported in Phlips and Weiserbs (1972).

form continuous time results into measurable discrete time equations.

In the same vein, a second approach is to simultaneously solve the allocation problem of y_t among the n commodities at each period t, and the allocation problem of income in year t between total consumption (or expenditures) y_t and savings. It suffices then to determine the optimal time path for each commodity $\{x_{it}\}$ and to aggregate over the n commodities to find optimal total consumption. This is the approach followed by Lluch (1973) in the construction of the so-called 'extended linear expenditure system', in which an equation explaining y_t in terms of exogenous income is added to the (static) linear expenditure system.

However, demand analysis generally proceeds otherwise. Most models dealing with the consumer's demand for goods and services at a disaggregated level study the allocation of a *given* budget y_t among different uses. It is therefore assumed that the intertemporal consumer choice can be *decentralized*. Once the budgets (y_t) are allocated to the different periods, the consumer is supposed to be able to allocate his budget of a particular period among the different goods and services *without reconsidering the entire intertemporal optimization procedure.*

This third route is the one followed here.[13] After discussing decentralizability with unchanging tastes – and discovering the usefulness of the Bergson family of utility functions for the practical solution of the allocation of income between total consumption and savings – we shall show that decentralizability can be maintained with changing tastes. Furthermore, we shall establish that the myopic dynamic linear expenditure system, derived in Chapter VII, is observationally equivalent with the rational dynamic linear expenditure system derived under the assumption of intertemporal utility maximization. Myopic systems can thus be given theoretical standing, at least in the sense that they provide a handy way of estimating rational intertemporal behavior. In the present state of the art, they probably provide the best way of estimating demand systems with a sound intertemporal foundation.[14]

By the same token, observational equivalence will be shown to exist between approaches which put *purchases* of durables in the utility function and more orthodox formulations in which the *services* rendered by durables

---

[13] The rest of this chapter is based on Phlips and Spinnewyn (1982).

[14] Or, to put it crudely: the route followed in Chapter X of the first edition of this book was a waste of computer time. The difference between the myopic and the intertemporal quadratic model (one additional time lag) was an optical illusion, due to the use of a discrete approximation in the measurement of the state variables.

appear as arguments in the utility function. Theoretical standing will thus be given to models of durable goods which use purchase prices instead of user costs. The vexing problem resulting from the difficulty of measuring user costs will thus be circumvented.

11.8.* Decentralization with unchanging tastes

Decentralization of the intertemporal decision problem is an attractive property for the empirically oriented economist. The computation of the budget to be assigned to a particular period may be difficult, requiring lots of information which is not directly necessary for the study of the allocation of the budget to the goods and services of a particular period. Since the budget of any period can be observed, a large part of the information which in one way or another determines the observed demand behavior can therefore be discarded by considering demand conditional on the budget assigned.

If the formal definition in Blackorby, Primont and Russell (1975) of decentralizability is applied to an intertemporal decision problem, one can say that decisions can be decentralized over time if in any period only prices of the current period are needed to determine demand, once the budget is known. Using a result of Gorman (1971), we know that decentralizability of decisions over time is then identical to requiring weak separability of the intertemporal utility function with respect to commodities relating to different periods.

Under separability, the allocation of an observed budget y_t can be considered as the second stage in a two-stage budgeting procedure. The empirically oriented demand analyst has, as such, no direct interest in the way budgets are assigned intertemporally. Yet, from a theoretical point of view, it is illuminating to be more explicit about this first stage.

It is impossible to allocate budgets intertemporally without some information about what is happening at the second stage. But it is sometimes possible to summarize this information in an efficient way, such that the intertemporal allocation procedure is simplified. Price aggregation turns out to be important. In an intemporal context, price aggregation may be defined as the possibility of computing the budget assigned to any period by knowing only the value of price indices (for all periods) in addition to initial wealth.

Let y_t be the budget and r_t be the interest rate. In discrete time and with a finite horizon T, an optimal budget allocation is the solution to

$$\max_{y_1, \ldots, y_{T-1}, w_{FT}} V(y_1, \ldots, y_t, \ldots, y_{T-1}, w_{FT}) \tag{11.23}$$

subject to

$$w_{Ft+1} = (1 + r_t)(w_{Ft} - y_t) \qquad (t = 1, \ldots, T-1), \qquad (11.24)$$

where V is the intertemporal indirect utility function.

Several assumptions have to be made to formulate the first stage allocation problem in this way. First of all, weak separability of the instantaneous direct utility function makes it possible to define an indirect representation $v(y_t, p_t)$. This is a natural way to derive an objective function in terms of budgets such as (11.23). The prices are not explicitly introduced in the objective function (11.23), but if we assume these to be constant, it is not necessary to do so.

One also assumes that the consumption-saving decision can be separated from the portfolio problem, in which the investment of wealth in different assets is considered. In other words, the interest rate r_t summarizes the information on the investment opportunities and this information is all one needs for the consumption–savings decisions. This problem is adequately dealt with by Samuelson (1969a) and Hakansson (1970), among others, and will not be considered here.

Wealth and total expenditures are defined in (11.24) in such a way that there is no exogenous income nor exogenous expenditures.[15] However, under the assumption that one can borrow or lend in the current period for any future period and that the borrowing rate is equal to the lending rate, it is always possible to take the discounted value of such exogenous outlays or receipts. This value can be considered to be part of initial wealth.

It does not suffice to represent preferences by a utility function in terms of budgets, as in equation (11.23): the functional structure of this utility function has to be further simplified if one wants to obtain closed form solutions. Since Phelps (1962), utility functions which are homothetic and additive in the budgets have received great attention.

If the intertemporal objective function is *homothetic* in the budgets, it follows that the budgets are proportional to initial wealth. This can be proved as follows (see also Mirrlees, 1974).

If $V(y_1, \ldots, y_t, \ldots, y_{T-1}, w_{FT})$ is homothetic, there exists by definition a positive increasing transformation of V which is positively homogeneous of degree one. A feasible plan that maximizes the normalization F will also maximize V, since the transformation is increasing.

Now let $y_1, \ldots, y_t, \ldots, y_{T-1}, w_{FT}$ be an optimal plan for initial wealth

---

[15] Compare this with equation (11.12).

w_{F1}. It follows from the wealth constraint (11.24) that $ky_1, \ldots, ky_t, \ldots ky_{T-1}$, kw_{FT}, is feasible for kw_{F1}. But it is also optimal. Consider any other feasible plan $k\bar{y}_1, \ldots, k\bar{y}_{T-1}, k\bar{w}_{FT}$, then

$$F(k\bar{y}_1, \ldots, k\bar{w}_{FT}) = kF(\bar{y}_1, \ldots, \bar{w}_{FT}) \leqslant kF(y_1, \ldots, w_{FT})$$
$$= F(ky, \ldots kw_{FT}).$$

The inequality follows from the feasibility of $\bar{y}_1, \ldots, \bar{w}_{FT}$ and the optimality of $y_1, \ldots, w_{FT}$ for initial wealth w_{F1}.

If, then, $y_t = f_t(w_{Ft})$ is the optimal plan for $t = 1, \ldots, T-1$, we have $ky_t = f_t(kw_{Ft}) = kf_t(w_{Ft})$, so that f_t is homogeneous of degree one. It follows that (for y_t non-negative)

$$y_t = \xi_t w_{Ft}. \tag{11.25}$$

Add the assumption of *additivity* to the assumption of homotheticity, and suppose V also to be increasing and strictly quasi-concave: you obtain the 'Bergson family', which can be written as

$$V = \sum_t C(t) \frac{1}{a} y_t^a + C^*(T) \frac{1}{a} w_{FT}^a \tag{11.26}$$

for $a < 1$, and as

$$V = \sum_t C(t) \ln y_t + C^*(T) \ln w_{FT} \tag{11.27}$$

for $a \to 0$. For these functions there exist closed form solutions.

A solution is obtained recursively (see e.g. Samuelson, 1969a). Let

$$\beta(t) = \frac{C(t+1)}{C(t)},$$

rewrite $C^*(T)$ for convenience as $C(T)\xi_T^{a-1}$ and consider the case where $a \neq 0$.

At time $T - 1$ we have to find y_{T-1} such that

$$\frac{1}{a} y_{T-1}^a + \beta(T-1)\xi_T^{a-1} \frac{1}{a} w_{FT}^a \tag{11.28}$$

is maximized subject to $w_{FT} = (1 + r_{T-1})(w_{FT-1} - y_{T-1})$. Since $y_{T-1} = \xi_{T-1} w_{FT-1}$, we have that

$$w_{FT} = (1 + r_{T-1})(1 - \xi_{T-1})w_{FT-1}.$$

Substitution into (11.28) yields, at $T - 1$,

$$\frac{1}{a} w_{FT-1}^a \{\xi_{T-1}^a + \beta(T-1)\xi_T^{a-1}(1 + r_{T-1})^a(1 - \xi_{T-1})^a\}. \tag{11.29}$$

The first order condition for ξ_{T-1} is

$$\xi_{T-1}^{a-1} - \beta(T-1)\xi_T^{a-1}(1 + r_{T-1})^a(1 - \xi_{T-1})^{a-1} = 0,$$

so that

$$\xi_{T-1} = \frac{b_{T-1}\xi_T}{1 + b_{T-1}\xi_T},$$

where

$$b_{T-1} = [\beta(T-1)]^{1/(a-1)}(1 + r_{T-1})^{a/(a-1)}.$$

Substituting the first order condition into (11.29) and multiplying by $\beta(T-2)$ yields the optimal value of the utility from $T-1$ onwards, as seen at $T-2$,

$$\beta(T-2)\frac{1}{a}\xi_{T-1}^{a-1}w_{FT-1}^a,$$

which is of the same form as the bequest function in (11.28).

At time $T-2$, we can again take (11.28) as the objective, after adjusting the time subscripts and repeat the procedure. For each period t, we therefore obtain

$$\xi_t = \frac{b_t\xi_{t+1}}{1 + b_t\xi_{t+1}}, \tag{11.30}$$

where

$$b_t = \beta(t)^{1/(a-1)}(1 + r_t)^{a/(a-1)}.$$

We may also look at the limiting value of ξ, when the interest rate (and β) are constant and the horizon is infinitely far. If b exceeds unity, we obtain

$$\xi = 1 - b^{-1} = 1 - \beta^{-1/(a-1)}(1 + r)^{-a/(a-1)}.$$

In the logarithmic case (11.27), we have $a = 0$, and therefore $b_t = \beta^{-1}$ so that in the limit $\xi = (1 - \beta)$. The argument is essentially the same as for $a \neq 0$. But the utility from t onwards has the form

$$\xi_t^{-1} \ln w_{Ft} + A_t, \tag{11.31}$$

where A_t is a constant which does not affect the allocation process.

Up to now, prices were supposed to be constant. With variable prices, additive and homothetic instantaneous utility functions have a corresponding indirect utility function of the form

$$\frac{1}{a}\left(\frac{y_t}{\pi(p_t)}\right)^a,$$

where $\pi(p_t)$ is a price index. Assume in addition that the intertemporal utility function is the discounted sum of the instantaneous (indirect) utility functions, with a constant discount factor. Then $C(t)$ can be specified as

$$C(t) = \rho^t[\pi(p_t)]^{-a},$$

so that

$$\beta(t) = \frac{C(t+1)}{C(t)} = \rho\left[\frac{\pi(p_{t+1})}{\pi(p_t)}\right]^{-a},$$

$$b_t = \rho^{1/(a-1)}\left[\frac{\pi(p_t)}{\pi(p_{t+1})}(1+r_t)\right]^{a/(a-1)}$$

$$= \rho^{1/(a-1)}(1+r_t^*)^{a/(a-1)},$$

where r_t^*, the real interest rate, is the solution to

$$(1+r_t^*) = \frac{\pi(p_t)}{\pi(p_{t+1})}(1+r_t).$$

Under these assumptions, the real interest rate (approximately the nominal interest rate r_t less the price inflation given by the price indices of the two periods) summarizes all the information about price changes.

The usefulness of the Bergson family of utility functions for the practical solution of our first stage allocation problem is thus established. True, these functions are highly unrealistic when defined in terms of quantities consumed or purchased. Nevertheless, they can be used in applied demand analysis through a change in variables, i.e. when defined in terms of transformed quantities, such as the committed quantities ($z_{it} = x_{it} - \gamma_i$) which appear in the Stone–Geary instantaneous utility function.[16] The intertemporal utility function is weakly separable in z, once the instantaneous utility function is written with these committed quantities as arguments. And the wealth constraint can also be redefined in terms of z.

Indeed, let the uncommitted expenditures (or supernumerary income) be

$$e_t = p_t'z_t. \tag{11.32}$$

---

[16] See exercise 1.14.

The indirect utility function is then

$$\frac{1}{a}\left(\frac{e_t}{\pi(p_t)}\right)^a.$$

Let $w_{HT} = 0$ and define w_{Ht} recursively as

$$w_{Ht} = Y_t - p_t'\gamma + \frac{1}{1 + r_t} w_{Ht+1}$$

for $t = 1, \ldots, T - 1$, where Y_t is exogenous labor income. The wealth constraint

$$w_{Ft+1} = (1 + r_t)(w_{Ft} + Y_t - y_t)$$

can then be rewritten as

$$w_{Ft+1} + w_{Ht+1} = (1 + r_t)(w_{Ft} + w_{Ht} - y_t + p_t'\gamma)$$

or as

$$w_{t+1} = (1 + r_t)(w_t - e_t), \tag{11.33}$$

where $w_t = w_{Ft} + w_{Ht}$. Equation (11.33) is in the same form as equation (11.24). The variable w_{Ht} will be given a concrete meaning later on (see (11.40)). What we wanted to show is that, by redefining the problem in terms of uncommitted expenditures e_t and an extended wealth concept w_t, the results obtained for our original problem, defined in (11.23) and (11.24), can be applied to the new problem. This insight will turn out to be very useful in the next section when we tackle the corresponding problem with changing tastes.

11.9.* Decentralization with changing tastes

The intertemporal utility function ceases to be separable when instantaneous utility is made to depend upon past purchases through the introduction of state variables, as in equation (7.11). This formulation indeed endogenizes taste changes, with the result that marginal rates of substitution in one period cease to be independent of purchases in another period. Is intertemporal decentralization therefore impossible when tastes change in the way described in Chapter VII? Do the myopic models of Chapter VII lack theoretical standing?

The orthodox attitude is to answer that, indeed, decentralization becomes impossible and to treat the first stage and the second stage allocation problem simultaneously. As indicated above, this amounts to solving the inter-temporal model w.r.t. to each argument in the direct utility function, i.e. finding the optimal path for each x_{it} and adding up optimal expenditures $p_{it}x_{it}$ over all i in each period, to find the intertemporally optimal budgets (total expenditures). This is the approach followed by Lluch (1974) and Phlips (1974, Chapter X).

Another attitude is to claim that decentralization is still possible, simply because the (static) concept of decentralizability defined above is too narrowly defined, when it requires the information of current prices to be sufficient to explain demand behavior once the budget is known. Why shouldn't past purchases (determined by past prices) be allowed to enter the problem through their impact on stocks?

Blackorby et al. (1975) introduced asymmetric restrictions on the structure of the utility functions. One can expect these to be particularly interesting in an intertemporal setting, since time runs in one direction. Myopic models could then be rationalized on the basis of what Phlips (1975) called 'forwards' separability (as distinguished from 'backwards' separability). More formally, write the intertemporal utility function as

$$U = U(u_{T-1}(x_{T-1}, u_{T-2}), w_{FT}),$$

with $u_t = u_t(x_t, u_{t-1})$ for $t \leq T - 1$. Once an intertemporal allocation of the budgets is determined in a first stage (a difficult problem compared to the assignment of the budgets considered in Section 11.8*), the instantaneous utility function can then be maximized subject to the familiar budget constraint. For the allocation of the preassigned budget among the different commodities, all one needs is current prices and past purchases, which is precisely the additional information used in dynamic demand systems.

But even in an intertemporal setting with time running in one direction, asymmetric separability imposes severe restrictions on the endogenous process in which tastes are formed. Forwards separability implies, by definition, that the effect of past purchases can be aggregated into one indicator, u_{t-1}, which, in the terminology used above, can be considered as a stock. Indeed, both the physical or psychological stocks and the instantaneous utility level of the previous period depend on past behavior, and determine (together with current purchases) the instantaneous utility of the current period. But unlike the state variable approach, which associates one state variable with each commodity, forwards separability channels all particular dynamic links through the same gate. This special structure of the intertemporal utility function introduces dynamic elements, and yet allows myopia in the allocation of a given budget. Of course, foresightedness will be required in the choice of an optimal intertemporal plan for the budgets.

Although myopic behavior in the allocation of a given budget can thus be justified, even if current tastes change endogenously, forwards separability will in many instances be too restrictive to deal with the dynamic links in the preference structure. Indeed, in the dynamic instantaneous utility functions introduced in Chapter VII, each commodity is linked to the past in its own way. In that case, even in allocating a preassigned budget, the rational consumer has to look both backwards and forwards. Unlike the case with forwards separability, myopia in the allocation of the budget becomes naive. Or, alternatively, forwards separability could be said to be present only if the instantaneous utility function were treated as if it represented an intertemporal preference ordering, which is of course hard to swallow: the rational consumer will be aware of the effect of current purchases on future tastes.

The attitude suggested here is to fully recognize the absence of separability and yet to point at the possibility of decentralizing. This possibility arises, as shown in Spinnewyn (1979a), when intertemporal models with state variables can be made formally equivalent with intertemporal models without state variables, so that rational habit formation ceases to be a problem *sui generis*.

When such formal equivalence exists, it is worth being investigated. First of all, it is a fact that all empirical knowledge of demand behavior, whether static or dynamic, is based on the assumption of decentralizability. If the latter can be shown also to exist in the dynamic case, then the myopic models of Chapter VII can be given a sound theoretical basis. Second, decentralizability simplifies considerably the empirical implementation of intertemporal models.

Formal equivalence can be obtained whenever it is possible: (a) to rewrite the non-separable intertemporal utility function so that it becomes weakly separable w.r.t. new variables, and (b) to redefine accordingly the cost of consumption and consequently to enlarge the wealth constraint in such a way that the latter takes the same form as the static wealth constraint defined in equation (11.24) above. The only difficulty is to find the appropriate change in variables.

The reader will have guessed that the appropriate change in variables is to write the utility function in terms of $z_{it} = x_{it} - \gamma_{it}$. As for the enlargement of the wealth constraint under rational habit formation, we summarize the procedure outlined in Spinnewyn (1979b). The generalization presented

here specializes to the type of dynamic models described in Chapter VII.
We start from

$$x_{it} = s_{it} - (1 - \delta_i)s_{it-1}, \tag{11.34}$$

$$\gamma_{it} = \theta_i + \alpha_i s_{it-1}, \tag{11.35}$$

$$w_{Ft+1} = (1 + r_t)(w_{Ft} + Y_t - y_t). \tag{11.36}$$

How is the wealth equation (11.36) to be enlarged to take account of rational habit formation?

It suffices to write the wealth constraint as

$$w_{t+1} = (1 + r_t)(w_t - c'_t z_t), \tag{11.37}$$

where

$$c_{it} = p_{it} - \left(\frac{1}{1 + r_t}\right)\mu_{it+1} \tag{11.38}$$

defines the user cost of a purchase as the difference between the purchase price (p_{it}) and today's value of one unit of stock tomorrow, while

$$\mu_{it} = \left(\frac{1}{1 + r_t}\right)(1 - \delta_i + \alpha_i)\mu_{it+1} - \alpha_i p_{it} \tag{11.39}$$

defines the value of a unit of stock. To check (11.39), remember that $k_i = \delta_i - \alpha_i = 1$ in statics, so that $\alpha_i = \delta_i - 1$. For a perishable good, $\delta_i = 1$, so that $\alpha_i = 0$ and $\mu_{it} = 0$. For $\delta_i < 1$, equation (11.39) reduces, in a static framework, to $\mu_{it} = p_{it}(1 - \delta_i)$, the purchase price corrected for depreciation, as it should. In addition,

$$w_t = w_{Ft} + w_{Ht} + \mu'_t s_{t-1} \tag{11.40}$$

postulates that total wealth (w_t) includes financial wealth (w_{Ft}), human wealth (w_{Ht}) *and* the wealth resulting from the accumulation of (durable and non-durable) state equations. We also define human wealth as

$$w_{Ht} = (Y_t - c'\theta) + \left(\frac{1}{1 + r_t}\right)w_{Ht+1}, \tag{11.41}$$

where ($Y_t - c'\theta$) is that part of income which is above the minimum $c'\theta$.

Now substitute (11.38) and (11.40) into (11.37), using (11.39) and (11.41), to find the static wealth constraint as written in (11.36). Decentralization remains possible.

If, furthermore, prices and the rate of interest are expected to be constant, then the rational consumer evaluates μ_i as

$$\mu_i = -\frac{\alpha_i p_i}{1 + \left(\dfrac{1}{1+r}\right)(1 - \delta_i + \alpha_i)},$$

and c_i as

$$c_i = p_i \varepsilon_i, \tag{11.42}$$

where

$$\varepsilon_i = \frac{r + \delta_i}{r + \delta_i - \alpha_i}.$$

EXERCISE

11.4. Check equation (11.42) by solving equations (11.39) and (11.38) on the assumption that $\mu_{it} = \mu_{it-1} = \mu_i$, $p_t = p$ and $r_t = r$.

Notice that the correction factor ε_i is very close to the myopic factor $\delta_i/(\delta_i - \alpha_i)$ which transforms the parameters β_i and θ_i of the short-run Stone–Geary function into the corresponding parameters of the utility function which rationalizes the myopic linear expenditure system in the long run (see equation (7.9)).

It is also illuminating to consider the value of μ_i and c_i under the assumption of total and immediate adjustment (such that $\delta_i - \alpha_i = 1$). Then

$$\mu_i = p_i(1 - \delta_i),$$

i.e. μ_i is the value of the depreciated stock of durable i, while

$$c_i = p_i\left[\frac{r + \delta_i}{1 + r}\right],$$

i.e. c_i is (the discrete version of) the traditional rental price of durable goods. This provides a justification for also interpreting c_i as a rental price when there is habit formation.

Note, finally, that μ_i is positive when $\alpha_i < 0$ (the stock effect dominates) and negative when $\alpha_i > 0$ (habit formation dominates).

11.10.* The linear expenditure system with rational habit formation

Equation (11.37) is the same form as the static wealth constraint (11.24). It is also in the form required for an application of the usual dynamic programming techniques, if we take e_t as the budget whose optimal path is to be determined and c_t as the vector of true prices. Suppose the instantaneous indirect utility function of a rational consumer is Stone–Geary:

$$v_t = \ln e_t - \sum_i \beta_i^R \ln c_{it}$$

$$= \ln\left[e_t \Big/ \prod_i \left(c_{it}^{\beta_i^R} \right) \right]$$

so that the optimal time path for e_t is found by maximizing

$$\sum_{t=0}^{T-1} \left[\rho^t \left(\ln e_t - \sum_i \beta_i^R \ln c_{it} \right) \right] + \rho^T \xi_T \ln w_T. \qquad (11.43)$$

This indirect intertemporal utility function belongs to the logarithmic Bergson family and has therefore all the properties required. In particular, it is separable in e_t. A straightforward application of the recursive procedure outlined in Section 11.8* gives, in the limit, $\xi = (1 - \rho)$ or

$$e_t^R = \xi w_t = (1 - \rho)w_t. \qquad (11.44)$$

The index R indicates that the consumer behaves rationally, i.e. looks both forwards and backwards.

The linear expenditure system with rational habit formation takes the form

$$x_{it}^R = \gamma_{it} + \frac{\beta_i^R}{c_{it}} e_t^R, \qquad (11.45)$$

where β_i^R is the marginal propensity to consume commodity i of a rational consumer who accumulates stocks and habits.

11.11.* Observational equivalence with myopic models

The variables e_t^R and c_{it} are not observable. However, the linear expenditure system with rational habit formation is easily transformed into a system that is observationally equivalent with the myopic linear expenditure system. Multiply system (11.45) by p_{it}, use (11.42) to obtain

$$p_{it}x_{it}^R = p_{it}\gamma_{it} + \frac{\beta_i^R}{\varepsilon_i} e_t^R,$$

and sum over all commodities, so that

$$\sum_i p_{it} x_{it}^R = \sum_i p_{it} \gamma_{it} + e_t^R \sum_i \left(\frac{\beta_i^R}{\varepsilon_i} \right)$$

or

$$e_t^R = \left(y_t^R - \sum_i p_{it} \gamma_{it} \right) \bigg/ \sum_i \left(\frac{\beta_i^R}{\varepsilon_i} \right).$$

Then

$$p_{it} x_{it}^R = p_{it} \gamma_{it} + \beta_i \left(y_t^R - \sum_j p_{jt} \gamma_{jt} \right) \tag{11.46}$$

with

$$\beta_i = \left(\frac{\beta_i^R}{\varepsilon_i} \right) \bigg/ \sum_j \left(\frac{\beta_j^R}{\varepsilon_j} \right). \tag{11.47}$$

System (11.46) is equivalent with the myopic demand version of the linear expenditure system discussed in Chapter VII. The instantaneous maximization of $u = \sum_i \beta_i \ln(x_{it} - \gamma_{it})$, subject to $y_t = p_t' x_t$, where y_t is on its optimal path (i.e. $y_t = y_t^R$), is thus equivalent to the maximization of $\sum_{\tau=t}^T \rho^{T-\tau} \sum_i \beta_i^R \ln(x_{i\tau} - \gamma_{i\tau})$ plus the utility of final bequests, subject to the wealth equation (11.27), if the consumer's expectations are constant and the horizon is sufficiently far away.

Observational equivalence (i.e. equivalence in terms of a regression model) is obtained when system (11.46) is rewritten as

$$p_{it} x_{it} = p_{it} \gamma_{it} + \beta_i \left(y_t - \sum_j p_{jt} \gamma_j \right) + \eta_{it}, \tag{11.48}$$

where η_{it} is an error term, on the assumption that $y_t = y_t^R$. Under this assumption, the condition that $\sum_i \eta_{it} = 0$, with the implied singularity of the contemporaneous variance–covariance matrix, can be maintained. However, if $y_t \neq y_t^R$, then this condition ceases to be applicable, as the budget constraint has no longer to be satisfied exactly. And the value of $\sum_i \eta_{it}$ could be interpreted as an estimate of the 'intertemporal' error made by the observed consumers, to the extent that they are not entirely rational in solving their first stage allocation problem. There seems to be no possibility of making y_t endogenous. Nor is it possible to estimate e_t^R, using (11.44) as an estimating equation, simultaneously with system (11.48), as e_t^R is defined in terms of true prices c_t. The logic of decentralizability suggests, however, that it is observed

y_t that has to be allocated, whether it contains an intertemporal error or not.

Equation (11.47) is homogeneous of degree zero in β_i^R. We can therefore compute β_i^R as

$$\beta_i^R = \frac{\varepsilon_i \beta_i}{\sum_i \varepsilon_i \beta_i},$$

(11.49)

where β_i is the short-run marginal propensity to consume which is estimated in the myopic linear expenditure system. Conversely, β_i can be reinterpreted as reflecting the behavior of a rational rather than a myopic consumer: this consumer can be thought of as transforming his true β_i^R coefficients into β_i when confronted with purchase prices p_t instead of correct prices c_t.

When confronted with purchase prices p_t, the consumer will give relatively less weight, in the myopic short-run utility function, to commodities which are strongly habit forming (high α_i) or for which habits are wearing off slowly (small δ_i). He knows that future consumption of these commodities will be stimulated through habit formation, so that he reduces the short-run marginal propensities to consume. The converse is true for commodities which are weakly habit forming (low α_i) and for which habits are wearing off quickly (high δ_i) or for which the stock effect dominates (α_i is negative). In other words, the rational consumer corrects the inadequate information provided by the observed budget constraint by readjusting the short-run marginal propensities to consume.

The reader may wonder whether the other structural parameters (α, δ_i and θ_i) of the dynamic linear expenditure system remain unchanged under rational habit formation. In fact they do. To see this, remember that the estimating equations of the myopic linear expenditure system are nothing but the first-order conditions, so that the marginal utility of money λ_t appears explicitly, and that the budget constraint is imposed through an iteration on λ_t. These equations are

$$x_{it} = K_{i0} + K_{i1} x_{it-1} + K_{i2} \frac{1}{\lambda_t p_{it}} + K_{i3} \frac{1}{\lambda_{t-1} p_{it-1}}.$$

(11.50)

On the other hand, the marginal utility of money is

$$\lambda_t = \frac{1}{y_t - p_t' \gamma_t}.$$

(11.51)

Using equation (11.45), which defines the rational linear expenditure system, we find the rational λ_t^R to be

$$\lambda_t^R = \frac{1}{e_t^R}$$

$$= \sum_i \left(\frac{\beta_i^R}{\varepsilon_i}\right) \bigg/ (y_t - p_t'\gamma_t) = \sum_i \left(\frac{\beta_i^R}{\varepsilon_i}\right) \lambda_t. \tag{11.52}$$

λ_t^R is thus proportional to λ_t. Inserting λ_t^R in the estimating equations (11.50), and replacing p_{it} and p_{it-1}, by c_{it} and c_{it-1}, we see that only K_{i2} and K_{i3} are affected, and that they change in the same proportion. A look at the equations which define the structural parameters in terms of the regression coefficients will convince the reader that α_i, θ_i and δ_i are unchanged:

$$\delta_i = \frac{2(K_{i2} + K_{i3})}{K_{i2} - K_{i3}}, \qquad \alpha_i = \delta_i - \frac{2(1 - K_{i1})}{1 + K_{i1}},$$

$$\beta_i = \frac{K_{i2} - K_{i3}}{1 + K_{i1}}, \qquad \theta_i = \frac{K_{i0}(K_{i2} - K_{i3})}{(1 + K_{i1})(K_{i2} + K_{i3})}. \tag{11.53}$$

All information about the future is thus summarized in the β^R coefficients. And all these coefficients are needed to define λ_t^R. This multiplier can thus be said to subsume all future information. An analogous idea was used by Heckman and MaCurdy (1979) in their analysis of a life cycle model of female labor supply.

Table 11.1 reproduces estimates of the structural parameters β_i, α_i and δ_i. These estimates are taken from Phlips and Pieraerts (1979) and were computed using Abbott and Ashenfelter's corrected data – see Pencavel (1979) – on expenditures for seven commodity groups and on hours worked in the U.S. during the period 1929–1967.

Table 11.2 gives the corresponding values of ε and β^R for $r^* = 0.03$, 0.05 and 0.10.

TABLE 11.1

Commodity group	β	α	δ
Durables	0.261	0.353	0.712
Food	0.248	0.014	0.245
Clothing	0.078	0.148	0.168
Other non-durables	0.089	0.387	0.511
Housing services	0.082	0.692	0.778
Transportation services	0.029	−0.012	0.038
Other services	0.102	0.170	0.148
Leisure	0.108	0.553	0.719

TABLE 11.2

Commodity group	$r^* = 0.03$		$r^* = 0.05$		$r^* = 0.10$	
	ε	β^R	ε	β^R	ε	β^R
Durables	1.909	0.109	1.864	0.167	1.770	0.209
Food	1.054	0.057	1.050	0.090	1.043	0.117
Clothing	3.990	0.068	3.130	0.084	2.239	0.079
Other non-durables	3.508	0.069	3.220	0.100	2.725	0.111
Housing services	6.968	0.125	6.090	0.172	4.722	0.175
Transportation services	0.851	0.005	0.881	0.009	0.921	0.012
Other services	21.234	0.476	6.974	0.246	3.163	0.146
Leisure	3.821	0.090	3.560	0.132	3.079	0.150

The values taken by ε are surprisingly high. 'Transportation services' is the only item for which the user cost is lower than the purchase price. Our interpretation is as follows. We notice, first, that the consumer's choice is limited, in every period, since he has first to satisfy habitual (i.e. committed) consumption. The true prices (user costs) are used to allocate uncommitted expenditures. On the other hand, the rational consumer recognizes that current consumption will induce future habitual consumption through its effect on future habit stocks. He knows therefore that, in his free choice for consumption now, he commits himself to consumption in the future. If a household switches from a black and white to a color TV set, or if it buys a second car, or if the housewife enters the labor market, it will be difficult to abandon the new consumption pattern, even when the car or the TV set has to be replaced, or when the family situation has changed. The rational consumer will therefore think twice and calculate the future costs of adopting a new consumption pattern.

What is the influence of the (real) rate of interest r^*? Let r^* pass from three to respectively five or ten percent: the rational correction factors ε_i tend systematically to one for all commodity groups. Less weight is given to the cost of future habit formation: the present value of future costs is lower.

When confronted with purchase prices instead of user costs, the rational consumer readjusts the weights in his myopic short-run utility function. For most commodity groups, and especially for 'food' and 'durables', β_i is larger than β_i^R when the real rate of interest is 3%. The reverse is true for two groups: 'housing' and 'other services', for which ε_i is particularly high. For these two groups, the user cost c_i is relatively much higher than the purchase price p_i used in the estimation of the myopic system. The cost of future habit formation is, indeed, important in expenditures on 'housing services' and on 'other services', which include medical care, cleaning, movies and higher education. The relative importance of the marginal propensity to consume 'other services' of the rational consumer who faces true user costs is impressive. Welfare comparisons made in terms of the vector β^R should lead to conclusions which are rather different from those made on the basis of the vector β.

There is a considerable reshuffling of the differences between β_i and β_i^R, however, when other values of the real rate of interest are considered. As of $r^* = 0.05$, there are five commodity groups for which β_i is smaller than β_i^R: 'clothing', 'other non-durables', 'housing services', 'other services' and 'leisure'. Given the normalization rule $\sum_i \beta_i^R = 1$, the number of commodities for which the *relative* difference between user cost and purchase price is higher, increases when the real rate of interest is higher.

The reader will have noticed that our reasoning starts from a given β_i^R, which is readjusted to a particular β_i for a given constant real rate of interest and a given historical sequence of purchase prices. As it is β_i which is parametrized, we had to do our computations the other way around, i.e. from estimated β's to alternative β^R's.

11.12.* Consistency and time preference

Time preference is implied in the postulates set up by Koopmans (1960) to derive the intertemporal utility function, and these postulates do '*not* imply that, after one period has elapsed, the ordering then applicable to the "then" future will necessarily be the same as that now applicable to the "present" future' (Koopmans et al., 1964). The rational consumer is 'impatient', whether his tastes change or not. But what about consistency?

Consistency is automatically achieved when future behavior is precommitted, even if utility is maximized instantaneously (as in the case of naive habit formation). And one way to achieve commitment is to have what Blackorby et al. (1973) call a preference inheritance mechanism according to which preferences of the next generation (or time period) are imposed by the previous generation (or period). Such a mechanism is in fact implied in the state variable approach, as the preferences today are endogenously determined by the consumption decisions made yesterday. One could say that the habit forming consumer is on a track and cannot get off it. The conditions for consistency for a naive consumer as well as for a 'sophisticated', i.e. rational, consumer are simply not applicable, since they refer to consistent planning in the absence of commitment.

Inconsistency can arise in the state variable approach only through the presence of a discount function, in addition to the inheritance mechanism described by the instantaneous utility function. It is only if the discount function changes that inconsistency arises. If we continue to assume an exponential discount function, this implies a change in the rate of time preference γ used in successive planning, given that $\rho = 1/(1 + \gamma)$.

Since Fisher (1930), we know that γ is a decreasing function of total consumption and an increasing function of the riskiness of future events. With a data set spanning a period as long as 1929–1967, in which there was a great depression, a world war and a Korean war, the rate of time preference must have jumped quite significantly. Can we verify this?

Optimal control theory shows (see equation (11.22)) that the rate of change of the Lagrangian multiplier associated with the wealth constraint is a function of the rate of time preference and of the rate of interest. Given estimates of the multiplier and given the real rate of interest, it should thus be possible to estimate γ.

This multiplier is nothing but our rational λ_t^R. Remember also that our consumer is maximizing

$$\frac{1}{a} e_t^a + \beta(t)\xi_{t+1}^{a-1}\frac{1}{a} w_{t+1}^a$$

with respect to e_t and w_t, subject to the wealth constraint

$$w_{t+1} = (1 + r_t)(w_t - e_t)$$

as can be seen on replacing y_t and w_{Ft} by e_t and w_t respectively in equation (11.28). In terms of the Lagrange multiplier associated with the wealth constraint, this maximization implies, at any t,

$$e_t^{a-1} = \lambda_t^R,$$

which leads to equation (11.52) above when $a = 0$, and

$$\beta(t)\xi_{t+1}^{a-1} w_{t+1}^{a-1} = i_t\lambda_t^R, \tag{11.54}$$

where $i_t = 1/(1 + r_t)$. The current value, at t, of the optimal value of utility is

$$\xi_t^{a-1}\frac{1}{a} w_t^a,$$

so that

$$\lambda_t^R = \frac{\partial}{\partial w_t}\left(\frac{1}{a}\xi_t^{a-1}w_t^a\right) = \xi_t^{a-1}w_t^{a-1}$$

and

$$\lambda^R_{t+1} = \zeta^{a-1}_{t+1} w^{a-1}_{t+1}.$$

Substituting into (11.54) yields

$$\lambda^R_{t+1} = \frac{1}{\beta(t)} i_t \lambda^R_t$$

$$= \rho^{-1} \left[\frac{\pi(c_{t+1})}{\pi(c_t)} \right]^a i_t \lambda^R_t$$

$$= \frac{1+\gamma_t}{1+r_t} \left[\frac{\pi(c_{t+1})}{\pi(c_t)} \right]^a \lambda^R_t. \tag{11.55}$$

In terms of the real rate of interest r^*, and for $a = 0$, this result can be rewritten as

$$\lambda^R_{t+1} = \frac{1+\gamma_t}{1+r^*} \left[\frac{\pi(c_t)}{\pi(c_{t+1})} \right] \lambda^R_t, \tag{11.55a}$$

with the implication that

$$\gamma_t = (1+r^*) \left(\frac{\lambda^R_{t+1}}{\lambda^R_t} \right) \left(\frac{\pi(c_{t+1})}{\pi(c_t)} \right) - 1. \tag{11.56}$$

We prefer to use (11.55a) rather than (11.55), because the nominal rate of interest on human and non-human wealth (r_t) is very hard to estimate, while the real rate of interest r^* can be assumed constant. Furthermore, we know that the price index is equal to

$$\pi(c_t) = \prod_i c^{\beta^R_i}_{it}$$

when the utility function is Stone–Geary. All we need in addition is a time series λ^R_t.

For r^*, we choose alternative constant values of 0.03, 0.05 and 0.10 as before. The series λ^R_t is proportional to λ_t according to equation (11.52), so that there is no point in computing λ^R_t separately, given that the marginal utility of money (here of full income) is defined up to a monotonic transformation. One series λ_t results from the iteration used in the estimation of the parameters in Table 11.1. This iteration refers to the budget constraint $\tilde{y}_t = \sum_i p_{it} x_{it} - p_{1t} h_t$, given the absence of data on leisure. (The variable h_t measures the number of hours worked and p_{1t} is the observed wage rate.) The λ_t series we are interested in is associated with full income $y_t = \sum_i p_{it} x_{it}$

$+ p_{1t}l_t$, where $l_t = T - h_t$ represents leisure. This λ_t is defined as

$$\lambda_t = \frac{1}{\tilde{y}_t - \sum_{i=1}^{7} p_{it}\gamma_{it} + p_{1t}\gamma_{ht}} \tag{11.57}$$

where $\gamma_{ht} = T - \gamma_{1t}$ is the maximum number of hours one is ready to work. The reader will readily check that

$$\tilde{y}_t - \sum_{i=1}^{7} p_{it}\gamma_{it} + p_{1t}\gamma_{ht} = y_t - \sum_{i=1}^{7} p_{it}\gamma_{it} - p_{1t}\gamma_{1t},$$

so that the λ_t series defined by (11.57) is identical with the λ_t series obtained in the iterative estimation procedure.

Table 11.3 reproduces the λ_t series and the corresponding γ_t and ρ_t values for r^* equal to 0.03, 0.05 and 0.10. When r^* is equal to three or five percent, many rates of time preference are negative. This is incompatible with the axioms of intertemporal consumer choice, which imply 'impatience' and therefore $\gamma > 0$. On the contrary, a real rate of interest of ten percent is compatible with impatience for most of the years in the sample. We interpret this to mean that ten percent is closer to the true value of the real rate of interest than three or five percent. In other words, we interpret our computations as an indirect way of estimating both the real rate of interest on human and non-human wealth (corrected for habit formation) and the rate of time preference. It should be clear, also, that equation (11.55) establishes the correct theoretical causal relationship: it is the difference between the rate of time preference and the (nominal) rate of interest which determines the time shape of λ.

With these provisos in mind, we may have a closer look at γ and ρ, given $r^* = 0.10$ and given our λ_t series. Notice first that λ climbs to impressive heights during the second world war. This is due to the fact that the opportunity cost of leisure is included in our budget constraint, and that working hours were pushed to the psychologically admissible upper limit in the war effort: h is practically equal to γ_h in 1943 (see Table 10.3 above). As a result, λ had to come down very sharply at the end of the war.

As for γ, we are glad to report that it is indeed very sensitive to economic conditions, as suggested by Irving Fisher. During the big depression, the rate of time preference was very high. With the recovery, it came down sharply. In 1941, Pearl Harbour made impatience rise again. The years 1943–45 were years of forced savings, so that γ became negative: the average American consumer was forced to prefer the future to the present. After

TABLE 11.3

Year	λ_t	$r^* = 0.03$		$r^* = 0.05$		$r^* = 0.10$	
		γ_t	ρ_t	γ_t	ρ_t	γ_t	ρ_t
1929	1.00000	0.42	0.70	0.44	0.70	0.50	0.67
1930	1.40330	0.14	0.87	0.16	0.86	0.21	0.83
1931	1.69213	0.21	0.83	0.22	0.82	0.27	0.78
1932	2.24272	0.22	0.82	0.26	0.80	0.32	0.76
1933	2.85584	0.03	0.97	0.05	0.95	0.10	0.91
1934	2.65407	0.03	0.97	0.05	0.95	0.10	0.91
1935	2.63643	0.02	0.98	0.04	0.96	0.09	0.92
1936	2.57572	0.08	0.03	0.10	0.91	0.15	0.87
1937	2.58247	−0.12	1.13	−0.10	1.12	−0.06	1.07
1938	2.21864	0.00	1.00	0.02	0.98	0.07	0.93
1939	2.17071	0.04	0.96	0.06	0.94	0.12	0.90
1940	2.16617	0.22	0.82	0.25	0.80	0.32	0.76
1941	2.40737	1.29	0.44	1.37	0.42	1.50	0.40
1942	4.86100	1.11	0.47	1.16	0.46	1.26	0.44
1943	9.30103	−0.42	1.73	−0.41	1.70	−0.38	1.62
1944	4.87569	−0.59	2.45	−0.58	2.39	−0.56	2.28
1945	1.87019	−0.53	2.11	−0.52	2.10	−0.50	2.01
1946	0.79195	0.11	0.90	0.12	0.89	0.17	0.85
1947	0.76857	0.10	0.91	0.13	0.89	0.19	0.84
1948	0.76314	−0.04	1.04	−0.03	1.03	0.01	0.99
1949	0.71295	−0.02	1.02	0.00	1.00	0.05	0.95
1950	0.66638	0.28	0.78	0.30	0.77	0.37	0.73
1951	0.77966	0.03	0.97	0.04	0.96	0.09	0.92
1952	0.75297	−0.06	1.07	−0.05	1.05	−0.01	1.01
1953	0.66059	−0.09	1.10	−0.08	1.08	−0.03	1.04
1954	0.57339	−0.02	1.02	−0.01	1.01	0.03	0.97
1955	0.53193	0.06	0.94	0.08	0.93	0.13	0.89
1956	0.53023	−0.01	1.02	0.00	1.00	0.05	0.95
1957	0.48991	−0.04	1.04	−0.02	1.02	0.03	0.97
1958	0.44744	0.03	0.97	0.04	0.96	0.09	0.92
1959	0.43314	0.05	0.95	0.07	0.93	0.12	0.89
1960	0.43359	0.00	1.00	0.02	0.98	0.07	0.94
1961	0.41567	0.01	0.99	0.03	0.97	0.08	0.92
1962	0.40331	−0.01	1.01	0.01	0.99	0.05	0.95
1963	0.38064	−0.01	1.01	0.01	0.99	0.05	0.95
1964	0.35706	0.01	0.99	0.03	0.97	0.07	0.93
1965	0.34360	0.06	0.94	0.08	0.93	0.12	0.89
1966	0.34249	0.06	0.94	0.08	0.93	0.13	0.89
1967	0.34062	−	−	−	−	−	−

four 'back to normal' years, the Korean war produced another sharp rise, possibly followed, in 1952–53, by a compensating movement in savings. Since 1954, the rate of time preference stabilized at values somewhere between zero and thirteen percent. The negative value of γ in 1937 seems hard to explain.

The corresponding movements of ρ can be followed in the last column of Table 11.3. When $\rho = 1$, $(1 - \rho)$ is no doubt equal to zero. According to equation (11.44), the rational consumer then reduces e^R, his uncommitted expenditures, to zero and restricts himself to committed expenditures. A higher rate of time preference implies a smaller ρ and therefore a higher level of uncommitted expenditures.

References

ABBOTT, M. and O. ASHENFELTER (1976), Labor supply, commodity demand, and the allocation of time, *Review of Economic Studies 43* (1976) 389–411.

AFRIAT, S.N. (1977), *The price index*, Cambridge University Press, Cambridge.

AITCHISON, J. and J.A.C. BROWN (1957), *The lognormal distribution with special reference to its uses in economics*. Cambridge University Press, Cambridge, England.

ALCHIAN, A. (1953), The meaning of utility measurement. *American Economic Review 43* (1953) 26–50.

ALLEN, R.G.D. (1938), *Mathematical analysis for economists*. Macmillan, London.

ALLEN, R.G.D. (1975), *Index numbers in theory and practice*, Macmillan, London.

ALLEN, R.G.D. and J.R. HICKS (1934), A reconsideration of the theory of value. II. *Economica*, N.S. *1* (1934), 196–219.

ALLEN, R.G.D. and A.L. BOWLEY (1935), *Family expenditure*. Staples Press, London.

ANDERSON, R.W. (1979), Perfect price aggregation and empirical demand analysis, *Econometrica 47* (1979) 1209–1230.

ANDERSON, R.W. (1980) Some theory of inverse demand for applied demand analysis, *European Economic Review 14* (1980) 281–290.

ANDERSON, R.W. and M. WILKINSON (1979), An evaluation of alternative consumer demand systems within an econometric model of the U.S. livestock sector, Columbia Business School Working Paper 175A, mimeo.

ARROW, K. and M. KURZ (1969), Optimal consumer allocation over an infinite horizon. *Journal of Economic theory 1* (1969) 68–91. Reproduced in ARROW and KURZ (1970).

ARROW, K, and M. KURZ (1970), *Public investment, the rate of return and optimal fiscal policy*. Johns Hopkins, Baltimore.

ASHENFELTER, O. (1980) Unemployment as disequilibrium in a model of aggregate labor supply, *Econometrica 48* (1980) 547–564.

ASHENFELTER, O. and J. HECKMAN (1974), The estimation of income and substitution effects in a model of family labor supply, *Econometrica 42* (1974) 73–85.

BALESTRA, P. (1967), *The demand for natural gas*. North-Holland, Amsterdam.

BALESTRA, P. and M. NERLOVE (1966), Pooling cross-sections and time series data. *Econometrica 34* (1966) 585–612.

BARNETT, W.A. (1977a), Pollak and Wachter on the household production function approach, *Journal of Political Economy 85* (1977) 1073–1082.

BARNETT, W.A. (1977b), Recursive subaggregation and a generalized hypocycloidal demand model, *Econometrica 45* (1977) 1117–1136.

BARNETT, W.A. (1979a) Theoretical foundations for the Rotterdam model, *Review of Economic Studies 46* (1979) 109–130.

BARNETT, W.A. (1979b), The joint allocation of leisure and goods expenditure, *Econometrica 47* (1979) 539–564.

309

BARTEN, A.P. (1964a), Consumer demand functions under conditions of almost additive preferences. *Econometrica 32* (1964) 1–38.

BARTEN, A.P. (1964b), Family composition, prices and expenditure patterns, in *Econometric Analysis for National Planning*, P.E. HART, G. MILLS and J.K. WHITAKER (eds.). Butterworth.

BARTEN, A.P. (1966), *Theorie en empirie van een volledig stelsel van vraagvergelijkingen*. Doctoral dissertation, Rotterdam.

BARTEN, A.P. (1967), Evidence on the Slutsky conditions for demand equations. *Review of Economics and Statistics 49* (1967) 77–84.

BARTEN, A.P. (1968), Estimating demand equations. *Econometrica 36* (1968), 213–251.

BARTEN, A.P. (1969), Maximum likelihood estimation of a complete system of demand equations. *European Economic Review 1* (1969) 7–73.

BARTEN, A.P. (1971), Preference and demand interactions between commodities, in *Schaarste en welvaart*, Opstellen aangeboden aan Prof. Dr. P. Hennipman. H.E. Stenfert Kroese, 1–18.

BARTEN, A.P. (1974), Complete systems of demand equations: some thoughts about aggregation and functional form, *Recherches économiques de Louvain 40* (1974) 3–20.

BARTEN, A.P. (1977), The systems of consumer demand functions approach: a review, *Econometrica 45* (1977) 23–51.

BARTEN, A.P. and S.J. TURNOVSKY (1966), Some aspects of the aggregation problem for composite demand equations. *International Economic Review 7* (1966) 231–259.

BARTEN, A.P., T. KLOEK, and F.B. LEMPERS (1969), A note on a class of utility and production functions yielding everywhere differentiable demand functions. *Review of Economic Studies 36* (1969) 109–111.

BARTEN, A.P. and E. GEYSKENS (1975), The negativity condition in consumer demand, *European Economic Review 6* (1975) 227–260.

BARZEL, Y. and R.J. McDONALD (1973), Assets, subsistence and the supply curve of labor, *American Economic Review 63* (1973) 621–633.

BASCHET, J. and P. DEBREU (1971), Systèmes de lois de demande: une comparaison internationale. *Annales de l'I.N.S.E.E.*, nr. 6, Jan.–April (1971) 1–39.

BECKER, G.S. (1965), A theory of the allocation of time, *Economic Journal 75* (1965) 493–517.

BERA, A.K., R.P. BYRON and C.M. JARQUE (1981), Further evidence on asymptotic tests for homogeneity and symmetry in large demand systems, *Economics Letters 8* (1981) 101–105.

BERGLAS, E. and A. RAZIN (1974), Preferences, separability and the Patinkin model: a comment, *Journal of Political Economy 82* (1974) 199–201.

BERGSON (BURK), A. (1936), Real income, expenditure proportionality, and Frisch's 'New methods of measuring marginal utility'. *Review of Economic Studies 4* (1936) 33–52.

BERGSTROM, T.C. (1976), Toward a deeper economics of sleeping, *Journal of Political Economy 84* (1976) 411–412.

BERNDT, E.R., M.N. DARROUGH and W.E. DIEWERT (1977), Flexible functional forms and expenditure distributions: an application to Canadian consumer demand functions, *International Economic Review 18* (1977) 651–675.

BLACKORBY, C., G. LADY, D. NISSEN and R.R. RUSSELL (1970), Homothetic separability and consumer budgeting. *Econometrica 38* (1970) 468–472.

BLACKORBY, C., D. NISSEN, D. PRIMONT and R.R. RUSSELL (1973), Consistent intertemporal decision making, *Review of Economic Studies 40* (1973) 239–248.

BLACKORBY, C., D. PRIMONT and R.R. RUSSELL (1975), Budgeting, decentralization, and aggregation, *Annals of Economic and Social Measurement 4* (1975) 23–44.

BLACKORBY, C., D. PRIMONT and R.R. RUSSELL (1978), *Duality, separability, and functional structure: theory and economic applications*, North-Holland, Amsterdam.

BLACKORBY, C. and R.R. RUSSELL (1978), Indices and subindices of the cost of living and the standard of living, *International Economic Review 19* (1978) 229–240.

BLINDER, A.S. (1974), *Toward an economic theory of income distribution*, MIT Press, Cambridge, Mass.

BLOKLAND, J. (1976), *Continuous consumer equivalence scales*, Stenfert Kroese, Leiden.

BÖHM-BAWERK, E. VON (1912), *Positive Theorie des Kapitals*, Dritte Auflage, especially Buch IV, Abschnitt I, Gegenwart und Zukunft in der Wirtschaft, p. 426–486. English translation in *Capital and interest*, Vol. II, *Positive theory of capital*, Book IV, Section I, p. 257–289. South Holland, Illinois, 1959.

BOYER, M. (1981), *Rational demand and expenditures patterns under habit formation*, CORE Discussion Paper No. 8118, Louvain-la-Neuve, mimeo.

BRANSON, W.H. and A.K. KLEVORICK (1969), Money illusion and the aggregate consumption function. *American Economic Review 59* (1969) 832–849.

BRECHLING, F.P.R. (1965), The relationship between output and employment in British manufacturing industries. *Review of Economic Studies* (1965) 187–216.

BRONSARD, C. (1971), *Dualité micro-économique et théorie du second best*. Vander, Louvain.

BROWN, J.A.C. and A. DEATON (1972), Surveys in applied economics: models of consumer behaviour. *Economic Journal 82* (1972) 1145–1236.

BROWN, M. and D. HEIEN (1972), The S-branch utility tree: a generalization of the linear expenditure system. *Econometrica 40* (1972) 737–747.

BYRON, R.P. (1968), Methods for estimating demand equations using prior information: a series of experiments with Australian data. *Australian Economic Papers 7* (1968) 227–248.

BYRON, R.P. (1970a), A simple method for estimating demand systems under separable utility assumptions. *Review of Economic Studies 37* (1970) 261–274.

BYRON, R.P. (1970b), The restricted Aitken estimation of sets of demand relations. *Econometrica 38* (1970) 816–830.

CARLEVARO, F. (1976), A generalization of the linear expenditure system, in L. SOLARI and J.-N. du PASQUIER (eds.) *Private and enlarged consumption*, North-Holland, Amsterdam.

CASS, D. (1965), Optimum growth in an aggregative model of capital accumulation. *Review of Economic Studies* (1965) 233–240.

CAVES, D.W. and L.R. CHRISTENSEN (1980), Global properties of flexible functional forms, *American Economic Review 70* (1980) 422–432.

CHAMPERNOWNE, D.G. (1969), *Uncertainty and estimation in economics*, Vol. 2. Oliver and Boyd, Edinburgh.

CHIPMAN, J.S. (1965), A survey of the theory of international trade: Part I: The classical theory. *Econometrica 33* (1965) 477–519.

CHIPMAN, J.S. (1974), Homothetic preferences and aggregation, *Journal of Economic Theory 8* (1974) 26–38.

CHIPMAN, J.S., L. HURWICZ, M.K. RICHTER, and H.F. SONNENSCHEIN (1971), *Preferences, utility and demand*. Harcourt Brace Jovanovich.

CHOW, G. (1957), *Demand for automobiles in the U.S.: a study in consumer durables*. North-Holland, Amsterdam.

CHOW, G. (1960), Statistical demand functions for automobiles and their use for forecasting, in *The demand for durable goods*, A.C. HARBERGER (ed.). University of Chicago Press, Chicago, 149–178.

CHOW, G. (1966), On the long-run and short-run demand for money, *Journal of Political Economy 74* (1966) 111–131.

CHRISTENSEN. L.R. (1977), Estimating U.S. consumer preferences for meat with a flexible utility function, *Journal of Econometrics 5* (1977) 37–54.

CHRISTENSEN, L.R., D.W. JORGENSON and L.J. LAU (1975), Transcendental logarithmic utility functions, *American Economic Review 65* (1975) 217–235.

CHRISTENSEN, L.R. and M.F. MANSER (1975), Cost-of-living indexes and price indexes for U.S. meat and produce, 1947–1971, in N. TERLECKYJ (1976).

COOPER, R.J. and K.R. McLAREN (1980), Atemporal, temporal and intertemporal duality in consumer theory, *International Economic Review 21* (1980) 599–610.

COURT, R.H. (1967), Utility maximization and the demand for New Zealand meats. *Econometrica 35* (1967) 424–446.

CRAMER, J.S. (1957), A dynamic approach to the theory of consumer demand, *Review of Economic Studies 24* (1957) 73–86.

CRAMER, J.S. (1962), *A statistical model of the ownership of major consumer durables.* Cambridge University Press, Cambridge, England.

CRAMER, J.S. (1970), Interaction of price and income in consumer demand. *European Economic Review 1* (1970) 428–436.

DEATON, A.S. (1972), The estimation and testing of systems of demand equations: a note. *European Economic Review 3* (1972) 399–411.

DEATON, A.S. (1974a), The analysis of consumer demand in the United Kingdom, 1900–1970, *Econometrica 42* (1974) 341–367.

DEATON, A.S. (1974b), A reconsideration of the empirical implications of additive preferences, Economic Journal *84* (1974) 338–348.

DEATON, A.S. (1975a), *Models and projections of demand in post-war Britain*, Chapman and Hall, London.

DEATON, A.S. (1975b), The measurement of income and price elasticities, *European Economic Review 6* (1975) 261–274.

DEATON, A.S. (1977), Involuntary saving through unanticipated inflation, *American Economic Review 67* (1977) 899–910.

DEATON, A.S. (1978), Specification and testing in applied demand analysis, *Economic Journal 88* (1978) 524–536.

DEATON, A.S. (1979), The distance function and consumer behaviour with applications to index numbers and optimal taxation, *Review of Economic Studies 46* (1979) 391–405.

DEATON, A.S. (1981), Theoretical and empirical approaches to consumer demand under rationing, in A.S. DEATON (ed.), *Essays in the theory and measurement of consumer behaviour in honour of Sir Richard Stone*, Cambridge University Press, Cambridge.

DEATON, A.S. and J. MUELLBAUER (1980a), *Economics and consumer behaviour*, Cambridge University Press, New York.

DEATON, A.S. and J. MUELLBAUER (1980b), An almost ideal demand system, *American Economic Review 70* (1980) 312–326.

DEATON, A.S. and J. MUELLBAUER (1981), Functional forms for labour supply and commodity demands with and without quantity restrictions, *Econometrica 49* (1981) 1521–1532.

DEBREU, G. (1954), Representation of a preference ordering by a numerical function, in *Decision processes*, R.M. THRALL, C.H. COOMBS, R.L. DAVIS (eds.). Wiley, New York, 159–165.

DEBREU, G. (1959), *Theory of value: an axiomatic analysis of economic equilibrium.* Cowles Monograph 17. Wiley, New York.

DEBREU, G. (1960), Topological methods in cardinal utility theory, in *Mathematical methods in the social sciences.* Stanford University Press, Stanford.

DE SOUZA, E. (1972), *Dynamic approaches to the true cost-of-living index.* M.A. thesis, Louvain, mimeo.

DE WOLFF, P. (1938), Demand for passenger cars in the United States. *Econometrica 6* (1938).

DHRYMES, P.J. (1970a), *Econometrics.* Harper and Row, New York.

DHRYMES, P.J. (1970b), *Distributed lags.* Holden-Day, San Francisco.

DIAMOND, P.A. and J. MIRRLEES (1971), Optimal taxation and public production II: tax rules, *American Economic Review 61* (1971) 115–122.

DIEWERT, W.E. (1971), An application of the Shephard duality theorem: a generalized Leontirf production function, *Journal of Political Economy 79* (1971) 481–507.

DIEWERT, W.E. (1974a), Applications of duality theory, Chapter 3 in M.D. INTRILIGATOR and D.A. KENDRICK (eds.), *Frontiers of Quantitative Economics*, Vol. II, North-Holland, Amsterdam.

DIEWERT, W.E. (1974b), Intertemporal consumer theory and the demand for durables, *Econometrica 42* (1974) 497–516.

DIEWERT, W.E. (1980), The economic theory of index numbers: a survey, in A.S. DEATON (ed.), *Essays in the theory and measurement of consumer behaviour in honour of Sir Richard Stone*, Cambridge University Press, Cambridge.

DORFMAN, R. (1969), Economic interpretation of optimal control theory. *American Economic Review 59* (1969) 817–831.

DUESENBERRY, J.S. (1949), *Income, saving, and the theory of consumer behavior*. Harvard University Press, Cambridge, Mass.

DUSANSKY, R. and P.J. KALMAN (1972), The real balance effect and the traditional theory of consumer behavior: a reconciliation, *Journal of Economic Theory 5* (1972) 336–347.

DUSANSKY, R. and P.J. KALMAN (1974), The foundation of money illusion in a neoclassical micro-monetary model, *American Economic Review 64* (1974) 115–122.

DUTTON D.S. and W.P. GRAMM (1973), Transaction costs, the wage rate, and the demand for money, *American Economic Review 63* (1973) 652–665.

EDGEWORTH, F.Y. (1881), *Mathematical psychics*. Paul Kegan, London.

ENGEL, E. (1857), Die Produktions- und Konsumptionsverhältnisse des Königreichs Sächsen. *Zeitschrift des Statistischen Bureaus des Königlichen Sächsischen Ministerium des Innern*, Nos. 8 and 9, 1857. Reprinted in *Bulletin de l'Institut International de Statistique 9* (1895).

FARRELL, M.J. (1952), Irreversible demand functions. *Econometrica 20* (1952) 171–186.

FARRELL, M.J, (1953–54), Some aggregation problems in demand analysis. *Review of Economic Studies 21* (1953–54) 193–203.

FARRELL, M.J. (1954), The demand for motor cars in the United States. *Journal of the Royal Statistical Society*, Series A (General) *117* (1954) 171–201.

FISHER, I. (1923), *The making of index numbers*. Houghton Mifflin, Boston.

FISHER, I. (1930), *The theory of interest*. Macmillan, New York.

FISHER, I. (1937), Note on a short-cut method for calculating distributed lags. *Bulletin de l'Institut International de Statistique*, 1937, 323–328.

FISHER, W. (1969), *Clustering and aggregation in economics*. Johns Hopkins, Baltimore.

FISHER, F.M. and K. SHELL (1969), Taste and quality change in the pure theory of the true cost-of-living index, in *Value, capital and growth, Essays in honor of J.R. Hicks*, J.R.N. WOLFE (ed.). Oxford, 97–139.

FOURGEAUD, C. and A. NATAF (1959), Consommation en prix et revenu réels et théorie des choix. *Econometrica 27* (1959) 329–354.

FRIEDMAN, M. (1949), The marshallian demand curve. *Journal of Political Economy 57* (1949). Reprinted in *Essays in positive economics*. Chicago University Press, Chicago, 1953.

FRIEDMAN, M. (1957), *A theory of the consumption function*. Princeton University Press, Princeton.

FRISCH, R. (1936), Annual survey of general economic theory: The problem of index numbers. *Econometrica 4* (1936) 1–38.

FRISCH, R. (1959), A complete scheme for computing all direct and cross demand elasticities in a model with many sectors. *Econometrica 27* (1959) 177–196.
FRISCH, R. (1964), Dynamic utility. *Econometrica 32* (1964) 418–424.

GARCIA DOS SANTOS, J. (1969), La demande d'appareils électroménagers en Belgique, 1956–1966. *Recherches économiques de Louvain 36* (1969) 111–132.
GARCIA DOS SANTOS, J. (1972), Estimating the durability of consumers' durable goods. *Review of Economics and Statistics 54* (1972) 475–479.
GEARY, P.T. and M. MORISHIMA (1973), Demand and supply under separability, in M. MORISHIMA (ed.), *Theory of demand, real and monetary*, Oxford University Press, Oxford.
GEARY, R.C. (1950–1951), A note on 'A constant utility index of the cost of living'. *Review of Economic Studies 18* (1950–51) 65–66.
GOLDBERGER, A.S. (1964), *Econometric theory*. Wiley, New York.
GOLDBERGER, A.S. (1967), *Functional form and utility: a review of consumer demand theory*. Systems Formulation, Methodology, and Policy Workshop Paper n⁰ 6703, Social Systems Research Institute, University of Wisconsin, mimeo.
GOLDBERGER, A.S. (1969), Directly additive utility and constant marginal budget shares. *Review of Economic Studies 36* (1969) 251–262.
GOLDBERGER, A.S. and T. GAMALETSOS (1970), A cross-country comparison of consumer expenditure patterns. *European Economic Review 1* (1970) 357–400.
GOLDMAN, S.M. and H. UZAWA (1964), A note on separability in demand analysis. *Econometrica 32* (1964) 387–398.
GORMAN, W.M. (1959a), Separable utility and aggregation. *Econometrica 27* (1959) 469–481.
GORMAN, W.M. (1959b), The empirical implications of a utility tree: a further comment. *Econometrica 27* (1959) 489.
GORMAN, W.M. (1961), On a class of preference fields, *Metroeconomica 13* (1971) 53–56.
GORMAN, W.M. (1967), Tastes, habits and choices. *International Economic Review 8* (1967) 218–222.
GORMAN, W.M. (1971), *Two stage budgeting*, London School of Economics, mimeo.
GORMAN, W.M. (1976), Tricks with utility functions, in *Essays in economic analysis*, M. ARTIS and R. NOBAY (eds.), Cambridge University Press, Cambridge.
GOSSEN, H.H. (1854), *Entwicklung der Gesetze des menschlichen Verkehrs*. Prager, Berlin.
GREEN, H.A.J. (1964), *Aggregation in economic analysis*. Princeton University Press, Princeton.
GRILICHES, Z. (1958), The demand for fertilizer: an economic interpretation of a technical change. *Journal of Farm Economics 40* (1958) 591–606.
GRILICHES, Z. (1960), The demand for a durable input: farm tractors in the United States. 1921–1957, in *The demand for durable goods*, A.C. HARBERGER (ed.). Chicago University Press, Chicago, 181–207.
GRILICHES, Z. (1967), Distributed lags: a survey. *Econometrica 35* (1967) 16–49.
GRILICHES, Z. (1971), *Price indexes and quality change: studies in new methods of measurement*. Harvard University Press, Cambridge, Mass.

HAAVELMO, T. (1944), The probability approach in econometrics. *Econometrica 12* (1944) Supplement.
HABERLER, G. (1927), *Der Sinn der Indexzahlen*. Tübingen.
HADLEY, G. and M. KEMP (1971), *Variational methods in economics*. North-Holland, Amsterdam.
HAKANSSON, W.H. (1970), Optimal investment and consumption strategies under risk for a class of utility functions, *Econometrica 38* (1970) 587–607.

HALL, R. (1973), Wages, income and hours of work in the U.S. labor force, in *Income maintenance and labor supply*, G. CAIN and H. WATTS (eds.), Markham, Chicago.

HANOCH, G. (1975a) Hours and weeks in the theory of labor supply, The Rand Corporation, R-1787/HEW, Santa Monica, California, mimeo.

HANOCH, G. (1975b), Theory and estimation of a complete labor supply model, The Rand Corporation, R-1869-HEW/ASPE, Santa Monica, California, mimeo.

HARMAN, H.H. (1960), *Modern factor analysis*. Chicago University Press, Chicago.

HECKMAN, J.J. (1974a), Life cycle consumption and labor supply: an explanation of the relationship between income and consumption over the life cycle, *American Economic Review 64* (1974) 188–194.

HECKMAN, J.J. (1974b), Shadow prices, market wages, and labor supply, *Econometrica 42* (1974) 679–694.

HECKMAN, J.J. and T.E. MACURDY (1979), A life-cycle model of female labor supply, Center for Mathematical Studies in Business and Economics, University of Chicago, mimeo.

HEIEN, D.M. (1969), Conceptual and practical issues in the measurement of cost-of-living changes. *Proceedings of the Business and Economic Statistics Section of the American Statistical Association, 1969*, Washington D.C.

HEIEN, D.M. (1973), *Some further results on the estimation of the S-branch utility tree*. Research Discussion Paper No. 10, Office of Prices and Living Conditions, U.S. Bureau of Labor Statistics Washington, D.C., January, 1973.

HENDERSON, J.M. and QUANDT, R.E. (1958), *Microeconomic theory*. McGraw-Hill, New York.

HICKS, J.R. (1936), *Value and capital*. Oxford University Press, Oxford.

HICKS, J.R. (1956), *A revision of demand theory*. Oxford University Press, Oxford.

HICKS, J.R. (1969), Direct and indirect additivity. *Econometrica 37* (1969) 353–354.

HOA, T.V. (1968), Interregional elasticities and aggregation bias: a study of consumer demand in Australia. *Australian Economic Papers 7* (1968) 206–226.

HOA, T.V. (1969a), Additive preferences and cost-of-living indexes: An empirical study of the Australian consumer's welfare. *Economic Record 45* (1969) 432–440.

HOA, T.V. (1969b), Consumer demand and welfare indexes: a comparative study for the United Kingdom and Australia. *Economica* (1969) 409–425.

HOUTHAKKER, H.S. (1950), Revealed preference and the utility function. *Economica 17* (1950) 159–174.

HOUTHAKKER, H.S. (1952), The econometrics of family budgets. *Journal of the Royal Statistical Society*, Series A (General) *115* (1952).

HOUTHAKKER, H.S. (1952–53), Compensated changes in quantities and qualities consumed. *Review of Economic Studies 19* (1952–53) 155–164.

HOUTHAKKER, H.S. (1953), La forme des courbes d'Engel, in *Cahiers du Séminaire d'Econométrie*, nr. 2 (1953) 59–66.

HOUTHAKKER, H.S. (1957), An international comparison of household expenditure patterns, commemorating the centenary of Engel's law. *Econometrica 25* (1957) 532–551.

HOUTHAKKER, H.S. (1960a), The influence of prices and incomes on household expenditures. *Bulletin of the International Institute of Statistics 37* (1960).

HOUTHAKKER, H.S. (1960b), Additive Preferences. *Econometrica 28* (1960) 244–257.

HOUTHAKKER, H.S. (1961a), Some problems in the international comparison of consumption patterns, in R. MOSSE, *L'évaluation et le rôle des besoins de biens de consommation dans les divers régimes économiques*. C.N.R.S., Paris, 1961, 89–102.

HOUTHAKKER, H.S. (1961b), The present state of consumption theory. *Econometrica 29* (1961) 704–740.

HOUTHAKKER, H.S. (1965a), New evidence on demand elasticities. *Econometrica 33* (1965) 277–288.

HOUTHAKKER, H.S. (1965b), A note on self-dual preferences. *Econometrica 33* (1965) 797–801.

HOUTHAKKER, H.S. and J. HALDI (1960), Household investment in automobiles, in *Consumption and savings*, I. FRIEND and R. JONES (eds.). University of Pennsylvania, Philadelphia, 1960, vol. I, 175–224.

HOUTHAKKER, H. and L.D. TAYLOR (1970). *Consumer demand in the United States 1929–1970*, 2nd ed. Harvard University Press, Cambridge, Mass.

HOUTHAKKER, H. and R.A. POLLAK, *The theory of consumer's choice*, Holden-Day, San Francisco, forthcoming.

INTRILIGATOR, M. (1971), *Mathematical optimization and economic theory*. Prentice-Hall, Englewood Cliffs.

IRONMONGER, D. (1972), *New commodities and consumer behaviour*. Cambridge University Press, Cambridge, England.

JOHANSEN, L. (1969), On the relationships between some systems of demand functions. *Liiketaloudellinen Aikakauskirja* (1969) 30–41.

JOHNSTON, J. (1963), *Econometric methods*. McGraw-Hill, London.

JORGENSON, D.W. (1966), Rational distributed lag functions. *Econometrica 34* (1966) 135–149.

JORGENSON, D.W. and L.J. LAU (1975), The structure of consumer preferences, *Annals of Economic and Social Measurement, 4* (1975) 49–101.

KAGEL, J.H., R.C. BATTALIO, H. RACHLIN, L. GREEN, R.L. BASMANN and W.R. KLEM (1975), Experimental studies of consumer demand behavior using laboratory animals, *Economic Inquiry 13* (1975) 22–38.

KAGEL, J.H., R.C. BATTALIO, H. RACHLIN and L. GREEN (1977), Demand curves for animal consumers, N.S.F. Technical Report No. 29, Department of Economics, Texas A&M University, 1977, mimeo.

KALMAN, P.J. (1968), Theory of consumer behaviour when prices enter the utility function. *Econometrica 36* (1968) 497–510.

KATZNER, D.W. (1970), *Static demand theory*. Collier–Macmillan, London.

KIEFER, N. (1977), A Bayesian analysis of labor supply and commodity demand, *International Economic Review 18* (1977) 209–218.

KLEIN, L.R. and H. RUBIN (1947–48), A constant-utility index of the cost of living. *Review of Economic Studies 15* (1947–48) 84–87.

KLEIN, L.R. (1962), *An introduction to econometrics*. Prentice-Hall, Englewood Cliffs.

KLEVMARKEN, A. (1977), A note on new goods and quality changes in the true cost of living index in view of Lancaster's model of consumer behaviour, *Econometrica 45* (1977) 163–173.

KLEVMARKEN, A. (1981), *On the complete systems approach to demand analysis*, The Industrial Institute for Economic and Social Research, Stockholm.

KLOEK, T. (1966), *Indexcijfers*. Doctoral dissertation, Den Haag.

KLOEK, T. and H. THEIL (1965), International comparisons of prices and quantities consumed. *Econometrica 33* (1965) 535–556.

KONUS, A.A. (1924), The problem of the true index of the cost of living. *Econometrica 7* (1939) 10–29. (Translation of a 1924 paper.)

KOOPMANS, T.C. (1960), Stationary utility and impatience. *Econometrica 28* (1960) 287–309.

KOOPMANS, T.C., DIAMOND, P.A. and R.E. WILLIAMSON (1964), Stationary utility and time perspective. *Econometrica 32* (1964) 82–100.

KOOPMANS, T.C. (1965), On the concept of economic growth, in *Study week on the econometric approach to development planning*. North-Holland, Amsterdam.

KOYCK, L.M. (1954), *Distributed lags and investment analysis*. North-Holland, Amsterdam

KRELLE, W. (1971), *Dynamics of the utility function*. Institut für Gesellschafts- und Wirtschaftswissenschaffen, Bonn, mimeo.

KUENNE, R.E. (1963), *The theory of general economic equilibrium*. Princeton University Press, Princeton.

KUH, E. and J. MEYER (1957), How extraneous are extraneous estimates? *Review of Economics and Statistics 38* (1957) 380–393.

LAITINEN, K. (1978), Why is demand homogeneity so often rejected?, *Economics Letters 1* (1978) 187–191.

LAITINEN, K. and H. THEIL (1979), The Antonelli matrix and the reciprocal Slutsky matrix, *Economics Letters 3* (1979) 153–157.

LANCASTER, K. (1966), A new approach to consumer theory. *Journal of Political Economy 74* (1966) 132–157.

LANCASTER, K. (1968) *Mathematical economics*. Macmillan, London.

LANCASTER, K.J. (1971), *Consumer demand: a new approach*, Columbia University Press, New York.

LAU, L.J. (1970), Duality and the structure of utility functions *Journal of Economic Theory 1* (1970) 374–396.

LAU, L.J., W.T. LIN and P.A. YOTOPOLOUS (1978), The linear logarithmic expenditure system: an application to consumption-leisure choice, *Econometrica 46* (1978) 843–868.

LEONI, R. (1967), An analysis of expenditures on private consumption. *Rivista di Politica Economica* (selected papers), 1967.

LEONTIEF, W. (1947). Introduction to a theory of the internal structure of functional relationships. *Econometrica 15* (1947) 361–373.

LESER, C.E.V. (1941–42), Family budget data and price elasticities of demand. *Review of Economic Studies 9* (1941–42).

LESER, C.E.V. (1963), Forms of Engel functions, *Econometrica 31* (1963) 694–703.

LEWIS, H.G. (1975), Economics of time and labor supply, *American Economic Review 65* (May 1975) 29–34.

LLOYD, C. (1964), The real balance effect and the Slutsky equation, *Journal of Political Economy 72* (1964) 295–299.

LLOYD, C. (1971) Preferences, separability and the Patinkin model, *Journal of Political Economy 79* (1971) 642–651.

LLUCH, C. (1971), Consumer demand functions, Spain 1958–64. *European Economic Review 2* (1971) 277–302.

LLUCH, C. (1973), The extended linear expenditure system. *European Economic Review 4* (1973) 21–32.

LLUCH, C. (1974), Expenditures, savings and habit formation, *International Economic Review 15* (1974) 786–797.

LLUCH, C., A.A. POWELL and R.A. WILLIAMS (1977), *Patterns in household demand and saving*, Oxford University Press, Oxford.

LUCAS, R.E. (1967), Adjustment costs and the theory of supply. *Journal of Political Economy 75* (1967) 321–334.

MANTEL, R.R. (1970), *On the utility of infinite programs when time is continuous*. Institute Torenato Di Tella, Buenos Aires, mimeo.

MARSHALL, A. (1920), *Principles of economics*, 8th ed. Macmillan, London.

MATTEI, A. (1971), A complete system of dynamic demand equations. *European Economic Review 2* (1971) 251–276.

MELTZER, A.H. (1963), The demand for money: the evidence from the time series, *Journal of Political Economy 71* (1963) 219–246.

MIRRLEES, J. (1974), Optimum allocation under uncertainty: the case of stationary returns to investment, in *Allocation under uncertainty*, J. DRÈZE (ed.), The International Economic Association, Macmillan, London.

MILLER, B. (1974), Optimal consumption with a stochastic income stream, *Econometrica 42* (1974) 253–266.

MODIGLIANI, F. (1949), Fluctuations in the savings-income ratio: a problem in economic forecasting, in *Studies in Income and Wealth*, vol. XI. N.B.E.R. New York, 371–443.

MODIGLIANI, F. (1966), The life cycle hypothesis of saving, the demand for wealth and the supply of capital. *Social Research 33* (1966), 160–217.

MODIGLIANI, F. and BRUMBERG (1955), Utility analysis and the consumption function: an interpretation of cross-section data, in *Post-Keynesian economics*, K. KURIHARA (ed.). Allen and Unwin, London.

MORISHIMA, M. (1965), Should dynamic utility be cardinal? *Econometrica 33* (1965) 869–871.

MORISHIMA, M. (1969), *Theory of economic growth*. Clarendon Press, Oxford.

MUELLBAUER, J. (1974a), Recent UK experience of prices and inequality: an application of true cost of living and real income indices, *Economic Journal 84* (1974) 32–55.

MUELLBAUER, J. (1974b), Household composition, Engel curves and welfare comparisons between households: a duality approach, *European Economic Review 5* (1974) 103–122.

MUELLBAUER, J. (1974c), Household production theory, quality, and the 'hedonic technique', *American Economic Review 64* (1974) 977–994.

MUELLBAUER, J. (1974d), Inequality measures, prices and household composition, *Review of Economic Studies 41* (1974) 493–504.

MUELLBAUER, J. (1975a), The cost of living and taste and quality changes, *Journal of Economic Theory 10* (1975) 269–283.

MUELLBAUER, J. (1975b), Aggregation, income distribution and consumer demand, *Review of Economic Studies 62* (1975) 525–543.

MUELLBAUER, J. (1975c), Identification and Consumer Unit Scales, *Econometrica 43* (1975) 807–809.

MUELLBAUER, J. (1976), Community preferences and the representative consumer, *Econometrica 44* (1976) 979–999.

MUELLBAUR, J. (1977), Testing the Barten model of household composition effects and the cost of children, *Economic Journal 87* (1977) 460–487.

MUELLBAUER, J. (1980), The estimation of the Prais–Houthakker model of equivalence scales, *Econometrica 48* (1980) 153–176.

MUELLBAUER, J. (1981a), Testing neoclassical models of the demand for durables, in *Essays in the theory and measurement of consumer behaviour in honour of Sir Richard Stone*, (ed.), Cambridge University Press, Cambridge.

MUELLBAUER, J. (1981b), Linear aggregation in neoclassical labour supply, *Review of Economic Studies 48* (1981) 21–36.

MUELLBAUER, J. (1982), *Why do empirical demand functions violate homogeneity tests?*, Birkbeck College Discussion Paper No. 113, mimeo.

MUTH, R.F. (1966), Household production and consumer demand functions. *Econometrica 34* (1966) 699–708.

NASSE, P. (1970), Analyse des effets de substitution dans un système complet de fonctions de demande. *Annales de l'I.N.S.E.E.*, nr. 5, Sept.–Dec. (1970) 81–110.

NEARY, J.P. and K.W.S. ROBERTS (1980), The theory of household behaviour under rationing, *European Economic Review 13* (1980) 25–42.

NERLOVE, M. (1956), Estimates of the elasticities of supply of selected agricultural commodities. *Journal of Farm Economics 38* (1956) 496–509.

NERLOVE, M. (1958), *Distributed lags and demand analysis.* Agriculture Handbook No. 141, US Department of Agriculture, Washington.

NERLOVE, M. (1960), The market demand for durable goods; a comment. *Econometrica 28* (1960) 132–142.

NOE, N.N. and G.M. von FURSTENBERG (1972), The upward bias in the consumer price index due to substitution. *Journal of Political Economy 80* (1972) 1280–1286.

O'BRIEN, J.M. (1974), The covariance measure of substitution: an application to financial assets, Review of Economics and Statistics *56* (1974) 456–467.

ORCUTT, G.H. and H.S. WINOKUR, Jr. (1969). First order autoregression: inference, estimation, and prediction. *Econometrica 37* (1969) 1–14.

OWEN, J.D. (1969), *The price of leisure*, Rotterdam University Press, Rotterdam.

PAELINCK, J. (1964), *Fonctions de consommation pour la Belgique 1948–59.* Facultés Universitaires N-D de la Paix, Namur.

PARETO, V. (1906), *Manuale di economia politica.* Societa Editrice Libraria, Milan. Second edition: *Manuel d'économie politique.* V. Giard et E. Brière. Paris, 1909. (English translation by A.S. SCHWIER, *Manual of political economy*, Macmillan London, 1972.)

PARKS, R.W. (1967), Efficient estimation of a system of regression equations when disturbances are both serially and contemporaneously correlated. *Journal of the American Statistical Association 62* (1967) 500–509.

PARKS, R.W. (1969), Systems of demand equations: an empirical comparison of alternative functional forms. *Econometrica 37* (1969) 629–650.

PARKS, R.W. (1971), Maximum likelihood estimation of the linear expenditure system. *Journal of the American Statistical Association 66* (1971) 900–903.

PARKS, R.W. and A.P. BARTEN (1973), A cross-country comparison of the effects of prices, income, and population composition on consumption patterns, *Economic Journal 83* (1973) 834–852.

PEARCE, I.F. (1964), *A contribution to demand analysis.* Oxford University Press, Oxford.

PENCAVEL, J.H. (1977), Constant-utility index numbers of real wages, *American Economic Review 67* (1977) 91–100.

PENCAVEL, J.H. (1979), Constant-utility index numbers of real wages: revised estimates, *American Economic Review 69* (1979) 240–243.

PESTON, M.H. (1967), Changing utility functions, in *Essays in mathematical economics, in honor of Oskar Morgenstern*, M. SHUBIK (ed.). Princeton University Press, Princeton, 233–236.

PHELPS, E. (1962), The accumulation of risky capital: a sequential analysis, *Econometrica 30* (1962) 729–743.

PHLIPS, L. (1971a). Substitution, complementarity, and the residual variation around dynamic demand equations. *American Economic Review 61* (1971) 586–597.

PHLIPS, L. (1971b), *Dynamic demand systems and the maximum principle.* Working Paper n⁰ 7104, Institut des Sciences Economiques, Louvain, mimeo.

PHLIPS, L. (1972), A dynamic version of the linear expenditure model. *Review of Economics and Statistics 64* (1972) 450–458.

PHLIPS, L. (1974), *Applied consumption analysis*, Advanced Textbooks in Economics, vol. 5, North-Holland, Amsterdam.

PHLIPS, L. (1975), Comment [on 'Budgeting, decentralization, and aggregation'], *Annals of Economic and Social Measurement 4* (1975) 45–48.

PHLIPS, L. (1976), Transactions demand for money and consumer behavior, in *Private and enlarged consumption: essays in methodology and empirical analysis*, L. SOLARI and J.N. DU PASQUIER (eds.), North-Holland, Amsterdam.

PHLIPS, L. (1978a), The demand for leisure and money, *Econometrica 46* (1978) 1025–1043.

PHLIPS, L. (1978b), A Taste-Dependent True Wage Index, in *Theory and Applications of Economic Indices*, W. EICHHORN, R. HENN, O. OPITZ and R.W. SHEPHARD (eds.), Physica-Verlag, Würzburg-Wien, pp. 401–415.

PHLIPS, L. and P. ROUZIER (1972), Substitution, complementarity and the residual variation: some further results. *American Economic Review 62* (1972) 747–751.

PHLIPS, L. and R. SANZ-FERRER (1972), *A dynamic true index of the cost of living.* Working Paper n⁰ 7201, Institut des Sciences Économiques, Louvain, mimeo.

PHLIPS, L. and D. WEISERBS (1972), *An intertemporal version of the linear expenditure system.* Working Paper N⁰ 7217, Institut des Sciences Economiques, Louvain, mimeo.

PHLIPS, L. and P. PIERAERTS (1979), Substitution versus addiction in the true index of real wages, *American Economic Review 69* (1979) 977–982.

PHLIPS, L. and F. SPINNEWYN (1979), True Wage Indexes and Rational Habit Formation, Cornell University, Department of Economics, Working Paper # 206, September 1979, mimeo.

PHLIPS, L., R. BLOMME and C. VANDEN BERGHE (1981), *Analyse chronologique*, 2nd ed. Cabay-Economica.

PHLIPS, L. and F. SPINNEWYN (1982), Rationality versus myopia in dynamic demand systems, in *Advances in Econometrics*, vol. 1, R.L. BASMANN and G.F. RHODES, Jr. (eds.), JAI Press, Greenwich, Connecticut.

PIGOU, A.C. (1952), *The economics of welfare*, 4th ed. Macmillan, London.

PLASMANS, J. (1970), *The general linear seemingly unrelated regression problem*, vol. 1 and 2, E.I.T., nr. 18 and 19, Tilburg.

POLLAK, R.A. (1968), Consistent planning. *Review of Economic Studies 35* (1968) 201–208.

POLLAK, R.A. (1969), Conditional demand functions and consumption theory. *Quarterly Journal of Economics*, February (1969) 60–78.

POLLAK, R.A. (1970), Habit formation and dynamic demand functions. *Journal of Political Economy 78* (1970) 745–763.

POLLAK, R.A. (1971a), Conditional demand functions and the implications of separable utility. *Southern Economic Journal 37* (1971) 423–433.

POLLAK, R.A. (1971b), Additive utility functions and linear Engel curves. *Review of Economic Studies 38* (1971) 401–413.

POLLAK, R.A. (1971c), *The theory of the cost of living index.* Research Discussion Paper, nr. 11, Office of Prices and Living Conditions, U.S. Bureau of Labor Statistics. June 1971.

POLLAK, R.A. (1972), Generalized separability. *Econometrica 40* (1972) 431–453.

POLLAK, R.A. (1975a), The intertemporal cost of living index, *Annals of Economic and Social Measurement 4* (1975) 179–195.

POLLAK, R.A. (1975b), Subindexes in the cost-of-living index, *International Economic Review 16* (1975) 135–150.

POLLAK, R.A. (1976a), Habit formation and long-run utility functions, *Journal of Economic Theory 13* (1976) 272–297.

POLLAK, R.A. (1976b), Interdependent preferences, *American Economic Review 66* (1976) 309–320.

POLLAK, R.A. (1977), Price dependent preferences, *American Economic Review 67* (1977) 64–75.

POLLAK, R.A. (1978), Endogenous tastes in demand and welfare analysis, *American Economic Review 68* (1978) 374–379.

POLLAK, R.A. and T.J. WALES (1969), Estimation of the linear expenditure system. *Econometrica 37* (1969) 611–628.

POLLAK, R.A. and M.L. WACHTER (1975), The relevance of the household production function and its implications for the allocation of time, *Journal of Political Economy 83* (1975) 255–277.

POLLAK, R.A. and T.J. WALES (1979), Welfare comparisons and equivalence scales, *American Economic Review 69* (May 1979) 216–221.

PONTRYAGIN, L.S., BOLTANSKII, V.G., GRAMKRELIDZE, R.S. and E.F. MISHENKO (1964), *The mathematical theory of optimal processes*. Pergamon Press, Oxford.

POWELL, A.A. (1966), A complete system of consumer demand equations for the Australian economy fitted by a model of additive preferences. *Econometrica 34* (1966) 661–675.

POWELL, A.A. (1974), *Empirical analysis of demand systems*, Heath, Lexington, Mass.

POWELL, A.A., T.V. HOA, and R.H. WILSON (1968), A multi-sectorial analysis of consumer demand in the post-war period. *Southern Economic Journal 35* (1968) 109–120.

PRAIS, S.J. and H.S. HOUTHAKKER (1955), *The analysis of family budgets*. Cambridge University Press, Cambridge (2nd ed. 1971).

PYATT, F.G. (1964), *Priority patterns and the demand for household durable goods*. Cambridge University Press, Cambridge.

RAJAOJA, V. (1958). *A study in the theory of demand functions and price indexes*. Societas Scientiarum Fennica, Commentationes Physico-mathematicae *XXI*, Helsinki.

ROOS, C.F. and V. VON SZELINSKI (1939), *The dynamics of automobile demand*. The General Motors Corporation.

ROSSIER, E. (1972), *Contribution aux explications dynamiques de la consommation semi-agrégée*. Doctoral dissertation, Geneva.

ROY, R. (1942), *De l'utilité – Contribution à la théorie des choix*. Hermann, Paris.

ROY, R. (1961), *Analyse de la demande*. Collectanea de Estudos nr. 10, Lisbao.

SALVAS-BRONSARD, L. (1978), Estimating systems of demand equations from French time series of cross-section data, *Annales de l'I.N.S.E.E.* No. 30–31 (1978) 543–564.

SALVAS-BRONSARD, L., D. LEBLANC and C. BRONSARD (1977), Estimating demand functions: the converse approach, *European Economic Review 9* (1977) 301–321.

SAMUELSON, P. (1974), Complementarity – An essay on the 40th anniversary of the Hicks–Allen revolution in demand theory, *Journal of Economic Literature 12* (1974) 1125–1289.

SAMUELSON, P.A. (1942), Constancy of the marginal utility of income, in *Studies in mathematical economics and econometrics*, O. LANGE, F. MCINTYRE and T.O. YNTEMA (eds.). Chicago University Press, Chicago.

SAMUELSON, P.A. (1947), *Foundations of economic analysis*. Harvard University Press, Cambridge, Mass.

SAMUELSON, P.A. (1947–48), Some implications of linearity. *Review of Economic Studies 15* (1947–48) 88–90.

SAMUELSON, P.A. (1950), The problem of integrability in utility theory. *Economica 17* (1950) 355–385.

SAMUELSON, P.A. (1965), Using full duality to show that simultaneously additive direct and indirect utilities implies unitary price elasticity of demand. *Econometrica 33* (1965) 781–796.

SAMUELSON, P.A. (1969), Corrected formulation of direct and indirect additivity. *Econometrica 37* (1969) 355–359.

SAMUELSON, P.A. (1969a), Lifetime portfolio selection by stochastic dynamic programming, *Review of Economics and Statistics 51* (1969) 239–246.

SAMUELSON, P. and S. SWAMY (1974), Invariate economic index numbers and canonical duality: survey and synthesis, *American Economic Review 64* (1974) 566–593.

SANZ-FERRER, R. (1972), Prévisions de la consommation privée en Belgique. *Recherches économiques de Louvain 38* (1972) 17–37.

SANZ-FERRER, R. (1973), *Teoria estatica y dinamica de la demanda. Una aplicacion al consumo privado espanol*. Instituto Iberamericano de Desarrollo Economico, Madrid.

SATO, K. (1972), Additive utility functions and double-log consumer demand functions, *Journal of Political Economy 80* (1972) 102–124.

SCHULTZ, H. (1938), *The theory and measurement of demand*. Chicago University Press, Chicago.

SCHULTZ, H. (1939), A misunderstanding in index-number theory. *Econometrica* 7 (1939).

SEADE, J. (1978), Consumer's surplus and linearity of Engel curves, *Economic Journal 88* (1978) 411–423.

SHELL, K., ed. (1967), *Essays on the theory of economic growth.* M.I.T. Press, Cambridge, Mass.

SIMMONS, P.J. (1979), A theorem on aggregation across consumers in neoclassical labour supply, *Review of Economic Studies 46* (1979) 737–740.

SIMMONS P.J. and D. WEISERBS (1979), Translog flexible functional forms and associated demand systems, *American Economic Review 69* (1979) 892–901.

SINGH, B. (1972), On the determination of economics of scale in household consumption, *International Economic Review 13* (1972) 257–270.

SINGH, B. and A.L. NAGAR (1973), Determination of consumer unit scales, *Econometrica 41* (1973) 347–355.

SLUTSKY, E. (1915), Sulla teoria di bilancio del consomatore. *Giornale degli Economisti,* 51 (1915). English translation in *Readings in price theory,* G. STIGLER and K. BOULDING (eds.). Allen and Unwin, London.

SOLARI, L. (1971), *Théorie des choix et fonctions de consommation semi-agrégées, modèles statiques.* Droz, Geneva.

SOLOW, R.M. (1960), On a family of lag distributions. *Econometrica 28* (1960) 399–406.

SONO, M. (1960), The effect of price changes on the demand and supply of separable goods. *International Economic Review 2* (1960) 239–271.

SPINNEWYN, F. (1979a), Rational habit formation, *European Economic Review 15* (1979) 91–109.

SPINNEWYN, F. (1979b), The cost of consumption and wealth in a model with habit formation, *Economics Letters 2* (1979) 145–148.

STAEHLE, H. (1935), A development of the economic theory of index numbers, *Review of Economic Studies 2* (1935), 173–188. (Comments by R.G.D. ALLEN and A.P. LERNER in the same *Review* (1935–36), 50–66.)

Statistical Office of the European Communities (1960), Prix, taux d'équivalence de pouvoir d'achat à la consommation et revenus réels dans les pays de la C.E.C.A. *Statistiques sociales,* nr. 2 (1960).

STEPHAN, P.A. (1975), Discussion [of Lewis (1975)], *American Economic Review 65* (May 1975) 35–36.

STIGLER, G.J. (1961), Report of the price statistics review committee, in *Price statistics of the federal government,* D. BRADY et al. (eds.). National Bureau of Economic Research, New York.

STIGLER, G. J. and G.S. BECKER (1977), De gustibus non est disputandum, *American Economic Review 67* (1977) 76–90.

STONE, J.R.N. (1947), On the interdependence of blocks of transactions, *Journal of the Royal Statistical Society 9* (1947, suppl.) pt. 1, 1–32.

STONE, J.R.N. (1953), *The measurement of consumers' expenditure and behaviour in the United Kingdom,* 1820–1938, vol. I. Cambridge University Press, Cambridge, England.

STONE, J.R.N. (1954), Linear expenditure systems and demand analysis: an Application to the Pattern of British Demand. *Economic Journal 64* (1954) 511–527.

STONE, J.R.N. (1964), Models for demand projections, in *Essays in Econometrics and Planning,* C.R. RAO (ed.). Pergamon, Oxford, 1965, 271–290.

STONE, J.R.N. and D.A. ROWE (1957), The market demand for durable goods. *Econometrica 25* (1957) 423–443.

STONE, J.R.N. and D.A. ROWE (1958), Dynamic demand functions: Some econometric results. *Economic Journal 68* (1958).

STONE, J.R.N. and D.A. ROWE (1960), The durability of consumers' durable goods. *Econometrica 28* (1960) 407–416.

STONE J.R.N., J.A.C. BROWN, and D.A. ROWE (1964), Demand analysis and projections for Britain 1900–1970: a study in method, in *Europe's future consumption*, J. SANDEE (ed.). North Holland, Amsterdam, 1964, 200–225.

STROTZ, R.H. (1956), Myopia and inconsistency in dynamic utility maximization. *Review of Economic Studies 23* (1956) 165–180.

STROTZ, R.H. (1957), The empirical implications of a utility true. *Econometrica 25* (1957) 269–280.

STROTZ, R.H. (1959), The utility tree- a correction and further appraisal. *Econometrica 27* (1959) 482–488.

SUMMERS, R. (1959), A note on least squares bias in household expenditure analysis, *Econometrica 27* (1959) 121–126.

TAYLOR, L.D. (1968), Personal consumption expenditure in Sweden 1931–1958. *Review of the International Statistical Institute 36* (1968) 19–36.

TAYLOR, L.D. (1974), On the dynamics of dynamic demand models, *Recherches économiques de Louvain 40* (1974) 21–31.

TAYLOR, L.D. and D. WEISERBS (1972), On the estimation of dynamic demand functions. *Review of Economics and Statistics 54* (1972) 459–465.

TERLECKYJ, N. (1976), *Household production and consumption*, N.B.E.R., New York.

THEIL, H. (1951), *De invloed van de voorraden op het consumentengedrag*. Poortpers, Amsterdam.

THEIL, H. (1954), *Linear aggregation of economic relations*. North-Holland, Amsterdam.

THEIL, H. (1965), *Economic forecasts and policy*. North-Holland, Amsterdam.

THEIL, H. (1967), *Economics and information theory*. North-Holland, Amsterdam.

THEIL, H. (1975), *Theory and measurement of Consumer Demand*, Vol. I, North-Holland, Amsterdam.

THEIL, H. (1976), *Theory and measurement of consumer demand*, Vol. II, North-Holland, Amsterdam.

THEIL, H. (1979), The effect of measurement errors on the estimation of demand systems, *Economics Letters 3* (1979) 373–376.

THEIL, H. and H. NEUDECKER (1958), Substitution, complementarity, and the residual variation around engel curves. *Review of Economic Studies 25* (1958) 114–123.

THISSE, J. and D. WEISERBS (1972), *Consumer behavior and Pontryagin's maximum principle*. Working Paper nr. 7216, Institut des Sciences Economiques, Louvain, mimeo.

THISSE, J. and D. WEISERBS (1973), *Existence et unicité d'une commande optimale pour une classe de systèmes linéraires en horizon infini*, Working Paper n⁰ 7303, Institut des Sciences Economiques, Louvain, mimeo.

TOBIN, J. (1952), A survey of the theory of rationing, *Econometrica 20* (1952) 512–553.

TOBIN, J. and H.S. HOUTHAKKER (1951), The effects of rationing on demand elasticities, *Review of Economic Studies 18* (1951) 140–153.

TÖRNQVIST, L. (1941), Review of work by H. WOLD. *Ekonomisk Tidskrift 43* (1941) 216–225.

TRIPLETT, J.E. (1973), A comment on: 'The upward bias in the consumer price index due to substitution'. Research Discussion Paper N⁰ 9, Office of Prices and Living Conditions, U.S. Bureau of Labor Statistics, February, 1973.

TRIPLETT, J.E. (1976a), Consumer demand and characteristics of consumption goods, in TERLECKYJ (1976).

TRIPLETT, J.E. (1976b), The measurement of inflation: a survey of research on the accuracy of price indexes, in *Analysis of inflation*, P.H. EARL (ed.), D.C. Heath, Lexington, 1976.

VAN BROEKHOVEN, E. (1971a), Short-term consumer behavior of individual Belgian labour households. *Tijdschrift voor economie 16* (1971).

References

VAN BROEKHOVEN, E. (1971b), De gezinsuitgaven, in *De behoeften van de mens en de belgische economie in de jaren tachtig*. C.E.M.S., Brussels, 215–257.

WALRAS, L. (1874), *Eléments d'économie politique pure*. L. Corbas et Cie, Lausanne. (English translation by W. JAFFE, *Elements of pure economics*. Allen and Unwin, London, 1954.)

WEISERBS, D. (1972), *Contributions à une analyse dynamique des choix du consommateur*. Doctoral dissertation, Anec, Louvain.

WEISERBS, D. (1974), More about dynamic demand systems, *Recherches économiques de Louvain 40* (1974) 33–43.

WEISERBS, D. (1975), A note on the discrete specification of the state-adjustment model, Working Paper No. 7514, Institut des Sciences Economiques, Louvain, mimeo.

WEIZSÄCKER, C.C. VON (1971), Notes on endogenous changes of tastes. *Journal of Economic Theory 3* (1971) 345–372.

WEYMARK, J.A. (1980), Duality results in demand theory, *European Economic Review 14* (1980) 377–395.

WILLIAMS, R.A. (1971), Demand for consumer durables: stock adjustment models and alternative specifications of stock depletion, *Review of Economic Studies 39* (1971) 281–295.

WILLIAMS. R.A. (1978), Demographic effects on consumption patterns in Australia: a preliminary analysis of the ABS 1974–75 household expenditure survey, Working Paper No. SP-11, Melbourne, February 1978, mimeo.

WINDER, J.W.L. (1971), A note on the Houthakker-Taylor demand analysis. *Journal of Political Economy 79* (1971) 368–371.

WOLD, H. and L. JURÉEN (1953), *Demand analysis*. Wiley, New York.

WORKING, E.J. (1927), What do statistical demand curves show? *Quarterly Journal of Economics, 61* (1927), republished in *Readings in Price Theory*, G.J. STIGLER and K.E. BOULDING (eds.). Allen and Unwin, London, 97–115.

WORKING, H. (1943), Statistical laws of family expenditure, *Journal of the American Statistical Association 38* (1943) 43–56.

YAARI, M.E. (1964), On the consumer's lifetime allocation process. *International Economic Review 5* (1964) 304–317.

YAARI, M.E. (1965), Uncertain lifetime, life insurance, and the theory of the consumer. *Review of Economic Studies 32* (1965) 137–150.

YOSHIHARA, K. (1969), Demand functions: an application to the Japanese expenditure pattern. *Econometrica 37* (1969) 257–274.

ZELLNER, A. (1962), An efficient method of estimating seemingly unrelated regressions and tests for aggregation bias. *Journal of the American Statistical Association 57* (1962) 348–368.

Index